CORRECTIONAL THEORY

THEORY

Second Edition

*For her courage, good humor, and
friendship in the face of adversity, this book is dedicated to
Wendi Goodlin-Fahncke.*

*We look forward to many years
of continued criminological companionship.*

CORRECTIONAL THEORY

CONTEXT AND CONSEQUENCES

Second Edition

FRANCIS T. CULLEN
University of Cincinnati

CHERYL LERO JONSON
Xavier University

Los Angeles | London | New Delhi
Singapore | Washington DC

Los Angeles | London | New Delhi
Singapore | Washington DC

FOR INFORMATION:

SAGE Publications, Inc.
2455 Teller Road
Thousand Oaks, California 91320
E-mail: order@sagepub.com

SAGE Publications Ltd.
1 Oliver's Yard
55 City Road
London EC1Y 1SP
United Kingdom

SAGE Publications India Pvt. Ltd.
B 1/I 1 Mohan Cooperative Industrial Area
Mathura Road, New Delhi 110 044
India

SAGE Publications Asia-Pacific Pte. Ltd.
3 Church Street
#10-04 Samsung Hub
Singapore 049483

Printed in the United States of America

Library of Congress Cataloging-in-Publication Data

Names: Cullen, Francis T. | Jonson, Cheryl Lero.

Title: Correctional theory : context and consequences / Francis T. Cullen, Cheryl Lero Jonson.

Description: Second Edition. | Thousand Oaks : SAGE Publications, Inc., 2016. | Revised edition of the authors' Correctional theory, 2012. | Includes bibliographical references and index.

Identifiers: LCCN 2015038735| ISBN 978-1-5063-0652-0 (pbk. : alk. paper) | ISBN 978-1-4129-8179-8 (cloth : alk. paper) | ISBN 978-1-4129-8180-4 (pbk. : alk. paper)

Subjects: LCSH: Corrections. | Corrections—United States.

Classification: LCC HV8665.C85 2016 | DDC 364.601—dc23
LC record available at http://lccn.loc.gov/2015038735

This book is printed on acid-free paper.

Acquisitions Editor: Jerry Westby
eLearning Editor: Nicole Mangona
Editorial Assistant: Laura Kirkhuff
Production Editor: Jane Haenel
Copy Editor: Kristin Bergstad
Typesetter: C&M Digitals (P) Ltd.
Proofreader: Christina West
Indexer: Michael Ferreira
Cover Designer: Gail Buschman
Marketing Manager: Amy Lammers

SFI Certified Sourcing
www.sfiprogram.org
SFI-00453

16 17 18 19 20 10 9 8 7 6 5 4 3 2 1

Brief Contents

Preface   x

Part I. Crisis in American Corrections

1. From Theory to Policy: Evidence-Based Corrections   2

2. Correctional Theory in Crisis: America's Changing Context   27

Part II. The Punishment Response

3. Just Deserts: Doing Justice or Getting Tough?   44

4. Deterrence: Scaring Offenders Straight   77

5. Incapacitation: Locking Up the Wicked   113

Part III. The Social Welfare Response

6. Restorative Justice: Reintegrative Shaming   146

7. Rehabilitation: What Works to Change Offenders   171

Part IV. Extending the Vision of Corrections

8. Reentry: Saving Offenders From a Life in Crime   206

9. Early Intervention: Saving Children From a Life in Crime   240

10. Six Correctional Lessons: Choosing Our Future   277

References   291

Index   317

About the Authors   335

Contents

Preface   **x**

Part I. Crisis in American Corrections

1. **From Theory to Policy: Evidence-Based Corrections**   **2**
    Theories of Corrections   6
    Seven Theories in Brief   7
        Retribution: Balancing the Scales of Justice   7
        Deterrence: Scaring Offenders Straight   8
        Incapacitation: Locking Up Predators   10
        Restorative Justice: Reducing Harm   11
        Rehabilitation: Saving the Wayward   12
        Reentry: Saving Released Prisoners   14
        Early Intervention: Saving the Children   16
    Utility, Opinion, and Evidence   17
    Evidence-Based Corrections   19
        Correctional Quackery   19
        Insider and Outsider Knowledge   20
        Evidence-Based Baseball   21
    Conclusion: What's Ahead?   25

2. **Correctional Theory in Crisis: America's Changing Context**   **27**
    What Is Rehabilitation?   29
    The Rise of the Rehabilitative Ideal   31
        The Rise of the "Penitentiary"   31
        The New Penology: The Cincinnati
            Congress of 1870   33
        Individualized Treatment: The Core
            of the Rehabilitative Ideal   35
        The Progressive Era: Theory Into Reality   36
        The Rise of Corrections   37
    Attacking Rehabilitation   38
    The "Nothing Works" Doctrine: Martinson and Beyond   39
    Conclusion: Crisis in Correctional Theory   41

Part II. The Punishment Response

3. Just Deserts: Doing Justice or Getting Tough? 44
    The Concepts of Retribution and Just Deserts: Punishing the Crime 47
    Retribution: Just and Painful 49
    Four Problems for Retribution 51
        The Prison Problem 51
        The Criminology Problem 52
        The Inequality Problem 54
        The Utility Problem 57
    The Justice Model: Restraining State Discretion 58
        The Failed Promise of Rehabilitation 58
        The Solution: Doing Justice 66
    What Went Wrong? Winning the Battle but Losing the War 68
        Winning the Battle 68
        Losing the War 70
    Conclusion: The Need for Crime Control 75

4. Deterrence: Scaring Offenders Straight 77
    The Concept of Deterrence 80
        Types of Deterrence: General and Specific 80
        Certainty and Severity of Punishment 81
    Is Deterrence a "Conservative" Theory? 82
    The Theoretical Assumptions of Deterrence 82
    Studying Whether Deterrence Works: Assessing Types of Evidence 84
    Policy Changes That Increase Punishment 85
    Macro-Level Studies of Punishment and Crime Rates 88
        Conducting a Macro-Level Study 88
        What Macro-Level Studies Find 90
    Perceptual Deterrence Studies 92
        Beware of the Ecological Fallacy 92
        Studying Individuals' Perceptions of Punishment 93
        Two Studies 95
    Deterrence in the Community 98
        Do Community Control Programs Work? 98
        The RAND ISP Study: A Classic Experiment in Corrections 103
    The Effects of Imprisonment 105
        Studying Imprisonment and Recidivism 105
        Does Imprisonment Deter? 107
    Conclusion: The Limits of Deterrence 111

5. Incapacitation: Locking Up the Wicked 113
    Too Many Prisoners 117
    More Than Enough Criminals 123
    The Concept of Incapacitation 126
        Collective Incapacitation 126
        Selective Incapacitation 127

Estimating the Incapacitation Effect: Studying Individual Offenders 131
    Inmate Self-Report Studies 132
    Longitudinal Studies 134
    Not So Quick: Don't Lock Up Everyone Yet 136
Estimating the Incapacitation Effect: Macro-Level Studies 139
    Spelman's Research 139
    Complicating Matters: Two Other Studies 140
Conclusion: Compared to What? 141

Part III. The Social Welfare Response

6. Restorative Justice: Reintegrative Shaming **146**
The Concept of Restorative Justice 148
The Appeal of Restorative Justice 151
Three Problems 154
    The Justice Problem 154
    The Prison Problem 156
    The Criminological Problem 158
Does Restorative Justice Work? 161
    Four Limits 162
    Five Studies 163
Conclusion: The Limits of Harm 169

7. Rehabilitation: What Works to Change Offenders **171**
The Concept of Rehabilitation 173
Knowing What Works 176
Challenging Nothing Works: Narrative Reviews 178
    Standing Up to Martinson: Ted Palmer's Rebuttal 178
    Bibliotherapy for Cynics: The Canadians Get Involved 182
Challenging Nothing Works: Meta-Analytic Reviews 184
    What Is a Meta-Analysis? 184
    The Overall Effect Size 186
    Heterogeneity of Effect Sizes 187
    The Impact of Meta-Analysis on the Nothing Works Debate 189
What Does Not Work 190
What Does Work: Principles of Effective Intervention 191
What Else Might Work? 196
    Desistance-Based Rehabilitation 196
    The Good Lives Model 198
Conclusion: Reaffirming Rehabilitation 201

Part IV. Extending the Vision of Corrections

8. Reentry: Saving Offenders From a Life in Crime **206**
From Parole to Reentry 209
The Reentry Problem 212
    Nature of the Problem 212
    Discovery of the Problem 217
    What's Going on Today 219

Reentry Programs   222
   Institutional Programs   223
   Community Programs   226
The Effectiveness Problem   229
   Four Barriers to Effectiveness   229
   Taking Stock of Effectiveness   234
Two Things to Keep in Mind   235
   Take Coming Home Seriously   235
   Confront Collateral Consequences   236
Conclusion: Saving Offenders From a Life in Crime   238

9. Early Intervention: Saving Children From a Life in Crime   240
Lessons From Child Criminology   242
   The Discovery of Childhood   242
   Beyond Adolescence-Limited Criminology   244
The Need for Early Intervention   246
Five Programs That Work—At Least When Done Right   249
   Nurse Home Visitation Program   251
   High/Scope Perry Preschool Program   254
   Functional Family Therapy   258
   Seattle Social Development Project   263
   Multisystemic Therapy   266
Two More Reasons to Support Early Intervention   269
   Cost Effectiveness   270
   Public Support   274
Conclusion: Beyond Adult-Limited Corrections   276

10. Six Correctional Lessons: Choosing Our Future   277
Three Themes   277
   Theory Has Consequences   278
   The Social Context Has Consequences   279
   Ignoring the Evidence Has Consequences   280
Six Lessons   281
   Punishment Does Not Work Well   281
   Prisons Work Somewhat   282
   Reaffirm Rehabilitation   284
   Reentry Matters   286
   Save the Children   286
   Things Can Change   287
Conclusion: Choosing Our Future   289

References   291

Index   317

About the Authors   335

Preface

The American correctional system is a virtual behemoth—a giant creature that seems to swallow an unending flow of the nation's population year after year after year. The numbers are cited so often—more than 2.2 million people behind bars on a daily basis and nearly 5 million under community supervision—that they risk descending into mere banality. Ho hum. But lest we become tempted to accept a huge correctional system and mass incarceration as minor facts of life, we should understand what is at stake. For one thing, elected officials from both ends of the political spectrum are concerned by how much corrections drains from the public treasury. For another, we should be troubled by the number of our fellow citizens, many of them poor and people of color, who find themselves in handcuffs and then peering through the cold steel bars of a prison cell. "Statistics," as Paul Brodeur eloquently reminds us, "are human beings with the tears wiped off."

Corrections is thus fundamentally a human enterprise; lives and futures are at stake. As we consider what to do with offenders, simple answers escape us. Two realities tug at our hearts and minds. On the one hand, offenders have harmed others and thus do little to inspire our sympathy. If anything, we have reason to be angry at them and to want to harm them in return. On the other hand, offenders too often are drawn from bleak circumstances. If we had inspected their plight when they were 10 or 15 years of age, we would have lamented that the deck was stacked against them and that they were destined for a life in crime and behind bars. Any sense of fairness—of social justice—thus tempers our desire for vengeance and perhaps leads us to see merit in saving them from a criminal future.

This matter is complicated still further by an understanding that corrections is not only about offenders but also about us—about we as a people. Of course, we cannot ignore the seriousness of a crime or the circumstances that shaped a person's decision to offend. But we also must be cognizant that our response to the criminally wayward is contingent on our own values and what Francis Allen calls our own sense of "social purpose." We certainly do not wish to stoop to the level of the criminal (whatever that might mean), but what we should do to those who break the law is debatable. As a number of commentators have remarked, however, how we treat the least desirable among us perhaps reveals what we truly stand for as a people.

Thus, when we pull law-breakers into the correctional system, we must have some reason for doing so—some idea of what we hope to accomplish. *Correctional Theory* addresses this compelling and complex issue. It identifies and evaluates the major competing visions—or theories—that seek to guide the correctional system's goals, policies, and practices.

Correctional Theory is informed by three core themes, two of which are represented in its subtitle: *Context and Consequences*. These themes, found across the book, are as follows:

- *Theory Matters.* This is the notion that *ideas have consequences.* That is, the theories we have about the purpose and structure of corrections can impact correctional policy and practice. Thus, changing theoretical assumptions can legitimize changing ways of treating and punishing offenders.

- *Context Matters.* The theories that are embraced and allowed to direct and/or legitimate correctional policies are shaped by the prevailing social and political context. An effort is thus made to show how the changes in the nature of American society have affected correctional theory and policy.

- *Evidence Matters.* In corrections, policies and practices are largely informed by common sense, ideology, and institutional inertia. This rejection of science in favor of popular beliefs leads to the practice of *correctional quackery*—of pursuing policies that have little chance of being effective. Accordingly, as others are now doing, we make the case for the utility of evidence-based corrections. This orientation provides a rationale for the inclusion of discussions of *evidence* across the chapters.

Again, these issues are salient because lives are at stake—those of offenders and those of past and future victims. If we do foolish things—such as place wayward youths in boot camps—we may feel self-righteous but surely we will do little to help these poor souls or those they may well harm down the road. What we do to, and for, offenders will affect their futures and our public safety. In making correctional decisions, we thus must have a clear sense of what we intend to accomplish and whether our prescriptions are backed up by empirical data.

In the United States—and elsewhere—there was a campaign for more than four decades to get tough with offenders. Many elected officials promised to place more offenders in prisons and for longer periods of time. To be sure, a variety of factors fueled the nation's imprisonment boom, but one contributing source certainly was this desire by policy makers to build and fill prison after prison. In scholarly terms, there was a call to subject offenders to stringent punishments so as to pay them back for their crime (retribution), scare them straight (deterrence), and get them off the street so they cannot hurt anyone (incapacitation). Was this punishment movement a good thing? Did it achieve justice and make us safer? Much of *Correctional Theory* is devoted to answering these questions.

Recently, political leaders from both parties have voiced substantial doubts that this "war on crime"—which included the embrace of mass imprisonment—was a good idea. Importantly, *Correctional Theory* also explores alternative visions of corrections—especially the theory of rehabilitation—that argue against inflicting pain on and warehousing offenders. Corrections by its nature is punitive. Offenders go to court, and their freedom is restricted either in the community or inside institutions. The larger issue is whether the sanction that is imposed seeks only to harm and restrain or whether it also seeks to improve offenders and restore them to the community. Cullen and Jonson, your esteemed authors, believe that the empirical evidence and the need to achieve a broader social purpose combine to provide a convincing rationale for embracing a type of corrections devoted to saving the wayward from a life in crime.

In the end, however, the purpose of *Correctional Theory* is not to indoctrinate readers into our way of thinking—though, of course, we would be delighted if our work proved convincing in this way. Rather, the ultimate goal is to motivate readers to become sophisticated consumers of correctional knowledge—to start to question what they are told, to become evidence-based thinkers, and to develop their own theory of corrections to guide them as citizens and perhaps as policy makers and practitioners.

Cullen and Jonson would prefer to take all the credit for this book—and none of the blame should something prove problematic! We would prefer to list all those who, in the case of difficulty, readers should immediately define as the responsible culprits. But, alas, we have been too well socialized—too guilt prone—not to confess that *Correctional Theory* is a volume whose faults are ours and whose existence owes much to others. Given that this is a second edition, we have virtually no excuse for not fixing whatever faults graced the pages of our first try at this book. But we remain cognizant that without the encouragement, support, and insights of a variety of parties, *Correctional Theory* would not have been possible, either initially or now in its new and improved form.

Developing a roster of folks to acknowledge is quite similar to devising a list of people to invite to a wedding. Where does one draw the line? So many of our colleagues, friends, and students—who have shared ideas, tracked down references, endlessly photocopied articles, proofread chapters, and kept our spirits high and sanity intact—could easily be mentioned here. But in an effort to keep our list to a manageable length, we will acknowledge only those who have been intimately involved in making *Correctional Theory* possible. To all others—and you should realize who you are—know well that Cullen and Jonson are grateful to have you in our academic and personal lives.

Robert Agnew of Emory University is most responsible for inspiring this book; it was his idea. Bob had borrowed the detailed lectures on various correctional theories that Cullen had developed for a graduate-level distance learning course. He encouraged Cullen to turn the notes into a book—which, given the incomplete state of the notes, proved a daunting task (and one that Cullen soon realized required a diligent coauthor, Jonson, to undertake). Cullen initially thought that Bob was pulling his leg. But Bob's persistent encouragement eventually led the project to move to a more concrete stage of development.

Jerry Westby at SAGE Publications made the first edition come to fruition and has insisted that we write this revised edition. Jerry's confidence in *Correctional Theory* and faith in its capacity to make an enduring contribution are heartening. He is the kind of editor that many authors hope for but few are fortunate to possess. Jerry's other talent is in recruiting a wonderful staff—competent and decent in every way. For shepherding this edition to print, we thus extend appreciation to Kristin Bergstad, Jane Haenel, and Laura Kirkhuff.

Our gratitude next goes to the five correctional scholars who agreed to review the first edition. Of course, Cullen and Jonson believe that these scholars are brilliant in large part because their comments were encouraging and moved SAGE once again to publish *Correctional Theory*! But we are also truly thankful for the set of scholars that took the time out of their crowded schedules to share an array of helpful insights with us that we trust have improved this edition. We are pleased to acknowledge our advisers for the second edition:

Jack Atherton
Northwestern State University of Louisiana

Addrain Conyers
Marist College

Jennifer Cobbina
Michigan State University

Lior Gideon
John Jay College of Criminal Justice

Krista S. Gehrig
University of Houston-Downtown

Todd M. Krohn
University of Georgia

Jennifer L. Lanterman
University of Nevada, Reno

Betsy Matthews
Eastern Kentucky University

Randolph Myers
Old Dominion University

Erin A. Orrick
Sam Houston State University

Elizabeth Perkins
Morehead State University

Caryn E. Saxon
Missouri State University

Charlene Y. Taylor
Boise State University

Sheryl L. Van Horne
Arcadia University

We wish to acknowledge that sections of three chapters include previously published material. Thus, portions of Chapter 2 were drawn from Francis T. Cullen and Shannon A. Santana (2002), "Rehabilitation," in Joshua Dressler (Ed.), *Encyclopedia of Crime and Justice* (Vol. 3, 2nd ed., pp. 1314–1327), New York, NY: Macmillan Reference USA. Portions of Chapter 7 were drawn from Francis T. Cullen and Paul Gendreau (2000), "Assessing Correctional Rehabilitation: Policy, Practice, and Prospects," in Julie Horney (Ed.), *Policies, Processes, and Decisions of the Criminal Justice System: Criminal Justice 2000* (Vol. 3, pp. 109–175), Washington, DC: U.S.

Department of Justice, National Institute of Justice. Portions of Chapter 8 were drawn from Cheryl Lero Jonson and Francis T. Cullen (2015), "Prisoner Reentry Programs," in Michael Tonry (Ed.), *Crime and Justice: A Review of Research* (Vol. 44, pp. 517–575), Chicago, IL: University of Chicago Press.

Cullen and Jonson are fortunate to work and live in supportive environments. We must note our appreciation to our colleagues in the School of Criminal Justice at the University of Cincinnati and the Department of Criminal Justice at Xavier University. For various reasons, we wish to give special thanks to Cecilia Chouhy, Teresa Kulig, Daniel Mears, Melissa Moon, Joan Petersilia, Travis Pratt, Lacey Rohleder, Mary Stohr, Paula Smith, and John Wozniak. Most notably, we recognize our family members, whose daily love and support enrich our lives in many ways. Cullen gives a big hug to Paula Dubeck and Jordan Cullen. Jonson gives a big hug to Paul Jonson, John and Linda Lero, and Chris and Josh Siler.

CALLING ALL INSTRUCTORS!

study.sagepub.com/cullenct2e

It's easy to log on to SAGE's password-protected Instructor Teaching Site for complete and protected access to all text-specific Instructor Resources. Simply provide your institutional information for verification, and within 72 hours you'll be able to use your login information for any SAGE title! Then, pick and choose from this list, depending on what each site offers.

Password-protected Instructor Resources include the following:

- A Microsoft® Word® test bank is available containing multiple choice and essay questions for each chapter. The test bank provides you with a diverse range of pre-written options as well as the opportunity to edit any question and/ or insert your own personalized questions to effectively assess students' progress and understanding.

- Chapter-specific discussion questions help launch classroom interaction by prompting students to engage with the material and by reinforcing important content.

- EXCLUSIVE! Access to certain full-text SAGE journal articles that have been carefully selected for each chapter. Each article supports and expands on the concepts presented in the chapter. This feature also provides questions to focus and guide student interpretation. Combine cutting-edge academic journal scholarship with the topics in your course for a robust classroom experience.

PART I

Crisis in American Corrections

1

From Theory to Policy

Doris Layton MacKenzie
Pennsylvania State University
Author of *What Works in Corrections*

Evidence-Based Corrections

O n any given day in the United States, more than 1.5 million offenders are imprisoned in state and federal institutions. When inmates in jails and other custodial facilities (e.g., juvenile institutions) are included in the count, the nation's incarcerated population surpasses 2.2 million (Carson, 2014). There are also approximately 3.9 million offenders on probation and more than 850,000 people on parole (Herberman & Bonczar, 2014). Taken together, nearly 7 million Americans are under the supervision of the correctional system (Glaze & Kaeble, 2014). To put this number in more understandable terms, 1 in every 110 American adults is behind bars, and 1 in 35 is under some form of correctional control. For African Americans, this latter figure is 1 in 12 (Glaze & Kaeble, 2014; Pew Charitable Trusts, 2008, 2009; Wolfers, Leonhardt, & Quealy, 2015).

It can be misleading to cite statistics and imply that some crisis is at hand. For example, on any given day in America, about 600,000 people are in hospitals and 19.5 million are enrolled in college degree programs (United States Census Bureau, 2014). Are these numbers cause for concern? But in this case, the United States clearly has grown remarkably fond of a massive correctional system that is, in Travis Pratt's (2009) words, "addicted to incarceration." Signs exist the United States is trying to kick the imprisonment habit—an issue that will we will consider. But the stubborn fact remains that other Western industrialized nations exercise more restraint in locking up their citizens, both in terms of how many and for how long (Tonry, 2007). It is hard to imagine that in the early 1970s, the number of inmates in state and federal prisons dipped below 200,000. If we turn to today's count—the 1.5 million cited above—we see that the United States has experienced more than a seven-fold increase in its prison population. Might this just be a product of the growth of the nation's citizenry? Yes, America's population has jumped from just over 200 million to just under 320 million. But this increase explains only a fraction of the expansion of the incarcerated population.

So, why do we place so many people in the correctional system? The simple answer, of course, is that they have committed crimes and been convicted, and thus some response by the government is required. But this explanation has two problems. First, it suggests that the amount of crime and the amount of corrections in a nation are tightly connected. But this is not the case. Within the United States, correctional populations do not rise and fall as crime rates rise and fall. Further, cross-nationally, nations with similar crime rates have incarceration rates that are dissimilar. To a degree, then, how many people are in prison or under community supervision is a policy choice. And this choice itself has a lot to do with what we hope to accomplish through a correctional intervention (Tonry, 2004, 2007).

This discussion thus leads us to the second problem with the simple notion that people are in the correctional system because they are offenders. This explanation begs the larger question of what *purpose* is served by intervening in the lives of offenders. What do we hope to accomplish? Our book is designed to address this very question. It is also intended to demonstrate that *theories matter because they affect correctional policy.*

Now, as just implied, across time in the United States competing visions have been set forth of *what corrections should be about.* We call these rival perspectives *theories of corrections.* They are comprised of three components. First, there is a statement of the *purpose or goal* of corrections. These tend to emphasize either restraining and inflicting pain on offenders or helping and reforming offenders. Another way to phrase this is that the purpose involves a *punishment response* or a *social welfare response.* Second, each theory has an implicit or explicit *blueprint* for how the correctional system should be arranged, including policies, practices, and organizational structure. Ideas thus matter; they influence what we do in corrections. Theories also breed conflict because each one demands that the correctional system be organized in a different way. Third, theories make a claim of *effectiveness.* Advocates assert not only that a theory's core goal is moral but also that their theory can be implemented effectively—in short, that it "works." For example, proponents of deterrence theory claim that we should place offenders in prison because it yields lower reoffending rates than a community sanction. Is this really the case? This is where *evidence-based corrections* comes in and proves critical in discerning what works and what does not work. Data, not mere opinions, should play the central role in guiding allegiance to any given correctional theory and the correctional system it proposes.

Importantly, correctional theories are not autonomous entities that exist in some virtual reality above the world they seek to guide. Rather, they are produced by and believed by humans who live in particular socio-historical times. If you were living in the first part of the 1900s rather than today, your view of the world and of offenders might be quite different. If you now reside in a Red State or a Blue State, or perhaps in an urban neighborhood wracked by crime or in a gated community in a ritzy suburb, your policy preferences might not be the same. One author of this book (Cullen) grew up in Massachusetts in an Irish family in which John Kennedy was admired and nary a Republican was in sight. He was schooled by the Sisters of Notre Dame who expertly inculcated not only a deep capacity for guilt but also a deep commitment to social justice. As a grade-school child, he learned the value of charity, donating coinage—and even the occasional dollar bill—to aid the poor and to help missionaries save "pagan babies" (yes, this is what the good Sisters called non-Catholic children in foreign lands!). Perhaps it is not surprising that his first book was called *Reaffirming Rehabilitation* (Cullen & Gilbert, 1982). Be forewarned: Cullen remains a supporter of rehabilitation—as is the case for coauthor Jonson, whose Catholic upbringing is a story for another time. We claim to be so now not because of nuns, priests, or the Pope, but because we are scientists who can read the empirical evidence. We will leave it to the readers to determine if this is indeed the case.

Thus, the chapters in this book are arranged—from front to back—in a rough timeline to show how the fate of correctional theories largely has hinged on the prevailing social context. For example, in politically liberal times, theories embracing offender reformation have flourished, whereas in more conservative times American corrections has been directed by theories advocating punishing offenders harshly and through incarceration.

In Chapter 2, we begin this story by showing how the theory of rehabilitation emerged in the Progressive Era of the early 1900s and dominated American corrections into the 1960s. The social turmoil of the sixties led to the attack on this therapeutic vision and resulted in theories emphasizing punishment. The conservative times of the 1980s, dominated by President Ronald Reagan, constituted a receptive context for seeing offenders as wicked super-predators beyond redemption and in need of caging. More recently, the limits, if not at times the bankruptcy, of political conservatism have created space for more reformist approaches to offenders. In fact, there is a growing consensus across political parties that mass imprisonment is no longer sustainable. The United States is now at a crucial policy turning point in trying to decide what the correctional system should seek to accomplish. Correctional theory promises to be at the center of the policy conversation that is ongoing across the nation.

The key intent of this analysis is to sensitize readers to the reality that *social context matters*. What people experience shapes how they see the world, which in turn makes them more receptive to certain correctional theories than to others. This is true of readers, of criminologists, and of us. Large shifts in the social context thus tend to produce shifts in the extent to which a given theory continues to "make sense" to the American public. It can also affect whether politicians believe that they can use specific crime control policies—such as favoring "law and order"—to advance their careers (Garland, 2001; Simon, 2007).

If context has a defining influence on correctional theory and policy, this may mean that, by contrast, something else plays only a limited role in guiding system practices. What might this "something else" be—something that is not paid attention to sufficiently? Some readers might anticipate the answer to this question: It is the *evidence* on whether a theory has merit. Does what the perspective proposes actually work? A huge problem in corrections is that many policies and practices have been based more on common sense rooted in individuals' experiences than on hard empirical evidence. This failure to consult the evidence has led to correctional interventions that either are ineffective or iatrogenic—a fancy medical term meaning that the "cure" actually makes the patient, in this case the offender, worse off. In medicine, we call using interventions not based on the scientific evidence *quackery*. As we note below, *correctional quackery* is widespread and its eradication is a key challenge for those hoping to make American corrections better for offenders and better for public safety (Latessa, Cullen, & Gendreau, 2002).

Thus far, then, we have identified the core themes that inform the chapters that follow. Let us summarize them clearly here:

- Correctional theories identify what the purpose of the correctional system should be and what policies should be implemented.

- Historically, the popularity of competing correctional theories has been shaped by the prevailing social context. People's experiences affect what ideas about crime and its control make sense to them.

- Theories should be judged in large part on whether the policies they suggest achieve what they promise. Is a theory guilty of false advertisement—of making claims it cannot produce?

- The key to knowing what does and does not work—to knowing which theories should be embraced—is to look at the data. Corrections should be evidence-based.

In the remainder of this chapter, we address two topics in some detail. First, we have already mentioned that there are different theories of corrections. Thus, we start out by explaining what these are and then discuss issues related to them. In particular, we show why knowing whether these theories work—whether they have utility—is essential to knowing whether we should endorse them. Second, this analysis leads us directly into an examination of evidence-based corrections, a movement that argues for the use of data to inform correctional policy and practice. A large part of this book is about using evidence to evaluate the relative merits of the competing correctional theories. We alert readers—as we have done above—that corrections is a domain in which those in charge do many things to those under their control *without ever consulting the research evidence on what the best practices might be.* Readers might think that we are joking or, in the least, exaggerating. We are not.

In a way, we are mystified by this reluctance to consult the evidence before intervening in the lives of others. We consider it unprofessional, especially when people's lives are at stake—including both offenders themselves and those they might victimize in the future (Latessa et al., 2002). Still, we realize that the evidence on what does and does not work in corrections is not always clear. Studies can reach conflicting conclusions, and those who must daily face real-life inmates and community-based offenders are often undertrained and overworked. Finding out what is a best practice—separating quackery from effective policy and practice—is often a daunting challenge.

In this context, this book attempts to present the evidence on rival correctional theories in what we hope is an accessible way. Make no mistake: Some issues are technical and some conclusions are, at best, provisional. But we trust that after taking an excursion through this volume's pages, readers will be more equipped to know the merits of the main correctional theories and will be more prepared to practice evidence-based corrections.

Theories of Corrections

What we call theories of corrections are often referred to as *philosophies of punishment*. This terminology is employed because each approach—for example, rehabilitation or deterrence—is seen as providing a philosophical justification for why it is legitimate for the state to punish someone through the criminal justice system. In the case of rehabilitation, the justification would be that the state sanctions in order to reform the wayward offender. We prefer the construct of *theories of corrections,* however, because it is broader in scope. It includes not only the goal or justification for sanctioning an offender but also the accompanying blueprint for how the correctional system should be *designed* in order to achieve a given goal. Thus, if rehabilitation is seen as corrections' main goal, then this will dictate a certain kind of sentencing, whether to have a separate juvenile court, the nature of community supervision, and the use of therapeutic programs in prison.

Thus, each philosophy or goal logically suggests a corresponding theory about which policies and practices should be pursued in the correctional system. This link between goals and what is done in corrections is often missed. In part, this is because most of us have multiple ideas of what the correctional system should accomplish—that is, we have *multiple goals* we want corrections to pursue. This is probably a practical way of viewing things, but it does mean that we often embrace goals that require *incompatible correctional policies and practices.* Take, for example, parole. The goal of "rehabilitation" would justify this policy (i.e., release inmates when they have been "cured"), whereas the goal of "deterrence" would not (i.e., parole would just teach inmates that they will not be fully punished for their crimes). Now, if we wanted the correctional system to deter and to rehabilitate, that might be a reasonable thing to desire. However, organizing the system to accomplish both goals fully is impossible. In this case, it is not feasible to both have and not have parole!

Again, in judging correctional theories, a key issue is that of effectiveness. Most often in corrections, we measure effectiveness—whether something works—by its impact on *recidivism* (although sometimes the focus is on *crime rates*). That is, if you follow a certain theory of corrections, does it make it less likely that offenders will return to crime? We could use other outcome measures, such as whether the theory saves money or makes offenders more employable and better citizens. But let's be serious here: The "biggie" criterion for measuring effectiveness in corrections is whether something reduces crime.

As noted above, it is a daunting challenge to determine whether a policy—say, placing youths in a boot camp or in a prison cell—works to diminish reoffending. This is why, as criminologists, we are driven to distraction when scholars, policy makers, media commentators, or people at the donut shop just glibly say that a certain policy "works." How do they know? Well, it's their "opinion." That is not good enough! Remember, we favor science over attitude. We want all readers to jump on the bandwagon of evidence-based corrections!

Seven Theories in Brief

The intent at this point is to give a brief introduction to the major theories of corrections. These will be reviewed in greater detail in chapters devoted to each one. There are seven main theories of corrections:

- Retribution or Just Deserts
- Deterrence
- Incapacitation
- Restorative Justice
- Rehabilitation
- Reentry
- Early Intervention

RETRIBUTION: BALANCING THE SCALES OF JUSTICE

At the core of this theory is the mandate to pay an offender back for his or her wrongdoing. This attempt to "get even" is sometimes called "retribution" and sometimes called "just deserts." Conservatives tend to favor the former term, liberals the latter. Why? Because conservatives wish to ensure that offenders feel the pain they have caused, they thus seek retribution. By contrast, liberals wish to make sure that offenders suffer no more than the pain they have caused; they want to see justice done but only that which is truly deserved. This distinction between retribution and just deserts is more than semantics—more than a war of words. Conservatives typically believe that retribution is achieved only when harsh punishments—especially lengthy prison terms—have been imposed, whereas liberals typically believe that just deserts is achieved through more moderate punishments and shorter prison sentences. Despite these differences, those in both political camps embrace the idea that the core purpose of the correctional system is to balance the scales of justice.

Note, however, that "getting even"—this balancing the scales of justice through a figurative eye-for-an-eye approach—is unrelated to the goal of reducing crime and of making communities safer. Offenders are punished as an *end in and of itself*—to achieve justice. Such pain or punishment is seen as warranted or "deserved" because the offender is assumed to have used his or her "free will" in deciding to break the law.

Because retribution or just deserts seeks to be an end in and of itself, this theory is called *non-utilitarian*. Theories that are *utilitarian* seek to sanction offenders not simply to sanction them, but for some other purpose. This purpose is most often to reduce crime. For example, I might put you in prison in hopes that someone else will learn of your fate and be too afraid to break the law. This is the so-called notion of punishing Peter to make Paul conform. To someone who believes in retribution, this action would be immoral. Peter should be punished only for what Peter personally has done. What Paul might or might not do should not be a consideration. In any event, hard as it is to keep straight, let us repeat the point: Principled advocates of retribution or just deserts could care less about how criminal sanctions affect crime. They are in the business of doing justice, not controlling crime.

As we will note shortly, utilitarian theories make the claim that their approach to corrections works best to reduce crime. This is an *empirical issue*. We can test these assertions by examining the data. This is where evidenced-based corrections becomes important. For the most part, evidence is not central to evaluating retribution or just deserts. This theory is based mainly on values—on the principle that people who harm others deserve to be harmed equally in response. We will not delve deeply into the issue here, but suffice it to say that this theory does make claims that can be evaluated with evidence—not about reducing crime but about other things.

For example, retribution or just deserts bases its morality on the assertion that people break the law due to their free will. This is why this theory demands that punishments should be calibrated to the seriousness of the crime; the more serious the crime, the harsher the punishment. Focusing exclusively on the crime presumes that all people are the same and thus face the same choice when it comes to crime. The only thing that separates them is how they decide to exercise their free will—to break the law or not. But what if criminological research shows—as indeed it does—that the propensity for crime begins in the first years of life and that offenders are, through no conscious choice of their own, quite different from non-offenders? What does this do to the free will assumption? In short, criminological evidence has implications for the claims of retribution theory whenever they are based on some view of how people and the world actually operate.

DETERRENCE: SCARING OFFENDERS STRAIGHT

Deterrence theory proposes that offenders should be punished so that they will be taught that "crime does not pay" and thus will not to return to crime. Note that deterrence theory assumes that offenders are rational. Accordingly, efforts to increase the cost of crime—usually through more certain and severe penalties—will cause offenders to choose to "go straight" out of fear that future criminality will prove too painful. They will refrain from reoffending so as to avoid the cost of the criminal sanction. This is called *specific deterrence*; sometimes, the term *special deterrence* is used. In any event, the key point is the assumption that punishing Mary—such as putting her in jail for a while—will make her less like to recidivate.

There is also the concept of *general deterrence*. Here, the assumption is made that people might decide to commit or not commit a crime depending on what they see happens to other people who break the law. One reason to punish Mary, then, is to make Paula think twice and not commit the crime she might have been contemplating. So, just to sum up: When *other people* in society refrain from crime because they witness offenders' punishments and fear suffering a similar fate, this is called *general deterrence*.

What kinds of correctional policies do you think deterrence theory favors? To start with, deterrence advocates oppose discretion—that is, giving people like judges the freedom to place, for example, one robber in prison but not another or allowing parole officials to release one robber earlier from prison than another. You and I might disagree with deterrence theory on this point; we might want to give judges and parole board members such discretionary powers because no two robbers are the same. The two robbers just mentioned might have offended for different reasons—one to get money to buy drugs and party all night, the other in response to a mental disturbance. Similarly, when sent to prison, one robber might have worked harder than the other to be rehabilitated. Does it make sense to keep them both behind bars the same length of time? Because people, including any two criminals, differ, treating them the same in corrections ignores this important reality. It can result in interventions that do not work. Your authors, Cullen and Jonson, do, in fact, believe this.

Such thinking by Cullen, Jonson, and most other criminologists, according to deterrence theory, is mistaken. (Cullen and Jonson will return to this issue later in this book.) Deterrence advocates believe—or at least are willing to assume—that offenders exercise rational choice when breaking the law. This view is akin to the idea of free will, only a bit more specific. Offenders are seen to use their free will but in a rational way: They assess the potential costs of committing a crime, such as going to prison, versus the potential benefits, such as stealing money or, say, a computer.

If people do in fact consciously weigh costs and benefits, then two things follow. First, in many criminal situations, the benefits of crime are staring offenders in the face: They can see the laptop computer that is there for the taking or a pusher's hand is displaying drugs to get high on if only they exchange some cash. Put another way, the gratifications tend to be immediate and often easily attained (Gottfredson & Hirschi, 1990). So why not succumb to temptation and grab these crime benefits? According to deterrence theorists, people will exercise self-control only when a little accountant in their heads pops up and says: "Hmm. Let's do the calculation. Not a good idea. If you steal that computer and get caught, you will go to jail. It's not worth it. Walk on by that computer, my foolish friend!"

Second, the critical issue thus becomes whether this little accountant thinks the crime—stealing the computer—will lead to an arrest and, if so, knows what punishment a subsequent conviction will actually bring. According to deterrence theorists, we cannot be ambiguous here. We cannot say, "Well, if you are caught, you might or might not go to prison. And if you go to prison, you might stay five years but you might get out in one year." Every time judges and parole boards exercise discretion, they claim, the cost of punishment is made either less certain or less severe. No wonder, then, that the little accountant often concludes: "Hmm. How the hell do I know what's going to happen to you? Take the damn computer, sell it for some hard cash, and then let's get high and party down, dude!"

Deterrence theory thus provides a basis for a particular kind of correctional system. Punish the crime, not the criminal. This is done not to achieve retribution or just deserts but to reduce crime. Deterrence is a utilitarian theory; it is all about crime control. Punishments are to be fixed tightly to specific crimes so that offenders will soon learn that the state means business. Do the crime and you will do the time. No wiggle room allowed; no parole once sent to prison. Instead, the sentences served are to be determinate, not indefinite or indeterminate. Convicted offenders should be told at sentencing precisely how long they will spend in prison; once the sentence is imposed, no early release—the cost is carved in stone and not mitigated later on. Ideally, if prison sentences are going to be imposed, they should be made mandatory for everyone convicted of a crime. To stop the behavior, it is held, make the cost clear and unavoidable: Possess an illegal firearm, sell drugs, rob a store, then it is automatically off to prison.

INCAPACITATION: LOCKING UP PREDATORS

Here, no assumption is made about offenders and why they commit their crimes. Instead, criminals are likened to wild, predatory animals, such as a tiger, whose essential natures are given and are not going to change. For whatever reasons, the argument goes, those we send to prison have shown that they are predatory. We do not really care why they got that way, and we should have no illusions that they can be reformed. Good sense mandates that we remove them from society. To keep us safe, we place predatory animals in cages and behind sturdy walls. We should do the same with predatory offenders.

Thus, the explicit utilitarian goal is to reduce crime by caging or incarcerating offenders. The amount of crime saved—that does not occur—because an offender is in prison and not in the community is called the *incapacitation effect*. When prison is used to lock up everyone who has committed a certain crime (e.g., all gun offenders), this is called *collective incapacitation*. When an effort is made to predict who will be high-rate offenders and lock up only them, this is called *selective incapacitation*.

Sounds good, huh? There is a compelling, virtually indisputable logic to incapacitation. If dangerous offenders are behind bars, then they are not in my community— or any community—committing crime. What could be wrong with that? Well, to an extent, nothing. But incapacitation theory confronts two daunting difficulties. First, its main correctional advice is to build more and more cages to house more and more offenders. This approach creates a correctional system that constructs prisons constantly and then fills them to the brim. We suspect that this is done because most offenders standing before the court manifest at least some risk of recidivating. If judges have an incapacitation mind-set, then it is logical to think: "Better safe than sorry; better send this one to prison." Other options—such as sending offenders into a community-based rehabilitation program—are not considered.

The issue of how to spend the public's money is important. Prisons are very expensive to build and maintain; they run 24/7, and guarding inmates is labor intensive. There is an immense *opportunity cost* to prisons. An opportunity cost is what you forgo—what you do not do—when you spend money on one thing (e.g., going out to eat) rather than on another (e.g., seeing a movie). In corrections, money devoted to prisons cannot be devoted to treatment programs or, perhaps, to creating early intervention programs. Closer to home, such funds also cannot be employed by the government to subsidize college education. In most states, students reading this book now pay higher tuition because tax dollars once used to defray such costs have been steadily siphoned off to pay for an ever-expanding prison complex. Whether many readers of this book realize it, they are paying indirectly to incapacitate offenders.

Second, the theory of incapacitation has nothing useful to say about what to do with the more than 620,000 offenders who return to society each year—most after serving about two to three years behind bars (Carson, 2014; Petersilia, 2003). In fact, the theory is deafeningly silent on this issue. Should we simply ignore this horde of prison veterans and hope for the best? Further, the theory has nothing useful to say about whether we might reduce ex-inmates' high chances of recidivating while the offenders are still in prison. Research evidence now shows that simply caging offenders, placing them in prison and doing little else, typically either leaves their criminal propensities unchanged or strengthens them (Cullen, Jonson, & Nagin, 2011; Nagin, Cullen, & Jonson, 2009). There is that darn iatrogenic effect again—a correctional practice that worsens an offender's criminality. This finding is not good for incapacitation theory.

RESTORATIVE JUSTICE: REDUCING HARM

When a crime takes place, *harm* occurs—to the victim, to the community, and to the offender. The traditional theories of corrections do not make rectifying this harm in a systematic way an important goal. Even with retribution—where the *state* punishes and balances the scales of justice—any reward or satisfaction to the victim is indirect. In contrast, in *restorative justice,* the state acts more as an arbitrator and less as an adversary. The goal is for all harms to be rectified and the injured parties to be restored. Offenders must restore the victims and community they harmed. This might be done by apologizing and by providing restitution to the victim and doing service for the community. In exchange, however, the offender is, ideally, forgiven by the victim and accepted back into the community as a full-fledged member.

Restorative justice is both non-utilitarian and utilitarian. It is non-utilitarian because there is an overriding concern for achieving justice in and of itself. In this case, the justice is not, as it is in retribution or just deserts, adversarial with the goal of inflicting pure harm on the offender. Think of Lady Justice with her scales tilted downward on one side. In retribution, the scales are balanced by pulling the offender down by having the individual experience pain—arrest, public stigmatization, prison, continued exclusion by the community. By contrast, in restorative justice, the scale tilted downward is pushed back up—restored to its previous position. The goal is thus to motivate offenders to admit their wrongdoing, apologize to victims, and take steps to compensate victims and the community for the harms suffered. The response of others is to hate the sin—it is condemned and shamed—but to love the sinner, if not literally, then at least in the sense of making reintegration possible. Restoration, not retribution—getting everyone back to normal, not getting even—is the goal.

Restorative justice is utilitarian, however, because it claims that its approach of harm reduction is more likely to lower recidivism than the typical correctional response. In fact, advocates of restorative justice wish to take offenders out of the traditional justice system, using prisons only as a sanction of last resort. They prefer to create a parallel justice system that is devoid of judges, prosecutors, defense attorneys, probation officers, and so on. Instead, when a crime occurs, the plan would be to have a "facilitator" call for a "restorative justice conference" (Braithwaite, 1998, p. 326). At this conference, multiple parties will be convened: the offender, the offender's family members, people from the community who know and will support the offender, the victim, and his or her kin and supporters. The victim's story, including harm experienced, will be told, and the offender will feel remorse and apologize. Guided by the facilitator, the group will develop a plan for restitution and for using members of the family and the community to build relationships with the offender so as to make recidivism unlikely.

There is much that is appealing about this theory, but also a good bit that is potentially problematic. One immediate difficulty is how to implement restorative justice in a nation that has more than 2.2 million offenders incarcerated—a number that may well decline but is unlikely any time soon to head south of 2 million. The other problem is that restorative justice theory is antiscientific. Its advocates believe, for example, that research on what works to make rehabilitation programs more or less effective is irrelevant. They are convinced that the key to reducing crime is the good faith efforts of non-professionals to construct a web of supportive relationships around the wayward that makes reoffending unlikely. We are all for social support and agree that the needless stigmatizing and rejection of offenders is counterproductive (Cullen, 1994; Cullen & Jonson, 2011a). Still, we are uncomfortable with any correctional theory that is not rooted in sound scientific criminology and in evidence-based corrections.

REHABILITATION: SAVING THE WAYWARD

As already intimated, Cullen and Jonson, your authors, are advocates of rehabilitation. We must let you in on a bit of a secret. When authors favor a certain theory, they usually discuss it toward the end of the book—as we do here. Why? Because they want to tell you what is wrong about all the rival theories before explaining why their perspective is the best! We are disclosing this information so that readers will understand where our potential biases might rest. We say "potential," because our goal here is not to be biased—to pull some ideological wool over the readers' eyes. Rather, we support rehabilitation for what we see as a good reason: the empirical weakness of the other theories of corrections and rehabilitation's consistency with what we know about the causes of offending and how best to reduce it. To be direct, Cullen and Jonson are convinced that a correctional system devoid of rehabilitation will increase recidivism and endanger public safety.

In the rehabilitation perspective, the goal is to intervene so as to *change those factors that are causing offenders to break the law.* The assumption is made that, at least in part, crime is determined by factors (e.g., antisocial attitudes, bad companions, dysfunctional family life). Unless these criminogenic risks are targeted for change, then crime will continue. Thus, crime is saved—recidivism is reduced—to the extent that correctional interventions succeed in altering the factors within or very close to offenders that move them to commit crimes (Andrews & Bonta, 2010).

What we have just outlined is not based on Advanced Rocket Science Criminology but is taught in Introduction to Criminology—a course readers might have taken. Every theory covered in the introductory course identifies a set of factors that is purported to increase the risk of crime: exposure to strain, differential association with antisocial peers, lack of social bonds or self-control, stigmatizing labeling, residing in a disorganized neighborhood, neuropsychological deficits, biosocial developmental trajectories, and so on. Does any of this sound familiar? Criminologists assume that crime is chosen but not according to some vague notion of rational choice. Rather, crime is held to be chosen for a reason—something is driving or shaping the choice. Again, criminological theories tell us what those reasons are (Lilly, Cullen, & Ball, 2015).

The implications of Introduction to Criminology are thus profound. If individuals do indeed commit crime because of the risk factors identified by criminologists, then it follows logically that their offending will continue unless they are cured of the criminal forces within and around them. This is why rehabilitation makes sense: It involves the use of correctional programs to cure what is wrong with offenders. In turn, this means that the system should be arranged to deliver effective treatment. We will describe the components of a rehabilitation-oriented system in Chapter 2, but for now we will note that it involves policies such as pre-sentence reports, indeterminate sentences and parole release, making prisons therapeutic, and having probation and parole officers provide or broker services for their supervisees. The overriding goal is to individualize treatment: Know what is criminogenic about each offender and try to fix it.

Introduction to Criminology is also why advocates of rehabilitation do not believe that inflicting harsh punishments on offenders is a prudent crime control policy. These approaches just do not change what makes criminals recidivate. Thus, rehabilitation theory predicts that if offenders are incapacitated—simply warehoused without treatment—then they will leave prison no better off, and worse off if they have been exposed to criminogenic risk factors while behind bars. The theory also predicts that deterrence-based policies will not be very effective in preventing reoffending because they are based on a limited, if not incorrect, theory of crime (crime is simply a rational choice). For the most part, these predictions turn out to be true.

To be fair, rehabilitation has its own challenges to overcome if it is to claim the mantle as the guiding theory of corrections. For one thing, it is not easy to change people who do not want to change and may have spent their whole lives developing into hard-core criminals. Further, saving people within correctional agencies is difficult. Prisons are hardly ideal therapeutic settings, and many correctional workers lack the professional orientation, therapeutic expertise, and organizational resources to deliver effective interventions. Many programs initiated under the guise of rehabilitation are non-scientific and have no chance of reducing reoffending. For those readers not inclined to like rehabilitation, there is plenty of grist for your mill. We believe, of course, that the alternative correctional theories are far more problematic. But this will be for each reader to decide.

REENTRY: SAVING RELEASED PRISONERS

Here is the difficulty of mass imprisonment—more than 1.5 million inmates are housed on any given day in state and federal prisons: When you send a lot of people to prison, a lot of people come out of prison! Duh! This is what Jeremy Travis (2005, p. xxi), called the "iron law of imprisonment: they all come back." Well, actually, it is about 95% of those sent to prison who come back—since a handful are executed, others—more than should—die due to medical reasons during their incarceration, and a fair number are serving life sentences that ban their release. But Travis (2005) got the big picture correct, which is why he titled his book on the subject, *But They All Come Back.*

It was not that Travis was the first to recognize this fact. Complaints that parole does not work and that recidivism rates for released prisoners are too high appeared regularly for years, if not decades. In the 1960s and 1970s, calls were made to "reintegrate" inmates returning to the community. Yet this concern was muted and unorganized. It was as though not paying attention to the obvious coming-back problem would make it go away. Maybe this neglect was possible because the numbers involved, although high, were not yet staggering. But this would change. Thus, the number of released inmates from state and federal prisons first topped 200,000 in 1983 and 300,000 in 1988. The annual count continued on a steep upward trajectory. New records were set in rather quick order: 400,000 was reached just two years later in 1990; 500,000 was surpassed in 1997; and 600,000 was attained in 2000 (Carson & Golinelli, 2013).

By the time Travis published his book in 2005, more than 700,000 inmates were being released annually—a figure that rose to a high mark of 729,749 in 2009 (Carson & Golinelli, 2013). This was a bad time for American corrections, but good timing for Travis's book. Along with Joan Petersilia (2003), who wrote a similar book around the same time (called *When Prisoners Come Home*), his message was now difficult to ignore: We have to do something about the horde of inmates returning to our communities who then often are arrested and sent back to prison

(Clear, 2007). The number of released inmates has fallen more than 100,000 inmates, down to 623,337 in 2013 (Carson, 2014). Still, we are talking about more than 620,000 people, which is a lot! In fact, it is equal to or higher than the populations of a bunch of major U.S. cities, including Atlanta, Boston, Cincinnati, Miami, New Orleans, and Minneapolis. If you do not believe us, just Google "major American cities," which is what we did!

But there was one more clever thing that Travis—and Petersilia—both did: They used the word *reentry* (actually in the subtitles of their two books) to describe the problem. Does a word really make that much of a difference? Well, in this case the answer is "yes." The word reentry captured the reality that inmates are not simply being "released" or "returning" to society. Rather, they undergo an inevitable experience of having to leave prison and reenter a social life that they have been kept away from for a lengthy period. Given that hundreds of thousands of inmates each year are confronted with this transition, they argued that this unique experience needs to be recognized and addressed seriously.

In a way, Travis and Petersilia were advancing a theory of corrections—a way of thinking that sought to guide policy and practice when it comes to releasing offenders back into prison. This theory is not the same as other theories that apply to virtually the entire correctional process, because it is focused on only one component of this system. Still, reentry cannot easily be placed under any other theory's umbrella—though it involves rehabilitation. Rather, it is its own unique entity and thus deserves its own unique examination.

Scholars have offered useful definitions of reentry (see, e.g., Gunnison & Helfgott, 2013; Mears & Cochran, 2015). For our purposes, as an event in inmates' lives, reentry is defined as the transition of offenders from an institution into the community, typically under some form of correctional supervision. As a *correctional theory*, reentry is a planned correctional intervention designed to facilitate an inmate's return to society so as to prevent further recidivism. Reentry programs can be undertaken in one of three phrases—or across all three phases: during incarceration; during a period that spans or immediately follows incarceration (e.g., a halfway house); or fully after incarceration.

Reentry also involves two central components. First, the *correctional component* covers the actions taken by officials to reduce the likelihood of recidivism. Typically, this intervention includes treatment programs aimed at reducing criminal propensity. However, another aspect would be the surveillance strategies used to control offenders in the community—such as during parole supervision. Second is the *reintegration component*. This involves taking positive steps to help released inmates assume core social roles (e.g., employment, family) and to acquire material support to survive in the "real world" (e.g., housing, medical services). It also involves trying to remove the negative "collateral consequences" that restrict reintegration into society. Often written into federal and state laws, collateral consequences are the rights (e.g., voting) and privileges (e.g., access to certain occupations) that offenders lose as a result of a criminal conviction, especially a prison sentence (see Alexander, 2010; Jacobs, 2015). Taken together, the correctional and reintegration components are intended to *save released inmates from a life in crime*.

EARLY INTERVENTION: SAVING THE CHILDREN

Early intervention involves placing children at risk for a criminal future into programs early in life so as to prevent them from developing into juvenile or adult criminals. For example, young, single, disadvantaged mothers are likely to smoke or ingest drugs during pregnancy, which in turn compromises the development of the fetus's brain. The resulting neuropsychological deficits can make the mother's offspring irritable as a baby, hard to discipline as a toddler, and unable to focus on schoolwork as a child. These behaviors often lead to harsh and erratic parenting, rejection by other children, and failing grades in school—and, as you might imagine, place the youngster on a pathway to early conduct problems, associations with like-minded antisocial peers, dropping out of school, and progressively deeper involvement in delinquent behavior. How might this criminal trajectory be prevented? David Olds (2007) ingeniously came up with the idea of sending experienced nurses to visit these at-risk expectant mothers both during pregnancy (to encourage healthy behavior) and after pregnancy (to help the mothers in parenting skills). This program has proven successful in achieving healthy pregnancies and thus in saving children from struggling with crime-inducing deficits that can be traced to the womb.

The appeal of early intervention lies in its inherent logic: If something can be prevented, then why not do so? Why wait until the child develops into a predator who hurts someone and must be incarcerated? Does not a "stitch in time save nine"? Of course, few things involving humans turn out to be as easy as they sound on the surface. It is a daunting challenge to identify who the future criminals of America will be. Further, unlike the correctional system, there is no early intervention system to take up this child-saving task. Still, there should be, and the persuasive logic of early intervention is becoming more difficult to ignore. It now appears that early intervention programs will be an increasing part of the effort to save at-risk children and adolescents (Farrington & Welsh, 2007). It is why we have chosen to include it in this book.

In a way, early intervention is not really a correctional theory in that it does not carry advice on how to organize the correctional system. Whereas corrections focuses on what should be done with people *after* they have broken the law, early intervention focuses on what should be done with people *before* they have broken the law. In a way, early intervention is the counterpart to rehabilitation—just that it takes place earlier in the life course. Thus, similar to rehabilitation, early intervention is based on the criminological reality that individuals with certain traits and exposed to certain social conditions develop propensities to engage in crime. Only if these propensities are diagnosed and cured through some treatment will the individual be diverted from crime. This is preferably accomplished in the beginning stages of life (early intervention) but, if not, then it must be accomplished later in life (correctional rehabilitation).

Finally, as readers proceed through the discussions of the various views on corrections, Table 1.1 might serve as a useful synopsis of the theories. For each theory, the table summarizes its core goal, whether it is utilitarian or non-utilitarian, whether it focuses on the crime or the criminal, and the key correctional policies it recommends.

Table 1.1 Theories of Corrections

Theory	Purpose	Utilitarian	Focus on Crime or Criminal	Key Correctional Policies
Retribution/ Just Deserts	Get even Do justice	No	Crime	Determinate sentence Limit discretion
Deterrence		Yes	Crime	Mandatory sentences Abolish parole
General	Scare the public straight		Crime	High levels of imprisonment
Specific	Scare offenders straight		Crime	Long prison sentences Intensive supervision Scared-straight programs
Incapacitation		Yes	Both	Imprisonment
General	Imprison all offenders		Crime	Mass incarceration
Selective	Imprison high-rate offenders		Criminal	Incarcerate career criminals
Restorative Justice	Reduce harm to offender, victim, and community	Yes	Criminal	Sentencing conferences Restitution Offender reintegration
Rehabilitation	Reform offender	Yes	Criminal	Treatment programs Probation and parole Juvenile justice system
Reentry	Reduce recidivism among released inmates	Yes	Criminal	Treatment programs Reintegration programs Reduce collateral consequences
Early Intervention	Treat at-risk youngsters to prevent a criminal career	Yes	Criminal	Nurse home visitation Head Start Family therapy Multisystemic therapy

Utility, Opinion, and Evidence

We live in a society that values justice. This is why we expect offenders to be punished at a level that is consistent with the seriousness of their crime. That is, we want a measure of "just deserts," with more serious crimes receiving harsher punishments. Any correctional system will thus have to pay attention to issues of retribution or just deserts. An offender's punishment must fall within acceptable lower limits (it cannot be too lenient) and acceptable upper limits (it cannot be too harsh). However, the difficulty with a system based exclusively on retribution or just deserts is that we also live in a society that values utility—that wants things to "work." Our correctional system thus is expected to balance these competing expectations: to do justice and to be utilitarian—that is, to exact retribution and to work to reduce crime.

Correctional policies and practices that violate these expectations of justice and utility risk being challenged. That is, one way to discredit a correctional policy— such as parole release—is to oppose it on the grounds that it creates injustice or increases crime. Of course, the opposite also holds: One way to advocate for a policy is to say that it promotes justice or reduces crime!

As we have seen, with the exception of retribution or just deserts, all other correctional theories embrace utility. They all claim that if their ideas are followed, crime will be reduced. Importantly, this claim is an *empirical issue* that can be decided by examining the existing evidence. Utilitarian goals only "make sense"—only seem worthy of our support—if, in fact, they have utility or benefits. If you advocate deterrence but the correctional system does not deter, then you are in big trouble! The same holds for the other correctional theories. In fact, philosophers would argue that if a utilitarian philosophy has no utility, then it has *no moral justification*. That is, the very morality of a utilitarian correctional philosophy hinges on its "coming through"—on it achieving the goals it states it will achieve.

At this point, we can see why a person's "opinion" is *irrelevant*. Whether a certain way of doing corrections has utility—for example, placing an offender in prison as opposed to a community cognitive-behavioral treatment program—is not a matter of what you, me, some politician, Snoop Dogg, or Snoopy might think. Saying that something works to reduce crime does not make it so. In fact, many people who set up correctional interventions suffer the sin of hubris—of unwarranted overconfidence. They easily delude themselves that some program they like—especially when they can give it a catchy name like *scared straight* or *boot camp*—will reduce recidivism simply because they think it will. But if we know anything about the history of failed programs in corrections, hubris typically is the first step to doing something stupid that has no chance of working.

Again, determining whether a correctional philosophy has its intended utility— whether it "works"—is not a matter of opinion but of *scientific evidence*—of research findings. This is why it is essential for us to take seriously the need for *evidence-based corrections*—a topic we examine in some detail in the next section. Before doing so, however, we want to emphasize that a major purpose of this book is to subject the utilitarian claims of the major correctional theories to empirical scrutiny. If we do what any given correctional theory advises, will these policies and practices result in less crime? Which theory is most supported by the empirical evidence? Which theory should guide American corrections in the 21st century? These are large and important questions, and ones that all students of corrections should take seriously. Again, our intent in this book is to provide readers with a careful assessment of these issues. Regardless of which theory readers favor at this book's end, we trust that mere opinions will be relinquished in favor of a serious understanding of the evidence.

Evidence-Based Corrections

Around the year 2000, a general movement was initiated to make criminal justice *evidence-based*. Lawrence Sherman (1998) was the first to use the term explicitly in this policy domain when he called for an evidence-based policing. Shortly thereafter, Cullen and Paul Gendreau (2000) and Doris MacKenzie (2000, 2006) set forth the case for evidence-based corrections. More broadly, there were calls to make policy and practice systematically evidence-based in other social domains, including education, medicine, and—as we will see below—baseball (Ayres, 2007; Davies, 1999; Timmermans & Berg, 2003).

In short, there was an emerging recognition in the United States and beyond that we had done a poor job of using the research we produced to help us make the best decisions possible—especially as these decisions impacted other people's lives. In some areas, such as medicine, scientific data were valued but often not organized in an optimum way to help doctors make correct, life-saving decisions. In others, such as criminal justice and baseball, the use of research was vigorously resisted and dismissed. These domains have had occupational traditions that value common sense and personal experience—sometimes called clinical judgment—over research evidence. Such ways of thinking and doing business die hard. Still, even in these more resistant areas, there is an increasing recognition that ignoring research data reduces effectiveness and exacts a high cost. This book thus is part of the effort to suggest that using the best evidence available to inform correctional policy and practice is a good idea.

CORRECTIONAL QUACKERY

Consider if medical doctors made decisions that affected the lives of patients without any reliance on medical research on "what works" to cure patients. We would call them "quacks." We would sue them in civil courts and perhaps cart them off to prison for needlessly injuring and killing people. Yet, in corrections, we often make decisions on the lives of offenders—which have implications for others, including future victims—based on myth, tradition, politics, convenience, personal opinion, and personal experience. The result is what Cullen and his good friends Edward Latessa and Paul Gendreau call *correctional quackery* (Latessa et al., 2002).

By correctional quackery, we are saying that much of what is done in corrections has the *scientific standing* that the practice of bloodletting would have in medicine! More formally, Latessa et al. (2002) define correctional quackery as "interventions that are based on neither (1) existing knowledge of the causes of crime nor (2) existing knowledge of what programs have been shown to change offender behavior. . . . The hallmark of correctional quackery is thus ignorance" (p. 43).

Our position is that correctional policy makers and practitioners (as well as those working in other agencies in the criminal justice system) have a *professional responsibility to seek out research evidence and to use this evidence to inform their decisions.* Corrections is not a "science" like medicine, but this does not mean that research evidence would not allow *better decisions to be made.* This is a theme we will revisit in this book.

INSIDER AND OUTSIDER KNOWLEDGE

Some readers might object that we should not place so much faith in "the evidence." What about "personal experience" that comes from working in agencies? Does not this count for something? In this regard, the late Robert K. Merton (1972), a former professor of Cullen's at Columbia University, distinguished between two kinds of knowledge: *insider* and *outsider.*

Insider knowledge refers to knowing about something because of all the personal experience an individual has had as an "insider"—as someone, for example, who has worked in a correctional agency or as a police officer. A person might have had many years to "make observations." The individual has *rich data,* so to speak, and is able to understand the *complexities* of working in a criminal justice environment. Sometimes, this is also called *clinical knowledge.* It is having an "experienced eye" and a "gut-level feeling" about what is going on and what one should do with, say, a particular offender.

Outsider knowledge refers to knowing about something because one applies a standard methodology—*the scientific method*—to determine what is "really true" in the world. "Outsiders" do not work in an agency but rather conduct studies to develop a body of research literature on the subject. They assume that if high-quality studies are conducted, the resulting knowledge will allow us to "know what is really going on." Personal experience is irrelevant because, in the end, faith is placed only in "what the data say."

Now, importantly, what kind of knowledge—insider or outsider—do you think is valued in this book? Right: It is outsider or scientific knowledge that counts as "evidence" here. In taking this position, we do not mean to be arrogant about what someone who works in the system—including readers—might know about corrections. Insider knowledge has a place in making decisions on the job. Sometimes, it is the only knowledge available. Sometimes, a situation is so unique that a worker needs to "put everything in the mix" and use his or her experience to make an informed *clinical judgment.*

But three problems typically are associated with "insider knowledge." When these occur, they can result in insider knowledge being incorrect or only partially correct. They can lead to "correctional quackery" (more generally, see Kahneman, 2011). First, there is the *N-of-1 problem.* This is the issue of *generalizability.* You and your experiences are, in essence, one case. In research, we use the letter "N" to refer to the number of cases—thus the idea of an "N of 1." Relying on personal experience—insider knowledge—means that you assume that *what you have experienced also holds for other people in other settings.* But this may not be the case, especially since you play a role in affecting your environment in ways that other people may not affect their environment (you are not a passive observer of "what's going on" but an active participant). Basing policy on your experiences thus may result in decisions that would not work for other people and in other places.

Second, there is the *conflicting-personal-experience problem.* What happens when the "knowledge" you draw from your personal experiences differs from the "knowledge" someone else draws from his or her personal experiences? Who is right? Whose "insider knowledge" should we believe? Science, however, has rules (i.e., the *scientific method*) for trying to figure out which knowledge is best. Science is messy, too, and there are disagreements. But, again, the scientific method at least provides an agreed-upon strategy for figuring out whose knowledge is correct.

Third is the *selectivity-of-perceptions problem.* In deciding what is true about your world, you do not have to record or take down every instance in which some practice is tried. Let's take baseball. Many managers use their personal experience and "gut feeling" about when, for example, to have runners steal a base. If they call a steal and it works, they believe that the strategy "works." But what about the three previous times when the runner was thrown out? If the manager had looked at all instances in which a steal was attempted, he might conclude that having runners steal is not a good strategy. But without such statistics—without a scientific approach—managers are free to *selectively perceive the events in their environment.* Now, the same *selective perception* can occur with personal experience. We may focus on the events that seem important to us—the successes or failures we have had—but ignore other events that were not as important (or pleasing) to us. We may thus form opinions about the world that are distorted by these selective perceptions.

The problem in corrections is, again, hubris: the belief by too many people—whether policy makers or practitioners—that their view of how to punish or rehabilitate offenders is correct because of all the personal experience they have had in the system. There is not a sense that their clinical judgment might be idiosyncratic, not shared by others, and focused on successes but blind to failures. Of course, if American corrections were a bastion of success—taking in the predatory on one side of the system and releasing them as angels on the other side of the system—we would be trumpeting insider knowledge and the clinical judgment it yields. In fact, Cullen and Jonson would not be writing this book. But the stubborn reality is that corrections is an area more often marked by failure than by success. On the face of things, it seems that we should be doing a better job. Phrased differently, ignoring research evidence has not produced much success.

EVIDENCE-BASED BASEBALL

Cullen and Jonson both like baseball and, as a result, think it holds important lessons for life. When Cullen was a youngster, his grandfather would take him to Red Sox games at Fenway Park, where bleacher seats were 50 cents. Jonson somehow became an Atlanta Braves fan. Growing up in Defiance, Ohio, her options for watching baseball on television were severely limited. With each and every Braves game televised on TBS, she became a die-hard Atlanta fan. If Cullen and Jonson were the Commissioners of Corrections, we thus would make everyone examine what has occurred in baseball over the past decade. This analysis would begin by having everyone read Michael Lewis's (2003) wonderful book, *Moneyball: The Art of Winning an Unfair Game.* Okay, see the 2011 movie version with Brad Pitt first and then read the book! We believe that this book holds important lessons for corrections (see also Cullen, Myer, & Latessa, 2009; Vito & Vito, 2013).

Moneyball is illuminating because it tells what happens when insiders who use insider knowledge run a baseball franchise as opposed to making decisions based on statistics or data—that is, decisions about who to draft, who to sign in free agency, and how to manage a game. As it turns out, major league baseball is—or at least traditionally was before *Moneyball* came on the scene—the ultimate insiders' game. Most general managers, managers, coaches, and scouts were, and still are, people who at one time or another played the game. They were socialized into and learned a culture that tells what are supposedly good baseball practices and what are bad baseball practices.

Strangely—that is, "strangely" for a sport that compiles reams of statistics—most of this insider wisdom is based not on statistics or *evidence* but on tradition rooted in personal experience (Gray, 2006; Schwarz, 2004). This involves the value of bunting late in a game, having a base runner try to steal, or perhaps advising a hitter to swing aggressively rather than work for walks (base on balls). On these and other things, it turned out that most of this insider wisdom is also wrong or true only under some circumstances (Tango, Lichtman, & Dolphin, 2007; see also Moskowitz & Wertheim, 2011). Decisions based on insider "gut feelings" rooted in personal "experience"—ignoring the evidence—were losing teams games and nobody realized it. Well, as true baseball fans might recall, Bill James, the guru of statistical baseball, understood this fact and tried to point it out, but almost nobody paid attention to him.

Insider perspectives also typically shaped who was drafted by major league teams. Teams have scouting departments because they believe that scouts—most of them having played in the major or minor leagues—can eyeball a player and tell who is likely to make it to the majors. Once again, this usually turns out to be an incorrect assumption. Scouts tend to be wowed not by statistical performances but by how a player "looks." They like players with a "major league body"—someone who is tall and rangy, who can run fast, or who can throw over 90 mph. This is because their job is not to read statistics but to use their "experience" to pick out the guy who will become a star. They can "tell" who is a baseball player when looking at prospects because they are insiders and their insider status gives them special expertise.

As you now can anticipate, this turns out not to be the case. Many highly effective ballplayers have been, and still are, overlooked by scouts because they are under six feet, a bit chubby and slow, and throw only 88 mph. This occurs even when their statistical performance is far superior to other players who "look better." This is because "everyone knows" that you can't be a major league player if you are undersized and not athletic in appearance. A key problem with the tradition of baseball is that those in charge are convinced they are right. It is that darn hubris thing again. They do not subject their knowledge to empirical test. When a bunt leads to a winning run being scored, they talk about "good strategy." When it does not, they do not wonder whether the strategy was stupid, but talk about players not hitting in the clutch with men in scoring position. Equipped with selective perception, their views about baseball are virtually impossible to falsify—to prove wrong.

As detailed in *Moneyball*, however, this situation changed when Billy Beane became general manager of the Oakland Athletics. He was once an athletic "phenom" who was drafted in the first round by the New York Mets (along with Darryl Strawberry!). Blessed with a "great body" and tons of athleticism, Billy Beane had one problem: When a pitch came his way, he could not tell a "ball" from a "strike." This meant that he did not do a good job getting on base. When Billy Beane became a general manager (GM), however, he realized that being an "athlete" (which he was) was not the same thing as being an *effective* baseball player (which he was not). He lost his trust in scouts and in accepted insider-baseball wisdom. He realized that what really mattered was not how a player looked, but how he *performed over long periods of time.*

Billy Beane also bought into a theory about baseball—in essence, the "theory of outs." The defining aspect of the game is that each inning has *three outs.* In effect, this means that anything that contributes to an "out" being made is bad for the offense and good for the defense because it limits the ability to score runs—and scoring runs is how baseball games are won! This means that what matters most for the offense is *getting on base.* Walks—long seen as irrelevant—are a very good thing. Not striking out is good, because any ball "put in play" has a chance of being a base hit. Hitting a home run is really good because it creates a run and prevents an out. In contrast, the best pitchers are those who strike out hitters, do not walk hitters, and do not give up home runs.

If these facts are true, then it would only make sense to draft, trade for, and sign free agent players who get on base a lot (i.e., have a "high on-base percentage") or, if pitchers, those who do not walk a lot of hitters and give up a bunch of home runs. In the end, it would *make almost no difference whatsoever* whether the players who do this are housed in athletic bodies or can throw 95 mph. Rather, you would know who the most effective players are by looking at their statistical history of performance. Preferably, you would mostly draft college players, because then you would have a longer statistical history to use in judging their performance. You would also scour the major leagues for undervalued players who performed well on key statistics (e.g., on-base percentage, slugging percentage) but were not the kind of athletic specimens who inspire awe. Further, if you used statistical data to select players—rather than insider knowledge—then arguably you would create a team that, collectively, produced a lot of runs and did not give up a lot of runs. Since scoring more runs than your opponent is what wins games, you would—over the course of a season—win a lot of games.

Now, Billy Beane was not the first person to argue that statistics should be used to make baseball decisions (Schwarz, 2004). Most famously, Bill James long advocated using statistics to manage baseball more effectively, and coined *sabermetrics,* a term that "married the acronym for the Society for American Baseball Research and the Latin suffix for measurement" (Schwarz, 2004, p. 127). However, the insider culture within baseball was so hegemonic—it dominated virtually everyone's thinking—that James was ignored for years (Gray, 2006). (He was eventually hired by the Red Sox before they ended an 86-year drought and won their two World Series championships in 2004 and 2006.)

Beane was innovative in that he was the first GM to use statistics systematically to control how he managed his team, the Oakland A's. Accordingly, he provided a test case for whether evidence-based baseball is more effective than insider-based baseball. Readers will have already figured out that Beane showed the value of an evidence-based approach—or Cullen and Jonson would not have devoted so much space to him. From 1999 to 2006, Beane's teams averaged 94 wins a season. By contrast, the New York Yankees averaged just 97 wins annually.

So what is the big deal? As Lewis points out in *Moneyball,* the issue is, well, money. During this time, the Yankees' payroll was three times higher—and yet they won only on average three games more per season. Between 1997 and 2005, the Oakland Athletics paid an average of $423,053 a win; the Yankees' cost per win in player salaries was over $1.2 million (Cullen, Myer, & Latessa, 2009). Further, during this time, the A's lost a cavalcade of all-stars to free agency or to trades made necessary by the threat of free agency. The only way that Beane would be successful on such a small budget was to practice evidence-based baseball: to use statistics rather than insider knowledge to make player-personnel decisions.

In short, the story of Billy Beane and the Oakland A's is a case study of what happens when decisions are based on *scientific evidence* and when those you are competing against base their decisions on custom and personal experience. Over the long haul, *rationality produces distinct advantages.* Other teams, for example, did not draft a pitcher like Barry Zito—an all-star pitcher—because he throws the ball only 88 mph. The Oakland A's did draft him because his past statistical performance was outstanding. They were more interested in how many batters Zito could get out rather than in how much "heat" he had on his fastball.

Billy Beane hired an assistant, Paul DePodesta, who had no professional baseball experience but did have a Harvard University education. In *Moneyball,* Lewis (2003) described DePodesta's thinking in this way:

> He was fascinated by irrationality, and the opportunities it created in human affairs for anyone who resisted it. He was just the sort of person who might have made an easy fortune in finance, but the market for baseball players, in Paul's view, was far more interesting than anything Wall Street offered. There was, for starters, the tendency for everyone who actually played the game to generalize wildly from his own experience. People always thought their own experience was typical when it wasn't. There was also a tendency to be overly influenced by a guy's most recent performance: what he did last was not necessarily what he would do next. Thirdly—but not lastly—there was the bias toward what people saw with their own eyes, or thought they had seen. The human mind played tricks on itself when it relied exclusively on what it saw, and every trick it played was a financial opportunity for someone who saw through the illusion to the reality. There was a lot you couldn't see when you watched a baseball game. (p. 18)

Since the *Moneyball* years, the Oakland A's have not always fared so well, which might lead some critics to question Beane's evidence-based approach to baseball management. Enduring baseball poverty and repeatedly losing star players did take a toll. But looks can be deceiving. After a few losing years, the A's averaged more than 92 wins a year from 2012 to 2014. Further, Benjamin Morris (2014) provides a broader perspective by calculating how Beane's teams performed from 2000 up to 2014 relative to the salary available and relative to other teams. He found that the A's led Major League Baseball with an annual average of 12 wins above payroll expectations. In financial terms, Morris (2014) concludes that "the A's have exceeded expectations by close to $1.38 billion"—yes, billion!

In the end, therefore, little doubt exists that Billy Beane's *Moneyball* approach was correct; the evidence is on his side. The greatest challenge, however, is that other general managers proved that they preferred to win games than continue to rely in incorrect insider knowledge! Alas, Lewis's *Moneyball* unmasked Beane's advantages—as two economists showed relative to the prior "underpayment of the ability to get on base" that "was substantially if not completely eroded within a year of *Moneyball's* publication" (Hakes & Sauer, 2006, p. 184). Now, all baseball teams have come to employ sabermetricians and to use statistics in personnel decisions. Even the scoreboards at baseball parks now report not only batting averages but also OBP (on-base percentage) and slugging percentage—statistics that relate to run production and winning games. "Analytics" also are increasingly used during games. As White (2014, p. C14) notes, a "proliferation of shifting defenses, shuffling lineups and statistically based efforts to identify the next edge or market inefficiency has impacted how the game is parsed and played." Although some may still hold on tightly to the traditional insider culture, the baseball world has had to become smarter—lest it fall prey to the data and rationality of GMs like Billy Beane.

Now, we trust that you can start to see—or even better, to start to truly feel—the connection between *evidence-based baseball* and *evidence-based corrections*. *Why not become the Billy Beane of corrections?* Of course, we well know that simple comparisons between baseball and corrections are a stretch. It is one thing to predict how many runs a team will score and quite another to predict the recidivism rate for a treatment program. But the broader point is worth truly contemplating: *In human endeavors—whether it is baseball, medicine, or corrections—ignorance is a dangerous thing.*

The special risk of insider knowledge is that it is a potential source of a particularly troublesome type of ignorance: beliefs that, because they are rooted in our personal experience, we just "know" to be true (or cannot believe are incorrect). The challenge for those of us in or who care about corrections, then, is to escape the blinders of mere personal experience, to take steps to learn about the existing scientific evidence, and to use this evidence to support interventions that are the most likely to be effective.

Conclusion: What's Ahead?

Corrections is serious business. People's lives are at stake—both offenders and potential victims. The harsh reality is that, similar to fighting cancer, success comes in small doses, incrementally, and only after careful research and experimentation. But corrections is not merely a matter of science and public health. It also is a political institution—an arm of *the state* (a fancy name for the government). As a result, it is vulnerable to being caught up in larger socio-political movements that change the social context and thus usher in new ways of thinking and new ways of doing.

Starting in the next chapter, we describe some major shifts in American society that have reshaped the nature of corrections. Perhaps the key transformation occurred in the late 1960s into the mid-1970s when rehabilitation came under attack and lost its status as the dominant theory of corrections. For this reason, we call Part I of the book—Chapters 1 and 2—"Crisis in American Corrections." What we mean by this title is that once rehabilitation was no longer widely accepted as *the* main way of thinking about how best to respond to offenders, a crisis existed as to what theory should govern correctional policy and practice. Despite many appropriate criticisms, Cullen and Jonson, your authors, would have preferred that rehabilitation did not lose its luster, because a lot of quackery and harm to offenders and innocent victims might have been avoided. Alas, not too many people bothered to listen to Cullen (see Cullen & Gilbert, 1982) and Jonson was still in grade school during much of that time.

As rehabilitation declined, however, other theories gained in popularity and increasingly guided correctional policy and practice. Most notably, the United States experienced the ascendancy of the theories of retribution or just deserts, deterrence, and incapacitation. These are distinct paradigms, but they shared a common element: They all rejected rehabilitation and embraced punishment as the preferred way to organize the correctional system. For this reason, they are considered together in Part II, which we have termed "The Punishment Response." It contains Chapters 3, 4, and 5.

These punitive-oriented theories provided a powerful justification for a mean season in American corrections—a time not only when mass imprisonment became a near-permanent state social institution but also when gleefully trumpeting the infliction of pain on offenders was celebrated (Clear & Frost, 2014). Only in more recent times have we seen the revitalization of competing approaches such as the theories of restorative justice, rehabilitation, reentry, and early intervention. Because they emphasize using the correctional system to improve the welfare of offenders, we have placed the theory of restorative justice (Chapter 6) and rehabilitation (Chapter 7) in Part III. We have labeled this section as "The Social Welfare Response." In recent years, an effort has been made to broaden this social welfare response to include two critical periods that might help save people from a life in crime—the time when prisoners reenter society and the time when future offenders are growing up. Discussions of reentry (Chapter 8) and of early intervention (Chapter 9) are contained in Part IV. This section, which also includes a review of the core lessons offered by this book (Chapter 10), is termed "Extending the Vision of Corrections."

Over the book's chapters, we thus tell this story of the struggle between two visions of corrections—one rooted in pain and prisons and the other rooted in betterment and social welfare. Again, our tour across history and into the bellies of these theories will be undertaken on a ship of science. The intent is to leave readers equipped with the knowledge and skills to be consumers of correctional research knowledge and thus able to practice evidence-based corrections. Let the trip begin!

David J. Rothman
Columbia University
Author of *The Discovery of the Asylum*

2

Correctional Theory in Crisis

America's Changing Context

O ur main goal is to have readers think seriously about the competing correctional theories. These theories are critical to study because *ideas have consequences*—that is, the belief in one versus another theory can lead to or justify vastly different correctional policies and practices. We also have urged that allegiance to any given theory be based on evidence—on the extent to which theoretical claims are rooted in empirical reality. The historical record suggests, however, that the emergence and fate of any given correctional theory has had less to do with science than with the prevailing *social context*. Ideas are not so much rational choices as they are ways of seeing the world inculcated during childhood and influenced by experiences, whether in school, on the job (something called occupational socialization), or in the larger society. In short, context affects theory, which in turn affects policy and practice.

This context → theory → policy linkage should not be seen as an iron law that governs corrections. It is more of a heuristic device, a helpful way of thinking about how this trinity of factors is interrelated. In reality, each component in this chain can affect the others; that is, there can be feedback loops or reciprocal effects. When policies fail, for example, this might open up political space for new theories to emerge that can rival existing ways of seeing corrections. The development of fresh and powerful ideas can create a different context by mobilizing reformers to change how a society is organized. And so on.

Still, as a rule of thumb, the context → theory → policy linkage will assist readers in understanding the general outlines of the United States' correctional history. Most important, when there are shifts in policies, readers will immediately realize that other things are up—and will be prompted to ask questions. What theoretical ideas have changed to justify these policy transformations? How might this be due to broader shifts in the nation's social context? In short, what occurs in corrections will not be seen in an insular, taken-for-granted way. There will be a constant understanding that a broader perspective is needed—that policies are rooted, implicitly or explicitly, in theoretical ideas and are enmeshed in an ongoing, dynamic context.

The context → theory → policy linkage also applies to all of us—to readers and to Cullen and Jonson. To think clearly about corrections, it is foolish to deny that we are somehow immune to the social forces that fill our consciousness with certain values, beliefs, and constructs. It is a touch amusing—and perhaps a touch arrogant—when we look to the past and wonder how our predecessors could have been so stupid to think the way they did. Here we are with 2.2 million fellow Americans behind bars, and we wonder how those in past times treated criminals so naïvely or inhumanely. Rather, the key to observing our world more accurately is, paradoxically, to admit that our observations will never be fully free of who we are and the times in which we live. Alvin Gouldner (1970) called this talent to observe ourselves *reflexivity*. We might add that the other limit on our biases is science. Science plays by rules that, though not free from individual values, require others to scrutinize what we do as a way of checking on our claims. Robert Merton (1973) termed this core principle of science *organized skepticism*.

As we move into this chapter, then, we attempt to place American correctional theory within a broader social context. We make four points:

- By the early part of the 1900s—in a time period called the "Progressive Era"— rehabilitation had emerged as the dominant philosophy of corrections. The emergent rehabilitative ideal shaped virtually every aspect of correctional policy and practice—including the components of the correctional system. We need to know, then, something about the *rise of rehabilitation*.

- In the later 1960s and early 1970s, rehabilitation was attacked by conservatives and liberals. Suddenly, no one seemed to believe in rehabilitation anymore. People claimed that "rehabilitation is dead." Why did this happen?

- A part of the attack on rehabilitation involved the claim that there was *no empirical support for correctional rehabilitation programs*. In a famous essay, Robert Martinson asserted, in essence, that "nothing works" in correctional treatment. The existing data seemed to confirm that rehabilitation was not humane or effective; it had no justification. Why were people so ready to accept the conclusions of Martinson's article?

- Once rehabilitation was called into question, this issue inevitably arose: If rehabilitation was not going to be the guiding philosophy of corrections, what would be? There was a *theoretical and ideological crisis in corrections!* Should the main goal of corrections be deterrence? Incapacitation? Some "get tough" combination of the two? Simply to do justice and not worry about crime control? Some argued that the answer should be to *reaffirm rehabilitation*—that the attacks on rehabilitation were not warranted. But that is another story for later in the book.

Thus, our analysis follows this sequence of topics: (1) the rise of rehabilitation; (2) the attack on rehabilitation; (3) the role of research evidence and the *nothing works doctrine* in this debate; and (4) the resulting crisis in corrections and the ensuing debate, which continues to this day, on what theory should guide the correctional system. Because rehabilitation is at the core of this story, we start out by defining and discussing this concept. This analysis builds on the brief overview of the theory of rehabilitation presented in Chapter 1.

Before moving forward, we want to make two points. First, obviously, this chapter does not pretend to present a full history of corrections. If we claimed that we could write such an account in a single chapter we would be either delusional or deceptive. Rather, this chapter uses the historical record for a more specific purpose: to frame the key developments that have influenced the course of correctional theory in the United States. Put another way, this is more of an intellectual history—that is, an examination of how a central idea about corrections—that offenders could be reformed—emerged and then, in a tumultuous social context, lost its legitimacy, throwing the field into a theoretical and policy crisis. Again, the rehabilitative ideal is important because it was the theory that provided the rationale for the invention of the main components of the modern correctional system (e.g., prisons, probation, parole, juvenile justice system). Because this ideal was so influential, its decline opened the way for other theories, especially those favoring a punishment response, to rival if not surpass its influence—at least for a while.

This leads to the second point. In Chapter 7, we return to the story about rehabilitation. At that point, we detail how rehabilitation eventually made a remarkable comeback, in large part because of the evidence its advocates marshaled showing its effectiveness. The other thing that has occurred since the first edition of this book is how much policy makers from both political parties have come to question the wisdom of mass imprisonment. This wavering of support for the punishment response is another reason why rehabilitation is regaining influence within corrections. So, consider this paragraph a trailer for a movie about rehabilitation that will not be released until a bit later. But you do know where this story is headed!

What Is Rehabilitation?

The concept of rehabilitation rests on the assumption that criminal behavior is caused by some factor. This perspective does not deny that people make choices to

NOTE: Portions of this chapter are from: *Encyclopedia of Crime & Justice*, 2E. © 2001 Gale, a part of Cengage Learning, Inc. Reproduced by permission. www.cengage.com/permissions.

break the law, but it does assert that these choices are not a matter of pure "free will." Instead, the decision to commit a crime is held to be determined, or at least heavily influenced, by a person's social surroundings, psychological development, or biological makeup.

People are not all the same—and thus free to express their will—but rather are different. These *individual differences* shape how people behave, including whether they are likely to break the law. When people are characterized by various "criminogenic risk factors"—such as a lack of parental love and supervision, exposure to delinquent peers, the internalization of antisocial values, or an impulsive temperament—they are more likely to become involved in crime than people not having these experiences and traits.

The rehabilitation model makes sense only if criminal behavior is caused and not merely a free willed, rational choice. *If crime were a matter of free choices, then there would be nothing within particular individuals to be "fixed" or changed.* But if involvement in crime is caused by various factors, then, logically, reoffending can be reduced if correctional interventions are able to alter these factors and how they have influenced offenders. For example, if associations with delinquent peers cause youths to internalize crime-causing beliefs (e.g., "it is okay to steal"), then diverting youths to other peer groups and changing these beliefs can inhibit their return to criminal behavior.

Sometimes, rehabilitation is said to embrace a *medical* model. When people are physically ill, the causes of their illness are diagnosed and then "treated." Each person's medical problems may be different and the treatment will differ accordingly; that is, the medical intervention is *individualized*. Thus, people with the same illness may, depending on their personal conditions (e.g., age, prior health), receive different medicines and stay in the hospital different lengths of time. Correctional rehabilitation shares the same logic: Causes are to be uncovered and treatments are to be individualized. This is why rehabilitation is also referred to as treatment.

Correctional and medical treatment are alike in one other way: They assume that experts, scientifically trained in the relevant knowledge on how to cure their "clients," will guide the individualized treatment that would take place. In medicine, this commitment to training physicians in scientific expertise has been institutionalized, with doctors required to attend medical school. In corrections, however, such professionalization generally is absent or only partially accomplished.

The distinctiveness of rehabilitation can also be seen by contrasting it with the three other correctional perspectives: retribution, deterrence, and incapacitation. As noted previously, rehabilitation differs from retribution, but is similar to deterrence and incapacitation, in that it is a *utilitarian goal*, with the utility or benefit for society being the reduction of crime. It fundamentally differs from the other three perspectives, however, because these other goals make no attempt to change or otherwise improve offenders. Instead, advocates of these theories want to inflict pain or punishment on offenders either for a reason (retribution in order to "get even" or deterrence in order to "scare people straight") or as a consequence of the penalty (incapacitation involves placing offenders in an unpleasant living situation, the prison). In contrast, rehabilitation seeks to assist *both offenders and society*. By treating the wayward, its advocates hope to give offenders the attitudes and skills needed to avoid crime and live a productive life. (Restorative justice and early intervention share this orientation with rehabilitation.)

At times, this attempt to help offenders exposes rehabilitation to the charge that it "coddles criminals." This view is short-sighted, however, because correctional rehabilitation's focus is not simply on lawbreakers but also on protecting society: By making offenders less criminal, fewer people will be victimized and society will, as a result, be safer.

As we will see below, the idea that we should rehabilitate criminals is not a new invention. In fact, it is deeply woven into the history and culture of the United States. This is one reason, perhaps, that public support for rehabilitation remains strong—an issue we revisit later in the book.

The Rise of the Rehabilitative Ideal

In this section, we trace the centrality in American corrections from the 1820s into the late 1960s. Covering approximately a century and a half in a few pages means that, as brilliant as Cullen and Jonson are, we leave out a few details! However, we establish the essential point that during this long period, the notion that efforts should be made to save the wayward from a life in crime became firmly entrenched in American culture. At the start of the 1960s, nearly all criminologists and members of the nation's political elite embraced the rehabilitative ideal as their chief theory of corrections (Toby, 1964; see also Menninger, 1968). To do otherwise, it was thought, would be to resist the march toward the creation of a civilized, enlightened society that would be the exemplar for the rest of the world to admire and follow.

Today, despite some recent policy improvements, America's correctional system is in crisis. If anything, it is (or should be) a source of national embarrassment. Commentators liken prisons to warehouses (Irwin, 2005) and, given their racial composition, see them as the functional equivalent of inner-city ghettos (Wacquant, 2001, 2009). Cullen and Jonson, your authors, believe that the attack on rehabilitation contributed to this disquieting situation (Cullen & Gilbert, 2013). If corrections is not devoted to reforming offenders, then what reason is there to be concerned about the quality of prisons and the quality of interventions? Why not just relish inflicting pain on those who have proven unworthy to be among us? We are getting ahead of ourselves. Even so, this perspective is perhaps worth keeping in mind as readers progress through this chapter and those to follow.

THE RISE OF THE "PENITENTIARY"

Those unfamiliar with the history of corrections might suspect that the idea that we should rehabilitate offenders is a modern invention, perhaps of the 1960s when social welfare programs were expanded and when liberal ideas, many of them advanced by secular humanists, shaped numerous governmental policies.

In actuality, however, a belief that a main purpose of corrections should be to save, and not merely punish, offenders extends to the first days of the American prison—back to the 1820s with the invention of the *penitentiary*.

Pause for a moment and think of the term reformers at this time chose for their invention: *penitentiary*. They might have called it a "house of pain," a "justice institution," or a "cage for criminals." But they did not. Rather, the selection of penitentiary was purposeful. It represented the view that prisons might be more than conduits for inflicting retribution, terrorizing to deter, or restraining to incapacitate. Prisons might be settings in which offenders might be transformed morally. In fact, Alexis de Tocqueville, who traveled from France in 1831 to visit these new institutions and would later (1835 and 1840) author the famous book *Democracy in America* (1969), was aware that penitentiaries reflected a fresh way of thinking. Although not uncritical, Tocqueville (1844/1968) realized that without this nobler purpose of reform, the punishments imposed on offenders would never be civilized. If offenders were merely the objects of our anger and scorn, what would inhibit the natural inclination to seek vengeance and make criminals suffer?

Indeed, before this time, most offenders were either banished to another community or, if not sent away, were fined, whipped, placed in the pillory, or executed. Incarceration, to the extent it existed at all, was used only to detain offenders for trial or, if convicted, for punishment that would soon take place (e.g., hanging). Jails looked more like a regular house in which the offenders, the jailer, and the jailer's family lived under the same roof.

What caused the people in the 1820s to switch to a radically different form of corrections that involved constructing high- and thick-walled prisons that were imbued with the mission of transforming law-breakers into law-abiders? Some scholars have suggested that prisons reflected the inevitable progress of civilization, of moving away from barbaric punishments—like the horror of the gallows and brutality of the whipping post—to an institution that did not physically disfigure offenders but instead sought to rescue them from crime. Although not without merit, this march-of-progress thesis does not explain why penitentiaries emerged in the early 19th century rather than, say, 50 years earlier or later.

In his classic work, *Discovery of the Asylum*, David Rothman (1971) offers a more creative account for both why prisons emerged when they did and why they were given the purpose of reforming the criminally wayward. He suggests that by the 1820s, the United States was making the transformation from the small, isolated communities of colonial America to a society in which communities were growing in size and in the diversity and transience of their residents. Enmeshed in this changing landscape, many Americans felt that their society was growing disorderly. Before, they had ascribed much crime and deviance to the sinfulness of individuals. Although not discarding this view fully, they supplemented it with the idea that the prevailing social chaos meant that people were not inculcated by the family and community with the moral fiber to resist the criminal temptations that had become rampant in society.

If social disorder was fueling crime, then the obvious solution was to take offenders out of this chaos and place them in an orderly environment—one much like the communities that used to exist in colonial America several decades before. And once this cognitive leap was made, then the ostensible rationality of the "penitentiary" became undeniable. If orderly communities no longer existed, the challenge was to create a pure community in which to situate offenders. The penitentiary would serve this purpose. Its impenetrable walls would function to keep offenders within this community and symbolically, if not pragmatically, to keep the forces prevailing in the larger society at bay.

This community would be built on the traditional values of religious training, discipline, hard work, and immunity from criminal influences. Reformers argued, often bitterly, over how best to keep offenders from criminal influences in a community comprised mainly of other offenders. In Pennsylvania, reformers favored the "solitary system" of keeping inmates in solitary confinement within individual cells; in New York, reformers favored the "congregate system," which allowed inmates to eat, work, and pray together but required total silence under the threat of whipping those who dared to talk with another offender. Regardless, these debates overshadowed the similarities of visions these reformers shared; the organizing principles of the prison were the same, even though the means of achieving these principles differed.

More importantly, however, the founders of the *penitentiary*—again, as this very word suggests—did not build prisons to scare offenders straight or to incapacitate them. Their reform was justified in nobler terms. They believed that if they could create the perfect daily regimen in the prison, this environment would have the power to transform the very moral character of inmates. The purpose of the penitentiary thus was to morally *reform* offenders.

We should note that some scholars believe that the motives of these reformers were more sinister or, in the least, more complex. One idea is that prisons were invented largely to control poor people (who, after all, inhabited penitentiaries) and to discipline them so that they could be more productive workers for the economic elites (after all, a well-behaved ex-offender was more useful than a banished, executed, or physically mangled offender). At the very least, this perspective cautions us that prisons would not have been embraced so readily if they were used to lock up rich folks or otherwise threatened the status quo.

Still, the motives of reformers—which were deeply rooted in Christianity and in the genuine belief that the penitentiary was far more humane than ravaging an offender's body—should not be dismissed as irrelevant. This form of extreme reductionism would miss the point of the penitentiary: The people who invented the prison truly believed that it was capable of rehabilitating the wayward.

THE NEW PENOLOGY: THE CINCINNATI CONGRESS OF 1870

Thus, from the inception of the penitentiary, prisons and rehabilitation were seen as inextricably mixed. Again, an important reason for this link was the *religious nature of the penitentiary*. For reformers, Christianity fostered the dual views that offenders both can and should be saved from a life in crime. To relinquish this optimism would be tantamount to condemning offenders to damnation on earth and in the afterlife. Again, this point is noteworthy because it suggests that the belief that a core function of prisons should be rehabilitation is woven deeply into the nation's cultural fabric. This belief in reforming offenders may become frayed at times, but it is durable enough to avoid becoming fully unraveled.

The aftermath of the Civil War was just such a period when the belief in rehabilitation might have been abandoned. The ideal of the orderly prison had fallen prey to the decision to crowd more and more offenders into institutions. More disquieting, the rise of social Darwinism made it comforting to attribute crime to the so-called dangerous classes, comprised mostly of immigrants, who were portrayed as biologically inferior and beyond redemption. Given this ideology, the temptation was strong simply to view prisons as convenient places to cage the innately wicked.

In the face of these daunting obstacles, however, prison reformers met in Cincinnati in 1870 at the National Congress on Penitentiary and Reformatory Discipline (Wines, 1870/1910). In their "Declaration of Principles," the Congress's members advanced a *new penology,* a blueprint for renovating American corrections. Reasserting Christian ideals, they argued that "the supreme aim of prison discipline is the reformation of criminals, not the infliction of vindictive suffering" (Wines, 1870/1910, p. 39). But if the orderly prison of the 1820s had proven to be a failure, what would work to reform offenders? The key, they argued, was that "the prisoner's destiny should be placed, measurably, in his own hands" (p. 39). And the means of accomplishing this goal was the *indeterminate sentence.*

In the past, prison terms had been determinate, which meant that offenders knew, at the time of sentencing by a judge, how much time they would serve behind bars. Given that even the most recalcitrant inmate would be released from prison when the sentence expired, where was the motivation for offenders to change? The indeterminate sentence, however, reversed this motivational calculus, because inmates could be retained in prison until they had been reformed. With freedom hanging in the balance, inmates would be inspired to change for the better. If not, they would remain incarcerated, and the safety of society would be ensured.

Many other features of the Congress's new penology were so forward looking that they would not be foreign to current-day penal discussions of correctional reform. Thus, the Congress favored the "progressive classification of prisoners"; the use of "rewards, more than punishments"; "special training" in order "to make a good prison or reformatory officer"; access to "education" and "industrial training"; and efforts to reintegrate offenders into society "by providing them with work and encouraging them to redeem their character and regain their lost position in society" (Wines, 1870/1910, pp. 39–45). Again, these recommendations were set forth as part of a plan to create prisons capable of reforming the wayward. The dangerous classes—the poor, the immigrant, the uneducated—were not to be warehoused or portrayed as beyond redemption. Rather, they were all God's children, and the mandate was to save them from a life in crime.

INDIVIDUALIZED TREATMENT:
THE CORE OF THE REHABILITATIVE IDEAL

Pregnant in the Congress's set of principles was the conclusion that rehabilitation should be *individualized*. This idea of individualized treatment, however, was expressed more clearly and forcefully closer to the turn of the century—about three decades after the 1870 Cincinnati meeting. At this time, the Congress's new penology was being elaborated by the emerging insights from the nascent social sciences of psychology and sociology. These disciplines brought a secular perspective to the enterprise of reforming offenders. They suggested that it was possible to study the causes of crime scientifically. This new science would become known as *criminology*.

Now, criminology revealed that for any given offender, *the causes were likely to be multifaceted and found in a unique combination*. Two people might commit the same crime—for example, robbery—but the reasons for their acts could be widely divergent (e.g., emotional problems as opposed to the exposure to gang influences). Once this premise was accepted, it led logically to the conclusion that successful rehabilitation depended on treating offenders on a *case-by-case basis*. A single treatment would not fit all law-breakers because, again, they were all different. Instead, interventions had to be *individualized* (Rothman, 1980).

Once the philosophy of individualized treatment or rehabilitation was embraced, it led directly to a *theory of how the correctional system should be organized*. What kind of system should be set up to deliver individualized rehabilitation? Several components were fundamental to this *theory of corrections*:

- Above all, individualization required that criminal justice officials have the *discretion* to fit correctional interventions to the *offender* and not base them on the offense.

- *Indeterminate sentencing*, of course, was essential because it meant that inmates would be released from prison only when they had been cured of their criminal propensities.

- To determine who should be released and when, a *parole board* would be necessary. The idea of parole in turn mandated that released offenders be supervised in the community by *parole officers* whose task it was to counsel parolees and, when necessary, to return offenders to prison who failed to go straight.

- Reformers, however, also argued that incarceration was not the appropriate intervention for all law-breakers; many could be rehabilitated in the community. This belief led to the creation of *probation*, a practice in which *probation officers* would both help and police offenders released to their supervision. These officers, moreover, would assist judges in deciding who to imprison and who to place in the community by amassing information on each offender. This portrait was compiled in a "pre-sentence report" that would detail not just the offender's criminal history but also his or her employment record, family background, and personal characteristics.

- Because juveniles differed from adults, it also made sense to create a separate *juvenile court*. This special court most fully embodied the ideals of individualized treatment. Wayward youths were not to be punished by the state, but rather "saved from a life in crime." The court would act as a kindly parent who would, in essence, step in and help not only youths already involved in illegal acts but also those at risk for a criminal life. The jurisdiction of the juvenile court thus was not limited to youths who had committed a crime. Instead, the court claimed jurisdiction over youths who engaged in deviant acts seen as precursors to crime (i.e., status offenses such as truancy, running away from home, and sexual promiscuity) and over those who were neglected or abused by their parents.

The paradigm of individualized treatment offered a persuasive rationale for reform. *This proposal offered to improve the lives of offenders and to protect society* by curing criminals who could be cured and by locking up those whose criminality proved intractable. Science and religion, moreover, meshed together to suggest that offenders could be transformed and that mere vengeance would be counterproductive.

But in advancing a seemingly enlightened correctional agenda, advocates remained blind to *two* potential dangers of individualized treatment. First, they assumed that judges and correctional officials would have the expertise to administer this new system—such as knowing what caused an individual's criminality and knowing what intervention would work to effect the offender's reform. Second, they assumed that the officials' discretion would be exercised to advance the cause of rehabilitation. They did not consider that the *unfettered discretion* given to judges and officials might be abused or used mainly to *control, not help,* offenders. These problems would later play a role in undermining the legitimacy of individualized treatment, but for the moment they either did not come to mind or were dismissed as nay-saying. We will return to these issues shortly.

THE PROGRESSIVE ERA: THEORY INTO REALITY

Persuasive theoretical paradigms do *not* always translate into concrete policy reforms. By 1900, however, the United States had entered the Progressive Era, which came to be called the "age of reform" because of the diverse social and governmental reforms undertaken in this time span. Critically important, there was a firm belief that the *state could be trusted to help solve a range of social problems— including crime!* In the area of corrections, this meant that the state could be trusted to work on behalf of offenders to ensure their rehabilitation. Concretely, this involved giving judges and correctional officials virtually *unfettered discretion* in making decisions about offenders' lives (e.g., who goes to prison, when an inmate is released from prison).

In any event, at this particularly receptive historical juncture of the Progressive Era, the new penology ideas—ideas that had been embellished since the Cincinnati Congress—presented a clear blueprint for renovating the correctional system. *The time was ripe for individualized treatment to be implemented.* During the Progressive Era, which lasted the first two decades of the 20th century, the power of this ideal transformed the nature of corrections.

As is well known, the first juvenile court was initiated in 1899 in Cook County, Illinois, home of Chicago (Platt, 1969). Two decades or so later, all but three states had a special court for hearing juvenile cases, and every state permitted probation for youths. Similarly, during this time period, two thirds of the states had begun probation and 44 states had initiated parole for adults. Meanwhile, in little over 20 years, the number of states that allowed indeterminate sentencing had risen from 5 to 37 (Rothman, 1980).

These changes were rapid and remarkable. The rehabilitative ideal would hold sway over corrections in the United States into the early 1970s. This is not to say that observers were blind to how infrequently this ideal was achieved in reality. The resources and the criminological knowledge to achieve this ambitious project of reforming offenders typically were lacking. Still, each generation of reformers— acknowledging the failures of the previous generation—did not cast doubt on the *possibility* of rehabilitating offenders if only enough funding and the "right" treatment program were used.

THE RISE OF CORRECTIONS

This continuing commitment to rehabilitation was reflected in reforms that occurred in the period that spanned, roughly, the 1950s to the late 1960s. During this time, prisons were relabeled *correctional institutions*, with the name *corrections* suggesting that the core task of working with offenders was to change or *correct* them. Again, what we call things makes a difference, because words often capture our unspoken beliefs.

Corresponding to this new vocabulary, a range of treatment programs was introduced into institutions. These included, for example, individual and group counseling, therapeutic milieus, behavioral modification, vocational training, work release, furloughs, and college education. New and more sophisticated systems to *classify* inmates as to their treatment needs were also implemented. Especially in the 1960s, *community corrections* became fashionable, as a movement emerged to *reintegrate* inmates into society through halfway houses and other community-based treatment programs. Reflecting the tenor of the times, the Task Force on Corrections (1967), part of a presidential commission studying the nation's crime problem, asserted that the "ultimate goal of corrections under any theory is to make the community safer by reducing the incidence of crime. Rehabilitation of offenders to prevent their return to crime is in general the most promising way to achieve this end" (p. 16).

These were optimistic times and using American know-how to rehabilitate offenders did not seem far-fetched. Within a few short years, however, this confidence would collapse and the very legitimacy of the rehabilitative ideal would be called into question.

Attacking Rehabilitation

The apparent invincibility of rehabilitation as the dominant correctional philoso-phy was shattered in less than a decade. Treatment programs did not suddenly disappear, and faith in rehabilitation did not vanish. Even so, a sea change in think-ing occurred seemingly overnight and policy changes followed close behind. Suddenly, it became fashionable to be against *state enforced therapy* (Kittrie, 1971; more broadly, see Cullen & Gilbert, 1982).

Beginning in the mid-1970s, states began to question indeterminate sentencing and to call for sentencing in which judicial and parole board discretion was elimi-nated or, at the least, curtailed. About 30 states still retain some form of indetermi-nate sentencing, but this is down from a time when every state had this practice (Tonry, 1999). Further, over the last quarter of the 20th century, every state passed mandatory sentences, truth-in-sentencing laws, three-strikes-and-you're-out laws, or similar legislation aimed at deterring and/or incapacitating law-breakers (Tonry, 2013). Meanwhile, state and federal prison populations ballooned from 200,000 in the early 1970s to eventually surpass more than 1.6 million (and to more than 2.4 million, counting offenders in other custodial institutions, such as local jails) (Sabol, West, & Cooper, 2009). Within the community, the treatment para-digm was challenged by programs that sought not to correct and reintegrate offenders but to *intensively supervise, electronically monitor,* or otherwise control them. Even the juvenile justice system did not escape the diminished confidence in rehabilitation. By the end of the 1990s, 17 states had changed the legal purpose of the juvenile court to de-emphasize rehabilitation, and virtually all states had passed laws to make their juvenile justice systems harsher (more generally, see Feld, 1999).

As noted previously, major shifts in correctional thinking are usually a product of changes in the larger society that prompt citizens to reconsider beliefs they had not previously questioned. The mid-1960s to the mid-1970s was a decade of enor-mous social turbulence and, in turn, thinking about many things changed. This period was marked by the Civil Rights Movement, urban riots, the Vietnam War and accompanying protests, the shootings at Kent State and Attica, Watergate and related political scandals, and escalating crime rates. In this *social context,* as the central state agency for controlling crime and disorder, the criminal justice system (including its correctional component) came under careful scrutiny. It was often seen as part of the problem—as doing too much, too little, or the wrong thing.

For conservatives, the reigning chaos in society was an occasion to call for *law and order.* To them, it was apparent that the correctional system was teaching that crime pays. Under the guise of rehabilitation, criminals were being coddled: Judges were putting dangerous offenders on probation, and parole boards were releasing predators prematurely from prison. *Rehabilitation was being blamed by conserva-tives for allowing the victimization of innocent citizens.* Thus, we needed to toughen sentences—make them longer and determinate—in order to deter the calculators and incapacitate the wicked (Cullen & Gilbert, 1982).

For liberals, however, rehabilitation was not the source of leniency but of *injustice and coercion.* The prevailing events contained the important lesson that *government officials could not be trusted*—whether that was to advance civil rights, to be truthful about why the nation was at war, to act with integrity while in political office, or to rehabilitate the wayward. This issue of *trusting the state* was critical because the reforms of the Progressive Era were based on the very assumption that the *state could be trusted to do good!* This is why correctional officials were given so much discretion to intervene in the lives of juveniles, in the lives of offenders on probation, and in the lives of inmates in prison and seeking parole.

In this context of the late 1960s and 1970s—with protest and conflict prevailing—trust in the state was hard to sustain. Indeed, judges and correctional officials were redefined as "state agents of social control" whose motives were suspect. Thus, judges were now portrayed as purveyors of unequal justice, using their discretion not to wisely individualize treatments but to hand out harsher sentences to poor and minority defendants. Similarly, correctional officials were accused of using the threat of indeterminate incarceration not to achieve the noble goal of offender reform but to compel offenders to comply obediently with institutional rules that had little to do with their treatment; maintaining prison order thus displaced rehabilitation as the real goal of indeterminate terms.

In short, *liberals believed that rehabilitation—and the discretion it gave to state officials—resulted in the victimization of offenders.* In the liberal critics' minds, it was time to forfeit rehabilitation and embrace a *justice model* that would limit incarceration to *short sentences* and would grant offenders an array of legal rights to protect them against the ugly power of the state. Notions of *doing good* were relinquished and replaced with the hope of creating a correctional system that would *do no harm* (Cullen & Gilbert, 1982). We will return to a more detailed discussion of the justice model in Chapter 3 where the theory of just deserts is reviewed.

Thus, both liberals and conservatives opposed rehabilitation, albeit for different reasons: conservatives because they thought it victimized society, and liberals because they thought it victimized offenders. These two groups also agreed that the discretion of correctional officials should be limited and determinacy in sentencing implemented. They both embraced the punishment of offenders. They parted company, however, on how harsh those sanctions should be, with conservatives wanting *long prison sentences* and liberals wanting *short prison sentences*. Given the get tough policies that have reigned in recent times, it is clear that the conservative alternative to rehabilitation prevailed most often and in most jurisdictions.

The "Nothing Works" Doctrine: Martinson and Beyond

The story about the attack on rehabilitation has one additional chapter to be told. In 1974, Robert Martinson published an essay in which he reviewed 231 studies evaluating the effectiveness of correctional treatment programs between 1945 and 1967. Based on this assessment, Martinson (1974) concluded that, "*With few and isolated exceptions, the rehabilitative efforts that have been reported so far have had no appreciable effect on recidivism*" (p. 25, emphasis in the original).

This rather technical conclusion might have been open to different interpretations—for example, that treatment programs were being implemented incorrectly or that inappropriate interventions were being used. But Martinson (1974) then proceeded to ask a more provocative question: *"Do all of these studies lead irrevocably to the conclusion that nothing works, that we haven't the faintest clue about how to rehabilitate offenders and reduce recidivism?"* (p. 48, emphasis in the original). He stopped short of claiming that "nothing works," but it was clear that "nothing works" was the message he was conveying.

Few scholarly studies, however, are without their limitations, and Martinson's work was no exception. Only about 80 of the studies he reviewed—not 231 as is commonly believed—actually examined the impact of treatment interventions on recidivism (some studies did not measure "treatment"—e.g., they measured simply being on probation—and others did not have measures of recidivism). About half of the studies reviewed, moreover, showed that the intervention actually reduced recidivism (Palmer, 1975). Further, his research covered only those evaluation studies undertaken between 1945 and 1967. But subsequent reviews of more recent literature—including one by Martinson (in 1979) himself—suggested that many programs do, in fact, "work" to lower the risk of offenders returning to crime.

It is instructive, however, that Martinson's (1974) nothing works idea was accorded spectacular credibility whereas evidence favoring rehabilitation's effectiveness—including, again, his own essay published but five years later—was virtually ignored. More broadly, after 150 years of the rehabilitative ideal being a dominant correctional theory, why would this approach be forfeited in the face of a single study?

After all, very little that is done in criminal justice in general and in corrections in particular is based on officials carefully weighing research evidence. As suggested previously, more often than not, correctional policies and practices are rooted in custom and common sense, and the existing "empirical evidence" is scarcely consulted. These observations suggest that Martinson's study was accepted as unassailable truth not because it told people something new but rather *because it told them something they wanted to hear—indeed, something that they already "knew to be true"*: Rehabilitation didn't work (see also Gottfredson, 1979).

Again, by the early 1970s, the United States was in the midst of a period of sustained turmoil. The previous decade had seen civil rights marches, riots in the streets, protests over the Vietnam War, the Watergate scandal, rising crime rates, and the Attica prison riot in which guards and inmates alike were shot down when law enforcement officials stormed the institution. Much as the disorder of the 1820s had led Americans to rethink how they responded to crime and to create the penitentiary, the disorder of this period caused people to rethink many issues, including the nature of the correctional system. As the main justification for this system, the rehabilitative ideal was the obvious focal point of attack. Martinson's study added fuel to the fire, so to speak. For those already doubting correctional treatment, it provided "proof" that "nothing works." In short, given the tenor of the times—given the prevailing social context—people were ready to hear Martinson's nothing works message and unprepared to question empirical findings that reinforced what they already believed. With scientific findings on their side, they now could declare that "rehabilitation was dead."

Conclusion: Crisis in Correctional Theory

In the end, rehabilitation did not die (Cullen, 2013; Listwan, Jonson, Cullen, & Latessa, 2008). There have been reports that the commitment to treatment programs has diminished over the past quarter century. The dearth of systematic data, however, leaves open the question of how deep the retreat from rehabilitation has been, whether it is especially applicable to some types of programs (e.g., college education courses), and how it might vary across states. Regardless, an examination of correctional institutions and community agencies across the nation reveals the presence of a diversity of programs and treatment revitalization in a number of jurisdictions (Cullen & Jonson, 2011b; Listwan et al., 2008). But looks can be deceiving. For example, research by Taxman, Perdoni, and Harrison (2007) shows that while most prisons have a range of services available (high prevalence), their limited capacity to actually deliver services means that only a small percentage of inmates are enrolled in them (low usage). As they note, "access is an issue with correctional programs in that few inmates are involved in any program" (p. 246). Similarly, commenting upon California's crisis-riddled system, Petersilia (2008) observed that the "vast majority of . . . prisoners do not receive the rehabilitation they need" (p. 235). In fact, "50 percent of existing state prisoners did not participate in *any* rehabilitation or work program" (Grattet, Petersilia, Lin, & Beckman, 2009, p. 3; emphasis in the original; see also Simon, 2014).

Still, if rehabilitation did not vanish, its role as the hegemonic or dominant correctional theory was severely damaged, with a host of get tough policies being implemented that were inconsistent with rehabilitation and individualized treatment (Cullen & Gilbert, 2013; Tonry, 2013). From the 1970s to this day there has been a *theoretical crisis in corrections*. Again, at one time, it was generally agreed among criminologists and enlightened policy makers that *of course corrections should be directed to rehabilitating offenders*. But over the past four decades, this consensus was shattered. Criminologists came to believe that nothing worked in corrections to change offender behavior (Cullen & Gendreau, 2001). They lost faith in rehabilitation but never gained faith in punishment. They ended up as correctional agnostics who believed in virtually nothing—except that what was being done was wrong.

Of course, American correctional policy moved in a decidedly punitive or conservative direction during this time. This movement was applauded by many but opposed by others, including most academic criminologists. Mass incarceration became a seemingly intractable reality—an addiction that could not be kicked (Pratt, 2009). The specter of so many people locked up was disquieting to many Americans. The fact that the faces staring through the bars were disproportionately people of color emerged as a cause for concern.

Starting around 2010, if not a bit before, a remarkable transformation began to unfold (about the time we were writing the first edition of the book) (see Cullen, Jonson, & Stohr, 2014). We will revisit this issue in later chapters, but the key change has been the extent to which conservative policy makers have come to say that mass imprisonment is no longer "sustainable." In fact, politicians in many so-called Red States are leading the way in reforming corrections (Thielo, Cullen, Cohen, & Chouhy, 2016). To be honest, Cullen and Jonson never thought we would see this occur! Still, let's not get giddy about all this. It remains to be seen if the United States is entering a new correctional era of true reform—or is now just stuck in a policy limbo that could lead in any number of directions (see Gottschalk, 2015; Petersilia & Cullen, 2015). Much like the dispute over the Patient Protection and Affordable Care Act (aka Obamacare), the future of corrections will be determined state by state. National trends may emerge, but disagreements will surface as well. The conversation about correctional policy is not over.

In short, we are locked in an intense debate—an ongoing crisis—over what theory should guide the nation's correctional system. Does it make sense to rid the system of any attempt to help offenders and concentrate on using the iron fist of the law to do justice, deter, and incapacitate? Should we think outside the box and consider restorative justice? Did we, as Cullen and Jonson think, make a grievous error in abandoning the goal of offender treatment? Should we reaffirm rehabilitation and, in the process, extend this approach to at-risk youngsters through early intervention? Most importantly, how might evidence-based corrections help us to resolve the existing theoretical crisis? The chapters ahead seek to address these questions.

PART II

The Punishment Response

3

Just Deserts

Doing Justice or Getting Tough?

An eye for an eye. Do the crime, you do the time. Break the law, you get what you deserve. Simple justice. Need we say more?

At first blush, justice does seem to be something that is uncomplicated and that we all understand. If people engage in harmful acts—if they tip the scales of Lady Justice downward—then they must suffer a commensurate amount of harm to re-balance those scales. There is, moreover, no surprise here. The law can specify in advance what punishment each criminal act will trigger. Choosing to commit a crime is thus tantamount to choosing the promised punishment. No reason to complain. The sanction is deserved. Just deserts. Simple justice.

In a way, Cullen and Jonson test the *theory of just deserts*—sometimes also called the *theory of retribution*—every year when, as professors, we design and then teach our courses. As you know, each course syllabus lists rules and consequences. If you choose to plagiarize a term paper, then you get a zero. If you miss a test, zero. If you are late in submitting an assignment, zero—or at least a grade reduction. This is just deserts. Especially for students who believe in just deserts for criminals, we should hear nothing when they violate the rules. Suck it up and take your punishment. Live your beliefs. We may be talking to you, the reader. Are you one of those just deserts, responsibility types?

Of course, Cullen and Jonson do not meet many students who beg us to inflict just deserts on them when they break a rule. Perhaps it is our fault. Every time Cullen and Jonson give an examination, a tsunami of misery suddenly befalls our students. Grandmothers, in particular, are in jeopardy; some die three or four times. Dogs become ill, usually from eating term papers or, now, the flash drives on which the papers are saved. Automobiles are prone to breaking down, typically in places where cell phone service is not available or where cell phones inexplicably die, rendering any calls to us impossible. And then there are those pesky alarm clocks that are programmed not to function on test days. Ouch. All that sickness! Give a test, and we unleash an epidemic of illness that sweeps across our students. We feel guilty that our tests cause such human wreckage.

But so what? Why should Cullen and Jonson care if a student misses an exam because a grandmother died, a dog ran away and had to be found, an automobile broke down, an alarm clock did not buzz, or a student got the swine flu? Why should we take these *circumstances* into account when deciding whether to mete out punishment and, if so, what kind? Why not just look at the action—did you take the test or not?—and grade the examination if taken or give a zero if not?

The obvious response is that Cullen and Jonson would be seen as *unfair* if we did not take these circumstances into account. An act cannot be understood without considering the context in which it occurs. Some reasons for missing an examination seem unavoidable, such as illness. Others, however, are choices students make, such as whether to attend a family funeral. And still others show an element of irresponsibility—such as not setting an alarm properly—but perhaps do not manifest a conscious intent to avoid the examination. To be direct, students do not like just deserts professors. They prefer professors who will listen to them, take the complexities of their life into account, and use faculty discretion to make a reasonable decision. Cullen and Jonson, who have bleeding hearts, are not just deserts professors. We also are not just deserts criminologists. If nothing else, we are consistent.

Now to the correctional system. Here, the issue of just deserts is of defining importance. Few among us would dispute that just deserts should generally govern how much or how little punishment we will allow. We would not wish to place a heinous murderer on probation or to execute a shoplifter. This would affront our sense of justice. But the harder question is whether we want a correctional system that is *guided only by the principle of just deserts or retribution*. It is easy to say that we should punish the crime. But when we are the criminal involved, we quickly want the correctional system to take into account our circumstances, why we acted the way we did, and our possible potential to behave differently in the future. At issue is whether *justice* is a matter of punishing bad acts or is more fully achieved by weighing the totality of factors that surround the choice of crime. We will return to this sticky—and fundamental—issue ahead.

The other consideration is that just deserts or retribution is a *non-utilitarian* theory of corrections. The only focus is on balancing the scales of justice. Offenders are punished for the mere sake of punishment. They have harmed, so in turn they suffer harm. This act of retribution—of inflicting harm—is what achieves justice, plain and simple. The difficulty, however, is that we often want our correctional system to do more than impose just deserts. Given the billions of dollars that we spend, we might also hope that this system might reduce crime and make society safer. Recall that crime control is a *utilitarian goal of corrections*.

A challenge for just deserts or retribution as a theory of corrections is *that it must be unconcerned with crime control*. Let us assume, for example, that we want to incapacitate offenders for years behind bars because we prognosticate that they will commit crimes in the future. This practice might be justified because it keeps predators off the streets and saves lives. But a retribution/just deserts advocate must reject such utilitarian thinking because people cannot be punished for what they *might do*, only for *what they have done*. Further, because our predictions are inexact, there will be *false positives*: those that we predict will offend but will not, in fact, do so. This is not fair; they are being punished for conduct that *they never would have committed*. Put simply, the demands of just deserts/retribution and the demands of crime control are often at odds with one another.

The difficulty in saying that *justice is all that matters* is that the public does not believe this. Opinion polls show that the public values retribution/just deserts but also expects the correctional system to take steps to reduce crime—whether through deterrence, incapacitation, or rehabilitation (Cullen, Fisher, & Applegate, 2000). In this context, discussions of retribution/just deserts might sound philosophically persuasive, but are they politically feasible? Will just deserts always be corrupted by concerns over public safety? This worry is a core theme of this chapter.

Thus, we begin with a discussion of the concepts of just deserts and retribution. Although philosophers might well turn over in their graves (where many of them now lie!), we will make this useful distinction: Conservatives believe in retribution, whereas liberals believe in just deserts. The concepts are really the same, with this exception: Retribution *demands* the imposition of punishment on offenders; just deserts *seeks to limit* the imposition of punishment on offenders. In practical terms, those favoring retribution want to get tough, whereas those favoring just deserts want to get lenient.

The chapter is then divided into a discussion of the conservative retribution version of this correctional theory and a discussion of the liberal just deserts version of the correctional theory. In both cases, we identify key problems with the theory being proposed. For the conservative version, the problems mainly revolve around a view of offenders and their lives that exists only in the minds of philosophers, not in empirical reality. For the liberal version, the problems mainly revolve around the failure to anticipate that the United States was entering a conservative political era in which getting lenient on crime was foolish to expect. Put another way, the liberals played right into the hands of their conservative opponents. We then close the chapter by reiterating the necessity for any theory of corrections to address the utilitarian goal of crime control. Ignoring this cultural requirement means that the theory of just deserts or retribution will be misshapen when, in the end, the demands for reducing the crime problem surface and must be addressed.

The Concepts of Retribution
and Just Deserts: Punishing the Crime

For all intents and purposes, *retribution* and *just deserts* are two names for the same correctional theory. At its core, this theory argues that the correctional system has no business trying to figure out why someone committed a crime and no business trying to scare the person straight or to fix the person in any way. In fact, retribution/just deserts theory does not care what happened in the offenders' lives before they committed a crime and does not care what happens in the offenders' lives once they have been punished and walk free in society. The only concern is arranging the correctional system so that the *punishment fits the crime*. This means two things. First, everyone who commits a crime—say, a robbery—is given exactly the same sentence—say, three years in prison. No more, no less. Thus, there is equal justice before the law. Second, it means that crimes that are more serious—that do more harm, in particular—are given more punishment.

Advocates of retribution/just deserts really despise *discretion*. Now, discretion means that officials who make decisions, such as judges and parole boards, can use their expertise to fiddle with how much someone is punished. It means that they have the power to give two people who commit the same crime different punishments. For example, they might decide to place on probation a mother who stole money to buy food for her baby but to lock up someone who stole money to get high on crack. You might think that this use of discretion makes sense. A crime is not an abstract event but something that occurs within a context. You might think that a judge should have some discretion to take such factors into account. If you think this way, then you have bleeding hearts like Cullen and Jonson! We think this way, too. But there is a good rejoinder to our view of the world: What if judges do not use their discretion fairly or wisely? What if they use their discretion to punish people of color or perhaps even rich kids more harshly? Discretion has a slippery slope. Safer, the retribution/just deserts crowd would argue, to take away discretion and make judges like computers: Look at the crime, read the criminal code, and hand out the sentence that is written down.

Advocates of retribution/just deserts also despise parole and parole boards. Why? Because once the judges' discretion is removed, they do not want some parole board to have the discretion to let offenders out early or to keep others locked up forever. Put another way, they do not like *indeterminate sentences* in which parole boards are supposed to release offenders based on whether they have been rehabilitated. According to the retribution/just deserts crowd, offenders may be born again or judged by Freud himself to be mentally healthy and they are still going to stay in prison the exact same amount of time as those who embrace Satan or say they want to molest children once released from prison. Cullen and Jonson believe that this logic is risky and robs offenders of the motivation to try to improve themselves. But equal justice demands that the crime—and only the crime—be punished. Whether a sinner or a saint, whether healthy or deranged—all this makes no difference. The crime determines what punishment is meted out.

The correctional theory of retribution/just deserts thus demands the use of *determinate sentences*. The legislature specifies in the written criminal code how much punishment an offender is to receive. A specific sentence is listed—either a precise number of years in prison or, at most, a very narrow range of years (e.g., three to four). Sometimes, judges are given *sentencing guidelines* in which they read across and down a grid and then assign a sentence based on a combination of the seriousness of the crime, number of prior convictions, and perhaps harm done (e.g., amount of money pilfered, number of victims hurt). They cannot go outside the guidelines unless there is a compelling reason to do so—and then they have to write the justification down. In any case, once offenders are convicted of a crime, then nothing remains but to read the criminal code. If the code states three years in prison for a burglary, then it is off to prison for three years—no more, no less. Put another way, there is *complete truth in sentencing*.

There is much to recommend about this approach. The corrections process becomes much less complicated—there is *simple justice*. The punishments are written out where everyone can see them. Everyone who comes before a judge gets the same punishment for the same crime. Everyone who is incarcerated serves the same sentence for the same crime. Further, when asked, the public is pretty clear on which crimes are more serious than other crimes and on which crimes should receive longer prison sentences than other crimes (Cullen, Link, & Polanzi, 1982; Jacoby & Cullen, 1998; Rossi, Waite, Bose, & Berk, 1974). That is, although not perfect, there is a general consensus among Americans (in fact, among people across the globe) as to which illegal acts warrant more or less punishment. It seems possible, therefore, to create a system in which citizens mostly agree on how punishments, including prison sentences, should be scaled to match different types of crime.

Up until this point, those who favor retribution and those who favor just deserts are in complete agreement. But at this juncture they reach a fork in the road and go their separate ways. The retribution folks take almost literally the principle of *an eye for an eye*. They realize, of course, that if an offender shoots someone in the leg, we cannot take the offender and plug him or her in the leg. Then we would have *leg for a leg* justice, which is just a generalization of *eye for an eye* justice! Even so, advocates of retribution *identify first and foremost with the victim and the loss and/ or pain that may have been suffered*. In a way, offenders have had their day—they have taken their eye. To balance the scales of justice, it is now necessary to exact enough pain on the wayward so that an eye or a leg—even metaphorically—is taken in return.

The retributionists thus are *not queasy about pain*. They like pain; they like to see offenders suffer. In practical terms, they are typically suspicious that criminals do not suffer enough. They tend to see probation and community-based sanctions as non-punishments. This is why they want virtually every offender to be placed in prison. It also is why they want prisons to be miserable places—lousy food, uncomfortable beds, no television, no exercise equipment, no air conditioning. In their moral equation, crime is bad and thus pain imposed on criminals is good. It is only through the imposition of pain, in fact, that offenders can pay their debt and regain their moral place in society.

Advocates of just deserts are horrified by such thinking, which is precisely why they travel a different path away from the fork in the road. These folks almost always say that they care about victims. But to be honest, Cullen and Jonson find these claims to be vacuous—as amounting mostly to socially appropriate fodder that can be ignored. When it comes down to it, the just deserts crowd looks into the correctional system and sees a whole bunch of people—mostly the poor and members of minority groups—getting the short end of the stick. A few have been railroaded and are innocent. (This is why they like Innocence Projects rather than Guilty Projects!) But even the guilty are often, in their eyes, serving overly lengthy prison terms in institutions that expose them to threats of and actual victimization, the risk of catching a range of infectious diseases (e.g., hepatitis), and degrading living conditions. In many ways, they identify with *the injustice offenders experience*. The only way to combat *injustice is with justice*. This is why they favor *just deserts*.

The just deserters also favor determinate sentences because this is the only way that rich and poor, Black and White, and male and female will be treated equally. But the key consideration that separates the retributionists from the just deserters is *how often prison sentences should be used and, when imposed, how long they should be*. Identifying with victims and liking offenders to suffer, the retribution crowd favors sending most every offender to prison and most of them for lengthy terms behind bars. Identifying with offenders and not wanting anyone to suffer much, the just deserts crowd favors the sparing use of prison terms and, for all but the most heinous criminals, short institutional stays.

So, in the end, the retributionists and the just deserters both embrace *proportionality in sentencing*, which means that punishment should be proportionate to the seriousness of the crime committed. The worse the crime, the worse the punishment. The punishment, again, fits the crime. Where they differ, however, is in the *absolute level of punishment*. How *much* punishment must be exacted to conclude that it fits the crime? Retributionists—who of course are all pain-loving conservatives—want stiff punishments; just deserters—who of course are all bleeding-heart liberals—want lenient punishments. In the 1970s, these two crowds set aside their differences and joined together to attack rehabilitation, discretion, indeterminate sentences, parole boards, and so on. As will be noted, they succeeded in getting the federal government and about half the states to throw out their existing criminal codes and replace them with this retribution/just deserts sentencing. The key issue was *which version of this approach*—retribution or just deserts—would guide the *level of punishment* in the new laws. Which crowd won this debate? Hint: We have more than 2.2 million offenders behind bars—a figure that not long ago got beyond 2.4 million! In the end, just deserts turned out to be the road less traveled.

Retribution: Just and Painful

Cullen and Jonson have no use for a strict retribution or even a just deserts model. We must quickly agree, of course, that offenders' punishments should be broadly controlled by retribution/just deserts. After all, we would not favor executing shoplifters or giving probation to mass murderers. In fact, we are okay with a system that tries, more or less, to make punishments proportionate to the harm done. We just think that retribution/just deserts cannot be the sole consideration. We think that there must be a lot of room for other things to be factored into how we wish offenders to be sanctioned. One of those things, as we will say later in more detail, is what we can do to rehabilitate the wayward so that they will live improved lives and so that public safety will be enhanced. We are persuaded that a correctional system that is devoid of this social purpose ends up miserable and ineffective. More on this in later chapters.

Still, even we have to admit that retribution is, on first blush, hard to argue against because it is so damned *principled*. It links together several sound bites that are convincing. For each one, it is easy to say: "Well, okay, I guess I can buy that idea." Four or five principles later, you are a card-carrying member of the retribution crowd. Here are some of their major ideas:

- *There are no secrets.* The punishments for every crime are written out in the criminal code so that everyone in society can see them.

- *Offenders have the right to break the law.* They are moral agents who can exercise their free will. They know the consequences of illegal acts. But they are free to choose crime over non-crime.

- *Society has the right to punish offenders who choose to break the law.* This is a promise that the state makes when enacting its criminal code. It is a promise to the offender, the victim, and the community.

- *Society needs punishment.* Members of the public need the punishment promise to be kept so that everyone will remain clear on moral boundaries. Censuring offenders and condemning their acts is fuel for society's moral gas tank; it is how we as a collective know that criminal codes are not legal fictions but the rules by which society works.

- *Punishment = justice; non-punishment = injustice.* The failure to punish—to inflict pain on offenders—means that the scales of justice will never be balanced. The infliction of pain is not an evil but a social good.

- *Punishment confirms the essential humanity of offenders.* Offenders are not beasts—controlled by instincts or, as is the case with Pavlov's dogs, by reinforcements. Woof! Woof! To be human is to have free will. To deny that offenders choose is to deny their free will. It is to deny their humanity by treating them as less than you and me. They are not objects of our pity but our moral equals who make choices with consequences. Such consequences might be unfortunate, even tragic, but they are outcomes that offenders have freely chosen to endure.

How can anyone be against free will, humanity, justice, and making victims and society whole? This is America—the good old USA—baby, and only some commie, red socialist punk can be against equal justice for all! Plus, the retributionists like to cite a lot of heavyweight philosophers, starting usually with Immanuel Kant who was justifying getting even back in the 1780s with fancy terms like the "categorical imperative" (Johnson, 2014). This essentially means that as rational, free-willed agents, we have an unconditional obligation to act morally (e.g., never steal, never tell a lie), and the state has an unconditional obligation to punish those who do not so act. Now, who can debate Mr. Kant, who obviously was a lot smarter than Cullen and Jonson? Well, as it turns out, a bunch of other smart philosophers have, particularly those known as utilitarians or consequentialists. They think that for the state to punish people unconditionally without regard to the punishment's consequences is, well, a bit nuts. For example, if punishing someone (e.g., putting them in prison), rather than helping them (e.g., showing some mercy or giving them some rehabilitation), makes them more criminal and causes more harm in the world, is this really such a good idea? Is it really something that is moral? Hmm. Not everyone thinks so (see Braithwaite & Pettit, 1990).

Now, we are going to avoid all this philosophical debate because this is not a philosophy book. But if you want to learn more about these issues—in a criminal justice context—we recommend that you read works by Braithwaite and Pettit (1990), Tonry (2011b), and von Hirsch, Ashworth, and Roberts (2009). Meanwhile, our intent in this chapter is to boil things down to a more concrete level. Toward this end, we will identify *four big problems* that retributionists cannot easily answer. As a result, their high-minded embrace of justice for all seems, in the end, not so convincing.

Four Problems for Retribution

THE PRISON PROBLEM

First, there is the prison problem. The retribution crowd is stuck with prisons and all their problems. If they want to speak of justice and morality, then they must also take responsibility for the kind of punishment that they say exacts justice. In the abstract, prisons seem to fit that bill because the amount of time spent behind bars can be transformed into a number, such as three years or five years. In turn, it seems a simple matter to scale the amount of punishment (length of imprisonment) to the seriousness of the crime. But the reality is that not all prisons are the same. Some are well run and pretty much ensure inmates' health and safety, whereas others are poorly run and cannot ensure inmates' health and safety (DiIulio, 1987). This reality means that the cost of imprisonment varies by how well institutions are administered. So much for treating all offenders equally!

More than this, however, is that the retribution crowd seems to relish the fact that prisons can be dangerous places. Once a sentence is handed out in court, they seem to be unconcerned about the *quality of justice that follows*. So, they are all for preaching individual responsibility and for holding offenders accountable as moral agents, but then they exercise their own free will by turning a blind eye to the realities of prison. Where is their moral responsibility? Although the language borders on hyperbole, Braithwaite and Pettit (1990) have a point when they argue:

A society which feels morally comfortable about sending thousands of terrified young men and women to institutions in which they are bashed, raped, and brutalized, stripped of human dignity, denied freedom of speech and movement, has a doubtful commitment to freedom. A theory which assures us that any human being can deserve these things is subversive of that commitment. (p. 6)

Even the occasional retributionist recognizes the prison problem. In his intriguing *Just and Painful,* Graeme Newman (1983) agrees that prisons are nasty places that are overused. His argument is that they should be reserved only for serious, repeat criminals that a local community is so troubled by that they are willing to pay for these offenders to serve a sentence of 15 years or a sentence of life. Such prisons, says Newman, should be purposefully miserable places because it is only through suffering that these criminals will be able to do penance and achieve a measure of expiation for their sins. Dante's inferno is his model! Okay, Newman is getting a bit weird with this recommendation since it will, after all, never happen. But wait until we tell you how Newman thinks the vast majority of offenders should be punished: He advocates *corporal punishment.* Specifically, after defendants are convicted, he favors publicly punishing them with electric shocks (for no more than a total of eight hours). Such punishment can be scaled to the seriousness of the crime because the shocks can vary in intensity, duration, and number of sessions in which they are administered.

Newman's views might seem a bit shocking (ha! ha!), even to the point of dismissing him as some sadistic punishment fiend. But a close reading of his book reveals something very different. Newman's work makes us wonder how anyone could be outraged by the acute but temporary infliction of pain through electric shocks but not be disturbed by the chronic and at times unjust pains inflicted by imprisonment. Newman is honest about the fact that he does not see pain as evil but as a necessary instrument to do justice and reaffirm society's moral codes. Corporal punishment, especially administered in public, makes us own up to how much suffering we wish offenders to experience. Thus, in the end, Newman is honest about prisons, pain, and retribution. Our point is that most others who speak righteously about retribution and balancing the scales of justice—and then turn a blind eye to the problem of prisons—are hardly exemplars of the principles of morality and justice.

THE CRIMINOLOGY PROBLEM

Second, there is the criminology problem. Retribution hinges on the empirical reality that human behavior is not determined by individual traits and social experiences but is a product of free will. To be sure, it is fairly easy to demonstrate that we all exercise free will—or, as it also is called these days, *human agency.* At this moment, Cullen and Jonson could get up off our behinds, turn off the computer, and stop writing this exhilarating chapter! As readers, perhaps with eyes glazing over, you could shut this book and drift off into a refreshing nap. Offenders are no different. They truly do know right from wrong (which is why some, seeking to exact their own just deserts, attack child molesters in prison). When committing crimes, they avoid police officers, do their best to conceal their identity, and are delighted when they are not caught (which is most of the time). Free will is present, and so their punishment is deserved.

But saying that offenders have *some free will* is not to say that their behavior is not partially, and sometimes massively, determined by factors *not of their own choosing*. For example, offenders do not choose to be born to mothers who ingest or are exposed to toxic substances that damage their offspring's brain in a way to make them less able to exercise self-control. They do not choose to have conduct problems in early childhood. They do not choose to have lower IQs than the general population or to fail and be rejected by other kids in elementary school. They do not choose to be in a neighborhood where they witness violence, including dead bodies on the sidewalk, and where gangs seek their membership. They do not choose to lack the skills to graduate from high school and to be employed in comfortable jobs that pay a lot. And on and on and on. Criminologists have amply documented how an antisocial pathway leading to life-course-persistent crime is not a matter of free will but embarked upon before choice is possible—as early as the womb where damage to fetal development can occur (Benson, 2013; Farrington & Welsh, 2007; Moffitt, 1993; Tremblay et al., 1999; see also Chapter 9 in this book).

The criminology problem for the retribution crowd is thus that science has demonstrated that *un-chosen* individual traits (e.g., temperament, self-control, IQ) and *un-chosen* social circumstances (e.g., family, school, community) can be powerful risk factors that greatly increase the likelihood of early antisocial conduct, delinquency, and adult criminality. Some scholars simply choose to ignore or downplay these criminological realities (see, e.g., Wilson, 2010). One strategy they employ is, again, to show that offenders know right from wrong and thus exercise some free will. The other strategy is to argue that without punishment, victims would be wronged and society would collapse into moral chaos. If nobody was held responsible because we assumed that offenders' criminal behavior was determined and beyond their control, we would have no basis for separating the evil from the good, the praiseworthy from the blameworthy. Commenting on advances in biological science as the basis for human behavior, James Q. Wilson (2010) eloquently makes this point:

> It would be a profound mistake to believe that science has made such a change unavoidable. For all the advances in neurobiology and genetics—and for all the many sure to come—we are nowhere near a refutation of the basic fairness of a system of laws that takes free will seriously, and treats human beings as responsible agents. Those who believe such a change is at hand are not better informed about the science involved; they are just not informed enough about the practical and philosophical foundations of our morality and justice. (p. 114)

But this line of argument is clearly fallacious—or in plainer language, this dog just won't hunt. The options are not stark and mutually exclusive: Assume free will versus assume determinism. We can take a step back and agree that the behavior of offenders is in most cases a mixture of agency and constraint, of free will and determinism. Cullen and Jonson simply believe that the correctional system should reflect this empirical reality. It should hold people responsible *and* it should try to fix the factors that have made a life in crime likely.

We should also add that appreciating why offenders break the law is not tantamount to excusing their behavior. More than this, the retribution crowd subtly suggests that if free will is in any way questioned, then offenders would be treated as victims and released with our deepest sympathy back into society—where their determined criminal dispositions would wreak havoc on the community. Quite the contrary is, in fact, true. Those of us who take the criminal propensity of offenders seriously would do no such thing. Thus, a strong rehabilitation position supports the arrest, conviction, and, if necessary, incarceration of offenders until they are cured. *Rehabilitation advocates do not excuse behavior but rather seek to change it.* One effective strategy—cognitive-behavioral treatment—demands that offenders recognize their "thinking errors" that excuse their victimizing conduct and learn skills to avoid crime in the future. By contrast, retributionists are comfortable with allowing unreformed offenders, once they have been punished, to be released from correctional supervision and to return to the community as dangerous as ever. Hmm. Cullen and Jonson call that not justice but stupidity.

THE INEQUALITY PROBLEM

Third, there is the inequality problem. Look inside our prisons. You will view a sea of minority and poor faces. This is not a coincidence or a rare occurrence. Prisons in the United States and elsewhere have always been—and likely always will be—receptacles filled up disproportionately with society's disadvantaged. This statement is not meant to excuse offenders' victimizing behavior, especially since they mainly victimize other minorities and poor folk (i.e., most crime is intra-racial and intra-class). The stinging reality of crime is that it hurts people by taking their property, damaging their bodies, and robbing them of a sense of security. Nonetheless, the other reality is that criminal justice penalties, especially prisons, reflect and exacerbate the *wide socioeconomic inequality that marks American society* (Wacquant, 2009; Wakefield & Uggen, 2010; Western, 2006; Western & Pettit, 2010).

Such inequality in society and its reproduction in the correctional system present a rough problem for the folks preaching responsibility and retribution: *If those who eventually turn to crime are raised in an unjust society, how can that society then turn around and hold these individuals fully responsible for their actions?* One weak response is that most of those who suffer the injustice of inequality do not go out and criminally victimize others. This is the *within-group variation argument:* If not everyone in a group who is exposed to an awful condition does something untoward, then you supposedly cannot blame that awful condition for anyone's bad behavioral outcomes. But the simple rejoinder to this flawed reasoning is that if these awful conditions were not consequential, then why would those making the within-group-variation argument never expose themselves or their kids to them? The reason, of course, is that these conditions are risk factors that greatly increase the likelihood of unhappy things happening to someone. To give another example, smoking leads to cancer only in a minority of smokers, but none of us would encourage our kids to puff away. Why not? Because we know that smoking increases the risk of illness and of an early death.

Cullen and Jonson would solve the inequality problem by recognizing that society's correctional system should not only exact justice but also take steps to rectify the psychological and social deficits of offenders. Rehabilitation programs are one means of producing human and cultural capital in offenders—of providing offenders with the education and parenting (so to speak) that they did not receive as kids. Put another way, we believe that a truly just system would not only exact retribution but also rectify the disadvantages that many offenders confronted due to their drawing a losing number (so to speak) in society's birth lottery. Conversely, we maintain that by ignoring inequality, those who are supposedly *all about justice*—those who embrace retribution—ultimately choose to ignore *injustice*.

There is a second part to the inequality problem: discretion. The reality is that at some point, someone in the justice system has to decide if a person has committed a crime and then what the criminal charge will be, if a guilty verdict is warranted, and what sentence should be imposed. The retributionists will pretend that it is possible to pass enough laws that will tell court actors what they must do—such as a mandatory sentence for a drug- or firearm-related offense. But as we discuss later in the chapter, this is like playing criminal justice "whack-a-mole"; once an effort is made to push discretion down in one place, it pops up somewhere else. For now, we will just talk about one form of unavoidable discretion that has never been, and most likely will never be, meaningfully quashed: prosecutorial discretion.

We are writing this just a few days after a University of Cincinnati police officer was indicted for murder for shooting an unarmed African American motorist during a traffic stop. Following the grand jury hearing, a charge of murder was filed, with the Hamilton County district attorney—the chief prosecutor—promising that there would be no plea bargain. Yet a prosecutor in another jurisdiction might have thought that the officer's intent was not so foreordained and rendered a charge of, say, voluntary manslaughter. Still, another prosecutor might have welcomed the murder indictment but then used this grave charge as leverage to securing a guilty plea on a lesser crime that still sent the officer to prison for years on end. The point is that prosecutors have extensive and typically unreviewable freedom to make decisions, especially because a high proportion of cases (upwards of 80% to 90% in most places) are plea bargained. This is sort of like buying a car where the sticker price is one thing but the customer's skill in bartering determines whether the person gets a good or a bad deal. We can use the term inequality to describe this differential treatment.

Moreover, research shows that plea bargaining and the use of prosecutorial discretion varies across jurisdictions, influenced by such factors as local politics, office policy on case processing, how high caseloads are managed, and the culture that might arise in a courtroom workgroup (Forst, 2011; McCoy, 2011). How is this legal autonomy enjoyed by prosecutors ever going to be constrained so as to produce equal punishment for all—the real-world outcome that must exist for the retributionists' theory to claim moral legitimacy? Various ideas for fundamental reform have been floated, but the sobering truth, as McCoy (2011, p. 686) states, is that "attempting to control prosecutorial discretion through well-established checks and balances inherent in the structure of democratic government and the operation of the adversary system in court is probably not working very well at this historical moment."

And there is a third part to the inequality problem: the Golden Rule. By this we mean the following: *Those who have the gold make the rules!* Retributionists implicitly assume that the legal system reflects societal consensus about what should be a crime. In their world, we all agree on what should be a crime, everyone has a chance to know right from wrong, and thus we are just in punishing those who freely choose to do criminal wrongs. But in making this assumption, they are either being naïve or duplicitous—stupid or deceptive. Take your pick! The reality is that although consensus exists to a degree (i.e., everyone thinks that shooting someone should be a crime), the law is a product of politics and it reflects the interests of the powerful in society. In turn, *inequality in law means that only some people—mainly those who lack power—are held responsible for their unlawful conduct.* Jeffrey Reiman (1984) captured this problem when he titled his critical analysis of the criminal justice system *The Rich Get Richer and the Poor Get Prison*.

Scholars have now amply demonstrated that the costs of white-collar crime, including corporate illegalities, rival if not surpass those of so-called street crime. A single financial scandal, such as the Enron and the Madoff affairs, can pilfer billions of dollars. But less well known is that the illegalities of corporations—selling defective products, maintaining unsafe work conditions, polluting the environment—sicken, injure, and kill at a disquieting rate (Cullen, Cavender, Maakestad, & Benson, 2006). Even so, most of these unlawful acts are not investigated by law enforcement officials or ever sanctioned with criminal penalties.

Similarly disturbing, corporations and white-collar professionals engage in clearly unethical behaviors that are not technically crimes and thus fully escape punishment. Anatole France understood this problem when he famously quipped: "Behold the majestic equality of bourgeois law which forbids rich and poor alike from begging in the streets and sleeping under bridges." The law is targeted to control the social harms perpetrated by the disadvantaged but not to protect us from the social harms perpetrated by the rich and powerful. For example, the 2008 collapse of the financial system was triggered in large part by inordinately risky schemes in which a range of consumers—from investors to new homeowners—were enticed to put large chunks of their resources (sometimes their life savings) into business deals that were doomed to failure (see, e.g., Lewis, 2010). Those responsible for most of these unethical practices not only were beyond the reach of prosecutors but also reaped huge profits and bonuses. Even with public outrage toward Wall Street at a fever pitch, the financial reform of banking and investment practices barely squeezed through the U.S. Congress, in large part because powerful interests lobbied against this so-called intrusion into the free market system (Hagan, 2010).

Cullen and Jonson are not calling on you to join with us in funding a lobbying group for robbers and burglars in which we pay off elected officials to allow a free market in crime! But what we are saying is that advocates of retribution try to extract offenders and the system that punishes them from the social context in which they are inextricably enmeshed. It is only by having readers focus on such de-contextualized offenders and their choice of crime that retributionists divert our attention away from the inequalities that bound this choice and that shape who we as a society choose to punish and not punish. In the end, the correctional system also has a decision to make: Should it pay attention to these inequalities and try to cushion their effects on offenders who enter the system or should it pretend that these inequalities do not exist and speak in high moral tones about the justice of exacting retribution? Cullen and Jonson prefer to pay attention to the stubborn fact that we live in an unequal society and that this has implications for how we should seek justice and operate our correctional system.

THE UTILITY PROBLEM

After all this, we get to the biggest problem of them all for retribution: *Fourth, there is the utility problem.* Why is this the biggest problem? This is why: Advocates of retribution (and just deserts as well) want the criminal justice system to do one thing and one thing only: Exact retribution. For them, *punishment is an end in and of itself.* But what about using punishment to achieve another crucial purpose— that of reducing crime? No, this would be seen as illegitimate because seeking *utility out of punishment* risks corrupting a system that *only wants to balance the scales of justice.* For example, let us say that there are two robbers—one that we are fairly certain will never offend again and one that we are fairly certain will be predatory once released. If you want the correctional system to make society safer, you would think it is reasonable to release the first offender and to keep the second one locked up—at least until treatment programs might reduce the person's propensity for crime. That is, you would want the correctional system to selectively incapacitate and to rehabilitate the offender. For retributionists, however, punishing two offenders who committed the same crime differently is a gross injustice. It violates the principle of equal justice. Better to let them both out of prison—or better to keep them both in prison. Or to put it another way, sentence the offenders and release them when they have paid their debt to society. If one of them breaks the law again, that is unfortunate. All we can do is to incarcerate that offender again.

For most Americans, this willingness to ignore public safety is, well, sort of nuts. This is because Americans—as well as people in most other nations—are *utilitarian*. Yes, they favor a measure of retribution, especially for those who commit heinous crimes. But they also want the correctional system they fund with their tax dollars to make criminals less criminal and to make the community safer (Cullen et al., 2000). Importantly, what this means is that a pure system of retribution—or of just deserts—is not possible in the United States (and elsewhere). It would be un-American, inconsistent with our cultural values, to have a system that is *unconcerned about crime control.* This is why any attempt to create a retributivist or just deserts system will *always be corrupted by utility—by the understandable desire to control crime and protect public safety.* In fact, as we will see shortly, this is precisely what occurred when the United States embraced retribution/just deserts sentencing starting in the middle part of the 1970s.

The Justice Model: Restraining State Discretion

Again, there are two versions of the punish-the-crime theory: retribution, favored by conservatives, and just deserts, favored by liberals. As we have seen, conservatives have long trumpeted retribution because it allowed them to be mean to someone! But those namby-pamby liberals, who do not like to inflict pain, have traditionally fought against get tough corrections in favor of rehabilitation. Here, we reiterate why liberals ended up joining with conservatives in opposing rehabilitation and in saying that the purpose of corrections should be—believe it or not—*punishment!* We start with why they became disillusioned with rehabilitation, focusing in particular on why they came to believe that treating offenders behind bars was a fruitless enterprise. We then describe the alternative theory of corrections they developed: *the justice model.* In the next section, we end this story by telling why liberals' embracement of just deserts was, in our view, a big mistake.

THE FAILED PROMISE OF REHABILITATION

It is an occupational imperative for academics and reformers (sometimes these being one and the same person) to scan the world, to identify problems, and then to make recommendations for how to fix those problems. Today, most criminologists and penal activists look at 2.2 million people behind bars, argue that such mass imprisonment is excessive and costly, and preach that we need to find ways to sanction non-dangerous offenders in the community. But we are now in the second decade of the 21st century and not in the late 1960s and 1970s. Back in that time—when Cullen was on protest marches and singing "All we are saying is give peace a chance," and when Jonson did not exist—the mass incarceration movement had not begun. Law-and-order and get tough rhetoric was just beginning to be voiced (Gottschalk, 2006). Instead, the reigning correctional theory was rehabilitation. So, when academics and reformers saw problems in the justice system, what do you think they blamed? You are correct, grasshopper: *They blamed rehabilitation.*

Giving Up on Rehabilitation. In this section, we are talking about *political liberals who came to embrace the theory of just deserts.* Historically, people of this ilk were the very sort who helped to transform corrections into a system that adopted rehabilitation as its guiding theory. They campaigned to modernize the system—to move away from uncivilized cries for vengeance voiced by uncouth mobs to a more detached, scientific approach to treating offenders. They wanted the treatment of offenders to mirror the treatment of the psychiatrically or physically ill. Crime was a problem, perhaps even a disease, and it was, like any problem or disease, to be understood and corrected, not punished (Menninger, 1968). This was the position taken by nearly all criminologists (Cullen & Gendreau, 2001; Toby, 1964).

But by the late 1960s, those on the political Left—which ranged from liberals to folks radicalized by the days' events, including the Vietnam War—did not like what they saw when they looked into courtrooms and when they peeked behind the high and sturdy walls surrounding most prisons. The nature of their attack on rehabilitation was detailed in Chapter 2. But to reiterate briefly, they did not see a system devoted to the reform of offenders. They did not see caring judges trying to individualize treatments or sparkling clean, quiet prisons that were organized as therapeutic communities. Instead, they witnessed judges who abused their discretion, all too often by discriminating against the poor and people of color. They witnessed parole boards that had no idea who was or was not cured and thus decided to keep offenders locked up based on politics and guesswork. They witnessed offenders who committed the same crime serving widely disparate sentences for no apparent reason whatsoever. And most disquieting, they witnessed prisons that were painful, chaotic, and often victimizing of weaker inmates. In short, they witnessed a whole lot of injustice and not much rehabilitation. No wonder that they lost faith in offender treatment and called for a system based on a *justice model of corrections*. We will return to this shortly.

The liberal critics' enmity toward prisons was especially pronounced. Aside from capital punishment, incarceration is the state's most ominous exercise of power over its citizens' lives. Here, the state deprives convicted defendants of their freedoms, for several years (about two to three, on average) and, in some cases, for the remainder of their time on this earth. For liberals who came of age in the 1960s, the state thus had a responsibility to fulfill its promise to run correctional institutions that "corrected." But critics at this time, seeking a more equal and humane society, were appalled by the reality of prison life. It simply was not palatable to throw offenders into these nasty penal environments under the guise of helping them when, in fact, the experience was manifestly harmful. They believed that if *doing good was not possible, then the least we should accomplish was to do no harm* (Gaylin, Glasser, Marcus, & Rothman, 1978). It was clear to them that inmates—and offenders generally—needed *to be protected from the potential excesses of state power over their lives*. This is another point we will return to shortly (so, just hold on to this idea for a moment longer!).

Criminologists had long known that prisons could be dreary and depriving places. In his classic *The Society of Captives,* Gresham Sykes (1958) had used participant observation in a maximum-security prison to document how the "pains of imprisonment" permeated inmates' lives and led them to cope by embracing an oppositional inmate culture. Even so, such scholars also believed that rehabilitation was an important means for blunting these deprivations and for making prisons more humane. By the late 1960s and early 1970s, however, this sanguine view of rehabilitation seemed naïve when juxtaposed with a new vision of prisons: *Correctional institutions were inherently brutalizing and inhumane.* Their improvement was not possible. They were not places where rehabilitation could ever be effective.

Stanford Prison Experiment. The 1971 Stanford Prison Experiment, led by Philip Zimbardo and his colleagues, seemed to confirm these views, providing stark and seemingly indisputable evidence that prisons were beyond any redemption (for accounts of the experiment, see Zimbardo, 2007; Zimbardo, Banks, Haney, & Jaffe, 1973). We are going to spend a bit of time reviewing this study because it proved to be really important. Once it was conducted, it seemed like everyone—at least everyone Cullen knew—was soon aware of the study and embraced its message that all institutions are, by their nature, coercive places. In no time at all, the Stanford Prison Experiment became an instant classic, with its findings assumed to convey gospel truth about the coercive nature of prisons. In fact, even today, the study is often cited by psychologists and criminologists uncritically (Griggs, 2014; Kulig, Pratt, & Cullen, 2015). Remember, 1971 was a long time ago, and things might have changed a bit. Further, treating any piece of research as sacred and beyond question is usually a bad idea. The findings of classic studies often are not repeated when efforts are made to replicate them—the "truth wears off" as Lehrer (2010, p. 52) puts it. Alas, the influence of Zimbardo et al.'s research has not worn off—true or not! In 2015, "The Stanford Prison Experiment" was released as a movie to strong reviews. The trailer to the movie started with the claim: "The results shocked the world." Because he was in the world then, Cullen can attest that this was the case!

So, let's get to the study. Psychology is sometimes called the *science of sophomores* because many students enrolled in introductory courses are bribed (e.g., with extra credit points) to participate in professors' experiments. Psychologists love experiments because they can control a lot of things that they cannot control in the real world and, by doing so, can reveal some fundamental truths about human behavior and the human condition. The challenge is in figuring out whether these revealed truths operate the same way in the real world as they do in the experimental world created by researchers.

Social psychologists, such as Zimbardo, spend a lot of time trying to figure out whether human behavior is shaped mainly by personality (also called dispositions or individual differences) or by social situations that present people with roles to play and that exert pressures upon them. This is why they call themselves *social* psychologists!

Prisons offer a confined social environment in which the personality–situation debate might be explored. A lot of bad things occur in prison. Inmates disobey rules and on occasion victimize one another—and the staff. The correctional officers get angry at inmates and, at times, disrespect or even physically abuse them. It is tempting to conclude that such untoward conduct occurs because inmates are, after all, criminals and because correctional officers are drawn to their work due to authoritarian dispositions (something, we might add, that Cullen and Jonson would find far-fetched). Zimbardo, however, wondered whether the coercion found in prisons was in fact a problem of *bad apples* (as the personality folks would argue) or a problem of a *bad barrel* (as the situation folks would argue). That is, he wondered whether prisons, due to their very nature, would produce conflict and coercion.

Cullen and Jonson think that our readers are pretty clever! So, we put this question to you: How could Zimbardo, as an experimental social psychologist, *control for personality* so as to find out for certain that any bad behavior in a prison was due *only to the situation of being incarcerated*? The answer was that he had to put *normal people*—those who were not criminal or psychologically troubled—*into prison* and, in turn, *see what occurred*. Would the prison be quiet—sort of like a bunch of folks taking a vacation retreat at a monastery? Or would the prison produce the same kind of pathology among normal people as it did among criminals and their custodians? If so, then a strong case could be made that the situation of imprisonment was inherently brutalizing and inhumane. It would drive even good folks to do bad things.

Zimbardo had two problems: He had to find normal people and he had to find a prison to put them into. Well, he managed to do both. First, we are back to the science of sophomores! It was summer break—August of 1971—and thus Zimbardo had no sophomores in his classes to recruit. Instead, he advertised in two newspapers for male college students wishing to participate in a prison experiment. He received over 70 inquiries. From this group, he culled 20 students, chosen on the basis of a solid law-abiding background and a solid performance on psychological tests, given to them by Zimbardo's graduate assistants. Students were randomly assigned to the groups—nine to the prisoner group and nine to the guard group, with two students serving as backup guards (Zimbardo, 2007, p. 56). The participants, most of whom wanted to be prisoners (it was the early seventies, a time when people identified more with oppressed inmates than with the "Man" running the government), were to be paid $15 a day for an experiment that was intended to last two weeks.

Second, because Stanford University was not in session, Zimbardo was able to build a mock prison—the Stanford County Prison—in the basement of Jordan Hall in which the Department of Psychology was located. To make the experience of incarceration comparable to life in a real prison, Zimbardo and his colleagues attempted to create roles into which "guards" and "prisoners" would now be encapsulated. For the students-turned-guards, he sought to achieve what psychologists call *deindividuation,* a fancy term used to mean that custodians would conceal their individuality behind a mask of "silver reflecting sunglasses" and "standard military-style uniforms" (Zimbardo, 2007, p. 301). For the students-turned-prisoners, he wanted them to face *dehumanization,* a fancy word used to mean that they would be seen as less-than-equal beings occupying a degraded, powerless status. To accomplish this role placement, he arranged to have Palo Alto police arrest the nine students-turned-inmates at their residences and to book them (blindfolded) at the police station. They were then led to the mock Stanford County Prison where they were stripped naked, sprayed with a powder they were told was a delouser, given uniforms with numbers (not names) on the front and back, told to don a pair of rubber clogs on their feet, and—to remind them of their inmate status—made to wear a locked chain around one ankle. Soon thereafter, they were read a list of 17 rules that they were to follow.

You probably know—or can guess—what transpired. In fairly short order, the psychologically healthy college students started to act their roles as guards and prisoners. To assert their control, the guards awakened inmates at 6:00 a.m., belittled them, forced them to sing the prison rules, insisted that they make their cots in military style, required shows of obedience by calling the guards "Mr. Correctional Officer," and placed recalcitrant inmates in the "Hole." A rebellion by a few inmates, who barricaded themselves within their cells, was quashed quickly, in part by stripping naked and taking the beds away from other non-rebellious inmates (Zimbardo, 2007). As the researchers noted, the guards regularly "insulted the prisoners, threatened them, were physically aggressive, used instruments (night sticks, fire extinguishers, etc.) to keep the prisoners in line and referred to them in impersonal, anonymous, deprecating ways" (Zimbardo et al., 1973, pp. 48–49). Less than 36 hours into the experiment, a disorganized and depressed student-turned-prisoner had to be sent home. On each successive day, it was necessary to release additional inmates. By the sixth day, Zimbardo (2007) reports:

> Half of our student-prisoners had to be released early because of severe emotional and cognitive disorders, transient but intense at the time. Most of those who remained for the duration generally became mindlessly obedient to the guards' demands and seemed "zombie-like" in their listless movement while yielding to the whims of the ever-escalating guard power. (p. 196)

None of the student-guards quit or wanted the experiment to end.

Zimbardo, who took on the role of prison "Superintendent," as well as other researchers and people who had visited the mock prison, seemed to have a moral blindness to what was transpiring. Zimbardo was moved to halt the experiment after six days only because Christina Maslach confronted him and stated poignantly, "*What you are doing to those boys is a terrible thing*" (Zimbardo, 2007, p. 171, emphasis in the original). Maslach, who had just completed her Ph.D. at Stanford, was about to start what would prove to be a distinguished career in psychology at the University of California, Berkeley (most notably studying the nature and measurement of "burnout"). She also was romantically involved with Zimbardo and would become Mrs. Zimbardo thereafter. Back in those days, nobody got too riled up over professor–student relationships—sometimes for the better (in this case), sometimes for the worse. In any event, on this occasion, Dr. Maslach had the personal standing to prompt Zimbardo to stop for a moment, take a step outside his Superintendent's role, and realize the need to end the project before more harm had occurred.

As in any classic experiment in which researchers try to re-create social reality in a laboratory setting, subsequent critical analysis questioned the generalizability of the study to real-world conditions and questioned whether peculiarities of the design might have made certain outcomes more likely. Limited attempts to replicate the study have produced divergent results—and divergent interpretations of the results (Reicher & Haslam, 2006; Zimbardo, 2006, 2007; see also Griggs, 2014). If anything, Zimbardo's findings received their strongest reaffirmation in Iraq, where the U.S. military undertook what amounted to a natural experiment when it created the prison at Abu Ghraib. In this real-world setting where a prison was created from scratch, the soldiers-turned-guards acted much as did the students-turned-guards, belittling and abusing the inmates (Zimbardo, 2007).

But for our purposes here, the generalizability of the Stanford Prison Experiment is not of chief importance. Rather, the key issue is how this experiment's results were viewed by academics and activists living in the early 1970s—a particular social context that already had led them to mistrust state power. Reflecting back on this context, Zimbardo (2007) juxtaposes living in the "western paradise" of Palo Alto with the prevailing turmoil that had coalesced by 1971:

> Yet, all around this oasis, trouble has begun brewing of late. Over in Oakland, the Black Panther Party is promoting black pride, backed by black power, to resist racist practices "by all means necessary." Prisons are becoming centers for recruiting a new breed of political prisoners, inspired by George Jackson, who is about to go on trial with his "Soledad Brothers" for the alleged murder of a prison guard. The women's liberation movement is picking up steam, dedicated to ending women's secondary citizenship and fostering new opportunities for them. The unpopular war in Vietnam drags on as body counts soar daily. That tragedy worsens as the Nixon–Kissinger administration reacts to antiwar activists with ever-greater bombings in reaction to the mass demonstrations against the war. The "military-industrial-complex" is the enemy of this new generation of people, who openly question its aggressive-commercial-exploitation values. For anyone who likes to live in a truly dynamic era, this Zeitgeist is unlike any in recent history. (pp. 23–24)

For liberals at this time, the lesson taught by the Stanford Prison Experiment was inescapable. Even when the most healthy and normal are placed within the roles typically populated by criminals and uneducated if not authoritarian guards, a humane environment does not ensue. Instead, the very structure of imprisonment is so inherently corrupting that it constrains even good people to brutalize one another. In the words of Zimbardo et al. (1973):

> The potential social value of this study derives precisely from the fact that normal, healthy, educated young men could be so radically transformed under the institutional pressures of a "prison environment." If this could happen in so short a time, without the excesses that are possible in real prisons, and if it could happen to the "cream-of-the-crop of American youth," then one can only shudder to imagine what society is doing both to the actual guards and prisoners who are at this very moment participating in this unnatural "social experiment." (p. 56)

With regard to rehabilitation, the indictment was equally clear. If prisons were inherently dehumanizing, then it is fanciful to call them "correctional" institutions and to assume that they are environments in which effective "treatment" that cures inmates could take place. As it turns out, quality programs can improve offenders within institutions, although they work better in the community (Andrews & Bonta, 2010). This note aside, for 1970s' liberals, it seemed unethical on their part to support any longer the policy of incarcerating offenders on the "noble lie," as Norval Morris (1974, p. 20) called it, that they would be saved from a life in crime.

In particular, liberals grew deeply concerned that the therapy was *state enforced* (Kittrie, 1971). Under a therapeutic system, inmates are given an indeterminate sentence, which means they earn release only when they prove to their captors—from guards and counselors to wardens and ultimately parole board members—that they have been "cured." But it was clear from Zimbardo's experiment that the primary concern of prison custodians was—and would always be—inmates' obedience to rules and authority as opposed to their personal growth and reformation. Again, David Rothman (1980) captured this reality with his historical demonstration that, when it came to relying on institutions to do good for the wayward, "conscience" was inevitably corrupted by "convenience."

So to get to the key point: For liberal critics, rehabilitation was state enforced because inmates could not be released until they had demonstrated to state officials that they were rehabilitated. The message was clear: We have a stick over your head. Do what we say or you will not be paroled. Again, as the Zimbardo experiment suggested, powerful incentives existed for means-goal displacement to take place. Obedience to rules was not a means to rehabilitation but rather became the goal in and of itself. The guards wanted inmates to do what they were told so as to make prisons orderly and the guards' lives easier. To achieve this goal, they would use coercive strategies that were inconsistent with offender treatment—such as telling inmates that they would never get out if they acted in uncooperative ways. Given this bureaucratic priority, liberals reluctantly gave up on rehabilitation as a worthy but naïve goal that could never be achieved in prisons where state interests, not inmate interests, prevailed. As we will see shortly, a key policy that followed from this way of thinking was the campaign: Replace indeterminate with determinate sentencing. This new scheme, liberals argued, would take away the discretion to release inmates from correctional officials and parole boards.

Being Sane in Insane Places. The difficulty of achieving effective treatment within institutional settings was reinforced by a natural experiment conducted by another Stanford University professor, David Rosenhan (1973), who reported his results in a poignantly titled article published in *Science*: "Being Sane in Insane Places." Rosenhan and seven confederates—all people without any history of mental illness—managed to gain admission to a range of psychiatric facilities on the East and West coasts. The study's participants had been instructed to complain of hearing voices during the screening process but to act perfectly normal thereafter. Despite being sane, their status as psychiatric patients rigidly shaped the treatment staff's interpretation of their conduct. Indeed, "despite their public 'show' of sanity, the pseudopatients were never detected" (Rosenhan, 1973, p. 252). Diagnosed as schizophrenic, they were kept hospitalized an average of 19 days and were discharged not as cured but as suffering schizophrenia "in remission" (p. 253).

But Rosenhan's experiment had a second act, so to speak. The staff at one psychiatric facility "had heard these findings but doubted that such an error could occur in their hospital" (p. 252). If they knew that sane confederates were coming, they would not be fooled—or so they thought. Taking up this challenge, Rosenhan agreed to send for admission one or more pseudopatients—healthy confederates—over the next three months. At the close of this period, staff members, including psychiatrists and psychologists, had identified nearly 10% of the patient population as feigning illness. Rosenhan, however, either was clever or had a nasty sense of humor—or both: In reality, *he had sent no pseudopatients to this facility!* These *treatment experts* had, in essence, found a bunch of sane people among the population of patients they would have typically defined as insane. As Rosenhan (1973) warned:

> But one thing is certain: any diagnostic process that lends itself so readily to massive errors of this sort cannot be a very reliable one. . . . It is clear that we cannot distinguish the sane from the insane in psychiatric hospitals. (p. 252)

Rosenhan's study showed that separating the cured from the ill was a daunting task that likely outstripped the treatment technology available even to therapists with Ph.D.s (psychologists) and with M.D.s (psychiatrists). If these highly trained experts made inexact decisions regarding patient health, how much worse were the decisions being made in prisons by ill-trained correctional officials? Again, liberals worried deeply about allowing inmates to rot in prison—for years on end—because some *non-expert* opined that they had not been rehabilitated. Their image was *One Flew Over the Cuckoo's Nest*—or, for a younger audience, *The Shawshank Redemption.*

Attica Prison Riot. Any glimmer of hope that the state was interested in the welfare of offenders was extinguished with the tragic end to the prison riot at New York's Attica Correctional Facility—an event that transpired less than a month after the Stanford Prison Experiment had concluded (for an account, see Wicker, 1975). The outbreak occurred shortly before 9 a.m. on September 9, 1971, and led to 1,281 of Attica's 2,243 inmates occupying D-Block in the prison yard and holding 38 guards hostage. Four days hence, an armed assault by state troopers and some correctional officers quashed the insurgency. But the carnage of this assault horrified the nation: more than 80 inmates wounded and 32 dead. Eleven guards also were slain, all but one killed not by their captors but by those retaking the prison (Wicker, 1975). The guards' deaths were particularly disturbing because they suggested that the state officials storming Attica used lethal force indiscriminately—firing weapons even when no threat to anyone's life existed.

Attica was not just a grisly event that would slip quickly from the nation's collective conscience. Rather, it came to symbolize, at least for liberals, state power run amok. Although the film is a touch dated, many readers might still recall the following classic scene in the 1975 movie *Dog Day Afternoon,* a story about a botched bank robbery that ends up with the offenders and hostages caught inside. Played by Al Pacino, Sonny Wortzik parades outside the bank slinging a rifle around and defiantly chanting to the police—and to the onlooking crowd's growing crescendo of cheers—"Attica! Attica! Attica!" A *Time* reporter captured the significance of Attica shortly following the event:

> . . . Attica. For some time to come in the U.S., that word will not be primarily identified with the plain upon which ancient Athens nurtured philosophy and democracy. Nor will it simply stand for the bucolic little town that gave its name to a turreted prison, mislabeled a "correctional facility." Attica will evoke the bloodiest prison rebellion in U.S. history. It will take its place alongside Kent State, Jackson State, My

Lai and other traumatic events that have shaken the American conscience and incited searing controversy over the application of force—and the pressure that provokes it. (as quoted in Cullen & Gilbert, 1982, p. 5)

Attica had profound consequences for rehabilitation as well. Indeed, Gresham Sykes (1978) observes that this tragedy served as "a symbol for the end of an era in correctional philosophy" (p. 476). Recall that liberals had long been the prime advocates of a system that would *correct* offenders. The promise of inmates' humane improvement often remained unfulfilled, but confidence persisted that, with constant incremental reforms, steady progress would allow this goal to be realized. Consider how Gresham Sykes (1958) concluded *The Society of Captives*—again, a book that detailed how the pains of imprisonment prompt either a "highly individualistic war of all against all" or prisoners' formation of "a close alliance with [their] fellow captives" so as to "present a unified front against the custodian" (p. 131). But for Sykes, this fact of prison life was not a recipe for disillusionment with the goal of treatment—only a caution to be realistic in what might be accomplished. As Sykes noted, "it is excessively optimistic to expect the prison to rehabilitate 100 percent of its inmates" (p. 133). However, he proceeded to argue that it would be mistaken to assume that "man's nature is largely fixed by the adult years" or that we should "condemn efforts to reform the criminal as singularly naïve" (p. 133). Indeed:

The greatest naïveté, perhaps, lies in those who believe that because progress in methods for reforming the criminal has been so painfully slow and uncertain in the past, little or no progress can be expected in the future. (pp. 133–134)

Attica shattered this hope. For liberals, the idea that the state would benevolently seek to rehabilitate offenders seemed, in the aftermath of Attica, ludicrous. They had lost any hope that incremental progress could be made in saving the wayward while incarcerated. Instead, the task at hand was more sober: Find a way to protect offenders, especially inmates languishing behind bars, from the state's willingness to abuse its immense power when dealing with the unfortunate souls caught within its clutches.

THE SOLUTION: DOING JUSTICE

If not rehabilitation, then what? What other theory could organize the correctional process in such a way that offenders could be treated equitably and not be victimized by state power? How might it be possible to *do justice*—to ensure that judges sentenced equally, that everyone convicted of the same crime received the same sentence, and that state officials could not act abusively toward offenders under their charge? At this time, a number of influential scholars agreed that the goal of the correctional system should not be to save the wayward—to rehabilitate them—but to ensure that they receive penalties that are fair and not excessive. These divergent scholars—with some idiosyncrasies to each of their proposals— reached a general consensus on what to do. This shared vision became known as the *justice model for corrections* (see, e.g., American Friends Service Committee Working Party, 1971; Conrad, 1973; Fogel, 1979; Fogel & Hudson, 1981; Hickey & Scharf, 1980; Morris, 1974; Singer, 1979; von Hirsch, 1976; see also Kittrie, 1971).

The key challenge was *how to control state power,* which was rooted in the discretion that judges, corrections officials, and parole boards exercised in their sanctioning of the offenders under their charge. Well, in its simplest terms, when state officials have the *discretionary freedom* to make unfettered decisions, the countervailing strategy is to *remove this freedom.* How could you do this, though—take away discretion? Well, the clearest approach was to *pass rules* that officials had to follow when making decisions about offenders' lives. In the 1960s, the *due process rights* movement took strides precisely in this direction. For example, when the police interrogated offenders in abusive ways, the court responded in 1966 in the so-called Miranda case that arrestees had to be apprised of their right to an attorney and right to remain silent. If police officers did not read or comply with these rights, then any confession they gained would be inadmissible. The state's power was thus limited: Follow the rules and respect offenders' rights or they go free.

The justice model was an extension of this approach, for it set its sights on constraining the state's discretion in corrections. It was an attempt either to eliminate decisions altogether (such as by abolishing parole) or to limit discretion by telling officials what rules to follow when dealing with offenders (such as telling judges what sentences they must pass out). There are six main components of the *justice model for corrections*:

- *Punish the crime, not the criminal, by narrowing the range of punishments a judge can impose.* This could be achieved by writing into law precisely what sentence each crime should receive or by creating sentencing guidelines that would have to be followed. In this way, discrimination would be eliminated because every defendant—advantaged or disadvantaged—would receive the same sentence (or, in the least, very close to the same sentence).

- *Replace indeterminate with determinate sentences.* At the time of sentencing, every defendant would be told by the judge precisely how long his or her prison sentence would be. Offenders would no longer enter prison not knowing how long they would be staying. They would no longer sit behind bars having no idea whether they would be released this year—or the next, or the one after that, or five years after that. Certainty would replace uncertainty in sentencing.

- *Eliminate parole boards and parole release.* With prison terms set at the time of sentencing, there would be no release based on so-called treatment progress. When a sentence was served, the offender would be released.

- *Any rehabilitation would be voluntary.* Because release from prison no longer would be based on supposed progress in being rehabilitated, participation in treatment would not be mandatory or enforced. Regardless of whether offenders attended programs, their release date would be exactly the same as it was on the day they entered prison. With inmates choosing rather than being compelled to pursue treatment, program participants would have a genuine motivation to change. In fact, they might benefit far more from interventions such as counseling or job training because these would be opportunities that were desired rather than forced on them.

- *Make prisons just communities.* This should involve removing all abusive practices, giving inmates full legal rights, and creating opportunities for self-governance. Prisons should be administered according to just principles and be organized to teach inmates to act in just ways.

- *Make certain that prison sentences are short and reserved for only the most serious crimes.* Because prisons are dehumanizing and likely criminogenic, their use should be discouraged. When a prison sentence is imposed, it should be as short as possible.

In the early 1970s, the population of state and federal prisons hovered around 200,000; today, as we point out in several places in this book, it has increased seven-fold. Get tough rhetoric, which was barely legitimate in the early seventies, now is voiced proudly and without any trepidation by politicians in both parties. Looking back, advocates of the justice model are appalled by what has since transpired. Their hope of doing justice—and, in particular, of *restraining state power*—was not realized, as the United States went on an imprisonment binge and descended into an orgy of mean-spirited correctional practices. In a real way, these well-intentioned reformers helped to usher in precisely the kind of system they detested. Hmm. Maybe rehabilitation was not so bad after all! What in the world went wrong?

What Went Wrong?
Winning the Battle but Losing the War

WINNING THE BATTLE

In many ways, the liberal advocates of the justice model initially achieved what they desired. On a broad level, they did much to discredit offender treatment and to place its advocates on the defensive. In part, they succeeded in tarnishing the theory of rehabilitation because their critiques were accurate: Many programs did not work; many judges sentenced in harsh and unprincipled ways. Many offenders were needlessly detained in prison longer than their more fortunate brethren. Many parole boards had no clue as to who was or was not cured. Asking for more accountability and seeking to protect offenders against poorly used discretion made a lot of sense. Cullen and Jonson think it still does today.

Thus, in the context of the 1970s, making the correctional system more justice oriented did not seem like a loony idea. This is why Cullen for a time called himself a justice model liberal. But, one day, he changed his mind. It was in 1979 when he was attending a summer faculty seminar at the University of Virginia run by Gresham Sykes. Cullen had a short paper to write for, and presentation to give to, the seminar. Searching for a topic, he was thinking about writing on rehabilitation. In reflecting on its fate, he wondered what would happen if, indeed, the correctional system was purged of treatment programs, of people who wanted to save offenders, and of the responsibility by the state not just to do something to offenders but for them. This questioning, which he had never done before, led him to the startling conclusion that the alternative to rehabilitation would likely be a disaster. Why would a system that was devoted only to inflicting pain on offenders—even in a just and reduced way—be better than a system that, at least to a degree, wanted to improve offenders? Several years later, this led Cullen to write *Reaffirming Rehabilitation* (Cullen & Gilbert, 1982; see also Cullen, 2013).

What Cullen understood in 1979 in Virginia was that any theory of corrections—whether rehabilitation or the justice model—could be corrupted; again, to use Rothman's (1980) terms, conscience (the theory) can fall prey to convenience (bureaucratic and political interests). Whenever someone criticizes an older theory (in this case, rehabilitation), they typically propose a new theory (in this case, the justice model) that they assume will be put into practice as envisioned. Duh! This is pretty stupid—and a touch arrogant. Cullen and Jonson use the word *arrogant* because critics get on their high horse and belittle opponents and then turn around and are blind to the powerful forces that can corrupt their "good" intentions. That is, it is dangerous to assume that of all the correctional theories out there, yours is the only one that will not be corrupted!

In the end, we must compare the merits of correctional theories that, when implemented, *are all* imperfect. We have to determine which theory, after all the corruption occurs, is the best. Back in 1979, this is the insight Cullen had. The justice model advocates, he lamented, did not consider whether their model, when put into practice, could achieve its goals and actually produce a more just and humane correctional system. After much reflection, Cullen concluded that despite the good will of its proponents, the justice model was a bad deal for offenders and a bad deal for those wishing to achieve crime control. Jonson, as it turns out, agrees with Cullen—which is one reason they have come together to write this book. They want you to agree with them, too! You should, because if you do, you will be a very smart criminologist!

At first, the justice model reformers seemed in good shape. Their ideas gained traction, and a number of states embarked on the process of sentencing reform. In 1975, Maine was the first state to embrace determinate sentencing. But, of course, nobody much pays attention to our neighbors in the far Northeast—after all, they are practically Canadians! The next year, however, the movement to transform corrections received an incredible boost when California passed determinate sentencing legislation. California is generally considered to be a bellwether state—a place that is a harbinger of things to come elsewhere in America. In this instance, as David Garland (2001) notes, the change was especially significant because California was a "state where indeterminate sentencing and individualized treatment regimes had been best established" (p. 60). Not long thereafter, determinate sentencing laws were passed in Indiana, Illinois, New York, and (in various forms) in other states. Sentencing commissions and guidelines went into effect on the federal level and in states such as Minnesota, Pennsylvania, Washington, and Oregon (Griset, 1991;

Tonry, 1996). Indeed, the model of individualized treatment, which had pretty much ruled corrections for seven decades, collapsed (Rothman, 1980). "Beginning with Maine's abolition of parole in 1974," notes Tonry (1996), "nearly every state in some ways repudiated indeterminate sentencing" (p. 4). Garland (2001) echoes this observation: "In 1970 all of the US states had indeterminate sentencing laws. In the thirty years since, nearly every state had in some way repudiated this, bringing about a major transformation in sentencing policy and practice" (p. 60).

Okay, time for the just deserts crowd to party down, dude! Out with rehabilitation, and in with justice! We won! We won! But in the end, the genuine desire to improve the quality of justice in the correctional system was, in most instances, not achieved. As Tonry (1996) painfully concludes, the "irony of 'just deserts' is that it backfired" (p. 13). The goal was to ensure that punishments were equitable and to use this principle of justice to lower the severity of harm visited on offenders. But the opposite transpired. "In practice," concludes Tonry (1996), "the result has been both to make punishment more severe and to create disparities as extreme as any that existed under indeterminate sentencing" (p. 14). And in Rothman's (2002) words, the "reformers proved wrong on all counts" (p. 429). "Fixed sentences" have merely "promoted prison overcrowding," and the "distaste for rehabilitation" has "contributed to making prisons into human warehouses" (pp. 429–430). *The just deserters thus won the battle against rehabilitation but lost the war against coercion and injustice* (see also Cullen & Gilbert, 1982; Garland, 2001; Griset, 1991).

LOSING THE WAR

So, *what went wrong?* Each state has its own story to tell, but Cullen and Jonson think that three factors intersected to make the failure of the just deserts approach virtually inevitable (Rothman, 2002).

First, when the justice model was concocted, it seemed as though the United States was in the midst of a prolonged liberal era. The U.S. Supreme Court had issued many rulings favorable to civil rights and to the rights of offenders. Great Society programs had extended opportunity and a safety net to many—from the poor to the aged. Prison populations were miniscule by today's standards and experiments with deinstitutionalization had taken place—most notably Jerome Miller's (1991) closing of Massachusetts's juvenile reformatories in 1972. Who knew that America was in the process of turning to the political Right? As conservative ideas and conservative officials came to dominate public policy discourse—including about crime—concerns about justice were supplanted with concerns about victims and making so-called super-predator offenders pay for their crimes. David Garland (2001) captures this transformation:

> Over time, the liberal concern with just deserts, proportionality and minimizing penal coercion gave way to more hard-line policies of deterrence, predictive restraint and incapacitation, and eventually to expressive, exemplary sentencing and mass imprisonment—policies that were completely at odds with principles and intentions of the original liberal reformers. (p. 61; see also Tonry, 2013)

The well-meaning justice model liberals simply did not realize that, in embracing punishment, they were playing with fire. They were taking the position that the state had no obligation to help and reform offenders. Instead, the only job of the state was to inflict pain on offenders so that justice would be served. The conservatives of this day agreed and were delighted to help liberals dismantle rehabilitation-oriented sentencing and corrections and replace them with a system that punished. But remember, the conservatives had a much different agenda. They did not think that criminals were punished too harshly but too leniently.

So, in a way, they sat back and watched liberals eat their own—they watched as just deserts advocates undermined the legitimacy of rehabilitation in a way they never could have. This liberal crowd called its traditional theory a noble lie and then showed that being nice to offenders—trying to rehabilitate them—did not work! The conservatives could only smile at what the just deserters achieved: Killing off a bleeding-heart theory that had been a thorn in their mean-spirited sides for decades.

Of course, in the end, what had to be decided was whether the determinate sentencing system being established would be arranged according to the justice model or according to the conservatives' preference for retribution and harsh punishment. At issue, in large part, was not whether offenders would be punished but rather *what the absolute level* of that punishment would be. In this conservative time, there was no constituency for *being lenient on crime*. Just deserts proponents thus helped to create a reform whose outcome they were unable to control. They simply opened the door to punishment and a mean-season in corrections.

Let us give two brief examples. When Illinois reformed its sentencing in the mid-1970s, David Fogel, who had extensive experience as a correctional administrator and as an academic, proposed a sentencing scheme based on his *justice model for corrections* (see Fogel, 1979; Fogel & Hudson, 1981). But Fogel's proposal, introduced in the Illinois Senate in April 1976, never emerged from committee. The law that eventually was passed did embrace determinate sentencing and, to a degree, proportionality in sentencing. But it also added in a new category of crimes—called "Class X" felonies—that were to be punished with prison sentences that ranged from 6 to 30 years. In the end, it was clear that getting tough, more than treating offenders fairly, was the agenda in Illinois (Cullen & Gilbert, 1982).

California is the other example. Similar to Illinois, the state passed its Uniform Determinate Sentencing Act in 1976, which repudiated rehabilitation as guiding correctional theory in favor of punishment. On December 31 of that year, California housed only 21,088 offenders. It did not take long for liberal hopes of greater justice to be dashed. The state went on a prison construction orgy, adding 22 new facilities between 1984 and 1997 (Cullen & Gilbert, 2013). As Petersilia (2008, p. 211) notes, "from 1984 to 1991, the legislature passed over 1,000 crime bills, with almost none of them reducing sentences and many imposing sentence enhancements.... Media-driven add-ons and enhancements ratcheted up penalties, and therefore the size of the prison population." In 1994, California's three-strikes-and-you're out law would pass (Zimring, Hawkins, & Kamin, 2001). Meanwhile, prison conditions deteriorated, as a focus on inmate rehabilitation and social welfare was replaced by a focus on punishment and custody (see Kruttschnitt & Gartner, 2005; Page, 2011). Eventually, California's prisons became so crowded (housing more than 174,000 inmates) and the conditions of confinement became so disquieting that the U.S. Supreme Court ruled in its 2011 *Brown v. Plata* decision that the state "bring its swollen prison population down to 137 percent of the capacity of its thirty-three prisons within two years" (Simon, 2014, p. 133). Writing for a 5–4 majority, Justice Kennedy noted that inmates "retain the essence of human dignity. . . . A prison that deprives prisoners of basic sustenance, including adequate medical care, is incompatible with the concept of human dignity, and has no place in a civilized society" (quoted in Simon, 2014, p. 133). This was certainly an outcome that liberal reformers in 1976 California did not see coming.

Second, the just deserts crowd wanted to *remove discretion from sentencing and corrections*. What they failed to understand is that discretion taken from one part of the system is, in effect, concentrated at another part of the system. In the traditional indeterminate sentencing system, discretionary power was dispersed. Legislators passed laws with ranges of sentencing attached; judges assigned sentences; and parole boards added their two cents in deciding when offenders got out. It was a system of checks and balances. Now, however, judges and parole boards lost their discretion. Accordingly, all the power was transferred to the *front end of the system*. Well, *who the heck do you think got to make all the decisions now?* You are correct, grasshopper: Legislators got all the power.

The problem with legislators is that they are elected officials who are very sensitive to the wishes of the electorate. Legislators figured out that when some heinous crime was committed or some crime wave spiked upward (e.g., crack cocaine use), they could take the side of the *innocent victim* and write a new law mandating longer prison terms. This is at times called *eraser justice*, because they could get out their pencils, erase the existing penalty, and write in a higher number of years to be served in prison. Jonathan Simon (2007) argues that legislators got so enamored with this strategy that they came to "govern through crime."

Again, under determinate sentencing, whatever is written into the law is what offenders serve (except for charge reductions through plea bargaining). Thus, when legislators wrote laws, they were deciding how long prison sentences would be. Because crime was politicized in this conservative environment, appearing lenient on crime made elected officials of both parties vulnerable to defeat at the polls. Better safe than sorry! Get on board the get tough bandwagon and advocate for statutes that mandate putting people behind bars. In past times, even if politicians wrote tough laws, their effects could be mitigated by judges and parole boards, who were less visible to the public and more insulated from direct political pressures; checks and balances were at work. Even in places where judges were elected, most of the public hardly knew who they were. But under determinate sentencing, nobody was left to smooth out the harshness of the new laws. Tough laws often had their intended consequences.

David Rothman (2002) makes another observation regarding the policies passed by legislators: Many of the get tough laws had a disproportionate effect on African Americans (see also Clear, 2007; Tonry, 2011a; Wacquant, 2001, 2009). Although we might wish it were not the case, the reality is that racial animus—not liking minorities—is a robust source of punitiveness both in the United States and in other Western societies (Unnever & Cullen, 2010a, 2010b; Unnever, Cullen, & Jonson, 2008). Quite consciously, conservative politicians too often capitalized on this racism–punitiveness connection by favoring get tough policies as a way of controlling "crime in the streets" or "urban crime." There were votes to be gained by forgetting about justice and passing mandatory laws that told *White folks* that their elected officials were fully prepared to protect them by putting bad folks— read *bad Black folks*—behind bars. Concern about drug use was especially racialized (Beckett, 1997; Gordon, 1994; Tonry, 2011a). As Rothman (2002) notes:

> Probably the most serious drawback of the 1970s reform program was the failure to anticipate the prominence that would be given drug control, the issue that now dominates criminal justice procedures.... Drug law enforcement and punishment are aimed mostly at minorities, and the "war on drugs" is in large part a war on blacks. The proportion of blacks among those arrested for drug possession increased from 22 percent in 1981 to 37 percent in 1990. (pp. 432–433)

We need to add a final touch of nuance to the discussion. The problem was not simply with the type of sentencing that was implemented. In fact, some evidence exists that determinate sentencing and similar initiatives (e.g., sentencing guidelines) might have slowed the rate of increase in incarceration in some states over the past decades (see, e.g., Stemen & Rengifo, 2011). Rather, the difficulty was that sentencing reform did not usher in, as justice model advocates had hoped, a new era in which there was, across America, an abiding concern about justice for offenders or about the dangers of excessive imprisonment. Instead, it was more like opening a Pandora's box—creating the opportunity for elected politicians to spout harsh rhetoric and to demonstrate how tough on crime they could be by grabbing control over sentencing.

Now, here is the nuance: Importantly, this punitive posture was not confined to officials in states that passed determinate sentencing. Legislators in other jurisdictions did not look at the growing sentencing reform movement and then rush out and ask how they could treat offenders more justly! Rather, they copied the behavior of the so-called reformers. Although they may not have fully renovated their states' entire sentencing structures, they embraced punishment and got involved in sentencing so that they, too, could curtail the discretion of judges and correctional administrators. A favorite tactic was to pass statutes mandating lengthy incarceration for a range of offenses (Tonry, 1996, 2009). Thus, regardless of whether determinate sentencing per se was undertaken, legislators across states traveled the similar path of moving away from rehabilitation and of neglecting concerns about justice.

Third, the justice model advocates were so concerned with how the correctional system victimized offenders that they had no answer whatsoever to the following question:

> Okay, just deserters. What is your plan for reducing crime? After all, it is 1977 and, over the past decade, serious violent crime has jumped 80% and serious property crime has jumped 75%. What are we going to do about this?

The answer from the just deserters was that they were *interested only in doing justice, not in crime control!* They did not care about *the utilitarian goal of reducing crime and protecting the public*. They just wanted to use deserts to make sure that the people victimizing you or your family were punished equitably and, by gosh, not sent to prison where they might suffer in that bad environment.

Conservatives, however, offered a different option. Essentially, they said that "as a victim of crime, you have been harmed by a predator and, as your supporters, we are going to exact retribution on this retrograde creature. Let's get even by making the offender suffer." But, they then went on to say that "by getting tough in this way, they could also make you safer." Why? Because the offender's sorry derrière would be sitting in an uncomfortable prison cell! He (or she) would soon learn that crime does not pay (deterrence) or, in any case, would be in no position while locked up to harm anyone (incapacitation).

The point is that, in the real world, *conservatives linked retribution to utility*. It was a two-fer: We will get even and protect society. In contrast, the liberal just deserters were offering a correctional platform that was out of sync with the times. They ignored the enduring reality that, although Americans like justice, they also want the correctional system to reduce crime (Cullen et al., 2000). In the end, the conservatives promised retribution (justice for victims) and safety, whereas the liberals offered only just deserts (justice for offenders) and no safety. Hmm. Which option do you think people found to be the most attractive?

So to sum up, this is what went wrong:

- The United States moved from a liberal era into a conservative era.

- The power to decide how much offenders should be punished was concentrated in the hands of legislators who had every incentive to seem tough on crime.

- The just deserts advocates made the crucial mistake of having no plausible crime control strategy at a time when crime was rising. Their model thus seemed unrealistic.

Cullen and Jonson will make one final point. Over the years, liberals always had a plausible crime control model to offer *as an alternative to getting tough:* rehabilitation. Remember, rehabilitation is not just about helping offenders but also about societal protection. This approach says that we want to protect the public by making criminals less criminal and by keeping them behind bars until they are reformed—however long that might take. This latter part of the treatment model—that offenders are not to be put back into society if officials believe that they are still likely to recidivate—is what bothered the just deserters, who felt that this policy was overly coercive. They did not like the fact that inmates could be kept for years in prison on the unproven prognostication that they might reoffend. This concern is reasonable. Even so, it is one thing to criticize this feature of indeterminate sentencing (not releasing offenders until they supposedly are cured), but quite another to argue that protecting public safety—fostering crime control—should not be a concern of the correctional system. To be blunt, those on the political Left will not be taken seriously if they do not have something convincing to propose about how to keep the community free from crime.

Conclusion: The Need for Crime Control

This latter point leads us, Cullen and Jonson, to reiterate that a purely retributive or just deserts theory of corrections is not plausible. We can have deep philosophical discussions about the ethics of retribution/just deserts versus utilitarian justifications for the state punishing its citizens. This discussion might be illuminating, but it is beside the point in one crucial regard: In the United States—and in virtually every modern society Cullen and Jonson know of—people expect the legal system not only to do justice but also to control crime. The idea that you would have a correctional system whose *sole purpose* was to ensure that retribution/just deserts had been exacted is, well, *sort of nuts*. Citizens of any community, whose taxes support corrections, expect that system to control crime as well. So, there are really two realities that must be confronted:

- *The correctional system must be organized to ensure that when a crime is committed, retribution/just deserts is exacted.* The punishment received must be generally proportionate to the nature of the crime. Research shows that the American public's attitudes about punishment are *mushy*, not rigid; people will be happy if the punishment falls within a range of acceptable options. For a lot of offenders, they would not object to these individuals receiving a prison sentence and they would not object to a probation sentence (Turner, Cullen, Sundt, & Applegate, 1997). They just want a *reasonable* punishment to be given. What citizens oppose are wildly disproportionate sentences—those that are obviously too excessive for minor crimes or obviously too lenient for serious crimes. In short, members of the public want punishments to be *in the ballpark of the seriousness of the crime*. Achieving retribution/just deserts is important, but this consideration only sets the upper and lower limits of the range in which a sentence should fall.

- *The correctional system must be organized to ensure that offenders do not recidivate and that public safety is a priority.* While offenders are in the correctional system—while we have them in our grasp—we should do things to make them less likely to recidivate. Thus, crime control is an important function of corrections. We must judge what we do with offenders on the basis of *utility—does it work?* More broadly, when corrections fails to protect community safety, the public gets concerned, if not outraged, and the system loses legitimacy.

We are left, then, with a mandate from the public—in virtually every society—to operate a correctional system that pays attention to justice and that pays attention to crime control. And this leads us to the final two points of this chapter (yes, you are almost done!).

First, the difficulty in mixing retribution/just deserts with utilitarian theories is that the *policies* that each theory proposes can be inconsistent with one another. For example, retribution/just deserts favors giving the same sentence to offenders who commit the same crime. But incapacitation and rehabilitation would, if the offenders differed in their risk of reoffending, keep the more dangerous inmate in prison longer—incapacitation so that these predators are off the streets and rehabilitation so that these predators can receive a higher dose of treatment. So, mixing inconsistent theories together can lead to a mixture of inconsistent policies in the system. Balancing competing or multiple theories of corrections thus is a daunting, if not impossible, challenge.

Second, once considerations of retribution/justice have been taken into account in sentencing, there is still the thorny issue of *which utilitarian theory of corrections* should be chosen to guide our efforts at crime prevention. One helpful fact is that each of these theories makes empirical claims that, if its policies are followed, offenders will be less likely to commit crimes. These claims can be assessed with data.

Of course, saying how they wish to reduce criminal conduct also matters—and can be, in part, a question of values. Conservatives, who are *into pain,* might favor deterrence because it promises to scare offenders straight by making them suffer. Liberals, who empathize even with predators, might favor rehabilitation because it promises to transform offenders into law-abiding folks by treating them nicely (e.g., giving them education, employment training, and counseling). But putting the *means of crime prevention aside,* the claims each utilitarian theory makes about *its effectiveness* is not a question of values. It is an empirical question that now falls within the domain of *evidence-based corrections.* The key issue is *whether the theories actually work to make offenders less criminal or less able to commit crimes.*

This empirical inventory of competing utilitarian theories of corrections is precisely what occupies our detailed attention in the chapters that lie ahead. So, join with Cullen and Jonson on our travels through the empirical world of correctional theory!

4

Deterrence

Scaring Offenders Straight

Daniel S. Nagin
Carnegie Mellon University
Scholar of Deterrence Theory and Research

D eterrence is based on the notion that people consciously try to avoid pain and seek pleasure. It follows that by making a choice painful enough—such as the choice of crime—individuals will choose not to engage in the act. Across society as a whole, this perspective would predict that crime rates would be lowest in those places where offending evokes the most "pain" (or costs) and highest in those places where offending brings the most "pleasure" (or benefits). In short, deterrence is held to explain why *individuals* do or do not offend and to explain why certain *places* in society—called by criminologists "macro-level" or "ecological" units—have higher or lower *crime rates*.

In turn, this way of thinking has clear implications for *correctional policy and practice*. If deterrence theory is correct, then to reduce crime, *the correctional system should be organized to maximize the pain of crime and to minimize its benefits*. Its whole aim should be to scare people straight—those who have engaged in crime (specific deterrence) and those who are thinking about committing crime (general deterrence). For the past three or four decades, the United States has been engaged in a costly experiment in which policy makers have bet literally billions of dollars that getting tough on crime—especially through mass incarceration—will reduce reoffending. When was the last time you have heard of any politician or judge campaign for office with the slogan, "I promise to get lenient on crime!" And would you vote for that public official? In contemporary America, Todd Clear (1994) has referred to this ongoing attempt to use the correctional system to be an instrument for inflicting pain as the *penal harm movement* (see also Currie, 1998).

Deterrence theory is attractive because of its *inherent intuitive appeal*. This is the *hot-stove phenomenon*. When growing up, we learn that when we touch a hot stove top, we get burned. So, we don't touch hot stoves. We are "deterred." We decide, in short, not to do things that are like "hot stoves." So, it seems like commonsense that if we could make committing crime like a hot stove, people would not do it. Break the law, and you get burnt right away. If crime were like this, then offenders would be too scared to touch the stove again. And if people in general saw someone with a burnt hand, they would be too scared to touch the stove in the first place.

Stoves are good at deterrence, because the pain they administer is immediate, certain, and severe. Touch a hot stove top, and it's "ouch"; lesson learned. Unfortunately, it is difficult for us to make corrections like a stove. Most correctional punishments are not immediate and not certain—although they may be severe (or may not). This inability to make punishments efficient is one hindrance to achieving large deterrent effects when attempting to put this *theory* into *practice*.

The other problem is that of *individual differences*. Not everyone experiences the threat of a correctional punishment the same way. In particular, some people pay attention to *future consequences* but others do not—or at least not as much. Some people are more impulsive, short-sighted, inebriated, under the sway of peer influence; alas, these people tend to be offenders! They are not good at paying attention to future consequences. But paying attention to future consequences is essential if someone is to be deterred by the threat or even the imposition of a criminal punishment. Scaring offenders straight is thus a difficult business.

This insight reminds us of the lesson taught to Cullen by his beloved family dog, Bartlett. Yes, Bartlett has passed away, but dogs are important and, in Bartlett's case, memorable. Right now, Cullen has two canines: Topspin (a golden retriever) and Deuce (a big mutt). For those of you who are tennis fans, you will notice the tennis reference (Topspin as in "topspin forehand"; Deuce as in "the score is deuce"). The dogs reflect that somewhat pathological addiction to tennis of those in the Cullen clan. Topspin also is a model of how to live a contented life. Unlike Cullen, Topspin does not worry about global warming, world hunger, wars, and who is the nation's president. He is quite happy, virtually all the time. He is also his own man—err, canine. He will not fetch a ball if thrown, but when people arrive at the front door, he will go retrieve one of Cullen's shoes and prance around the house with the shoe in his mouth. He is a retriever high on self-efficacy, not on a need to please. But, alas, neither Topspin nor Deuce has taught Cullen anything about criminology. This is what made Bartlett so special!

Now, back to Bartlett's lesson. As Cullen was walking Bartlett one day, he thought of how we are commonly taught that when a dog poops on the rug, we should rub his nose in it. Yet as Bartlett meandered down the street, Cullen noticed that every time he came to a pile of poop on someone's lawn, what did he do? He stuck his nose in it! And every time he came to another dog, where did he smell?

This is an *individual difference*, because Cullen, and especially Jonson, certainly would be deterred by the prospect of their noses going into a pile of poop! That is, Bartlett versus Cullen and Jonson differ in their assessment of whether poop sniffing is a cost or a benefit. Economists call this a difference in our *tastes*, a concept we would not want to apply too literally in this example! But the serious point here—the criminological lesson—is that what we think might deter *those most likely to offend* may not have the intended effect. What we think would deter *us,* in short, may *not deter those with different personalities that predispose them to crime.* In fact, some criminologists worry that *sticking people's noses in it*—being nasty and punitive—actually makes offenders more criminogenic (Sherman, 1993). There is that iatrogenic effect again.

The appeal, and danger, of deterrence is that it seems so darn simple: *just increase the punishment and crime should go down.* Of course, if it were that simple, we would be a crime-free society. This has not happened.

We do not wish to push the anti-deterrence point too far. Punishing offenders in society almost certainly has some deterrent effect (Apel & Nagin, 2011; Nagin, 1998, 2013). Imagine, for example, if we did away with the criminal justice system and there was no threat of any punishment. Break the law, and unless some vigilante shoots you, you get away with it. Might crime increase? Cullen and Jonson think so and, as prudent criminologists, would greet this abolitionist experiment by heading to Canada! Still, as the "Bartlett incident" cautions, these *deterrent effects are complex.* In particular, it is questionable whether deterrence-oriented *correctional policies and programs* reduce the recidivism of those who enter the correctional system as serious or chronic offenders. In a point we will reiterate later, it seems that criminal sanctions have a general deterrent effect but not much of a specific deterrent effect (see also Paternoster, 2010).

With this context set up, what's the strategy for the remainder of this chapter? Well, we start out with three introductory-type sections:

- We go over key definitions, telling the difference between general deterrence and specific deterrence.

- We discuss whether deterrence theory is necessarily politically conservative. The answer is "no," although in practice conservatives like the idea of scaring offenders more than bleeding-heart liberals do.

- We explore the theoretical assumptions about crime that underlie deterrence. This analysis is important because *every correctional intervention is based on some underlying theory of crime* (i.e., a theory of why people commit crime). In the case of deterrence, the framework is rational choice theory. The key issue is whether this criminological explanation is multifaceted enough to base a whole correctional system on; Cullen and Jonson do not think so.

After these issues are considered, we turn to the heart of the chapter: subjecting deterrence theory to evidence-based analysis. Readers should realize that nobody on this planet truly knows in a precise way whether deterrence works to reduce crime. It is not one of those clear-cut matters. Studying human behavior—especially a behavior like crime that people try to conceal from the police and even researchers—is a daunting challenge. One option is to throw up our hands and go read philosophy on the meaning of life. Or perhaps to find happiness in retrieving shoes like Topspin does. The other option, which Cullen and Jonson believe in, is to amass as much evidence as possible to supply the most plausible answer possible as to the likely deterrent effect of correctional interventions. So, in this key section of Chapter 4, we review different *types of evidence*.

Deterrence theory will make certain predictions. Mainly, the predictions are all the same: The more punishment there is, the less crime there should be. The more offenders are watched and threatened with punishment, the less crime there should be. The more people think they will be punished, the less crime there should be. Remember, advocates of deterrence theory truly believe that *consequences matter*. They truly believe that only fools would touch the stove—or commit a crime—if they had been burned for doing so in the past. All of us would like to believe this because corrections would be really simple: Punish people and crime will vanish. Unfortunately, offenders seem more like Bartlett than they are like the rest of us. Sticking their noses in it just is not that effective. When we look at various types of evidence, for the most part, deterrence theory proves to be either incorrect or only weakly supported.

The Concept of Deterrence

TYPES OF DETERRENCE: GENERAL AND SPECIFIC

How do we prevent someone from committing a crime? Deterrence theory suggests that people will commit a crime if it gratifies them—if it is experienced as *beneficial*. Conversely, the assumption is made that people will not commit a crime if it brings unpleasant consequences—if it is experienced as *costly*. In everyday language, people commit crime *if it pays* and will not commit crime *if it does not pay*.

In this context, *deterrence* is said to occur when people do not commit crimes because *they fear the costs or unpleasant consequences that will be imposed on them*. In this sense, we can say that people are *scared straight*. The *deterrence effect* is how much crime is saved through the threat and application of criminal punishments.

Now, which people do we wish to deter or to scare straight? Well, two kinds. First, there are the people who have not yet broken the law but are thinking about it (or might think about it). Second, there are the people who have broken the law and might do it again (i.e., who might *recidivate*). Depending on the focus of who we are trying to scare, a different type of deterrence is said to be involved.

Thus, when we punish an offender *so that other people do not go into crime,* this is called *general deterrence*. As noted in Chapter 1, this is "punishing Peter to deter Paul." We are, in essence, making an example of offenders so that other people in society figure out that "crime does not pay." Some philosophers—especially those who believe in retribution or just deserts—think that this practice is morally reprehensible, because "Peter" is being used as a means to benefit society. Why should we punish Peter in such a way in the hope of stopping another party (Paul) from engaging in a behavior that has not yet occurred? Peter is getting punished for what

Paul *might do*. We will leave the philosophical debates to others, but it is an issue that general deterrence must confront.

The wonderful thing about *general* deterrence is that its effects are *potentially general!* If it works, then it is a very efficient and cost-effective way of controlling crime: By punishing a limited number of offenders, we may persuade a whole bunch of other *potential offenders* not to break the law.

The other type of deterrence, of course, is *specific deterrence* (sometimes also called *special deterrence*). Here, we punish Peter so that Peter will not recidivate. That is, the deterrent effect is *specific* to the person being punished. Importantly, when we focus on specific deterrence, we are moving more closely to what precisely the correctional system does with offenders. If specific deterrence is effective, we might expect to see these kinds of findings:

- Offenders sentenced to prison would be less likely to recidivate than offenders put on probation.

- Offenders given longer prison terms would be less likely to recidivate than offenders given shorter prison terms.

- Offenders placed in community programs that emphasize close supervision and the threat of probation/parole revocation should be less likely to recidivate.

As we will see, however, the research does *not* support any of these three propositions. This leaves deterrence theory with a lot of explaining to do!

CERTAINTY AND SEVERITY OF PUNISHMENT

Certainty and severity of punishment are fairly simple concepts that may, however, be related in complex ways. As the term implies, *certainty of punishment* involves the *probability that a criminal act will be followed by punishment*. The greater the probability that crime prompts punishment, the greater the certainty of punishment. The *severity of punishment* involves the *level of punishment that is meted out*. The harsher the punishment, the greater the severity of punishment. (There is also something called the *celerity of punishment*, which is how quickly a punishment follows a criminal act. It is rarely studied in the research.)

Now, can you anticipate what predictions deterrence theory would make regarding the certainty and severity of punishment? Here they are:

- The greater the certainty of punishment, the less likely crime will occur.

- The greater the severity of punishment, the less likely crime will occur.

Some authors like to combine certainty and severity of punishment into a *single concept*, like the *expected utility of crime*. Again, the prediction would be the same: The more combined certainty and severity there is (the lower the expected utility of crime), the less likely it is that crime will occur.

In general, which component of deterrence—*certainty or severity*—do you think is more important in deterring crime? The answer is clear: *certainty* of punishment. It appears that people do not become concerned (or as concerned) about the severity of punishment if they do not believe that they will ever get caught (if they think the probability of arrest and sanctioning is low).

Is Deterrence a "Conservative" Theory?

Is deterrence theory conservative? The answer to this question is "yes" and "no." It is "yes" because deterrence is typically associated with imposing more punishment on offenders—that is, it is justified by the claim that we have high crime and recidivism rates because offenders are punished too *leniently*. This leads to the view that reducing crime should involve getting tough. Conservative politicians have generally embraced this rhetoric. They have argued that we must make crime not pay by implementing a range of laws that increases the costs of crime (e.g., mandatory minimum penalties). Regardless of the wisdom of these approaches, it should be realized that deterrence is not *inherently* a conservative theory. That is, it does not inevitably lead to a justification of harsh correctional policies.

Now, when most advocates look at deterrence, they tend to focus on two factors: first, the cost of crime as measured by the certainty and/or severity of punishment; and, second, the benefits of crime as measured by how much money crime may bring. But the decision to go into crime is not just an assessment of the costs and benefits of *crime*. It also involves an assessment of the costs and benefits of *conformity*—that is, *of non-crime*. If deterrence theory is based on an accurate theory of human behavior, it must explain not only why crime is chosen but also why someone chooses to commit a crime rather than do what the rest of us do: go to school, obtain a job, settle down with a family, and so on. It also means that the reason why people go into crime is not only that crime is attractive but also that conformity or non-crime is unattractive.

Can you see what implication this has for correctional interventions? The answer is that offender recidivism might be reduced if interventions increased the likelihood that conformity would be beneficial! If making conformity attractive were the focus, then corrections might not concentrate on inflicting pain. Rather, the goal would be to make the choice of conformity more possible and profitable by placing offenders in programs that would increase their education and employment skills. Such programs as these are often called "liberal" because they seek to improve offenders. In general, however, advocates of deterrence focus almost exclusively on *manipulating the costs of crime through punishment*. To the extent that this is their limited perspective, they embrace a conservative political ideology.

The Theoretical Assumptions of Deterrence

Every utilitarian correctional intervention (except incapacitation) has, embedded within it, a criminological theory. Logic demands it! This is because the state is doing something to an offender with the expectation that this person will not go back into crime. By applying criminal sanctions, the state is trying to affect the *reasons why the person offends*.

Deterrence is based on the belief that people go into crime because *it pays—the benefits outweigh the costs*. This approach thus assumes that before offending, people sit back—if only for a moment—and *calculate the likely consequences of their action*. It is sort of like a *business decision*: Am I going to make a profit from this crime or not? This is when the little accountant in our head is supposed to pop up, calibrate the cost-benefit ratio, and tell us whether to invest in crime.

This view of offenders can be traced back to the Enlightenment Era (1700s) and the work of theorists within the Classical School of criminology, especially Cesare Beccaria and Jeremy Bentham (Bruinsma, in press). These theorists differed from one another, but their writings shared common themes. The big question of the day (and perhaps of today as well) is how to achieve social order. They were appalled at the arbitrary, unfair, and often brutal legal system of their day; they argued that its enlightened reform was needed for this system to contribute to crime prevention and thus order. Now, for our purposes, here is the key: Humans were viewed as self-interested and as seeking to maximize gain in any situation. They pursued happiness—they wished to secure pleasure and avoid pain. In turn, this view of human nature informed the theorists' proposals for a reformed legal system. To prevent crime, punishments should be arranged to make crime more painful than pleasurable. Because punishment was a potential evil, the amount of harm done to offenders should be just enough to outweigh the benefits a criminal act might accrue. Certainty of sanction was seen as critically important. In this way, they argued that an enlightened legal system would be both morally defensible and be a deterrent to crime (see Geis, 1972; Monachesi, 1972).

The Classical School's linking of human nature and deterrence remains relevant today. In particular, economists who have studied crime have embraced this way of thinking. This is because when economists study *any behavioral choice*—whether it is investing in the stock market, taking a job, getting married, or committing a crime—they assume that people's choices are affected by the likely consequences (or by their self-interest). You would not invest in a company's stock if you thought you would lose money. Or you would not cheat on a test if the professor was watching you like hawk and you thought you would get caught and earn a grade of zero. We think you get the point.

Most often, the underlying criminological theory is called *rational choice theory*. This term implies two things: first, that crime is a choice; and, second, that this choice is *rational*—that is, based on a calculation of costs and benefits. From the very fact that someone engages in an act, we can infer that a choice has been made. But the key issue is *why* has this choice occurred? The distinctive thing with rational choice theory is that it assumes that choices are rooted in a *conscious assessment of costs and benefits*.

Note that rational choice theory—at least in its pure form—*assumes that offenders and regular citizens are exactly the same*. The only thing that differs is that offenders happened to be in situations where crime is rational and regular citizens—*we*—are not.

There are no individual differences that distinguish offenders from non-offenders—that make some people more likely to be criminals. We are all self-interested rational decision makers. Thus, all of us would commit a crime if we were confronted with the same set of costs and benefits. Not committing the crime would be irrational; committing the crime, rational. What differs are not individual traits but the costs and benefits we confront.

As you might imagine, nearly all of modern criminology *rejects* rational choice theory. Most believe in the approach of the Positivist School of criminology first developed by Cesare Lombroso and fellow Italian scholars in the last quarter of the 19th century. Here, the assumptions about crime are quite at odds with rational choice theory:

- Crime is not a rational choice but is *caused*.

- Crime is caused by biological, psychological, and/or sociological factors.

- Offenders are different from non-offenders; there is something special about them or their social situation that makes them commit crimes.

It is possible that rational choice theory is *partially correct*. That is, a range of factors might create a person's propensity to commit crimes, but that *one factor* in determining whether a crime takes place is the person's perception of the likely certainty and severity of punishment. If this were the case (and we suspect it is), this is *good news* and *bad news* for deterrence theory: The good news is that increasing certainty/severity of punishment should have some deterrent effect (because part of the reason for crime is the view that it pays). The bad news is that the deterrent effect is likely to be *modest* (because other factors involved in the causation of crime are not changed by punitive interventions).

A key issue in corrections is what factors are being *targeted for change in an intervention*. If a theory about crime is wrong or only partially correct, then an intervention is likely to be targeting for change either (1) *the wrong factors* or (2) *only some of the factors that should be altered*. Again, rational choice theory has some merit, but its fundamental weakness is its willingness to ignore a mountain of evidence that other factors are involved in the causation of crime (more generally, see Thaler & Sunstein, 2008). In turn, a key limitation of deterrence as a correctional approach is that it is based on an *incomplete understanding of crime causation*. It follows that its proposed interventions are necessarily also incomplete, if not incorrect.

Studying Whether Deterrence Works: Assessing Types of Evidence

Now we have arrived at that point where we focus on the guts of the issue of deterrence. What do the studies say about the effectiveness of deterrence? The key point here is that there are different *types of studies* that may be used to assess the extent to which the punishments handed out by the courts and correctional system deter. We examine *five types of studies*. Note that although all the studies are important, the most significant assessments are drawn from the last three types of studies. This research is most relevant to corrections because it assesses how sanctions and correctional interventions affect individuals and, in particular, offenders brought into the system.

- *Studies of policy changes that increase the level of punishment.* If crime goes down after get tough policies are implemented, then this would be evidence in favor of deterrence theory.

- *Macro-level (or ecological level) studies of punishment and crime rates.* If geographical areas (e.g., cities, states) that have higher levels of punishment have correspondingly lower crime rates, then this would be evidence in favor of deterrence theory.

- *Perceptual deterrence studies.* If individuals who perceive punishment to be certain and/or severe are less involved in crime, then this would be evidence in favor of deterrence theory.

- *Studies of correctional interventions that are control or punishment oriented.* If offenders who are exposed to more control or punishment are less likely to recidivate, then this would be evidence in favor of deterrence theory.

- *Studies of the effects of imprisonment.* If offenders who are exposed to prisons (as opposed to probation) or to longer terms or harsher conditions are less likely to recidivate, then this would be evidence in favor of deterrence theory.

The strategy underlying this assessment is to try to determine if the predictions made by deterrence theory are consistently supported. If so, then this would be compelling evidence that punitive policies and interventions reduce crime. However, if the evidence is weak and contradictory, then deterrence theory would be judged to be less viable. As a guide through this assessment process of the five types of evidence, we have developed Table 4.1.

Policy Changes That Increase Punishment

There are lots of times in which legislators, the police, or the courts make policies or practices more punitive in order to "crack down on crime" and to "get tough." These efforts might involve laws that increase punishments for particular crimes (e.g., selling crack, possessing a gun) or policy decisions that increase arrests (e.g., mandatory arrests for domestic violence, police crackdowns on open-air drug markets in a high-crime neighborhood, roadblocks to test for drunk driving). These policies are meant to heighten either the certainty or severity of punishment.

Often, these studies fall into a category of research called *interrupted time-series studies* (Nagin, 1998). This term is used because the data on crime are collected over time—over a series of months or years. At some point, the punitive intervention

Table 4.1 Researching Deterrence—Types of Knowledge

Types of Research	Examples	Specific Method(s)	General Results
Policy changes that increase the level of punishment	Three-strike laws; mandatory sentencing laws; mandatory arrest for domestic violence; police "crackdowns" on drug markets.	Before–after evaluations; interrupted time-series studies; experimental or quasi-experimental studies comparing more and less punishment conditions.	(1) Short-term effects, then decay of effects. (2) Many interventions show weak or no effects. (3) Some "brutalization" effects reported—crime increases.
Macro-level studies	Compare how levels of punishment influence crime rates across ecological units.	Multiple regression studies; time-series studies that compare effects of changes in punishment.	(1) Some evidence of deterrent effects (likely a "general" deterrent effect). (2) The effects are complex, inconsistent, and often weak. (3) Effects of punishment outweighed by social factors. (4) Attribute incapacitation effects to deterrence effects.
Perceptual deterrence	Surveys—mostly of students but at times of community members and inmates—measuring how perceptions of the certainty and severity of punishment influence self-reported crime or "intentions" to offend.	Self-report surveys measuring for each respondent's perceptions and self-reported offending; vignette scenario surveys.	(1) Weak to no support on longitudinal, multivariate self-report survey studies. (2) More support on scenario studies. (3) Stronger effects for the certainty than the severity of punishment.
Correctional interventions with offenders	Scared straight programs; boot camps ("shock incarceration"); intensive supervision programs; electronic monitoring; drug testing.	Evaluation studies using experimental or quasi-experimental designs; meta-analyses that assess the effects of these punishment-oriented interventions across all available studies.	(1) Studies find no support that punishment-oriented programs appreciably reduce recidivism rates. (2) Some interventions appear to increase recidivism. (3) No evidence of a "specific" deterrent effect.
Effects of imprisonment	Prison versus probation; longer versus shorter sentences; harsher versus less harsh prison conditions.	Evaluation studies comparing levels of punishment; longitudinal studies examining effects of being in prison.	(1) Imprisonment has no effect or increases recidivism. (2) Harsher conditions tend to increase recidivism.

occurs that "interrupts" this "time series." The researcher then examines crime rates *before* the intervention and compares it to crime rates *after* the intervention. If crime goes down, then the evidence would favor the existence of a deterrent effect. If not, then deterrence theory is not supported.

Scholars differ in how they interpret these existing studies—some being more favorable to deterrence theory than others (Apel & Nagin, 2011; Doob & Webster, 2003; Levitt, 2002; Pogarsky, 2009; Tonry, 2008, 2009; Wikström, 2007). Cullen and Jonson read the evidence more on the negative side, seeing the deterrent effects as weaker than some other scholars may; but we are not alone in our views. The results are complex, but we believe that four main conclusions can be drawn:

- There appear to be real short-term deterrent effects.
- The deterrent effects tend to *decay* over time—to "wear off."
- Many interventions show weak or no effects on crime, or they vary by context. For example, studies of mandatory arrest for domestic violence find results in some places but not in others. Other studies suggest that arrest mainly works for people with social bonds to the community (i.e., those who are employed). Those without such bonds, which includes many serious offenders, are not deterred by increased arrest.
- In some instances (not frequent), there may be a "brutalization effect," in which increased punishment is associated with increased crime (this has been seen, for example, in studies of capital punishment in which certain crimes increase following executions).

Taken together, these studies suggest that when punishment increases in a *visible* way, it has the potential to deter offenders (or would-be offenders) for a limited period of time. Limited deterrent effects are not unimportant from a policy standpoint. Still, as a general strategy for reducing crime, the *decay in effects* is a problem. It suggests that get tough interventions cannot sustain enough *fear of punishment* to have long-term effects on crime. The fact that the effects tend to decay suggests that people may return to crime when:

- They find out they can, after all, escape detection.
- They no longer think about the punishment as the publicity around a new punishment subsides.
- The factors causing them to go into crime (e.g., antisocial attitudes) reassert themselves in the offenders' lives—that is, criminal propensities overpower temporary worries about punishment.

We want to be clear that we are not saying that people's decisions are not affected at all by sensitivity to costs and threats of sanctions. There is a whole field called *environmental criminology* in which scholars plot and scheme to figure out ways to divert offenders from committing crime. These scholars engage in something known as *situational crime prevention*. Here, the focus is on doing things in a particular place that make it impossible or inconvenient to offend. Such preventative strategies might involve installing locks or burglar alarms, placing surveillance cameras, or having an attendant at the door of an apartment complex. Offenders tend not to break the law where they think that they might get detected or have to work too hard to steal a desired good (see, e.g., Felson, 2002; Welsh & Farrington, 2009).

Importantly, the genius of situational crime prevention is that it is *situational*. The threat of possible punishment through detection or the cost of offending is *immediate*—at the precise time when the decision to break the law is being made. By contrast, many policy changes that increase punishments for criminal acts are typically not situational. Rather, they involve passing laws that heighten punishments that may never be applied to a specific offender and, even if so, only come into play after the crime is already committed. Situational crime prevention is much like the hot stove top: The cost is immediate and certain—that is, the burglar alarm goes off, the camera points right at you, the attendant at the door does not allow you to enter. The point we are making is likely clear: When policies that enhance punishment cannot operate like a hot stove, then they are not likely to have a strong deterrent effect.

Macro-Level Studies of Punishment and Crime Rates

CONDUCTING A MACRO-LEVEL STUDY

In a *macro-level* or *ecological-level* study, the *unit of analysis* is not the individual. Instead, it is some geographical area—a macro or ecological unit—such as a state, a county, a Standard Metropolitan Statistical Area (SMSA), a city, a neighborhood, or a census tract. In this research, the outcome or *dependent variable* is the *crime rate for each unit*. Usually, the FBI's crime statistics are used for the study, because they are one of the few sources that has data on crime across things like states, counties, SMSAs, and cities.

The researcher then tries to see what characteristics about the macro-level unit might explain why some areas have high rates of crime and why others have low rates of crime. Can you think about what factors researchers might consider in their models? Well, crime rates might plausibly vary by the level of poverty in areas, by the composition of the area (i.e., age, gender, race), by the density of living conditions, by the stability of families, and so on. In fact, studies have included variables such as these in their empirical analyses.

Now, if we want to show that criminal punishments deter, then we would have to show that *above and beyond these other variables*, differences in levels of punishment account for differences in levels of crime across the macro-level areas. Thus, to conduct a good study, the model would have to be *multivariate*, containing all at once the many factors that could potentially influence crime rates. Keep this point in mind; we are going to get back to it in one moment.

As we have said, crime rates are typically measured by using crime statistics compiled by the FBI and published annually in *Crime in America: Uniform Crime*

Reports. The trickier matter, however, is to measure the variable of *deterrence.* This is no simple matter. There are different possibilities that would "get at" a person's risk of being caught and punished for a crime in a given area. These include:

- The size of the police department.

- The size of the police department relative to the population size.

- Money spent on police activities.

- The percentage of arrests made once crimes become known to the police (this is often called the *arrest ratio*).

- The rate of imprisonment in an area.

What would deterrence theory predict? Well, you guessed it: the more police, arrests, and incarceration, the lower the crime rate.

There are a couple of important *methodological issues* that we need to consider before discussing what the macro-level research reveals. First, one daunting problem is how to *interpret findings from research on levels of imprisonment.* This is a problem because *we do not know what this variable actually measures!* Can you think about what it could measure other than deterrence? Tough question, but here's the answer. It could measure *incapacitation*—or how much crime is saved simply by having offenders locked up and off the street. In fact, it is highly likely that most of any imprisonment effect is due to incapacitation and not to deterrence (i.e., it comes from getting offenders off the street rather than scaring people straight).

Second, beware of studies that are *bivariate.* Do you know what a "bivariate" study is? It is a study that has only *two variables in it.* The two variables would be (1) some measure of deterrence and (2) some measure of crime rates. Can you figure out what the problem is with bivariate studies? It is that the world is *not bivariate but multivariate.* Accordingly, for a meaningful scientific study to be conducted, it is essential to include in the study measures of all variables that might influence the dependent variable—in this case, crime rates. What happens if some important variables are left out of the analysis? Well, the study potentially suffers from something called *specification error.* That is, the model is likely *misspecified.* In plain language, it means that we just cannot know if the results that are reported are true—an accurate reflection of reality—or would change if all relevant variables had been included in the statistical model.

To be direct, bivariate studies that include only (1) levels of punishment and (2) crime rates are unreliable; they have no scientific credibility. This does not mean that the bivariate findings are wrong; it only means that we can never know if they are right. They may be suggestive—even plausible—because the relationship between two variables may persist (to a degree) even when the full multivariate analysis is undertaken. Still, there really is no reason to do a bivariate study. Solid science demands that scholars undertake multivariate studies that provide the most accurate picture of reality that the existing data sources can make possible.

Now, why have we subjected you to all this methodology stuff? Well, it is because bivariate studies and bivariate thinking are commonplace when assessing the relationship between levels of punishment and crime rates. Conservatives are likely to select a state and show how a rise in imprisonment resulted in a decrease in crime (e.g., Texas), whereas liberals are likely to select a state and show how a rise in imprisonment resulted in an increase in crime (e.g., California). Again, these results are meaningless unless other variables that could influence the crime rate are also included in the statistical analysis.

WHAT MACRO-LEVEL STUDIES FIND

As it turns out, criminologists have done a number of macro-level studies on how a whole bunch of factors influence crime rates. Along with Travis Pratt, Cullen thought it would be an excellent idea to try to organize all existing studies so that we would know what, taken as a whole, they told us about what influences crime rates. Accordingly, Pratt and Cullen (2005) reviewed 214 macro-level studies conducted between 1960 and 1999. This study synthesizes the results using a statistical technique called *meta-analysis*.

In Chapter 7, what a meta-analysis is will be discussed in more detail. For now, we will note that this technique is like computing a batting average. Each study is similar to a time up at bat. When a study is conducted, the variables get to swing at the dependent variable—so to speak. If a variable—such as a measure of deterrence or inequality in an area—is found to influence the crime rate in the study's analysis, then it is like a batter getting a hit. If a variable does not influence the crime rate, then it is like making an out. What we try to determine is the batting average for that variable across all studies. The higher the average—or *effect size*—the more confident we are that the variable is a cause of crime. In essence, meta-analysis tells us quantitatively the relationship of predictor variables to crime—including deterrence variables—across all studies that have been undertaken.

Back to our specific concerns—meta-analysis answers this question: *If you look at all the deterrence studies that have been done, what is the average size of the relationship between (1) measures of punishment and (2) crime rates?* Pratt and Cullen's (2005) meta-analysis examined 31 predictor variables. Of these, 6 could be considered measures of deterrence: incarceration, the arrest ratio, police expenditures, get tough policy, police per capita, and police size. Each of these variables assesses either the level of punishment imposed or chances of being caught for a crime committed. The results are presented in Table 4.2. Several conclusions are warranted:

- Of the 31 predictors of crime rates measured, the deterrence measures were among the weakest predictors (see numbers 27, 28, 30, and 31).

- The only punishment variable to have strong effects was the *level of incarceration* (see number 5). However, this is most likely a measure of incapacitation and not deterrence. The very fact that the effect of incarceration was so different from the other deterrence variables suggests that it is measuring incapacitation (i.e., its results are inconsistent with the other deterrence measures).

- Overall, macro-level studies suggest that the deterrent effect on crime rates is modest at best.

- The variables that most account for macro-level differences in crime rates are social variables, especially the concentration of social disadvantage.

- If this finding is correct, it suggests that efforts to control crime through deterrence are likely to be only minimally successful. Why? Because the other causes of crime will remain unchanged.

Again, some scholars might read this evidence a bit more positively, especially if they examine only a limited number of the macro-level studies that focus only on deterrence. But overall, our assessment seems reasonable: Measures of deterrence have effects, but they are not among the stronger macro-level predictors of crime. Many other things matter. We will note one other consideration as well.

Measures of deterrence such as the arrest ratio or the size of the police force are mainly measures of certainty of punishment—of an offender's chances of being caught. Let us agree that these effects exist. But in and of themselves, they say nothing about what to do with offenders *after they have been arrested*. Virtually every theory of corrections starts with the assumption that it is a good thing to arrest criminals, especially those offending at a high rate. Take rehabilitation, for example. There can be no rehabilitation if offenders do not enter the correctional

Table 4.2 Rank-Ordered Mean Effect Size Estimates of Macro-Level Predictors of Crime (Deterrence Variables Ranked 5, 23, 27, 28, 30, 31)

Rank	Macro-Level Predictor	Rank	Macro-Level Predictor
1	Strength of non-economic institutions	17	Residential mobility
2	Unemployment (length considered)	18	Unemployment (with age restriction)
3	Firearms ownership	19	Age effects
4	Percent non-White	20	Southern effect
5	Incarceration effect	21	Unemployment (no length considered)
6	Collective efficacy	22	Socioeconomic status
7	Percent Black	23	Arrest ratio
8	Religion effect	24	Unemployment (no age restriction)
9	Family disruption	25	Sex ratio
10	Poverty	26	Structural density
11	Unsupervised local peer groups	27	Police expenditures
12	Household activity ratio	28	Get tough policy
13	Social support/altruism	29	Education effects
14	Inequality	30	Police per capita
15	Racial heterogeneity index	31	Police size
16	Urbanism		

SOURCE: Pratt and Cullen (2005, p. 399).

system. The crucial *correctional policy issue,* therefore, is not certainty of arrest but rather whether the subsequent response is one that emphasizes the infliction of pain—deterrence theory's embrace of severity of punishment—or one that emphasizes doing something productive with the offender (such as rehabilitation advocates). As we will see, studies have been conducted that directly address this debate. We will review this research after the following section.

Perceptual Deterrence Studies

BEWARE OF THE ECOLOGICAL FALLACY

Thus far, most of the research we have reviewed has as its *unit of analysis* macro-level areas (i.e., geographical areas like cities and states). This research is important in allowing us to draw inferences about the relationship of levels of punishment to crime. Still, this methodological approach has one weakness: It does not directly measure how punishment affects *individuals* and the *decisions they make about crime.*

In macro-level studies, the *inference* is made that if a relationship between punishment and crime rates exists in ecological units or areas, it is because *individuals in these areas are being deterred either specifically or generally.* This inference is plausible but risky. Unless one measures *individuals directly,* we really do not know for certain that processes observed on the macro or ecological level actually occur as we think they do on the individual level. In fact, when researchers make inferences about *individuals based on macro-level* data, this opens them up to what has been called the *ecological fallacy.* That is, they assume that what is found in macro-level data reflects what is occurring among the individuals living in that macro-area.

Often, there is a consistency between what one finds on the macro level and what happens to individuals; that is, the inferences are correct. But this is not always the case. Let's take one example from Table 4.2. As we noted, the research reveals that macro-level units (e.g., states) with high levels of incarceration have low rates of crime. A deterrence theorist would conclude that this is because the *individuals* living in places with different levels of imprisonment calculate the costs of crime differently. The little accountant in their heads sits up and tries to decide if crime pays. In the get tough geographical locations, the little accountant advises against offending and thus crime rates are lower. In the get lenient geographical locations, the advice is to go ahead and break the law and thus crime rates are higher.

But do macro-level researchers know for sure that *individuals* look at the risk of incarceration and then make a *rational decision* about whether to commit a crime? How do they know what *individuals are perceiving and thinking*? Of course, they do not! Rather, based on the theory of deterrence, they simply *infer* that people in high incarceration states *must be aware of the high costs of crime.* Remember: They obtain their data from statistics collected by the FBI and other government agencies. They never talk to a single living human being.

This interpretation is plausible, but as we have seen, it is almost surely *incorrect*. In all likelihood, the reason why higher levels of incarceration result in lower crime rates is *not because they make people fear punishment* but because more offenders are *incapacitated*. That is, even if no one changed his or her perceptions of the risks associated with crime, crime would go down where he or she lives simply because more people are in prison and not on the street. Again, this is an example of the *ecological fallacy*: the use of data from the macro or ecological level to make statements—incorrect statements—about *individuals*.

STUDYING INDIVIDUALS' PERCEPTIONS OF PUNISHMENT

Now, here is an interesting question: How do you think we can avoid the ecological fallacy? How can we know whether individuals are affected by the certainty and severity of punishment? This is *not* a trick question. Actually, the answer is a matter of common sense. The answer is that we need to conduct studies where *the unit of analysis is the individual respondent!*

Lo and behold, many scholars figured this out! In fact, this insight has led to numerous studies being done in which individuals are surveyed about punishment and criminal involvement. These studies have been called *perceptual deterrence studies*—and we will return to this issue right below. The other way of studying individuals is to examine correctional interventions in which *individual offenders* are exposed to different levels of punishment. We will focus on this later in this chapter.

In any event, a whole bunch of studies have been conducted that investigate how *perceptions of the certainty and severity of punishment are related to delinquent/ criminal involvement*. The standard study is conducted in this way:

- Develop questions that measure what a respondent thinks will happen if a crime is committed in terms of: (1) the probability of getting caught—the *certainty of punishment*—and (2) the amount of punishment that will occur once detected—the *severity of punishment*.

- Measure involvement in crime through a *self-report survey* (a series of questions about crimes that a person may have committed "in the past year"). Most often, the measure is of "delinquency," because the sample is drawn from a high school. Some studies of adults, however, do exist.

- Include on the same survey questions measuring other possible causes of crime. These might include, for example, measures of moral beliefs, attachment to parents, commitment to school, association with delinquent peers, and so on.

- In a multivariate model that also controls (i.e., takes into account the effects of) these other variables, see if the measures of certainty and severity of punishment are related to crime in the predicted direction (i.e., with more punishment resulting in lower involvement in delinquency).

Importantly, these studies focus on individuals' *perceptions of punishment*. But why the focus on *perceptions*? Well, there are two reasons. First is a *theoretical reason*. This is the belief that what precedes a decision to commit a crime is not simply how much punishment actually exists in objective reality but what a person *thinks* or *perceives* to be the risks at hand. There is, out there in the world, an *objective level of risk of punishment*. And we would expect that there would be some correspondence between objective levels of risk and *perceived* levels of risk. But in the end, individuals make decisions not based on objective risks but on what is inside their own heads—what they *perceive to be the risks of committing a crime*.

Second is a *practical reason*. In a survey, perceptual deterrence is relatively easy to measure if one develops appropriate questions. But how would one measure the objective risks to individuals who were completing a questionnaire? In short, methodologically, it is a lot easier to measure perceptions of punishment than objective levels of punishment in the environment.

In any event, in our view, the findings in perceptual deterrence studies are inconsistent. Again, different scholars might read the evidence differently. Why is this so? Well, they may give more weight to some studies than to others. Thus, readers should realize that when scholars are making *qualitative judgments* about a research literature, their conclusions may differ to a degree. We will return to the point below when we talk about a meta-analysis conducted by Pratt, Cullen, and a bunch of other people.

In Cullen and Jonson's view, the influence of deterrence on criminal behavior *diminishes* as the *quality of the research study increases*. The better the design, the weaker the relationship that exists between perceived deterrence and crime (see also Paternoster, 1987). Three factors are especially relevant here:

- *Controlling for other predictors of crime.* When studies include a full range of variables *in addition to measures of deterrence*—variables like peer influences, antisocial attitudes, and relationships with parents—the strength of the relationship of deterrence variables to crime decreases. That is, the more fully specified the model is, the weaker the relationship of deterrence to crime.

- *Longitudinal studies of crime.* Studies that follow a sample over time tend to find that perceptions of deterrence at "time 1" are not a strong predictor of delinquency at "time 2."

- *The experiential effect.* There is also the problem of *causal* ordering. Deterrence theory predicts that perceptions lead to behavior. But it is also the case that participating in delinquent behavior lowers the perception of deterrence. Studies that control for these prior delinquent experiences—called the experiential effect—tend to report weaker relationships between deterrence and delinquent involvement.

Where does this leave us, then, in assessing what perceptual deterrence studies teach us about whether deterrence works to reduce criminal involvement? This is a hard question to answer, but our readings lead to three conclusions:

- It is likely that perceptions of punishment are related to criminal involvement.

- Perceptions of certainty of punishment are more strongly related to criminal involvement than are perceptions of the severity of punishment.

- Compared to other known predictors (i.e., causes) of crime, perceptions of deterrence are a *relatively weak to moderate cause* of criminal involvement.

This last conclusion—the third one—has *important policy implications*. It means that get tough policies are likely to have some effect on crime if they can increase perceptions of deterrence. Even so, such policies are likely to *leave untouched a range of strong predictors of crime that have nothing to do with punishment*. If true, this means that deterrence is a narrow or limited approach to reducing crime.

TWO STUDIES

Are Cullen and Jonson, your authors, correct? Well, relatively recent research seems to confirm our assessment of the existing literature. We will review two studies here—one by Pogarsky et al., which seems to provide a complex investigation of key issues, and one by Pratt et al. (Cullen is an "et" in this study!), which is the most systematic summary of studies in this area.

First, Pogarsky, Kim, and Paternoster (2005) examined waves 6 and 7 (1984 and 1987) of the National Youth Survey, which involved a national sample of over 1,200 youths, to see if being arrested affected perceptions of the certainty of punishment. What would deterrence theory predict? Well, obviously that sanctions directly affect perceptions—that youths who were arrested would now perceive that offending would place them at greater risk of detection and punishment. But the data did *not* support the deterrence hypothesis. As Pogarsky et al. (2005) note, "Arrests had little effect on perceptions of the certainty of punishment for stealing and attacking" (the two offenses examined in their analysis) (p. 1). They did find, however, that if youths and/or their peers engaged in offending, then the youths' perceptions of certainty of punishment tended to decline.

What this means, then, is that deterrence theory is likely half correct: (1) If youths offend and get away with it—or see their friends get away with crimes—then perception of certainty declines. But (2) if youths offend and get arrested, this sanction does not cause them to change their perceptions of the certainty of punishment. It is thus unlikely that sanctioning has effects on behavior through perceptions—a core thesis of deterrence theory.

It is risky, of course, to evaluate deterrence theory—or any theory—based on a single study, which is why in a moment we will turn to a meta-analysis that considers the literature as a whole. The issues Pogarsky et al. address are complex, and conflicting evidence exists (see, e.g., Matsueda & Kreager, 2006; Matthews & Agnew, 2008; Pogarsky, 2010). It is clear, however, that the impact of being arrested and receiving a criminal justice sanction on perceived risk of punishment is complex and not fully unraveled (Nagin, 1998; Pogarsky & Piquero, 2003). Now, this situation is complicated even more by a related finding: Consistent with labeling theory, an increasing number of studies are showing that arresting—and then perhaps convicting and processing individuals in the justice system—is associated with greater criminal involvement (for summaries, see Cullen, Jonson, & Chouhy, 2015; Farrington & Murray, 2014). Hmm. Not good news for deterrence theory!

Further, we do not have much of an understanding of the extent to which get tough policies or, alternatively, reductions in enforcement affect people's perceptions of the risks of offending. Policy makers assume that when they pass new laws that escalate punishments (e.g., longer prison terms), offenders will somehow know about this, change their risk perceptions, and refrain from crime. The causal assumptions underlying each link in this chain (new law → changed perceptions → lower crime) are questionable and hardly established. As Daniel Nagin (1998) notes, "knowledge about the relationship of sanction risk perceptions to actual policy is virtually nonexistent" (p. 36). This point is important. Even if the perceived risk of punishment is related to the level of criminal involvement, it is not known whether, for most street offenders, policy changes ever reach their minds, affect their thinking, and alter their behavioral choices.

Second, Travis Pratt, myself (Cullen), Kristie Blevins, Leah Daigle, and Tamara Madensen (2006) set out to examine the results of all studies that had examined perceived deterrence. In this case, we again used a meta-analysis. As alluded to above, part of the problem in the existing reviews of the deterrence literature is that authors conduct a *qualitative* assessment. This means that they use their judgment to discuss those studies that they think are most important. By necessity, they include or emphasize some studies and exclude or de-emphasize other studies. Such qualitative assessments are likely to lead to scholars reaching different conclusions, if not in kind (i.e., they reach opposite conclusions) then at least in degree (i.e., in the extent to which they find the evidence is favorable to deterrence). One way around this difference in interpretation is to use a meta-analysis, as Pratt et al. (2006) did. Again, a meta-analysis seeks to review all studies and measures their effects *quantitatively*. Although all approaches have their limits and potential biases, meta-analysis has two advantages. First, it is inclusive of all studies and thus is not susceptible to a scholar's qualitative judgment—or bias— about what research is important enough to review. Second, it can be replicated by scholars who might question the findings. If you think the data are cooked, then re-do the study!

This project examined 40 studies. The main findings are summarized in Table 4.3, which is taken from the Pratt et al. (2006, p. 385) article. We can boil down what the table says into three essential points:

- Multivariate studies—ones that study how deterrence variables stack up against predictors from other theories—suggest that the effects of certainty of punishment are weak (stronger in samples of college students) and the effects of severity of punishment are weak to non-existent.

- Perception of punishment is thus likely to be a minor cause of criminal involvement.

- Legal sanctions might have effects on future crime not through fear of sanctions but through the non-legal or social costs they evoke. This might include rejection by family members, feelings of shame or guilt, loss of a job, and so on. More research and theory on this possibility are needed.

One final observation: Reality is not always simple; sometimes it is awfully complex. It takes scholars a while to figure this out and then to try to unpack all this complexity. This is now happening in perceptual deterrence research. As social psychologists have long understood, a lot of things affect people's perceptions and then the decisions that they reach (see, e.g., Kahenman, 2011; Mischel, 2014). For example, people who are impulsive or have low self-control might go into crime because

Table 4.3 Summary of Methodological Conditioning Effects for Variables Specified by Deterrence Theory

Predictor	Overall Magnitude and Variation by Effect Size Weighting	Sample Characteristics	Model Specification and Research Design
Certainty	Substantially overestimated in bivariate form; sensitive to weighting by sample size.	Varies significantly by gender (strongest in mixed samples) and much stronger in college student samples.	Effects are significantly reduced when competing theories and experiential effect are controlled; varies considerably according to the dependent variable.
Severity	Substantially overestimated in bivariate form; loses significance in multivariate designs.	Varies little by sample characteristics; effects are generally weak across all categories.	Varies little by model specification and research design characteristics; effects are generally weak across all categories.
Composite	Generally non-significant; multivariate effect sizes sensitive to unobserved heterogeneity.	Varies little by sample characteristics; effects are generally weak across all categories.	Varies little by model specification and research design characteristics; effects are generally weak across all categories.
Non-Legal Costs	Substantially overestimated in bivariate form; not sensitive to weighting procedures.	Varies significantly by gender and race (strongest in mixed gender and race samples) and from samples drawn from the general population.	Effects are stronger (although not significantly) when experiential effect is controlled and in cross-sectional designs.

SOURCE: Pratt, Cullen, Blevins, Daigle, and Madensen (2006, p. 385).

they focus on the immediate benefits that this decision provides (e.g., drugs, money) and ignore potential longer term costs. But it could also be that among people with low self-control, one of the few things that restrains them from offending is if they believe that their chances of getting caught are high. People might also differ in their capacity to avoid making bad decisions. Well, you get the point: It is complicated! Importantly, in a systematic review essay, Piquero, Paternoster, Pogarsky, and Loughran (2011) have detailed a variety of ways in which "individual differences" can affect perceptions and decision making. Much theoretical and empirical work remains to be done to determine how and to what extent "deterrability" varies across individuals (p. 356) (see also Paternoster & Bachman, 2013).

So, let us return to the crucial point. We have been examining different *types of evidence* to see if we can marshal evidence to show that criminal sanctions deter offenders from reoffending. From what we have reviewed in this section, however, *the research on perceptual deterrence does not offer strong and consistent support for deterrence theory.* While perceptions of deterrence might have some relationship with offending, the effects of such perceptions are likely to be limited and to occur only under specific conditions.

Deterrence in the Community

The research reviewed thus far provides important insights into the nature of deterrence and its likely effects on criminal decision making. In our view, however, this research is largely removed from the *correctional system.* If deterrence theory is correct, then punishment should work best—and be most easily detected in research—when it is applied *directly to offenders within the correctional system.* That is, deterrence should be most visible when we compare interventions that impose more punishments on one group of offenders than on another, preferably using an experimental design in which the effects of punishment can be isolated from other potential causes of crime.

In the next section, we will examine whether imprisonment versus non-custodial sanctions achieves deterrent effects. In Chapter 7, we will examine so-called treatment programs that use a get tough, deterrence-oriented approach (e.g., scared straight programs). In this section, however, we review the evidence on attempts to deter offenders in the community by increasing control over them. Just so that readers are aware of the punch line, here is what we will report: Punishment-oriented or control-oriented correctional interventions have little, if any, impact on offender recidivism. This is bad news for correctional deterrence theory.

DO COMMUNITY CONTROL PROGRAMS WORK?

Most Interventions Do Not Deter. In the 1980s, a movement emerged to bring deterrence into community corrections. This occurred in the *intermediate punishment* movement. These sanctions were called *intermediate* because they fell in between prison, which was a harsh penalty, and probation, which was often seen as a lenient penalty (Morris & Tonry, 1990). These sanctions were called *punishment* because the goal was to increase control over offenders in the community—more surveillance over and more discomfort imposed on them. As a result, this movement was part of the attack on rehabilitation discussed in Chapters 2 and 3. Since nothing worked in rehabilitation—the thinking went—it was foolhardy to deliver treatment services in probation and parole. Better to use probation and parole officers to police and punish the offenders on their case loads.

Intermediate punishments were particularly attractive to conservatives, because using these sanctions allowed them to have their cake and eat it too. In general, conservatives want to get tough on crime. But they also like to keep government taxes and expenditures down. The problem, however, was that rising prison populations were straining state budgets. So, how could one be tough on crime but do so in an inexpensive way? The answer to this seeming riddle: *Punish offenders not in prison but in the community!* The high expense of imprisonment would be avoided, but offenders would still feel the sting of the law.

Liberals also embraced this movement. That's because liberals like any reform that does not send offenders to prison! In fact, almost all writings by liberals on corrections are about the evils of prisons and why their use should be limited. Intermediate punishments may be punishment, but they are administered in the community or for only short times behind bars (such as in boot camps). Again, for liberals who embraced the nothing works doctrine and forsook rehabilitation—including, by implication, treatment in the community—the policy options that remained were limited. Anything that might provide judges with a reasonable alternative to imposing a prison sentence seemed like a good idea.

So, it seemed as though everyone—from Right-wingers to Left-wingers—liked the proposal to try to punish or control offenders in the community (Cullen, Wright, & Applegate, 1996). At the heart of this movement was the assumption that if offenders in the community were more closely monitored and threatened with punishments, they would refrain from going into crime. That is, these programs would be cost effective only if offenders *were, in fact, deterred.* If this did not occur, then offenders initially placed in the community rather than in prison would recidivate and end up in prison anyway. This would upset conservatives: There would be no cost savings, and a bunch of resources would have been wasted trying to monitor offenders in the community. This also would upset liberals: There would be no diversion from imprisonment if offenders were revoked and incarcerated.

Could intermediate punishments be designed that would deter offenders? Four main interventions were implemented:

- Intensive probation and parole programs in which offenders were watched closely by officers who had small caseloads and increased contacts.

- Electronic monitoring and home confinement (which often went together).

- Drug testing.

- Boot camps, which are military-style programs that last for a limited period of time (e.g., three to six months); sometimes this intervention is called *shock incarceration.*

Did these programs work? In 1993, Cullen undertook a project to find all the studies that had evaluated the impact of intermediate punishment programs on recidivism. Cullen was not an expert in the area, but he received a call from Alan Harland, who asked him to prepare a paper for an upcoming conference; the papers were to be published in a book as well (see Harland, 1996). Cullen was about to decline the invitation when Harland said that the participants, including Cullen, would be paid $6,000 to review various aspects of corrections. Readers should realize that except when academics write books, they rarely get paid for anything they publish, including journal articles. Not being independently wealthy, Cullen immediately decided to become an expert in community deterrence programs. He enticed John Paul Wright and Brandon Applegate, then trusted graduate assistants who have gone on to become well-known criminologists, to collaborate on this project (see Cullen et al., 1996). He even told them about the $6,000 and shared some of the loot with them.

When the review began, we—Cullen, Wright, and Applegate—did not know what we would find. But as we secured both published and unpublished studies evaluating intermediate punishment interventions from around the nation, the results did not seem promising. Indeed, in the end, the studies revealed that the deterrence-oriented programs had little impact on offender recidivism. We were able to find a few isolated successes, but these mainly occurred when rehabilitation services were grafted onto the control programs. As we concluded from our review of existing studies: "Intermediate punishments are unlikely to deter criminal behavior more effectively than regular probation and prison placements" (Cullen et al., 1996, p. 114).

It is also possible that Cullen and his collaborators were biased or incompetent criminologists. But even if true, these traits did not affect our reading of the evidence! Indeed, other scholars who have reviewed the extant evaluation literature on this topic have reached virtually the same conclusions (see, e.g., Byrne & Pattavina, 1992; Caputo, 2004; Gendreau, Goggin, Cullen, & Andrews, 2000; MacKenzie, 2006; Tonry, 1998; see also Cullen, Blevins, Trager, & Gendreau, 2005; Cullen, Pratt, Micelli, & Moon, 2002). This is, again, *troubling news for deterrence theory.* Some of the programs evaluated failed because they were poorly implemented. But even when the programs increased control over offenders, they did not have much of an impact on recidivism. For offenders *who are already in the correctional system, there is just not much evidence that trying to punish them makes them less criminogenic.* This is a conclusion we will state again in the section on the effects of imprisonment on reoffending. More generally, as noted briefly above, it appears that bringing offenders into the criminal justice system does little to reduce their criminality and, if anything, worsens it (see, e.g., Bernburg & Krohn, 2003; Bernburg, Krohn, & Rivera, 2006; Chiricos, Barrick, Bales, & Bontrager, 2007; Doherty, Cwick, Green, & Ensminger, 2015; Gatti, Tremblay, & Vitaro, 2009; Lieberman, Kirk, & Kim, 2014; McGuire, 2002; Petrosino, Turpin-Petrosino, & Guckenburg, 2010).

A Few Interventions Might Deter. Before moving forward, however, we do need to add one final qualification. Cullen and Jonson do not contend that deterrence-oriented community programs can never reduce recidivism. The impact of interventions is complex, and it can vary by whether or not the program's administrator is charismatic and competent, the resources allocated to the program, the quality of the program's implementation, the nature of the offenders, the specific intervention used, and the context in which the intervention is taking place.

For example, Padgett, Bales, and Blomberg (2006) studied Florida offenders on home incarceration, some of whom were placed on electronic monitoring and some of whom were not. They found data consistent with a specific deterrence effect. Offenders on electronic monitoring (whether GPS or radio frequency) were less likely to have their probation revoked for a technical violation or for a new offense. They also were less likely to abscond from supervision (see also Di Tella & Schargrodsky, 2013). But let's not jump to conclusions about this intervention. "A large body of research, including random assignment," cautions MacKenzie (2006, p. 322), "consistently shows the failure of . . . EM programs to lower recidivism." Omori and Turner (2015, p. 875) similarly conclude in their review of relevant research that "evidence has been relatively weak for electronic monitoring's success" (see also Renzema & Mayo-Wilson, 2005).

Correctional life is thus complicated, which is shown by another evaluation of electronic monitoring by Susan Turner and her colleagues (Turner, Chamberlain, Jannetta, & Hess, 2015; Omori & Turner, 2015). All participants were high-risk sex-offender parolees assigned to "small, specialized caseloads" (Turner, Chamberlain, et al., 2015, p. 7). To assess the effectiveness of added monitoring, a quasi-experimental design was used in which some offenders were equipped with a one-piece GPS ankle unit. Based on a 12-month follow-up, the results were, well, complicated. Deterrence advocates would be heartened by the finding that compared to the control group, GPS-monitored offenders were less likely to abscond and less likely to fail to register as a sex offender as required by law. Alas, they should not be too celebratory. Turner, Chamberlain, et al. also found that, overall, the study's "findings coincide with previous research in which intermediate sanctions were found to have no effect on recidivism" (p. 18). There were "no significant differences between comparisons and GPS parolees with regard to *criminal* sex and assault violation" (p. 18, emphasis in the original). Further, a subsequent analysis revealed that the use of GPS tracking was not cost effective (Omori & Turner, 2015).

Another so-called deterrence program receiving publicity is an initiative carrying the acronym of "HOPE"—or "Hawaii's Opportunity Probation with Enforcement" (Hawken & Kleiman, 2009; Kleiman, 2009). Upon his appointment to the bench in 2001, Judge Steven S. Alm noticed that probationers regularly failed drug tests, missed appointments with probation officers, and broke the law. Most often, these violations triggered no sanction because revoking probation typically meant sending offenders to prison for 5 or 10 years. So, in essence, misbehaving probationers either were treated with the utmost of leniency or, if they had the misfortune of lightning striking, they were whacked with a severe prison sentence.

This approach struck Judge Alm as being, well, stupid. Instead, he succeeded in implementing a much different system that involved two steps: (1) drug-test and other probation violations would lead to immediate, on-the-spot detention, followed shortly thereafter by a hearing (within 72 hours); (2) all offenders would then be punished, but with very *short* jail sentences (typically several days, at times served on the weekend so as not to interfere with employment). The program thus was oriented to the certain, swift, and mild punishment of probation infractions (Kleiman, 2009). But would the program work or would the system be overwhelmed with violations, hearings, and sending too many offenders to jail? A rigorous randomized experimental evaluation discovered that compared to those on regular probation, the HOPE probationers failed fewer drug tests, missed fewer appointments, and committed fewer new crimes (Hawken & Kleiman, 2009; Kleiman, 2009). Unfortunately, long-term behavioral change—did this approach reduce drug use and recidivism after offenders left probation supervision?—was not examined. However, if post-program reoffending is unaffected, then the cost of focusing on short-term compliance with conditions of probation might mean that interventions aimed at more durable offender reform (e.g., treatment programs) are being sacrificed—a trade-off Cullen and Jonson would not wish to make.

In any event, advocates of deterrence can rightly point to this program and say: "See, Cullen and Jonson—you bleeding hearts—deterrence works!" And Cullen and Jonson would have to admit as much. But three rejoinders are crucial to share. First, deterrence is effective in the HOPE program *precisely because punishment is applied in a way that is not typically followed in the regular criminal justice system!* In the HOPE program, punishment was certain because the probation officers can read a drug test report and can know when someone is not sitting in their office for a scheduled appointment! A sanction can then be applied right away and be kept very short. Again, punishment is certain, swift, and mild. (HOPE offenders are also urged to be responsible and have access to rehabilitation services—so the context is supportive, not mean-spirited.) In the regular system, however, crimes are committed that are never detected (i.e., certainty is low), the sanction might take months or longer to be applied (i.e., swiftness is low), and the punishment can be harsh (i.e., severity is high). The lesson to be learned is that under very narrow or special conditions, it might be possible to deter some offenders for a while (probationers while under supervision). Achieving such a deterrent effect more generally is doubtful and would, ironically, call for *getting lenient* on crime (see also Durlauf & Nagin, 2011; Kleiman, 2009).

Second, "H" in the word "HOPE" has been changed from Hawaii to "Honest," a way perhaps to ease its use in other places. And, indeed, similar models have been initiated, according to Hawken, in "at least 40 jurisdictions in 18 states" (quoted in Pearsall, 2014, p. 3). This is worrisome because this intervention is being implemented based on a limited evaluation study. In fact, along with Stephanie Duriez and Sarah Manchak, Cullen has voiced serious concerns about the possibility that Project HOPE might be "creating a false sense of hope" (Duriez, Cullen, & Manchak, 2014). If interested, consult this article (Duriez et al.) and the following exchange in the same journal issue between Cullen, Manchak, and Duriez (2014) and Kleiman,

Kilmer, and Fisher (2014); it might prove interesting to hear both sides! In any event, it is possible that Project HOPE could work in jurisdictions other than Hawaii, especially if Kleiman and Hawken help to monitor its implementation. Researcher involvement tends to help interventions work more effectively. But when the program "goes to scale" and is tried in other places, the risk of failure is likely to mount (see Welsh, Sullivan, & Olds, 2010).

One example is a HOPE-like program tried in Delaware called "Decide Your Time" (DYT). The program "was designed to manage high risk substance-using probationers by focusing on the certainty of detection through frequent drug tests and graduated but not severer sanctions" (O'Connell, Visher, Martin, Parker, & Brent, 2011, p. 261). Implementing DYT, however, strained resources, which may have contributed to its participants having recidivism outcomes comparable to those receiving standard probation. As the program evaluators concluded, "swift and certain sanctions can work (see HOPE)" and "swift and certain sanctions can also not work (see DYT)" (O'Connell, Visher, Brent, Bacon, & Hines, 2013, power point slide 34).

Third, and more broadly, occasional findings such as those reported for Project HOPE in Hawaii cannot be taken as proof that deterrence theory should be the foundation of corrections. Such studies might provide insights on where deterrence strategies might prove effective—if the results can be replicated in other settings. But in establishing any social policy, it is important to consider the *totality of the research*. This is one reason why Cullen and Jonson put great faith in works that try to *assess all the available evidence on a topic*. And in this instance, the vast majority of the evaluation studies cast serious doubt that meaningful reductions in recidivism can be achieved by using correctional interventions that try to get tough with offenders.

THE RAND ISP STUDY: A CLASSIC EXPERIMENT IN CORRECTIONS

Again, advocates of deterrence theory should be troubled by the failure of correctional programs to specifically deter offenders to whom more punishment and control is applied. If deterrence were to work anywhere, it should be in *controlled experiments where researchers ensure that offenders are subjected to increased control*. But this does not seem to be the case.

To illustrate this point one final time, we will alert you to one of the greatest studies ever undertaken in corrections—an evaluation of control-oriented intensive supervision programs (ISP) across multiple sites. Joan Petersilia and Susan Turner, who at that time worked for RAND, directed the study. (They are now well-known professors at Stanford University and the University of California, Irvine, respectively.) Why was this study so important? Here are some reasons why we view this investigation as a criminological classic:

- *The study used an experimental design in which offenders were randomly assigned to intensive supervision or to regular supervision (in 12 sites) or to prison (in 2 sites).* This is important because it means that the risk of selection bias was eliminated. In many programs, the treatment effect is contaminated because researchers allow offenders to volunteer for the program. But if those most amenable to the intervention volunteer for it, then the program may appear to be a success not because it works but because offenders more amenable to change joined the treatment group.

- *The study was conducted across 14 sites in nine states.* Since findings can be affected by the context in which a study was conducted, research studies on only one agency are unable to see if the findings reported may not generalize to other places (this is another example of the *N-of-1 problem*). However, the RAND study examined ISPs across many contexts. Accordingly, it could assess whether findings were specific to certain contexts.

- *The study was conducted in jurisdictions that agreed to have a control-oriented ISP intervention and in which increased monitoring (contacts with offenders) was going to occur.* This is the issue of the integrity of the intervention. Is it going to be implemented as intended? If not, then we are back to wondering whether the program failed because it was based on a faulty theory (it could never work) or because it was poorly implemented (it could work if done correctly). Importantly, although having problems in two sites, the RAND study was conducted in a way that the intervention had integrity. Offenders randomly assigned to the ISP condition were subjected to more surveillance and control (i.e., some combination of weekly contacts, drug testing, electronic monitoring, and strict probation conditions).

The upshot of all this is that the methodology of the RAND study was rigorous. This means that the study's findings almost certainly reflect empirical reality and cannot be attributed to some methodological problem. So, what did Petersilia and Turner find? Remember, for deterrence theory to be supported, we would anticipate that offenders placed on intensive supervision would have a lower rate of recidivism.

Alas, this did not occur. "At no site," reported Petersilia and Turner (1993), "did ISP participants experience arrest less often, have a longer time to failure, or experience arrests for less serious offenses than did offenders under routine supervision" (pp. 310–311). This result is stunning. By chance alone, we might have expected to find some deterrent effect at one of the sites. But this was not the case. Indeed, Petersilia and Turner realized that they had produced a "strong finding, given the wide range of programs, geographical variation, and clientele represented in the demonstration projects" (p. 311). In fact, in terms of recidivism, the ISP group had a *higher* rate of official arrest (37%) than the non-ISP group (33%). In short, the control-oriented programs did not work.

In supplementary analyses on programs in California and Texas, Petersilia and Turner explored one more issue. Although the ISPs across the sites were designed to deliver control and deterrence, offenders differed in whether they received treatment services. Petersilia and Turner (1993) found that recidivism was lower among offenders who participated more extensively in rehabilitation programs.

As they noted, "higher levels of program participation were associated with a 10–20 percent reduction in recidivism" (p. 315). It thus appears that decreasing offenders' criminality requires programs that move beyond punishment and deliver treatment services to offenders—a finding detected by other researchers as well (Bonta, Wallace-Capretta, & Rooney, 2000; Lowenkamp, Flores, Holsinger, Makarios, & Latessa, 2010; Lowenkamp, Latessa, & Smith, 2006; Paparozzi & Gendreau, 2005; see also Gendreau, Cullen, & Bonta, 1994). Notably, Gill's (2010, p. 37) meta-analysis of ISP interventions examined 38 randomized trials and nine quasi-experiments, but was "unable to find any evidence to contradict prior reports that suggest that ISP 'does not work'" (see also Hyatt & Barnes, 2014). Consistent with prior research, the analysis revealed that ISP increased technical violations. When potential moderator variables were examined, "no policy-relevant program features that indicated any circumstances under which ISP may be more successful" were detected (2010, p. 37).

Given all these findings, we might have expected that jurisdictions around the nation would have avoided surveillance-only ISPs. But this is not the case; people running corrections do not always embrace evidence-based practices. Thus, in Hamilton County, Ohio—the home county of Cincinnati—the state of Ohio spent $1.7 million to fund an ISP meant to keep offenders in the community and out of prison. In the program, 23 officers supervise between 68 and 80 offenders. They "function like a law enforcement unit," having offenders visit their offices once a week and seeing supervisees in the community once a month (Coolidge, 2009, p. A1). Predictably, the evaluation results were dismal, with the program being "so ineffective that the convicts in it are more likely to commit crimes than others convicted of similar crimes who never receive supervision" (p. A1). Only 29% of offenders completed the ISP successfully. A county official lamented that his "biggest frustration is that while the state pays for probation officers, it does not provide money for the programming needed to help rehabilitate people" (p. A10).

Cullen and Jonson feel compelled to note that this insight on the need to supplement control with treatment services has been known for the better part of two decades. Hmm! Should we pay attention to this research? Nooooo! Instead, let's not go to the library, read the research, and see if ISPs are a good idea. Let's rely on commonsense deterrence thinking (don't hot stove tops deter?). And let's spend $1.7 million of the taxpayers' money and then wonder why the law enforcement–oriented ISP does not work. Does the concept of correctional quackery come to mind?

The Effects of Imprisonment

STUDYING IMPRISONMENT AND RECIDIVISM

"Okay," deterrence fans might say, "we have just been warming up with all these other studies. Let's get down to what really matters: putting offenders in prison. All these other correctional sanctions—including intensive supervision—leave law-breakers in the community. They will never learn their lesson until they are incarcerated. After all, prisons are painful and virtually nobody wants to be there. That's why there are bars, locks, guard towers with armed correctional officers, barbed-wire fences, and high walls."

The effects of imprisonment, then, are the litmus test for deterrence as a correctional theory. Its advocates bet that people who go to prison will be less likely to recidivate than those who are given a non-custodial sentence. Further, they bet that those sent to prison for longer rather than shorter sentences and who live in harsher rather than softer conditions will also be less likely to reoffend. Okay, the bets are made. Let's roll the dice—look at the data—and see who the winner is: the get tough crowd or the bleeding-heart liberals who do not like prisons?

Well, deciding the winner is not simple due to an amazing criminological oversight. Despite more than 2.2 million people behind bars on any given day, we know remarkably little about how prisons affect recidivism. Cullen and Jonson are not saying that we criminologists know nothing; some decent studies have been undertaken—and they are being published more regularly these days. But given the human and financial cost of America's 40-year policy of mass incarceration, it is incredible that our knowledge base in this area must be considered suggestive rather than definitive. Still, given what we do know, the data are not overly favorable to deterrence theory. The dice have come up mostly snake eyes.

An initial problem for deterrence theory is the high levels of recidivism among those who go to prison. There is variation in recidivism across states, jurisdictions within states, and prisons, but there is a rule of thumb that seems to hold true across time. First, among those who enter prison for the first time, the recidivism rate is about one third. Second, among all those sent to prison—which include first-time, second-time, and multiple-time inmates—the recidivism rate is about two thirds. The follow-up period is typically three years. Now, offenders can be returned to prison for new crimes or for not obeying the conditions of parole, such as failing to show up for scheduled meetings with the parole officer, absconding from the jurisdiction, getting drunk, or affiliating with other criminals. Either way, it seems right off that a lot of offenders are not scared straight by their prison experience. We revisit this issue in Chapter 8 where we focus on the issue of prisoner reentry.

Of course, the empirical issue is whether such offenders are more likely to refrain from crime than those given sentences in the community. Again, deterrence theory predicts that prison is a higher cost than a community-based penalty. A custodial sentence is thus seen to deter more than a non-custodial sanction. The problem is a shortage of really good studies that use a randomized experimental design to place offenders in the community versus in prison. Readers might see the ethical problems of using the luck of the draw—random assignment—to determine who does or does not go to prison. As a result, criminologists typically study this issue through a quasi-experimental design in which a group of inmates is compared with a group of offenders under community supervision. In making comparisons between offenders sent to prison versus the community, a special challenge is to account for selection bias. Thus, if more serious or higher-risk offenders are sent to prison ("selected" for prison), then, of course, the prison group will have higher recidivism rates. Studies account for these effects by controlling statistically for these risk differences.

One more point is important to share. Because correctional deterrence theory is based on rational choice theory, prison is conceived of as a *cost* of committing a crime. Criminologists, however, see this approach as truncating reality. For them, imprisonment is not a cost but a *social experience*. This experience exposes offenders not only to pains (costs) but also to a range of experiences that may make crime more likely. These might include socializing with other antisocial offenders for years on end or having conventional social bonds to families cut off. Criminologists are concerned that these experiences may overwhelm concerns about punishment and result in the net effect of prisons being criminogenic. This perspective is sometimes called *labeling theory*. It makes the opposite prediction to deterrence theory: Labeling and treating people as offenders—especially sending them to prison—sets in motion a number of processes that increase, rather than decrease, criminal involvement.

DOES IMPRISONMENT DETER?

When Cullen was a criminological pup—just starting out in the field—he read a fascinating book by Gordon Hawkins (1976) called *The Prison,* which contained a fascinating chapter called "The Effects of Imprisonment." Hawkins criticized the easy acceptance by virtually all criminologists that institutions were schools of crime and that inmates all suffered prisonization. Yet he also rejected the notion that prisons somehow reduced criminal propensities. While "inmates are not being corrupted," concluded Hawkins, "neither their attitudes nor their behavior are being affected in any significant fashion by the experience of imprisonment" (pp. 72–73). With some qualifications added, the gist of his message was that prisons may not have much of an enduring effect on offenders' future criminality.

Cullen thought that this was an intriguing possibility and, as inmate populations expanded, he waited for a wealth of empirical studies assessing this null effect conclusion reached by Hawkins. And he waited, and waited, and waited. Somewhat shockingly, although criminologists continued to decry prisons and assume that they had bad effects on people's lives—something Cullen wanted to believe—they did not conduct much research to confirm this belief. Did it really matter, though, that criminologists felt comfortable believing, but not empirically validating, their prisons-as-schools-of-crime ideology? It did for one important reason: Policy makers from across the nation did not share this view. In particular, many conservative legislators thought that incarcerating offenders was a neat idea because it would scare bad people into acting like good people. If criminologists had presented compelling evidence that this was not the case, it might have curbed this insatiable appetite to lock up more and more people.

Over the years, Cullen kept an eye out for studies that might provide data on the effects of imprisonment. Then, in 1993, Sampson and Laub published their classic book, *Crime in the Making*. They had found data originally collected by Sheldon and Eleanor Glueck in the subbasement of the Harvard Law School library, which followed 1,000 boys born in the 1930s' Boston area for nearly two decades (starting in 1939–1940). Sampson and Laub reconstructed and reanalyzed the data, with their main interest devoted to understanding what led some, but not other, boys to follow a criminal life course. Embedded in their larger study, however, Cullen found an assessment of what happened when boys were sent to prison, controlling for all other factors. Importantly, Sampson and Laub discovered that serving time in prison weakened conventional social bonds (e.g., to quality marriage and work), which in turn *increased* recidivism. In short, imprisonment did not deter; this experience was criminogenic.

A 2002 study by Cassia Spohn and David Holleran reached a similar conclusion. Using 1993 data from offenders convicted of felonies in Jackson County, Missouri (which contains Kansas City), they compared the recidivism rates of 776 offenders placed on probation versus 301 offenders sent to prison. They followed offenders for 48 months. Here are their major findings:

- Being sent to prison increased recidivism.
- Those sent to prison reoffended more quickly than those placed on probation.
- The criminogenic effect of prison was especially high for drug offenders, who were five to six times more likely to recidivate than those placed on probation.

These findings are not limited to the United States. Thus, questions about the deterrent effects of prisons also are raised by Paula Smith's (2006) study of 5,469 male offenders in the Canadian federal penitentiary system. Smith discovered that imprisonment increased recidivism among low-risk offenders. Similarly, in a study that compared first-time inmates with a matched sample of non-imprisoned offenders in the Netherlands, Nieuwbeerta, Nagin, and Blokland (2009) found that imprisonment increased recidivism over three years. And just to give one other example, we can cite Cid's (2009) research on offenders given either a prison sentence or a suspended sentence by the Criminal Courts of Barcelona in Spain. Cid notes that the study's findings support labeling theory over deterrence theory. Thus, his analysis showed "that prison sanctions do not reduce recidivism more effectively than suspended sentences. On the contrary, the risk of recidivism increases when the offender is imprisoned" (2009, p. 471).

Several literature reviews of existing studies on prison effects have been conducted, including one that Cullen and Jonson published with Daniel Nagin, who headed up the project (Nagin, Cullen, & Jonson, 2009; see also Cullen, Jonson, & Nagin, 2011; Gendreau et al., 2000; Jonson, 2013; Smith, Goggin, & Gendreau, 2002; Ritchie, 2011; Villetez, Gillieron, & Killias, 2015; Villetez, Killias, & Zoder, 2006). Most notably, Jonson (2010) herself conducted a comprehensive meta-analysis of published and unpublished investigations of the effects of imprisonment on recidivism—85 studies, which is a lot of work! It is difficult to reach definitive conclusions because of the lack of studies using random experimental designs. Still, no matter who did them or what strategy for synthesizing findings was used, the clear consensus of the reviews is that *imprisonment versus a non-custodial sanction either has a null effect or slightly increases recidivism.* The policy implications of this growing body of research are quite important. As economist Levitt (2002) notes, "it is critical to the deterrence hypothesis that longer prison sentences be associated with reductions in crime" (p. 443). When such critical evidence cannot be found—as is the case here—it is time to rethink deterrence theory.

Deterrence advocates could take solace in the fact that the effects of imprisonment—virtually like the effects of every possible sanction!—are likely to be heterogeneous (Mears, Cochran, & Cullen, 2015). This gives them hope that they might find a deterrent effect of prisons somewhere. One possibility is to say that what really matters in deterrence is not a prison sentence per se but how long offenders stay in prison. Cullen and Jonson wish to remind everyone that if deterrence theory was as awesome as its get tough policy advocates think it is, signs of its effects would be popping up all over the place and easy to find! But let's put that aside for the moment and focus on whether the *dose of incarceration*—as researchers now call it—makes a difference. The answer is "not really." Mostly, the effect of length of imprisonment on recidivism tends to be weak and inconsistent. When effects are found, they occur under specific circumstances that mostly are unique to the study in which they are found—such as some effect after an inmate has served more than five years or for prisoners locked up for some crimes but not others (see, e.g., Loughran et al., 2009; Meade, Steiner, Makarios, & Travis, 2013; Rydberg & Clark, 2015; Snodgrass, Blokland, Haviland, Nieuwbeerta, & Nagin, 2011).

Maybe the clearest test of the dose thesis is found in a study by Hunt and Peterson (2014). In 2007, the United States Sentencing Commission decided, in essence, to revise federal sentencing guidelines and reduce the recommended prison terms for those convicted of possessing certain quantities of crack cocaine. They also voted to allow these revised guidelines to be applied retroactively to offenders currently behind bars. As of June 29, 2011, the courts had granted motions to more than 16,000 inmates that led to their release. The purpose was to reduce racial disparities linked to types of cocaine used by Whites (powder) and Blacks (crack). Thus, most of those released were African American and male.

Now, here is the key thing: These offenders were released earlier than would have been the case if they had served their assigned sentence. This created the opportunity to conduct what is called a *natural experiment*—that is, a study that is possible because of some fluke of nature. The fluke here was that a historic ruling—adjusting for racial inequities—allowed inmates to be let out of prison unexpectedly. We do not usually do such things in the United States (well, California is now another example!). Remember, there had been a whole bunch of inmates convicted for the same crime who before this time had to serve their entire sentence. They were in prison longer and thus had a higher dose of punishment. Do you see where this discussion is headed? It now became possible to compare the inmates released early (less punishment) with those released later (more punishment). Alas, the findings were bad news for deterrence! As Hunt and Peterson (2014, pp. 1–2) report, "there is no evidence that offenders whose sentence lengths were reduced . . . had higher recidivism rates than a comparison group of crack cocaine offenders who were released before the effective date of the 2007 Crack Cocaine Amendment and who served their full prison terms."

A final possibility exists: Maybe it is not a prison sentence or a longer prison sentence that matters, but rather in an institution that has particularly harsh living conditions. Maybe we have to make inmates suffer to make them realize the folly of reoffending. No country clubs, just dungeons! Admittedly, the evidence here is scarce. But, again, the studies that do exist report results contrary to the predictions of deterrence theory. Research reported by economists Chen and Shapiro (2007) explored whether inmates sentenced to easier prison conditions (minimum security level) or harsher prison conditions (higher security level) within the Federal Bureau of Prisons were more likely to recidivate. They concluded that harsher prison conditions did not reduce recidivism and, "if anything . . . may lead to more post-release crime" (2007, p. 1). Drago, Galbiati, and Vertova (2008) report similar results with Italian inmates, finding no evidence that harsher living conditions decrease recidivism. Other studies also show similar results (Gaes & Camp, 2009; Listwan, Sullivan, Agnew, Cullen, & Colvin, 2013; cf. Windzio, 2006).

Let us drive home this point with one final example. In Maricopa County, Arizona (home of Phoenix), Sheriff Joe Arpaio has earned national attention for his administration of the county jails. He is a conservative's dream correctional official, keeping costs at a minimum while creating harsh living conditions for offenders. Many inmates live in tents and thus are exposed to the extreme Arizona summer heat. He dresses them in pink underwear and striped uniforms. They work on chain gangs. Television is limited to the Disney and Weather channels. His philosophy is that discipline and discomfort will teach offenders a lesson and deter their offending. As Sheriff Arpaio proudly asserts in his autobiography, carrying the subtitle *America's Toughest Sheriff*:

> Most—and I mean 70 percent—choose to learn nothing, choose to keep breaking the law, choose to keep returning to jail. If all those inmates who comprise the 70 percent are just too stupid or corrupted or just plain vicious to go straight for their own good or the good of their families, then maybe my jails will convince a few, or maybe more than a few, to obey the law and get an honest job just to stay out of the tents and away from the green bologna. (Arpaio & Sherman, 1996, p. 50)

As he continues about his jail's tough regimen:

> That might sound harsh to you. I don't know. If it sounds harsh, that's all right, because jail is a harsh place. Jail is not a reward or an achievement, it is punishment. Amazingly, much of society seems to have forgotten that unvarnished reality. If you've ever visited my jails, tent or hard facility variety, you know I haven't forgotten. I promise the people I never will. (Arpaio & Sherman, 1996, p. 51)

Sheriff Arpaio was so confident in the deterrent powers of his jail that he enlisted Arizona State University criminologists John Hepburn and Marie Griffin (1998) to conduct an evaluation of his practices. A random assignment experiment was not possible, but a comparison could be made of jail inmates' recidivism before and after Sheriff Arpaio took office and instituted his get tough living conditions. As Hepburn and Griffin (1998) noted, the key research question was this: "To what extent do recent changes in the policies and programs that affect the conditions of confinement in the jail add to the deterrent effect of detention?" (p. 6).

After reading this chapter, we suspect you can predict what the study found. The first problem for Sheriff Arpaio is the high recidivism rate of his jail population. As Hepburn and Griffin (1998) report, "within 30 months following release from jail, 61.8% of the offenders studied were rearrested for some new offense and 55.2% of the offenders studied were rearrested for a felony offense" (p. 38). No magic bullet cure for recidivism was found. The second problem for Sheriff Arpaio was that the recidivism rate before and after he implemented his regimen remained virtually the same. As Hepburn and Griffin concluded, "there is no indication here that the policies and programs recently initiated by the Sheriff's Office add to the deterrent effect of detention" (p. 40).

Sheriff Arpaio's hubris about his correctional theory was undaunted by these data. So much for evidence-based corrections. But why should he change? We are certain he passionately believes in what he does. The electorate seems to love him, reelecting him without worry and repeatedly. He also has a national reputation (Arpaio & Sherman, 1996, 2008). His treatment of offenders is celebrated and often seen as amusing, especially the tent city and the pink underwear. Ha! Ha! What is not appreciated—what is not so funny—is the potentially high cost of running a jail based on a correctional theory with limited empirical support. What if Sheriff Arpaio had used his charisma, his organizational skills, and political acumen to implement correctional practices supported by the evidence? How many offenders' lives might he have saved? How many victimizations might he have prevented? What a shame.

Conclusion: The Limits of Deterrence

We have taken a lengthy excursion across the types of evidence that can be used to assess deterrence theory. We will boil our conclusions down to four take-away points:

- There is evidence of a *general deterrent effect* of both having a criminal justice system and of having a criminal justice system that does a better, rather than a poorer, job of catching offenders. The size of this effect is in question, and whether this "size" is seen as larger or smaller may depend on your vantage point. Thus, the effect of deterrence versus that of other causes of crime is limited. Still, it would seem better to have a system that catches offenders than one that does not. None of us, Cullen and Jonson suspect, would like to live in a community that was marked by the lawlessness of the Wild West. Letting people offend with impunity is not a good idea—especially if they are allowed to go on a crime spree where Cullen and Jonson live!

- We cannot discount that criminal sanctions have a deterrent effect with some offenders. Criminologists have not developed a systematic theory of the criminal sanction (Cullen & Jonson, 2011b; Sherman, 1993). We need to understand the conditions under which punishing offenders makes them more or less likely to recidivate.

- Most important, there is no consistent evidence that punitive-oriented correctional sanctions—such as ISPs, prisons as opposed to community-based placements, lengthier versus shorter sentences, and harsher living conditions—reduce recidivism. The failure of deterrence theory to be supported when punitive correctional interventions are evaluated is damning evidence. The existing evidence, in fact, leads us to doubt whether, across all offenders, punishment has a *specific deterrent effect*.

- Deterrence theory appears to be based on a limited understanding of criminal behavior. Criminologists, especially life-course scholars, have documented an array of factors that are implicated in criminal participation in different stages in life. When correctional interventions ignore these causes of reoffending, their impact on recidivism will be weak, if not non-existent.

In the end, correctional deterrence theory seems to rest on a shaky evidentiary foundation. In designing the content of interventions with offenders, better options exist. In the chapter to follow, we explore another get tough option: If offenders cannot be scared straight, then we can save crime by locking them up and getting them off the streets.

5

Incapacitation

Locking Up the Wicked

James Q. Wilson
Harvard University and
University of California at Los Angeles
Author of *Thinking About Crime*

I n January of 2010, Arnold Schwarzenegger rose to give his final State of the State address as Governor of California. Arnold, as he was fondly known from his Terminator days, might have organized his speech around many topics, including the enduring recession that left the economy in shambles and the state facing record budget deficits. But he did not. Instead, Arnold chose to talk about the folly of mass incarceration—of making the policy choice to invest scarce resources in sturdy bars and walls rather than in people and human capital. He proposed a state constitutional amendment that would require allocating more of the public treasury to colleges than to prisons:

> Spending 45% more on prisons than universities is no way to proceed into the future. What does it say about a state that focuses more on prison uniforms than caps and gowns? It simply is not healthy. I will submit to you a constitutional amendment so that never again do we spend a greater percentage of our money on prisons than on higher education. (Schwarzenegger, 2010)

What was the reaction? Did Californians wonder if Arnold was suddenly juicing up on steroids and going a bit nuts? Was he thinking oddly because the Kennedy family connection through then-wife Maria Shriver had finally warped his mind? Were there calls to deport him to his native land of Austria where he could find comfort among European socialists? Had the Terminator become flabby on crime? Strangely, the answer to these questions is a resounding *no*. Indeed, the *Los Angeles Times* captured the response with its headline, "Arnold Schwarzenegger Hits the Right Note" (Skelton, 2010, p. 1).

Back in 1975, James Q. Wilson, a famous Harvard University political scientist, had resonated with a different national mood in the final words to his provocative book, *Thinking About Crime*. "Wicked people exist," said Wilson (1975), and "nothing avails except to set them apart from innocent people" (p. 235). At that time, crime rates had soared, and the state and federal prison population was still hovering "at only" around 240,000. Locking up wicked people did not seem like such a bad idea. Today, however, prison populations are more than six times higher. Paying for this mass incarceration is a daunting challenge. As Arnold notes, money spent on "prison uniforms" does mean money not spent on "caps and gowns"—or on mental health services, health care, elementary schools, or highways. Is this the choice we want to make?

As Arnold recognized, California corrections was in crisis (Petersilia, 2008). The system, Joan Petersilia wrote in 2008, "has deteriorated from being one of the best systems in the country to being dysfunctional" (p. 211). A state's inmate population that stood at just 23,264 in 1980 now came to exceed 174,000 (Cullen & Gilbert, 2013; West & Sabol, 2008). Once, California spent only 3% of its budget on prisons and 10% on higher education. Now corrections had jumped up to the 10% figure, and higher education had slipped to 7% of the budget. In raw numbers, the allocation to corrections exceeded $9 billion a year, or over $34,000 per adult inmate per year behind bars (Petersilia, 2008). For this investment, Californians saw about two thirds of released inmates returned to prison within three years. To use Reiman's (1984) words, this seemed like a system "designed to fail" (p. 9).

Alas, Arnold did not prove to be the Terminator of mass imprisonment in California. Few signs existed at the time of his farewell address that the state's prison population could be substantially rolled back or that prison conditions would markedly improve (Page, 2011; Simon, 2014). Not long before, California had been a bellwether state in using prisons as a central means of crime control, including passing three-strikes-and-you're-out legislation (Kruttschnitt & Gartner, 2005; Page, 2011; Simon, 2014; Zimring, Hawkins, & Kamin, 2001). Still, as the reception his remarks received indicated, there was a growing sense that mass imprisonment was not such a great idea after all. Indeed, across the nation, enthusiasm for incarceration showed signs of waning. In 2009, state prison populations did not rise for the first time since 1977 (West & Sabol, 2010). The number of inmates had grown a lot (77%) in the 1990s, but in the decade starting in 2000, the average yearly increase dipped to 1.3% per year (Matthews, 2014, p. 120). The deep financial crisis that started in 2008 further heightened concern about the associated mass imprisonment (Aviram, 2015). Political rhetoric about prisons being economically "unsustainable" became commonplace. The United States also was in the midst of a lengthy decline in crime, extending from the early 1990s into the present time (Tonry, 2014; Zimring, 2007). Law and order receded as a political issue, rarely being mentioned in elections (more generally, see Petersilia & Cullen, 2015). Meanwhile, scholars at this time wrote book after book decrying the stupidity of the nation's orgy on incarceration. The titles of their books give a powerful message. Here we will list only five of them:

- Sasha Abramsky (2007), *American Furies: Crime, Punishment, and Vengeance in the Age of Mass Imprisonment.*

- Todd R. Clear (2007), *Imprisoning Communities: How Mass Incarceration Makes Disadvantaged Neighborhoods Worse.*

- Michael J. Lynch (2007), *Big Prisons, Big Dreams: Crime and the Failure of America's Penal System.*

- Bert Useem and Anne Morrison Piehl (2008), *Prison State: The Challenge of Mass Incarceration.*

- Travis C. Pratt (2009), *Addicted to Incarceration: Corrections Policy and the Politics of Misinformation in the United States.*

Put another way, it was as though someone jammed on the brakes of the mass imprisonment train, slowing it to a crawl but not fully halting its momentum. Then something truly dramatic happened. The U.S. Supreme Court assumed Arnold's role as the Terminator of California's mass incarceration. In May of 2011, the Court issued a historic decision in *Brown v. Plata.* In a 5–4 decision, with Justice Kennedy writing the opinion, the justices "required California to bring its swollen prison population down to 137 percent of the capacity of its thirty-three prisons within two years by any means the state chose" (Simon, 2014, p. 133). Numerically, this meant reducing the prison population by about 35,000 inmates. As Justice Kennedy notes, conditions inside the state's prisons had deteriorated so much as to be unconstitutional: "A prison that deprives prisoners of basic sustenance, including adequate medical care, is incompatible with the concept of human dignity and has no place in a civilized society" (quoted in Simon, 2014, p. 133).

Later in 2011, Governor Jerry Brown signed the Public Safety Realignment Act. The goal of "realignment"—as it has become known—was to have more convicted offenders penalized in local counties than transferred to the state system (Petersilia & Cullen, 2015). The story of how this will all work out remains to be told. For our purposes, the critical impact of realignment is that "California has embarked on a prison downsizing experiment of historic proportions" (2015, p. 27). Or as Simon (2014, p. 135) notes, "California has instantly become the leading example of the shift away from state prison." As such, downsizing—moving away from mass imprisonment as the central correctional policy of our era—is now a viable option. As the California experience unfolds, downsizing will remain on the agenda across the nation (see Turner, David, et al., 2015). Indeed, what seemed impossible not long ago—not just the end of mass imprisonment but seeing prisons as a problematic response to offending—is now part of contemporary correctional discourse. Put another way, it is no longer taken for granted in policy circles that locking up the wayward is a prudent thing to do. To borrow the title of Simon's (2014) recent book, mass incarceration is now on trial.

All this does not mean that mass incarceration is ended—only the *movement* to keep prison populations endlessly rising seemingly has halted. With more than 1.5 million inmates in state and federal prisons and a couple of million behind bars as you read this book, it is not as though we have embarked on a mass deinstitutionalization movement. Mauer and Ghandnoosh (2013) put this matter in perspective. They note approvingly that between 2011 and 2012, the U.S. prison population declined 1.8%. Then they calculate a sobering empirical fact: "Still, at this rate, it will take until 2101—88 years—for the prison population to return to its 1980 level."

But again, we cannot jump to conclusions. Reality can be complex. Take, for example, the field of medicine. Tens of millions of operations are undertaken in the United States every year, with 230 million surgeries occurring worldwide. Not only are the costs exorbitant, but each year these procedures leave 7 million people disabled and 1 million dead—"a level of harm that approaches that of malaria, tuberculosis, and other traditional public health concerns" (Gawande, 2009, p. 87). Are we addicted to surgery? Maybe. But, of course, the key consideration is how many people would have been disabled or died had the surgeries not been performed. That is, the surgical numbers seem high, but is the *health effect* worth it?

This same consideration must inform the debate over incarceration—mass or otherwise. Cullen and Jonson think we lock up way too many people in the United States. Nonetheless, we also are scientists who believe that the wisdom of mass incarceration ultimately must be decided on the basis of evidence. If the *incapacitation effect* is large—that is, if the amount of crime prevented by keeping offenders behind bars rather than on the street is large—then having more than 2.2 million criminals incarcerated on any given day might be a good thing. If there are 2.2 million wicked people out there, then maybe we should be locking them all up. Maybe we should be spending more on prisons than on universities. Maybe we should tell Arnold to shelve his constitutional amendment—that for California, it is better to have a state that is safe and stupid than a state that is dangerous and smart.

The key issue, then, is how much crime is saved by incapacitating people. Deciphering the size of the *incapacitation effect of imprisonment* is not easy. It involves complex statistical estimations, most of which involve using funny Greek letters (it is a good thing that Jonson married into a Greek family, because Cullen now assumes she can read and understand all the funny Greek symbols in the statistical equations). The other problem is that the numbers do not speak for themselves. Let's assume that locking up an offender for a year prevents four crimes that would have been committed had this person roamed free on the street. Would you say that *only* four crimes were saved or that *fully* four crimes were saved? Guess what? Liberals tend to use the word *only*, whereas conservatives tend to use the word *fully*.

But for now, we will give you the punch line of what we find when scrutinizing the evidence in the remainder of the chapter. It comes in three parts:

- There is an incapacitation effect, and it is meaningfully large. Prisons prevent crime. Letting people out of prison will increase criminal victimization.

- It is deceptive to compare the amount of crime saved by placing an offender in prison compared with *doing nothing* and allowing the offender to *roam free on the street*. The proper comparison, which is never done in incapacitation research, is how much crime would be saved if we used a similar amount of money and *invested it in alternative correctional interventions*.

- Prisons should be used judiciously and only as part of a comprehensive plan to intervene effectively with offenders.

In this chapter, we first discuss two issues that form the basis of a policy conundrum when it comes to incapacitation: We have too many prisoners, but also too many criminals who could easily be put into prison. Solving this problem—we lock up offenders excessively but there is no shortage of people to lock up—is not easy. Even the scholars who use Greek symbols do not help us much with this challenge. After this analysis, we spend some time on the concept of incapacitation, reminding the reader of the difference between selective and collective incapacitation. We then turn our attention to the core of the chapter: estimating the size of the incapacitation effect.

Too Many Prisoners

On any given day, America imprisons more than 2.2 million offenders. Already, we have cited this figure about 10 times. I think that, as readers, you get the point: There are a whole bunch of Americans behind bars. We do not really need to beat it into the ground, do we? Still, some perspective is needed to reinforce Cullen and Jonson's conclusion that the current use of imprisonment in the United States is exceptional. We make three observations.

- *First, other nations do not use prisons nearly as much as we do.*

This does not mean that the United States is an inordinately vindictive country. Still, when cross-national comparisons are conducted, America is especially harsh in its treatment of drug offenders (Bewley-Taylor, Hallam, & Allen, 2009). For most other crimes, the United States is at or near the top of the international list when it comes to handing out prison sentences. For example, Blumstein, Tonry, and Van Ness (2005) assessed eight advanced nations' punitiveness for the crimes of homicide, rape, robbery, residential burglary, assault, and motor vehicle theft. (In addition to the United States, the countries were Australia, Canada, England and Wales, the Netherlands, Scotland, Sweden, and Switzerland.) Blumstein et al. (2005) concluded that the "United States was the most punitive country for nearly all the crime types, especially when punitiveness is defined narrowly as expected time served per conviction" (p. 375). Cullen and Jonson put it this way: When in doubt, America incarcerates; other nations tend not to do so.

Table 5.1 presents some very telling numbers. We should note that these figures vary slightly year to year and by the source of the data. As we write this, some reports have the United States' incarceration figure as just north of 2.2 million. But regardless of slight variations in the details, the story is the same.

Now, as seen in Table 5.1, in terms of raw numbers, the United States incarcerates roughly 559,000 more individuals than China and roughly 1.5 million more than Russia (*World Prison Brief,* 2013). Such raw numbers can be deceiving because they do not standardize for population size. Of course, big countries will have lots of prisoners because they have lots of people to start with. To get around this statistical problem, scholars compute an *incarceration rate*—in this case, the number of those locked up per 100,000 people in the population. No problem; the United States ranks first in the world with an incarceration rate per 100,000 of 698. (Actually, Seychelles ranks first with a rate of 799 per 100,000 people, but the country is so small that it only incarcerates 735 people—so it does not make too much sense to put them into the rankings here.) Notably, Russia lags behind the United States with an incarceration rate of 455. In Europe, after Russia, the highest imprisonment rate is found in Belarus with a rate of 335, followed by Lithuania with a rate of 315, and Georgia with a rate of 281. These rates are all less than one half of the rate found in the United States (*World Prison Brief*, 2013). So, let's all chant: "We're number 1; we're number 1."

Indeed, we are. Although accounting for only 5% of the world's population, the United States houses almost 22% of the over 10 million people incarcerated worldwide. Thus, more than one in five people incarcerated in the world are locked up in the United States (*World Prison Brief*, 2013). With four times America's population, China houses only 16% of the world's incarcerated offenders. Together, China and the United States are cornering the prison market. They control roughly 40% of the world's imprisoned population, with the remaining 193 countries accounting for the other 60%.

As we have noted and will do again shortly, the rise in America's prison population over the past 40 years has been remarkable. But the majority of nations worldwide have not followed our example (Tonry, 2007). In Europe, the Scandinavian countries of Denmark, Norway, and Sweden have had stable imprisonment rates of between 40 to 71 prisoners per 100,000 population for the last half century (Lappi-Seppala, 2007; *World Prison Brief*, 2013). Germany also has had stable imprisonment rates for the last 25 years; it has hovered around 90 inmates per 100,000 population and has lowered in recent years (Weigend, 2001; *World Prison Brief*, 2013). Imprisonment rates in Finland actually decreased substantially from 1965 to 1990 and now have stabilized around 60 inmates per 100,000 population (Lappi-Seppala, 2007; Tonry, 2007; *World Prison Brief*, 2013).

Admittedly, the United States is not the only nation to have increasing incarceration rates. But what makes America exceptional is the length and the enormity of its prison expansion. For example, although England and Wales and New Zealand have shown substantial increases in their imprisonment rates, this has occurred only since the 1990s (Newburn, 2007; Pratt, 2007; Tonry, 2007). Similarly, after approximately three decades of falling or stable prison populations, the number of inmates in Japan increased 15% between 1990 and 2005 (Johnson, 2007). The key fact, however, is that even with these changes, other nations' use of prisons remains substantially below the United States'. Thus, as of 2013, the imprisonment rate per 100,000 population for England and Wales stood at 148, New Zealand at 190, and Japan at 49 (see Table 5.1) (*World Prison Brief*, 2013). One other telling fact: The United States still has an incarceration rate roughly 3 to 14 times higher than these nations.

What about Canada, our friendly neighbor to the north? Cullen, in particular, likes Canadians because they are serious about ice hockey, a sport Cullen played in college. Cullen was a fairly inept goaltender, which meant he spent a lot of time on

Table 5.1 The Prison Population Rate and the Raw Number of People Incarcerated for Various Countries Around the World, 2013

Country	Prison Population Rate per 100,000 National Population	Raw Number Incarcerated (including pre-trial detainees/ remand prisoners)
United States	698	2,217,000
Russia	455	656,618
Mexico	214	256,941
New Zealand	190	8,641
Australia	151	35,804
England and Wales	148	85,743
Spain	141	65,581
China	119	1,657,812
Canada	106	37,864
France	100	66,761
Germany	76	61,872
Netherlands	75	12,638
Norway	71	3,710
Japan	49	61,794

SOURCE: *World Prison Brief* (2013).

the bench. Cullen was not very good at stopping pucks shot at the "five hole," which is between the goalie's legs (holes one to four are at the corners of the net). Discussing his prowess in the nets, Cullen made the mistake one day of telling his teammates that he was "weakest between his legs." This comment was repeated to him the rest of the season.

Cullen likes Canada not only for its ice hockey but also because it sits to the north of us and presents a good case for comparison. Americans feel superior to Canadians, but Cullen and Jonson notice that our northern neighbors tend to do things that we do not. They succeeded in getting health care for all their citizens put into place, whereas we are still struggling to do so. Want to see Niagara Falls? Go to the Canadian side. Canada also has a lower crime rate. However, its crime rate tends to follow the United States'—though at a much lower level. If our crime goes up, so does Canada's. This is important because it means that Canada's incarceration rate also should track ours. Of course, it does not.

In his cross-cultural comparison, Brodeur (2007) demonstrates that countries that cluster together geographically and culturally seem to incarcerate people at roughly the same rate. Specifically, he found that within five clusters (e.g., Nordic Council countries, Central European countries, the Baltic countries, the Caribbean, and the Indian subcontinent), the countries had remarkably similar imprisonment rates. The United States and Canada share one of the world's longest common borders, second only to the border shared between Russia and China (Brodeur, 2007).

Due to this geographic proximity, one would expect Canada to be similar to the United States in terms of its incarceration rates (Brodeur, 2007). Again, this is not the case; the cluster rule does not apply. While the United States' incarceration rate has skyrocketed since the 1970s, the rate in Canada has remained relatively stable at around 100 inmates per 100,000 population (Ouimet, 2002; Webster & Doob, 2007). The latest figures place the rate at 106. Despite the cultural, economic, and geographic similarities between the two countries, America's rate of imprisonment is about 6.5 times higher than that of Canada (*World Prison Brief,* 2013).

- *Second, the United States' incarceration rate is high because we want it that way.*

To be sure, a bunch of factors have contributed to America's exceptionally high use of prisons. These factors include, for example, the growth from 1970 to today in the nation's population from around 200 million to about 320 million and increases in the total number of arrests. More inputs result in higher prison populations. Still, over the past four decades, politicians have promised us that they would get tough on crime. They have urged that more offenders be arrested and that more be convicted. They have instructed community corrections officials to watch offenders more closely and to return them to prison not just for new criminal acts but for a host of infractions that have little to do with the supervisees' dangerousness. They have participated in a virtual orgy of legislative punitiveness, passing law after law that sought to put more offenders behind bars for longer periods of time. Unless our elected officials were inept, they have succeeded in what they intended: They have made the United States the leading prison industry in the world. Again, why did this happen? "In the most literal sense," notes Michael Tonry (2004), "the explanation is that American politicians adopted unduly harsh policies and the public let them do it" (p. 11).

Another way to understand this issue is to envision the *counterfactual.* That is, what would America's incarceration rate look like today if elected officials had not spouted get tough rhetoric for nearly 40 years and had been deeply concerned about the possible over-use of imprisonment? To be sure, prisons would still exist and house hundreds of thousands of offenders. But we also might have had the political will to create a vast system of high-quality community corrections agencies that might have intervened earlier and more effectively in the lives of offenders. Even if some form of *mass corrections* was difficult to avoid, *mass incarceration* was not inevitable.

- *Third, because the size of the prison population is a choice, Americans could decide to use imprisonment more judiciously.*

Anyone at all familiar with imprisonment in America is likely to assume that prison populations have *always* been rising in the United States. Why is this so? Well, because for the last four decades—the better part of many of our lives—this certainly has been the case. Indeed, prison populations have risen so much that, on any given day, there are more than *2.2 million* offenders behind bars—oops, there is that darn figure again! A study by the Pew Charitable Trusts in 2008 made a lot of headlines by reporting that this big figure means that, on any given day, 1 in 100 Americans is behind bars. Today, the gap has widened a bit to 1 in 110 (Glaze & Kaeble, 2014). But you get the point: Whether the statistic is 1 in 100 or 1 in 110, the ratio is astounding and makes us pay closer attention to the real human costs of mass imprisonment.

Furthermore, until the last few years, inmate populations in the United States had been steadily rising. Between 1990 and 1999—the space of a decade—the federal prison population increased over 100%, from 65,526 to 135,246. The state prison population rose from 708,393 to 1,231,475—an increase of about 74%. The rise thereafter has been slower, but still is pushing forward. By yearend 2008, the federal prison population had jumped more than 60,000 to 198,414, whereas the state prison population stood at 1,320,145 (Sabol et al., 2009). The latest available figures—for yearend 2013—place the count at 195,098 federal inmates and 1,321,781 state inmates (Carson, 2014). But let's go back even further in time. Let's start, again, in 1990, where the total number of inmates in state and federal prisons was 773,919. In 1980, the total was less than half this number: *315,974.* Now, get this: In 1970, the total in state and federal prisons was *under 200,000* (196,429). Thus, in the last four decades, prison populations have increased more than *seven-fold.*

Right now, then, the size of America's prison population seems on an unstoppable march upward. But, again, it was not always the case. There was a time when the country was not ensnared in this upward spiral of imprisonment. Different choices were made about how much to use prisons as a possible solution to crime.

In fact, in 1973, two well-known criminologists—Alfred Blumstein and Jacqueline Cohen—wrote a theoretical article to explain why America's prison populations always seemed to be *stable!* They called it "A Theory of the Stability of Punishment." Blumstein and Cohen (1973) were amazed to discover that there had been relative stability in punishment in the United States between 1925 and the early 1970s. In the half century following 1925, the imprisonment rate per 100,000 Americans averaged under 108, and the number of inmates rose mainly in proportion to the growth of the general population.

Take a look at Figure 5.1. This is what Blumstein and Cohen saw. If you were in their shoes in 1973, you would have been wearing bell-bottom pants! And you would have authored a theory of stability and assumed that this pattern would have continued. Why? Because we always assume that what has existed in the past will exist in the future. Unfortunately for Blumstein and Cohen, the past was not to be the future. Talk about bad timing to write a theory prognosticating the stability of punishment!

So, take a look at Figure 5.2. What happened after 1970? The incarceration rate per 100,000 did not remain stable. Instead, it started on a four-decade steep upward trajectory. Again, there are complex reasons for this dramatic shift in the use of prisons. But as we have said, a key sustaining force nurturing the mass imprisonment movement was that a whole bunch of politicians were telling American voters that they were going to lock up offenders and passed a host of laws to see that this happened. Put another way, being number one in the world in imprisonment is not an Act of God but a policy choice. In the time ahead, we could choose a different path.

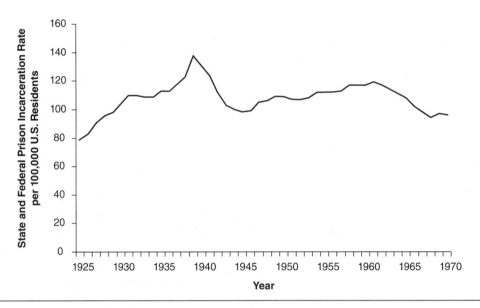

Figure 5.1   State and Federal Prison Incarceration Rates, 1925–1970

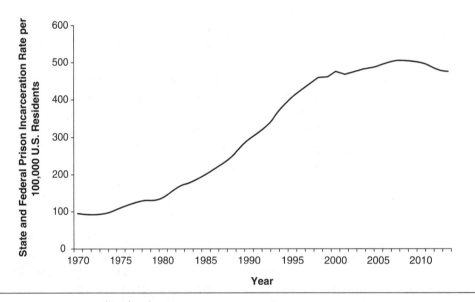

Figure 5.2   State and Federal Prison Incarceration Rates, 1970–2013

Importantly, the issue arises as to *why we wished to lock up so many Americans.*
What did policy makers hope to accomplish? They favored lengthy prison sentences in
part out of a desire for retribution—to exact just deserts on offenders for the harms
they caused—and for deterrence—to teach folks that crime does not pay (see Chapters
3 and 4). But the logic behind many laws aimed at increasing the use of imprisonment
was simply to *get offenders off the street.* That is, to *incapacitate* offenders.

This view is built on the premise that if offenders are not in society, then they cannot victimize innocent citizens (apart from correctional staff and each other). The beauty of this approach is that it can promise to reduce crime *without ever having to change offenders*. Whereas rehabilitation wants to change who offenders are and deterrence has the task of making offenders worry about getting punished, incapacitation can ignore the offender altogether. It merely has to put offenders in a cage to stop their ability to commit crime.

The logic is much like that of a zoo in which dangerous predators—like lions— are placed behind sturdy bars. To be safe from victimization, we do not need to tame the lion ("rehabilitate the lion") or make the lion afraid of us with a whip and a chair ("deter the lion"), but rather to stay on the other side of the bars. And if we just lock up enough offenders, then the population of active criminals loose in society will dwindle to the point that crime rates will bottom out. We can, in short, incapacitate ourselves out of the crime problem!

The power of incapacitation, then, is its appeal to our *common sense*. But as with other policies in corrections, the issues surrounding incapacitation are complex and cannot be adequately assessed merely by appealing to common sense. In general, there are two considerations that are intimately involved in any assessment of the merits of incapacitation as correctional philosophy:

- Imprisoning offenders is expensive; it costs a lot of money. In most state budgets, money spent on prisons cannot be spent on other needs. At issue, then, is how much incapacitation we can afford.

- As we will see, it is indisputable (in our view, at least) that prisons reduce crime rates. The key issue, however, is: *How much?* Further, we must ask whether crime saved due to incapacitation exceeds that saved due to other interventions with offenders. That is, the issue is: *Compared to what?*

As might be anticipated, the financial costs of prisons and how much crime is saved by prisons are often interrelated in policy discussions on imprisonment. Thus, the more crime that prisons prevent from occurring through incapacitation, the more "cost effective" they will be. That is, if a substantial amount of crime is saved by locking up offenders, then the money spent on massive imprisonment might well be a prudent investment. If the crime savings are minimal, then devoting immense sums of money to building and maintaining prisons would be difficult to justify.

More Than Enough Criminals

As a nation, we like to speak of *American exceptionalism*. This means that the United States is different. By *different*, we really mean *better*—as in, for example, that we, as a people, value freedom and accept others from all over the globe to become Americans.

But in corrections, American exceptionalism is more a source of national embarrassment than pride. It entails using prisons more than any of the other 194 nations on the planet. With over 170,000 residents locked up, California and Texas have a *state* prison population that exceeds that of all but six *nations* worldwide, not counting America (*World Prison Brief,* 2013). We also seem to have lost our way. Once, American corrections was the exemplar for the world. We used our prisons judiciously and led the way in efforts at offender treatment. Now, we have prisons filled to the brim, well over capacity. Many inmates sit idle and return to society unprepared for reentry. As John Irwin (2005) calls it, we have created the *warehouse prison.*

Cullen and Jonson thus think we have lost our way and have too many prisoners. This troubles us because our research shows—as reviewed in Chapter 4 on deterrence—that imprisonment either has no effect on, or increases, recidivism. Does it make sense to keep cramming offenders into warehouses when the result is that they come out no better or even worse?

This way of putting things is, of course, a loaded question meant to elicit the answer "no." But because Cullen and Jonson are honest scientists, we have to admit that there is a way to respond to this question with a "yes." Thus, if there is a large *incapacitation effect,* then the crime saved *while the offenders are behind bars* might make this nasty business worth it. Prisons might have become warehouses, but if they function to lock up truly wicked people, then so be it. As Americans, we may not be proud of our prison warehouses, but they will make us safer in our neighborhoods. Better to be safe than sorry.

The conundrum for bleeding hearts such as Cullen and Jonson is that incapacitation advocates among us have a point: *At any given moment, there are more than enough criminals available that most of us would like to see locked up.* So, we have too many prisoners but more than enough criminals to be prisoners. Let's probe this conundrum a bit further.

What this debate hinges on is this: *Who is in prison? How criminal are inmates? Are they mostly low-risk losers or wicked super-predators? If released, will they mostly use and sell drugs, take property if left unguarded, and get into stupid fights (the losers)? Or will they rape, rob, and shoot (the predators)?* To be honest, despite more than 2.2 million inmates sitting behind bars every day of the year, neither criminologists nor policy makers can tell you with any precision the level of criminality among the nation's prison population. This is an amazing oversight—an incredible gap in our basic knowledge when so much money and human lives are at stake. But if ignorance and corrections are two circles in a Venn diagram, the unfortunate reality is that they overlap a great deal.

Most criminologists ascribe to the view that prisons are filled with low-level chronic property offenders and a whole bunch of drug offenders needlessly incarcerated in the nation's ill-conceived war on drugs (see, e.g., Irwin & Austin, 1994; cf. Matthews, 2009). The gist of this educated guess is that about half the people in prison now are low-risk offenders who we could release without increasing the crime rate in any serious way (for an informed analysis, see Sabol & Lynch, 1997).

The alternative view is that offenders have to work hard to earn their way into prison. One study of persistent offenders (based on self-reported crime) found that only 63% are ever arrested (Barnes, 2014). Even for those brought into the system, they often repeatedly break the law and escape imprisonment until a frustrated judge sees no option except to lock them up. Most have lengthy criminal records not only as adults but also as juveniles. Many will have engaged in hundreds of crimes never detected (Farrington, Jolliffe, Loeber, & Homish, 2007). Indeed, over half of state prison inmates were sentenced for a violent crime. When those sentenced to prison for property and drug offenses are examined closely, it is discovered that they often have committed a range of other criminal acts—the kind of victimizations none of us would define as unserious (Bennett, DiIulio, & Walters, 1996; see also Matthews, 2009). Recidivism rates of released inmates also paint a discouraging picture. Depending on the state and how recidivism is measured, upwards of two thirds of offenders end up back in prison. And this is only for what they were caught doing. We explore this issue in Chapter 8 on prisoner reentry.

The scary thing is that there is also a whole bunch of people not in prison who the average citizen would think should be. Remember, there are more than 4.7 million offenders on probation (3.9 million) or parole (more than 853,200)—1 in every 51 adults in the United States. Let's just look at the probationers (Herberman & Bonczar, 2014). About one in five (19%) is on probation for a violent offense. Hmm, that's a touch disconcerting. If there are 3.9 million offenders on probation and one fifth committed a violent crime, then this means that there are well over 700,000 violent criminals not behind bars. Half of those on probation, in fact, were convicted of a felony—and this is after plea bargaining reducing their charges had taken place for most of them (Herberman & Bonczar, 2014). Nationally, the number of felony offenders not sentenced to prison was 30% for robbery, 41% for sexual assault, 53% for burglary, and 59% for aggravated assault (Petersilia, 2008). Although their 1991 data are a bit old now, Bennett et al. (1996) put the matter in stark terms that remain true today:

> Based only on the latest conviction offenses that brought them to prison, the 162,000 probation violators committed at least 6,400 murders, 7,400 rapes, 10,400 assaults, and 17,000 robberies while "under supervision" in the community an average of 17 months. (p. 185)

So, again, there is the policy conundrum we face: The United States has too many prisoners but also more than enough criminals who are excellent candidates for being locked up. Whether we should keep or place all these offenders in prison is a tough question to answer. It depends on two considerations. First, how much crime do we really save if we imprison offenders? What is the size of the *incapacitation effect*? We deal with this crucial empirical issue shortly. Second, what else might we do with these offenders that is as effective as incapacitation but that involves more than warehousing them? We address this matter in later chapters.

The Concept of Incapacitation

To reiterate, incapacitation is the use of a criminal sanction to physically prevent— or make impossible—the commission of a crime by an offender. It is possible to do this through sanctions such as home confinement or capital punishment (which is pretty damn preventative!). But to be realistic, when we talk about incapacitation, we are talking about putting offenders in prison. Also to reiterate, the *incapacitation effect* is the *amount of crime that is saved—or does not occur—as a result of an offender being physically unable to commit a crime.* Finally, there are two types of incapacitation. These really are different ways or strategies for how to do incapacitation. These are *collective incapacitation* and *selective incapacitation.* We discuss each of these below.

COLLECTIVE INCAPACITATION

Christy Visher (1987) defines *collective incapacitation* as "crime reduction accomplished through traditional offense-based sentencing and imprisonment policies or changes in those policies, such as imposing mandatory minimum sentences" (pp. 514–515). What the heck does that mean? Well, essentially, it means two things:

- First, we take *everybody* who falls into a certain category. This might be *everybody* who commits a crime carrying a gun; or everybody who commits a third serious felony; or everybody who sells drugs over a certain limit. Now, the notion of *everybody* is important because it is this feature that makes the incapacitation *collective.*

- Second, we then take everybody in this *category* and we put them in prison— we *incapacitate* the collective.

As we will see in more detail below, any *category of offenders* is made up of people who commit crimes at different rates—that is, there are high-rate offenders and low-rate offenders (and others in between!). Thus, when a third felony in a three-strikes-and-you're-out law causes an offender to receive a mandatory life sentence, it may be that a lot of crime will be prevented because a high-rate offender is off the streets. But some three-strikes offenders commit crimes at low rates. Imprisoning them for life makes little sense.

The main *benefit* of collective incapacitation is that it does not care if low-rate offenders are kept in prison for lengthy periods of time. That cost is worth it, because in casting the net wide, all high-rate offenders in the group are put behind bars. However, the main *problem* of collective incapacitation is—*surprise, surprise!*—the same thing: It does not care if low-rate offenders are kept in prison for lengthy periods of time. But the long-term incarceration of low-risk offenders is an inefficient crime control strategy. When low-rate offenders remain endlessly behind bars, we must spend enormous sums of money to pay for prison cells that are not giving us much crime savings. Of course, there is also the issue of *justice.* We are imprisoning these low-risk offenders for what they *might do in the future— even though they would never have committed these prognosticated criminal acts.*

Now, do you see where this discussion is headed? How might we make incapacitation more efficient (and just)? The answer is that we should not lock up everyone in a category. Instead, we should *select out* the high-rate offenders and give them the lengthy prison terms. This is, of course, the notion of *selective incapacitation.* We will return to this issue shortly. Before doing so, however, we wanted to note that most policies using imprisonment in America have been based mainly on the idea of *collective incapacitation.* This means that many high-rate offenders are taken off the streets, but it also means that the cost of this policy has been inflated prison populations that have drained tax monies. This is a trade-off. Whether this trade-off is worth it—whether this money has been wisely spent—is a policy decision for you to consider as we proceed through this chapter.

SELECTIVE INCAPACITATION

Criminologists note that when it comes to how much people offend, there are *individual differences* or *heterogeneity in criminal propensities.* One possibility is that when people break the law, they all commit the same number of offenses. In this case, there would be homogeneity, rather than heterogeneity in offending. But this is generally not how human behavior "works." In most types of behavior— whether it is crime, playing sports, or drinking alcohol—some people do not do it at all, many people do it a little (or in moderation), and a few people do it a lot. Again, this is what we mean by individual differences or heterogeneity.

What are the implications of the heterogeneity insight for criminology? It is that a relatively small group of people tend to commit a high proportion of the crimes, especially serious crimes. Where did we get this idea? A number of studies have shown this pattern in offending, but one of the earliest—and the most famous—is a now-classic study conducted by Marvin Wolfgang, Robert Figlio, and Thorsten Sellin. This study was published in 1972 in the book *Delinquency in a Birth Cohort.*

Wolfgang et al. studied the criminal records of a "cohort" of nearly 10,000 boys born in 1945 who had lived in Philadelphia from the age of 10 to 18. A cohort means all the kids born in a single year. By age 18, almost 35% of their sample had a criminal record. But most of this group had only one or two police contacts. Among the cohort, however, 627 youths had five or more offenses. The researchers called this group *chronic offenders.* And despite constituting only *6% of the cohort,* these chronic offenders accounted for over half the crimes committed: 69% of all aggravated assaults, 71% of all homicides, 73% of all rapes, and 82% of all robberies! What an amazing finding!!!

Now, we want to call your attention to the 6% figure. This figure is often cited in news reports on crime. It is the most *incorrectly* cited figure in the history of criminology—maybe in the history of all social sciences! You probably think

Cullen and Jonson are kidding, but we are not. Almost always, this figure is cited in this way: "6% of the *offenders* accounted for over half the crime." Is this what we said above about the study? The answer is, "No." Instead, we said "6% of the *entire cohort* accounted for over half the crime."

You are probably sitting there wondering why we are going into this criminological minutia. You might be thinking that we preparing you for *Jeopardy*. "Well, Alex, I'll take irrelevant criminological facts for $200." But we are not. What is the difference between (1) 6% of a cohort and (2) 6% of the group of kids in the cohort who were offenders? Well, one refers to 6% of all the kids studied—offenders and non-offenders alike. And the other refers to 6% of those kids in the cohort who broke the law. These numbers are *not the same*. Why? Because 6% of the cohort actually means about *18% of the offenders in the sample*.

We are getting closer to the punch line here: Why was the 6% figure so important—the figure that is repeated over and over again? How does this help to make the practice of "selective" incapacitation possible? Well, think of it this way: If *only* 6% of the offenders account for most of the serious crime, all we have to do in order to reduce crime is to incapacitate this *small group of offenders*. That is, select out the chronic offenders for imprisonment and put the less serious offenders in the community (or give them short prison sentences). This also will be *cost effective* because we will be using just a little prison space to save a bunch of crime!

But what if the figure is not 6% but *18% of the offenders* who are *chronic*. You may still want to selectively incapacitate high-rate offenders, but the figure in question is now *three times higher* than that quoted in article after article! It is not going to be such an easy task to imprison only the chronic offenders because it is not that small of a group. Again, you still may want to do it, but the challenge would be more daunting.

Just to show you what we mean by the 6% figure being the source of much misunderstanding, let us cite a passage from a story in the *Los Angeles Times* that was published on August 23, 2001. Here California's Secretary of State was justifying the use of three-strikes laws: "So when you are talking about affecting the crime rate, we decided with three strikes to go after the 6% or so of criminals who do 60% of the crime" (Krikorian, 2001).

In the Wolfgang et al. study, the authors also noted that the chronic offenders were disproportionately non-White and poor, had low school achievement and IQ scores, and belonged to families that frequently changed residences. By implication, officials might have targeted these risk factors for intervention. We are digressing a bit here, but with a point. Just because a group of chronic offenders exists does not mean that the *only* policy implication is that they should be locked up. We can also identify their *root causes*—that is, the conditions that produce chronic offenders—and attack them. Thus, the Wolfgang et al. Philadelphia cohort study could have led to a policy agenda that stressed not locking people up but fundamental social reform.

The scholar who did most to link the Wolfgang et al. study—and its 6% finding—to incapacitation was James Q. Wilson. You might recall Wilson from the first part of this chapter. He is that one who said in his classic *Thinking About Crime* (1975) that "wicked people exist" and that "nothing avails except to set them apart from innocent people" (p. 235). What he meant more precisely is that 6% of us are wicked and we should set these folks apart. Wilson (1975) put it this way:

> Out of the ten thousand boys, however, there were six hundred and twenty-seven—
> *only* 6 per cent—who committed five or more offenses before they were eighteen. Yet
> these *few* chronic offenders accounted for over half of all recorded delinquencies and
> about two-thirds of all the violent crimes committed by the entire cohort. (p. 224;
> emphasis added)

Again, few among us would argue with the general point that prison space should be reserved for serious, chronic offenders. But the cleverness of Wilson's argument was that he made incapacitation seem easy. Note his use of the words *only* and *few* in the above quote. There is just a small group of wicked people out there. Let's just select them out and incapacitate them. But what if Wilson had been more forthcoming and had not used the 6% statistic? What if he had said that 18% of the offenders in the cohort were chronic criminals, which would have been more accurate? This percentage would not have seemed so tiny and so easily managed. Imprisonment might not have seemed like the only or the best option.

As a Harvard political scientist, Wilson gave considerable credibility to the idea that we could substantially reduce crime by *selectively incapacitating* the wicked 6%. Whereas most criminologists at that time were calling for broader social reform, Wilson's policy prescription seemed easily within reach. In short, he legitimized imprisonment as the central tool for controlling crime in the United States. His analysis also placed the 6% figure into the public policy culture where, again, it has been misused in the defense of imprisonment for more than four decades.

Throughout this discussion, we have largely assumed that the definition of *selective incapacitation* was understood. But let us turn again to Visher (1987) for a formal definition of this concept:

> Selective incapacitation is an attempt to improve the efficiency of imprisonment as a
> crime control strategy by tailoring the sentencing decisions to individual offenders.
> A collective incapacitation strategy would require similar sentences for offenders
> convicted of the same offense. . . . when a selective incapacitation strategy is at work,
> however, offenders who are thought to pose the greatest risk of future crimes become
> the prime candidates for incarceration and for longer prison sentences. (p. 515)

What this means, of course, is that if 100 robbers are standing before the court, a collective incapacitation approach would be to imprison *everybody*. A selective incapacitation approach would be to imprison *only* the subgroup of robbers who will turn out to be *chronic offenders*. Importantly, as Visher (1987) notes, the "key to reducing crime through selective incapacitation policies is the ability to identify offenders who will commit serious crimes at high rates in the future" (p. 525). This leads us into the quagmire of prediction. That is, can we predict which of the offenders about to be sentenced by the court will be the chronic offenders, especially if they have similar criminal records?

There are *three* problems that prediction—as used for selective incapacitation at the time of sentencing—faces:

- *Can we do better than judges already are doing?* Judges already make predictions about who will be a recidivist and who will not. To improve on what prisons are already accomplishing, the instrument would have to out-predict the judge. Of course, this assumes that even if an accurate instrument were available, judges would use it in place of their own judgment. Remember that legal training is not scientific; judges are not required during or after law school to take a single course in criminology or corrections. They sentence based on the law and predict future criminality based on personal experience—not hard data. No evidence-based sentencing for them. I think you can guess what Cullen and Jonson think about this!

- *The prediction instrument can include only certain factors.* Let us assume that factors such as race, age, and gender predicted recidivism. If we wanted to predict future criminality, we would want to include these factors in our prediction instrument. Why couldn't we do this? Ever hear about *discrimination*? Would it be fair, for example, to give an *individual* man a longer sentence just because, *as a group,* men are more criminal than women? Our point is that some predictors of recidivism just cannot be included in a prediction instrument used by the courts.

- *The prediction instrument is likely to rely only on static factors, not dynamic factors.* A static factor is something such as a person's criminal record. It is static because an offender can never change it (i.e., can never reduce it). A dynamic factor is something such as *antisocial attitudes.* Those can change; an offender can reduce antisocial attitudes and replace them with prosocial attitudes, which does, in fact, lower his or her chance of recidivating. Notably, the best prediction instruments used in corrections (mainly for treatment) combine static and dynamic predictors (Andrews & Bonta, 2010; Smith, Cullen, & Latessa, 2009). At the time of sentencing, however, the prediction instruments tend to use only static factors; this is a one-time assessment and thus they do not follow offenders to see if dynamic factors do actually change. As a result, these prediction instruments are often not very predictive.

This is not to say that some prediction is not possible. Even so, being able to build an instrument to predict accurately—with only certain information available and doing so *at the time of sentencing*—is very difficult. Later in the process, where one can collect and use more information about an offender, prediction becomes more accurate. But at sentencing, the ability to predict with accuracy is not easy.

This leads us, finally, to another problem that is inherent in selective incapacitation: the problem of *false positives.* False positives are offenders that an instrument predicts (falsely) will become recidivists who, in fact, do not. As an analogy, think of a drug test: These offenders come up positive in the test (i.e., on the prediction instrument). But the problem is that they are not actually positives—they actually will not reoffend. As such, the *positive* result is *false.*

The prediction instruments developed for selective incapacitation are so limited that they often do not predict much better than chance. In the best cases, they still have a large number of false positives. This raises two issues:

- When the proportion of false positives is large, the efficiency of selective incapacitation is low. Selective incapacitation is cost effective only if it picks out the high-rate offenders. But if the prediction instrument falsely identifies low-rate offenders as being in the high-rate category, a lot of offenders end up sitting in prison—and costing money—who should not be there.

- There is the issue, again, of justice: Is it fair to lock up someone for many years on the basis of a prediction instrument that cannot tell who is and is not a false positive? A false positive is sort of like a false conviction. To be sure, the offender is not innocent. But he or she is innocent, so to speak, of being a chronic offender. Even so, the offender may be given a prison sentence that covers most of his or her life.

Estimating the Incapacitation Effect: Studying Individual Offenders

As we probe the relative merits of competing correctional theories, it is clear that readers who suffered through those boring social science courses on *methods* will now see that their suffering was not wasted! We constantly have to think carefully about what *methodology* needs to be employed to measure accurately the *effects* of various correctional policies. In most cases, trying to show what actually exists out there in reality is a significant challenge. We often have to use different strategies, conduct multiple studies, and overcome biases in the data to estimate these policy effects.

What really aggravates Cullen and Jonson is when policy makers (*who often don't know any better*) and criminologists (*who should know better*) make pronouncements about the effects of policies in which they fully ignore the many methodological factors that might make their pronouncements either misleading or just plain wrong. In the end, we have to make policy decisions as to what to do with offenders. But make no mistake about it. Knowing what the evidence says on these issues takes considerable analysis of the data or, in the least, listening to those scholars who have actually done considerable analysis of the data.

This discussion is a prelude to our attempt to assess the size of the incapacitation effect. As we embark on this task, it is important to appreciate *three* things:

- Making an estimate of incapacitation involves very complex methodological issues.

- Despite the methodological challenges, we probably have a general sense of what the incapacitation effect might be.

- Whether this effect is large enough and/or can be specified precisely enough to be the basis of an effective correctional policy remains to be seen. In fact, it is something that cannot be settled definitively.

Finally, as we explain shortly, there are two strategies for estimating the incapacitation effect. First, the *top-down approach* involves a macro-level analysis of punishment and crime. Remember, when we study macro-level data, *think of circles!* The unit of analysis is some ecological area, such as a state (which can be represented as a circle!). As in macro-level deterrence studies, this strategy examines how levels of incarceration across states predict crime rates. A negative correlation—higher incarceration leads to lower crime rates—would suggest the existence of an incapacitation effect. We review this approach in the section after this one.

Second, the *bottom-up approach* involves studying individual offenders and trying to use their offending patterns to estimate how much crime would be prevented if they were locked up. Remember, when we study individuals, *think of stick figures—not circles!* The unit of analysis is the individual, and thus we collect data on individuals, usually through surveys that ask them questions. We review this approach in this section. This discussion is divided into two parts. One focuses on *inmate self-report surveys*; the other focuses on *longitudinal studies*.

INMATE SELF-REPORT STUDIES

Do you know what a *self-report survey* is? Well, it is when members of a sample—it could be students in a high school, people drawn from the community, or prison inmates—are given a list of questions that ask them to report how many crimes they have committed. They are usually asked about their participation in criminal activity for a specific period of time (e.g., in the last month, over the last year, in their lifetime). Most often, they are asked about crime in the past year. This period is called the *reference period* for the survey. Each question on the self-report survey would correspond to a particular kind of offense. Here are some examples:

In the last year (before being imprisoned), how many times did you do any of the following:

- Armed robbery—threatened someone with a weapon in order to get money or something else.
- Beat up or physically hurt someone badly.
- Cut someone with a knife.
- Burglary—broke into a home or business in order to take something.
- Got into a fistfight.
- Forced someone to have sex with you.
- Threatened to hurt someone with a gun, knife, or other weapon.
- Sold hard drugs.
- Forged a check or other paper.
- Stole a car.

The list of offenses on a self-report survey could be short or could be long (e.g., 50 or more questions). Now, here is a methodological question for you: Do you think that the number and types of offenses listed on the self-report survey could affect one's findings on how much crime people commit? Yes! Depending on what offenses are listed, the study could come up with differing counts of how many crimes people in the sample commit. So, in any self-report study, be aware that how questions are asked can affect what the study finds.

There are, of course, other potential problems with self-report surveys (e.g., people not telling the truth when asked to report the amount of their offending). Criminologists have studied these issues in detail, and we are not going to go into the issues here (or we might never finish this chapter!). But let us offer this general conclusion: Although some biases exist, self-report surveys are a pretty good way of measuring participation of the *crimes listed on the survey*. Obviously, they cannot measure crimes that are not listed on the survey.

With this as a background, think of yourself as a criminologist who is asked to find out *how many crimes per year are saved simply by taking offenders off the street and imprisoning them*. What, in short, is the *incapacitation effect*? How would you find this out?

As has been discussed, one way is to ask offenders how many crimes they commit in a given period, such as a year. That is, we could give offenders a self-report survey and ask them to disclose how many crimes they committed the previous 12 months. If the survey were constructed well—such as to cover the crimes that most concern us (e.g., robbery, burglary, violence, drug offenses)—we might be able to estimate how many of these specific crimes offenders commit each year. And once we had this information, we could take the number of crimes the offenders reported committing each year and compute how much crime would be prevented by locking up each of these offenders.

One problem we would confront is finding enough offenders to fill out our survey. Can you think of a place where a bunch of criminals are located and are sitting around all day with nothing to do but fill out some criminologist's survey? Right—we have the researcher's dream: *the prison!* So, as noted, one way criminologists have used to estimate how much crime is saved through incapacitation is a *self-report survey of offenders who are in prison*. Ideally, this survey would be conducted as soon as inmates arrived in prison. In that way, their memories would be fairly fresh about the offenses committed over the survey's reference period (e.g., past 12 months).

Again, the empirical goal is to calculate the number of offenses the entering inmates committed over the past year. In this way, it is possible to estimate how much crime would be saved by taking them off the street and locking them up. The assumption is that offenders' criminality is stable: that the number of crimes in the past year would equal the number of crimes the offenders would have committed if not arrested and incarcerated.

Finally, criminologists use a fancy Greek term to label the rate of offending per offender per year: *lambda*. There is a funny symbol (sort of like an inverted "Y") that is used to indicate *lambda*—λ.

A number of inmate studies have been conducted to try to calculate λ (Visher, 1987). We will discuss but one here, a study by John DiIulio and Ann Morrison Piehl (1991), with the knowledge that the findings from this research are fairly consistent. In 1990, DiIulio and Piehl took a random sample of 7% of the male inmate population in Wisconsin. They then gave the inmates a self-report survey that asked mainly about theft, robbery, burglary, assaults, and drug offenses. What did they find?

DiIulio and Piehl report both (1) the average or mean number of offenses and (2) the *median* number of offenses. The problem with mean scores is that a few outliers—respondents who report an enormous number of crimes—can inflate the mean score. This can give a misleading portrait of what the criminality is for the typical offender. As you may recall from your statistics class, another statistical measure of central tendency is the *median*. The median is the *midpoint* in the distribution of cases (which in our study is the distribution of how many crimes offenders report committing in the past year, which might range from zero to several hundred or more). The median is the point at which half the cases fall below and half fall above. (For example, let's say that five offenders were surveyed and they reported committing this many crimes: 2, 3, 8, 15, and 39. The median or midpoint of this distribution of offending would be 8. There are two cases below 8 and two above.)

Here is the punch line. When DiIulio and Piehl use the median as their measure, the typical yearly crime rate per offender is 12. This number excludes drug offenses. When drug offenses are included, the median rises to 26. We can debate whether or not we want to include drug offenses when computing *crimes saved*. In a way, this depends on what kind of incapacitation effect you wish to compute and what you hope prisons to accomplish from a policy perspective. The value in having both figures is that it allows you to say how many regular crimes prisons save and how many drug offenses prisons save. This information may be relevant to different policy discussions.

But let's just take the *median* number of *crimes* saved: 12. This means that if a typical offender remains on the street, this individual will commit, on average, a *dozen* crimes or *one per month*. Cullen and Jonson certainly would not want this offender living in our neighborhoods! From this vantage point, the *incapacitation effect* thus seems pretty meaningful. For advocates of prison, this is good news. For bleeding-heart liberal criminologists, this empirical reality is disconcerting and cannot be ignored. But there is more to this story, as readers might have already imagined.

LONGITUDINAL STUDIES

As noted in Chapter 4 on deterrence, it is critical to examine different *types of evidence* when trying to calculate the effects of a criminal sanction. In this regard, the use of prison inmates is a potential problem because they are a select group of offenders and they are being asked to recall what might have occurred over the previous year. Put another way, the inmate self-report studies are valuable, but we would have more confidence in their findings if similar results were produced by using an alternative method.

This is where longitudinal studies become relevant. This methodological approach follows a group of people—ideally a random sample of some population—for a number of years. Innovative researchers figured out that these data sets might allow them to investigate incapacitation. Why? Because some members of the sample would end up in prison at some point during the study. It might then become possible to estimate how many crimes they would have committed if they had not been locked up (see, e.g., Bhati, 2007; Blokland & Nieuwbeerta, 2007; Owens, 2009; Sweeten & Apel, 2007; see also Bushway & Paternoster, 2009).

Gary Sweeten and Robert Apel (2007) give an excellent example of this type of research. They decided to reanalyze the National Longitudinal Study of Youth (NLSY) data set. They were able to come up with 262 usable cases of sample members incarcerated between the ages of 16 and 19 in a jail, juvenile institution, or prison. What makes Sweeten and Apel's approach pretty neat is that it used a fancy statistical technique called *propensity-score matching*. Read their article if you are high on statistical prowess or statistical masochism, but we can explain their approach simply.

- First, take the 262 incarcerated youths.

- Second, based on a host of variables, match this group to youths in the sample fortunate enough not to have been incarcerated. The key issue is to make the two groups as similar as possible in their criminal propensity (which is why this is called propensity-score matching).

- Third, then look at how many offenses the matched sample of non-incarcerated offenders committed while the incarcerated group was locked up.

- Fourth, if the two groups—those locked up and those not locked up—are the same in their propensity to offend, then the number of crimes committed by the matched sample should be an excellent proxy for what those who were incarcerated would have committed. This is the *incapacitation effect*—the number of crimes saved.

From the National Longitudinal Survey of Youth, Sweeten and Apel used self-reported offenses to calculate criminal participation in:

- Intentional destruction of property.
- Petty theft (under 50 dollars).
- Major theft (over 50 dollars, including automobile theft).
- Other property crimes (e.g., fencing stolen goods).
- Attacking someone with the intent to commit serious harm.
- Selling illegal drugs.

The selection of these offenses is potentially problematic in two ways. First, it excludes a range of other kinds of crimes (e.g., robbery, burglary). Second, it includes offenses that are relatively non-serious and, as such, may not be of much concern to us when talking about putting offenders in prison (e.g., petty theft). Be that as it may, what did Sweeten and Apel find?

Although their lambda (λ) is lower than that found for the inmates, they too report a meaningful incapacitation effect of between 4.9 and 14.1 offenses. Specifically:

- For juveniles ages 16 and 17, the annual incapacitation effect is between 6.2 and 14.1 offenses saved.

- For adults ages 18 and 19, the annual incapacitation effect is between 4.9 and 8.4 offenses saved.

NOT SO QUICK: DON'T LOCK UP EVERYONE YET

So, studying incapacitation may seem simple. We do a self-report study and then calculate how many crimes per offender per year we save. The results seem straightforward. We are ready to tell what the incapacitation effect is and ready to make correctional policy. Right? Well, *not so quick!*

The problem is that we are assuming several things that may not be totally true. For example, we are assuming that each year an offender stays in prison, his or her lambda—his or her rate of offending—remains constant. That is, we get the same crime savings the first year an offender is locked up as we do the last year an offender is locked up. But this may not be true. There are a bunch of fine points like this that suggest that the incapacitation effect reported by these self-report surveys—such as that conducted by DiIulio and Piehl—is *inflated.* There are three issues to consider.

- *First, let us consider the issue just mentioned, which criminologists call the aging effect.*

We know that participation in crime declines with age (this is sometimes called the age–crime curve). The older people get, the less crime they commit. Can you figure out what implications this has for estimating the incapacitation effect? Well, it means that on a self-report survey, an offender—we will call him James—tells how many crimes he committed in the last year he was free in society. But how old was James at this time? Say he was 25. Now, as this inmate ages—gets older—what would his yearly crime rate (lambda) have been if he were still in the community? Say he was 35 or 45 years of age?

What this means, of course, is that putting James in prison might have saved 12 crimes a year at age 25, maybe 5 crimes a year at age 35, and 0 crimes a year at age 45. So, the incapacitation effect may well decline with age. Studies that do not take this into account, like the one by DiIulio and Piehl, mislead us as to how much crime will be saved. They do not figure into their calculations the aging effect. To be sure, Sweeten and Apel's (2007) research did examine two age groups, but note that the estimated incapacitation effect for one year declined markedly from the 16- to 17-year-old group (between 6.2 and 14.1 offenses prevented) to the 18- to 19-year-old group (between 4.9 and 8.4 offenses prevented). This suggests that as offenders age in prison, the incapacitation effect diminishes.

- *Second, there is also something called the replacement effect.*

These studies assume that when offenders are in prison, the crimes they committed will no longer be committed. This assumes, however, that no offender's place will be taken by another person. But, in fact, it is possible that the crime position vacated by the offender might be filled—and filled by someone who might not have committed any crime had not this crime position become open (sort of like filling a job position after someone leaves; the same amount of work continues to be done by the person's replacement).

We do not really know what the size of the replacement effect is. Most obviously, the replacement effect is probably high for drug-selling offenses. When one offender is locked up, there is a supply of others willing to take his or her place. For homicide or rape, the replacement effect may be low and hover near zero. For crimes committed in groups—like, say, burglary or robbery—unless all members of the group are imprisoned, some replacement is likely to occur. Group members are likely to recruit a replacement and keep committing the same number of crimes as they did before one of their members was sent to prison. The upshot of all this is that locking up a single offender does not always prevent as much crime as advocates of incapacitation suggest.

- *Third, there is something called the labeling effect.*

This idea comes from labeling theory and was discussed in the last chapter. We do not know for certain that imprisonment is criminogenic, but there is a likelihood that the prison experience has an overall effect of increasing reoffending (Nagin et al., 2009). If so, then any incapacitation effect is eroded by this labeling effect.

Another consideration is the effect that incarcerating lots of people from one community has on that area's crime rate, such as when a high percentage of African American, inner-city males are locked up. Clear (2007, p. 5) calls this *concentrated incarceration*. The data on the racial divide in incarceration are disquieting. In their lifetimes, about one third of African American males will serve time in prison compared to about 6% of Whites (Nagin et al., 2009). On any given day in the United States, 11.9% of Blacks are behind bars—a rate that is "5 to 7 times greater than those for white males in the same age groups" (Harrison & Beck, 2006, p. 10). Most instructive in terms of inner-city communities are the statistics for men ages 20 to 40 who are high school dropouts. For Whites, 6.7% are in prison or jail on any given day. For African Americans in this category, the figure is a whopping 32.4% (Western, 2006). As Wacquant (2009) summarizes the issue:

An astonishing 60 percent of African Americans born between 1965 and 1969 who did not complete high school had been convicted of a felony and had served time in a state penitentiary by 1999. This nationwide rate suggests that the vast majority of black men from the core of the ghetto pass through the prison at the beginning of the twenty-first century. (p. 207)

There are basically two views on this matter:

- *Mass incarceration lowers crime in poor neighborhoods.* This is the view of John DiIulio (1994). When many African American offenders are incarcerated, the primary beneficiaries are their likely victims: Residents of minority, inner-city communities. DiIulio sees incarceration as a form of government investment in the inner cities. It costs money, but predators—each of whom commits 12 or more crimes a year—are off the streets. Imprisoning Black super-predators saves Black lives.

- *Mass incarceration increases crime in poor neighborhoods.* This is the view of Todd Clear and Dina Rose (Clear, 2007; Rose & Clear, 1998). In their view, the policy of incarcerating large numbers of young minority males ultimately backfires. No community can survive, let alone thrive, when a high proportion of its male population—generation after generation— spends critical parts of their lives in prison. Job markets fall apart, families do not form, and the community must constantly try to reintegrate men who have been in prison. In the long run, whatever benefits one gets from incapacitation are overwhelmed by the breakdown of the very fabric of communities.

To be honest, we do not know for certain which of these views is correct. It seems certain that incarcerating African American offenders has an incapacitation effect that should reduce crime in local communities where they are most likely to victimize others. Even so, it also seems plausible that, as described by Clear and Rose, a simultaneous community-level effect exists that is criminogenic (see also Lynch & Sabol, 2000). If so, then the incapacitation effect depicted in self-report surveys overestimates the amount of crime that is saved through mass imprisonment, at least in inner-city neighborhoods.

So, there is an important point that we want you to take from this discussion: *Computing the incapacitation effect based on self-report surveys is complex.* Thus, we start out computing an incapacitation estimate based on a self-report survey. But before settling on this estimate, we have to take into account aging, replacement, and labeling effects. Wow! That's a lot! And that is also why we really do not know what the incapacitation effect is, based on self-report surveys. We have an idea, but precise estimates are difficult.

Cullen and Jonson do not deny that there is an incapacitation effect. Even if it is at the lower end of the estimates—say somewhere between 4 and 12 offenses a year—that is a lot of crime saved. Again, if you were the judge and you knew that the offender standing before you would commit four crimes if released into the community, what would you say? Would you say: "Well, because you will break the law only four times in the next year, I am happy to let you roam free in my community. Have a nice day." Or would you say: "Well, because you will break the law four times in the next year, I am going to put your stupid rear end in jail. See you in a year." Of course, there is more to it than this—an issue we return to at the chapter's end.

Estimating the Incapacitation Effect: Macro-Level Studies

SPELMAN'S RESEARCH

As noted, in studying incapacitation, scholars distinguish between *bottom-up* and *top-down* approaches. A *bottom-up* approach is the one described above in the self-report survey. It is called *bottom-up* because it starts out by surveying individual offenders and then tries to estimate from these data how much crime offenders commit and, in turn, how much crime prisons save. A *top-down* approach never talks with or surveys individual offenders. Rather, it infers from *macro-level data* what the incapacitation effect is.

Macro-level incapacitation studies are identical to macro-level deterrence studies: Both try to see how the level of incarceration is related to the level of crime. If crime is lower where prison use is higher, they both have an effect. It is just that some scholars claim a deterrence effect (which is why they are called deterrence scholars), whereas others claim an incapacitation effect (which is why they are called incapacitation scholars).

As alluded to in Chapter 4, top-down macro-level studies cannot tell us whether there is lower crime because (1) people are being scared straight or (2) offenders are locked up and thus not committing crimes. Politicians really do not care whether crime reductions are due to deterrence or incapacitation. Lower crime, after all, is lower crime. But criminologists do care because the effects are analytically different and may have different implications for policy. Although nobody knows for sure, most scholars think that when imprisonment and crime rates are inversely related—prisons ↑ and crime rates ↓—it is really an incapacitation effect (largely because other measures of deterrence do not seem to have strong effects).

A number of really good top-down, macro-level analyses of incapacitation exist (for a listing, see Spelman, 2000a, p. 102). Nonetheless, the best is a complex and comprehensive essay by William Spelman (2000b). So, how much crime do prisons actually save? One way of talking about this issue is to use the term *elasticity*. Spelman (2000b) defines elasticity as "the percentage change in the crime rate associated with a 1 percent change in the prison population" (p. 421). That is, if we increase the prison population by 1%, how much does the crime rate change? After much analysis, Spelman provides his best estimate—based on the most rigorous macro-level studies available.

- He states that a 1% increase in the prison population decreases crime between 0.16% and 0.31%.

- If we calculate this out to some larger numbers, it may be more understandable. Thus, a 10% increase in the prison population would reduce the crime rate by between 1.6% and 3.1%. A 100% increase—a doubling of the prison population—might reduce crime between 16% and 31%.

What Spelman's research shows, therefore, is that there is an incapacitation effect and that it can be large if we decide to have large increases in the size of our prisons. For example, in another analysis, Spelman (2000a) examined the impact of imprisonment on what has been called "the great American crime drop" (Blumstein & Wallman, 2000; Rosenfeld, 2009). Crime rates had shot up in the early 1990s and then, suddenly and largely inexplicably, declined rapidly over the next decade. They have stayed at low levels since that time (Rosenfeld, 2009). Why did this occur? Did mass imprisonment play a role? The answer is "yes."

According to Spelman (2000a), however, this is a qualified "yes," not a resounding call for more prison expansion. As he notes, even without a prison boom, violent crime would have declined markedly. Incarceration was but a contributing factor—not unimportant but not all-powerful. Thus, Spelman (2000a) argues that the "crime drop would have been 27 percent smaller than it actually was, had the prison buildup never taken place" (p. 123). He reminds us of the trade-off for this crime savings:

> Over the past twenty years, the fifty American states have engaged in one of the great policy experiments of modern times. In an attempt to reduce intolerably high levels of reported crime, the states have doubled their prison populations, then doubled them again, increasing their costs by more than $20 billion per year. . . . That $20 billion could provide child care for every family that cannot afford it, or a college education to every high school graduate, or a living-wage job to every unemployed youth. (p. 97)

Whether the trade-off was worth it, of course, is what policy makers and voters must decide.

COMPLICATING MATTERS: TWO OTHER STUDIES

As good as Spelman's research is, it is but one study. As other research has appeared, the incapacitation waters have become muddied a bit. We review two studies that complicate matters—making it harder to have a clear view of the incapacitation effect.

First, as Spelman (2000b) realizes, one problem with most top-down studies is that they use the same data set: 50 states in which imprisonment rates and crime rates are analyzed either at one given time (a cross-sectional study) or over time (a longitudinal or time-series study). This approach makes sense because each state has a prison system and a crime rate. Still, if the incapacitation effect is real or at least stable, then it should be found when other kinds of data are collected and analyzed.

In this regard, Kovandzic and Vieraitis (2006) argue that there is a need to examine the incapacitation effects of imprisonment using smaller units of analysis where measurement error might not be as pronounced. Using state-level data may result in something called *aggregation bias* and in the inability to control for relevant factors. As an alternative, they examine 58 Florida counties from 1980 to 2000. Somewhat astoundingly, they conclude that in contrast to previous studies, there was "no evidence that increases in prison population growth covary with decreases in crime rates" (p. 213).

To be sure, this is only one study in one state. It needs to be replicated. But if the same results were produced over multiple jurisdictions, it would call into question the finding that locking offenders up always leads to reductions in crime.

Second, Liedka, Piehl, and Useem (2006) explored whether elasticity or the amount of crime saved from each percentage growth in incarceration was stable or changed depending on the size of the prison population. They discovered that over the past 30 years, the expansion of prisons saved crime in the early years. However, as prison populations have grown, their effects have reached a point of *diminishing returns*.

That is, when prison populations are low, locking people up has a high elasticity—it saves crime. When prison populations are high, locking people up has a low elasticity—it does not save much crime. Their findings thus call into question the wisdom of further prison expansion. As Liedka et al. (2006) conclude:

> Prison expansion is expensive in the costs it imposes on both those who serve time behind bars and in absorbing tax dollars. Policy discussion should be informed by the limitation of the fact that prison expansion, beyond a certain point, will no longer serve any reasonable purpose. It seems that that point has been reached. (p. 272)

Conclusion: Compared to What?

Looking back, Cullen and Jonson understand that traveling through this chapter has been more like climbing a mountain, scaling flat walls, trudging through rugged terrain, and gasping for air as the peak was in sight. Now that you are standing on the peak, what do you see?

Well, the view of incapacitation is a bit cloudy. Still, when all the evidence is stacked together, it is clear that locking offenders up prevents crime. Because most people who enter prison are in the middle of a criminal career, sending them to prison interrupts their illegal activities and saves society a bunch of crime. This conclusion is supported by individual-level bottom-up studies and macro-level top-down studies. When different types of data reach the same conclusion, the finding must be seen as reliable. Prisons have a meaningful incapacitation effect. Even bleeding-heart criminologists such as Cullen and Jonson can see that. The evidence is, after all, the evidence.

We do not know precisely how large the incapacitation effect is. Criminologists, who as we have admitted do not like imprisonment, do their best to explain why prisons do not prevent crime by highlighting a bunch of effects that counteract incapacitation: aging, replacement, labeling, and so on. These are important, as we have discussed. Still, it is likely that putting someone behind bars prevents somewhere between 4 and 10 crimes a year, depending on how crime is measured. If an average of about 2.2 million offenders are in prison over the course of a year, the annual savings in crime would rise into the millions. Do the math: 2.2×4 or 2.2×10. That is a multiplication problem that might make you a strong advocate of prisons!

But before running out to campaign for new prison construction, realize that all incapacitation studies have a major assumption hidden within them that makes them *fundamentally flawed*. After all this, are Cullen and Jonson saying that incapacitation studies are misleading? The answer is "yes." Why? Because these studies *compare imprisonment to doing nothing with the offender* (Spelman, 2000b). Huh? Believe it! Cullen and Jonson are telling the truth! When scholars compute the incapacitation effect, they assume that if offenders are not in prison, the alternative would be *allowing the offender to roam free on the street*.

Of course, this is a ridiculous comparison that wildly inflates the incapacitation effect *relative to some other sanction*. If offenders are not sent to prison, the judge does not say: "Go ye forth and victimize, young chap!" Rather, some form of supervision is enacted. Thus, the proper comparison ought to be *how much crime is saved by locking someone up as opposed to using an alternative correctional intervention*.

What else might be done with an offender? In the least, one might expect that an offender would be placed under some form of community supervision. Although limited, research suggests that criminal activity declines when offenders are placed on probation versus no intervention at all (MacKenzie, Browning, Skroban, & Smith, 1999). But let's go one step further: How about placing the offender in a high-quality, intensive rehabilitation program?

Thus, the problem with current studies is that in estimating whether incapacitation works—is a prudent crime control policy—they *ignore the key policy question: Does incapacitation work better than what might be used in its place?* Could the money spent on prisons be used to purchase more crime savings through other means? Elliott Currie (1998) captures this point nicely in his book when he asks whether a prison sentence:

> "works" better for an addicted burglar than a course of drug treatment outside prison walls. . . . If the question is whether marginal increases in incarceration of repeat nonviolent offenders "work" better than investment in high-quality prevention programs for at-risk adolescents, it is increasingly clear that the answer is "no." And if the question is whether an overall national strategy of sinking more and more resources into the prisons while slighting other crucial public investments can effectively protect us from violent crime, then history would seem to offer a particularly compelling negative. (p. 55)

In a like vein, Joan Petersilia (1992) makes a similar assessment when she notes that "every additional prison guard may mean one less teacher employed, and every prison cell constructed may mean a gang-prevention program unfunded" (p. 33).

In short, we have seen by the research reviewed in this chapter that prisons do have an incapacitation effect. Even so, taken by itself, this research is virtually meaningless. In formulating correctional policy, we must consider whether the crime savings from prisons outweigh what might be achieved through (1) other correctional sanctions or programs and/or (2) other social programs that might attack the root causes of crime (i.e., early intervention programs). In the chapters to follow, we consider what some of these alternative approaches to saving crime might entail.

Let us close with one cautionary remark. A powerful attraction of prisons is that they can achieve an incapacitation effect without much effort. Yes, they cost a lot of money. But they also exist and we can cram a lot of people into them. Unless the anti-prison crowd can develop effective alternatives to warehousing offenders, then warehousing it might well be (Petersilia & Cullen, 2015).

PART III

The Social Welfare Response

6

Restorative Justice

Reintegrative Shaming

John Braithwaite
Australian National University
Author of *Crime, Shame and Reintegration*

Cullen and Jonson like many of those who embrace restorative justice. Why? Because they are nice people. They believe in making peace rather than war on crime. It is not that they are blind to the harm crime causes. Rather, they just believe that responding to harm with harm only begets more harm. They are persuaded that we should, as the saying goes, "hate the sin and love the sinner." That is, we should morally condemn a harmful criminal act but not give up on the person who committed this act. If we can find a way to restore rather than to reject wayward individuals, then they might be able to take steps to restore their victims, make amends to the community, and become good and productive citizens.

Advocates of restorative justice truly favor justice—for victims and the offender—but believe that the justice will not be found by seeking retribution. Again, retribution or just deserts seeks to balance the scales of justice by inflicting harm on an offender commensurate with the harm caused. Restorative justice thinks this is nuts and doomed only to make matters worse. All one is left with is two harmed parties—the victims and the offender. Nobody is made whole or bettered by this experience.

John Braithwaite is one of Cullen and Jonson's favorite restorative justice advocates. In 1989, Braithwaite wrote a classic book that provided the theoretical basis for restorative justice titled *Crime, Shame and Reintegration*. Braithwaite was already a well-known scholar from Australia, but this volume made him really famous. Unknown criminologists rarely get asked to do anything, but universities like to have influential scholars stop by and give talks on their research. They even pay them to do so. Once Braithwaite became really famous, he was invited to visit the University of Cincinnati and to lecture on his perspective. He gave a marvelous presentation.

During his visit, Braithwaite stayed in Cullen's third-floor guest room. Cullen's golden retriever, Topspin, pilfered various pieces of Braithwaite's clothing. True to his convictions, Braithwaite did not ask that retributive justice be meted out to Topspin. He merely asked that his shoes and underwear be restored to his room. But he would suffer a deeper victimization that would test his convictions even further.

While out jogging one morning (Cullen was eating a jelly donut at the time), Braithwaite was assaulted, leaving his glasses bent and his face bloodied. How could this occur in a peaceful, safe neighborhood? Apparently, a squirrel—we will call him Rocky—was walking across a telephone wire and fell off. As fate would have it, the squirrel landed on Braithwaite's face—good for the squirrel whose fall was broken but not so good for the famous Australian criminologist.

Braithwaite managed to hobble back to Cullen's house, where he was greeted by Cullen's kind-hearted daughter. She rushed upstairs to Cullen who, having finished his jelly donut, was at his computer, in deep thought, and not wishing to be disturbed. She told Cullen that Braithwaite had been attacked by a squirrel. Thinking his daughter was joking—thinking that this must be some odd ruse that is humorous back in Australia—Cullen laughed, declined to be duped by such an absurd story, and went back to work. Braithwaite was not impressed. He accused Cullen (1994), author of social support theory, of not being appropriately supportive. With the help of Larry Travis, Cullen would make amends later, sending Braithwaite a University of Cincinnati hat with a stuffed-animal squirrel sewn to the top of the hat. Braithwaite has worn this hat proudly.

Notably, Braithwaite did not call for his attacker, Rocky the squirrel, to be hunted down and punished for the vicious assault. He was more upset that Cullen thought this was all amusing. Instead, Braithwaite merely wanted his glasses straightened, his cuts cleaned, and his life returned to its former state of happiness. This was done. Restorative justice was achieved! He was relieved to depart Cullen's house. Topspin still plays with someone's underwear. It looks Australian, but we are not certain it is Braithwaite's.

Cullen and Jonson know that this story, though true, is sort of ridiculous. But in an odd way, it leads us directly into the topic of restorative justice. In everyday life, many of us experience harms—usually small (as in the case of Braithwaite) but at times large. How should we respond when these harms occur? If our property is stolen or our bodies assaulted, it is natural to be angry and to succumb to the impulse to make our victimizer suffer some harm. Only saints do not feel this way.

But apart from individual personal sentiments, the question writ large is whether a criminal justice system will make sense if it is the embodiment of this outrage and thirst for vengeance. Will this system end up making victims better off? Will it give them true justice? And beyond this consideration, will it make society safer? Advocates of restorative justice, such as Braithwaite, answer these questions "no," "no," and "no." As a result, they urge us to implement a system that does not fall into the trap of seeing harming offenders as the only way to achieve justice. There is, they fervently believe, another way: restorative justice.

We thus begin this chapter with a section probing in a bit more detail what restorative justice is and why it has enjoyed a measure of popularity. We then discuss three concerns that Cullen and Jonson have about this correctional theory: the challenge of achieving justice, the difficulty of doing restorative justice in an age of mass imprisonment, and the weak scientific foundation of restorative justice. Despite these reservations, the existing evaluations of restorative justice programs have yielded some promising results. These are reviewed. We end the chapter by examining the core lesson of restorative justice—the limits of harm.

The Concept of Restorative Justice

In recent years, a number of jurisdictions in a number of countries have been experimenting with a sentencing philosophy called *restorative justice* (Sullivan & Tifft, 2008; Van Ness & Strong, 2010). Now, if you want to be a cool dude—or cool dudette—you need to know that none of the perspective's insiders use the term *restorative justice*. Instead, they refer to their correctional theory by its two-letter acronym, "*RJ*." Thus, Cullen and Jonson will occasionally use RJ when we do not want to write out restorative justice. We are not RJ insiders, but we are cool. Cullen is the cool dude; Jonson is the cool dudette!

What is *restorative justice* or, as we cool folks call it, *RJ?* Well, to answer this question, it is necessary to contrast it with the traditional system we now use—regardless of whether we seek to punish or rehabilitate. In the traditional criminal justice system, the government (or "state") acts as an *adversary.* Its role is to convict the defendant and then to do something to him or her. This invariably involves imposing some type of punishment or "harm" on the offender, although the sentence can incorporate attempts to improve the offender through rehabilitation.

In this whole process, however, one must wonder: *Where is the victim?* Where is the person or persons *who have been harmed by the offender?* Why are they *virtually invisible* in this process? How do they *benefit from the offender's punishment?*

In an ideal situation, the state represents the interests of the victim. The victim's harm is balanced by the state *punishing the offender.* At times, judges might require offenders to make restitution to the victim. (The victim can also sue the offender for damages in civil court—as happened in the O. J. Simpson case—but the relative poverty of many offenders makes this an infrequently used option.) But situations often are not ideal. The state most often plea bargains with offenders, treats victims as third parties with little say in what is done with the offenders, and does little to help victims—other than the psychic satisfaction victims draw from what punishment is doled out to the offenders. In the end—and this is a key criticism of the existing system voiced by advocates of restorative justice—the process ends with victims living with the harm that has befallen them and often with offenders more likely to harm again.

What, then, is the alternative? Well, RJ starts with a very different understanding of what sentencing and corrections should seek to accomplish. The thrust of restorative justice can be summarized in three central principles:

- *Crime causes harm*—to victims, to the community, and to the offender.
- The goal of sentencing/corrections should be to reverse the harm that has been caused by the criminal act.
- This goal is accomplished by sentencing and correctional practices that seek to *restore victims, the community, and the offender to their original state* (i.e., to what they were like before the crime inflicted its harm).

Now, how does *RJ* hope to accomplish this *restoration?* On a broad level, it involves two approaches:

- *The victim becomes central to the sentencing process.* The state acts more as an arbiter than as an adversary. Its role is to provide victims with a chance to have their voice heard and their interests represented.
- *The goal is to reintegrate the offender into the community.* The offender's action—his or her crime—is shamed and must be compensated for. But the special challenge is to shame the act without forever stigmatizing the person. The goal, that is, is "to hate the sin but to love the sinner." The offender, for better or for worse, is a member of the community. Unless he or she is reintegrated into the community, further crime—further harmful behavior—is likely to result.

Of course, the critical question is how these goals—how all this *restoration*—will be accomplished. Tony McCold (2008) suggests that the restorative process must involve two key components: "(1) victims and their offenders in face-to-face meetings, where (2) they determine the outcome" (p. 23). These requirements can be met in different ways, but a common RJ approach is the *victim–offender conference,* a meeting that brings together, in one place, the victim, offender, relatives of the victim and offender, community members, and a mediator (also sometimes called a facilitator).

The purpose is for the offender to show contrition, to develop a strategy for the offender to restore the victim (e.g., restitution), and to develop a strategy for the offender to restore the community (e.g., community service). At these conferences, the victim conveys how the crime has harmed him or her. The offender sees, first-hand, the harm that has been caused. The offender is unable to ignore what he or she has done. An offender's family members might express their shame and apologize. The offender might also apologize (but this does not always occur). At the end of the conference, a plan is devised as to how the offender will compensate the victim (e.g., pay for property damaged). The offender might also be required to do community service. It is possible as well that efforts will be made to enlist the offender's family members to take steps to ensure that their wayward relative will not recidivate. Promises might be made to help the offender if he or she fulfills the requirements for restitution and community service.

In essence, there is an *exchange* that occurs. The offender will be given the chance to reintegrate into the community if the offender does his or her part in being genuinely contrite and in restoring harm through restitution and community service. Restoration, in short, is contingent on the restorative actions of the offender. There is no "free lunch," so to speak.

Based on his extensive experience with RJ and conferences, John Braithwaite (1998) has provided a scenario of how restorative justice would work with a teenager arrested for robbery, who he calls "Sam." You should read the original to capture the full flavor of what RJ and a conference entail (see 1998, pp. 326–328). We only have space to pull out some key quotations to convey a sense of the realities of RJ.

Braithwaite (1998) notes that the conference brings together a facilitator, the victim and her daughter, and Sam. Sam rejects efforts to invite his parents (he was abused and is now homeless) and teachers (he is a school dropout). He agrees to have at the conference an older sister, Uncle George who was always good to him, and a former hockey coach who had treated him fairly. These six people thus sit in a conference to seek restoration. Braithwaite describes how the victim shares the inconvenience of having to cancel her stolen credit cards and of not having money to shop on the day of the robbery. Her daughter explains how her mother fears going outside on her own.

Sam's first reaction, however, is simply to "sneer" and to "appear callous throughout" (p. 327). At a break, Sam's sister is upset but also tells Sam that, similar to him, she also was abused by their parents. Here is what Braithwaite says happens next:

> When the conference reconvenes, Sam's sister speaks to him with love and strength. Looking straight into his eyes, the first gaze he could not avoid in the conference, she says that she knows exactly what he has been through with their parents. No details are spoken. But the victim seems to understand what is spoken of by the knowing communication between sister and brother. Tears rush down the old woman's cheeks and over her trembling mouth. (p. 327)

Sam is not immune to the conference's emotional transformation. Here is how he responds:

> It is his sister's love that penetrates Sam's callous exterior. . . . He says he is sorry about what the victim has lost. He would like to pay it back but has no money or job. He assures the victim he is not stalking her. She readily accepts this now. (p. 327)

Reassured, the victim now starts to reach out to her victimizer:

> She wants her money back but says it will help her if they can talk about what to do to help Sam find a home and a job. Sam's sister says he can live in her house for a while. The hockey coach says he has some casual work that needs to be done, enough to pay Sam's debt to the victim and a bit more. (p. 327)

In the end, the victim's harm is mitigated. Sam takes responsibility for his bad acts and is restored to a life with possibilities:

> When the conference breaks up, the victim hugs Sam and tearfully wishes him good luck. He apologizes again. Uncle George quietly slips a hundred dollars to Sam's sister to defray the extra cost of having Sam in the house, and says he will be there for both of them if they need him. (p. 328)

What would have occurred in the regular criminal justice system? The offender would have been arrested and perhaps sent off to an institution for six months, where his callousness would have deepened and where he would have associated with other troubled teens. He would not have reconnected with his sister, uncle, or former coach. He would have left the correctional institution with no job or place to live. His likelihood of recidivating would have been high. Meanwhile, the victim would likely have received no restitution from her destitute victimizer, would have experienced no closure on this bad event, and might have remained afraid of this unknown offender and been unable to leave her house with peace of mind (see Braithwaite, 1998, p. 326). In the end, harming the offender would only have begotten more harm.

Why would anyone wish to defend a system of this sort—a system that produces high rates of recidivism and does little to truly help victims? What is worse, punishing offenders—harming offenders—is often sold to the public, including those who experience crime, as being *for the victim*. There might be some satisfaction in knowing that a thief or predator is suffering behind bars. But such satisfaction, if it does in fact exist, is mostly fools' gold. The victim receives little material compensation, receives no expression of contrition from the offender, and receives no opportunity to participate in saving the offender from a life in crime. If anything, the victim—and those who know the victim—are enticed to hate the offender and to take pleasure in vengeance. Little good, in short, is produced by a correctional process that is committed to inflicting pain.

The Appeal of Restorative Justice

Okay, be honest. Similar to Cullen and Jonson, don't you want to just run out and hug Sam, too? Yes, you would have to go to Australia and stay at Braithwaite's house to do so. But John is a generous guy! We might even be able to travel together—dudes and dudettes!—and do a group hug with Sam. We could all become mates. RJ rocks, doesn't it?

Part of restorative justice's appeal is that the current adversarial system is at times so mindlessly punitive that it seems to have lost its way. It has no broad social purpose (Allen, 1981). It seems to feed our baser instincts—the desire for vengeance—but it does not encourage us to allow our nobler, altruistic instincts to play a role in shaping how we react to people who have done bad things. It leaves no space for people of faith and good will to move beyond their understandable anger and ask, as Christians often do, "What would Jesus do?" We might justify the infliction of pain by evoking fancy terms such as "just deserts" and "retribution." But a close inspection of what actually goes on in the correctional system reveals an enormous amount of effort and money wasted on inflicting pain on offenders that accomplishes very little. Or so say the advocates of RJ.

These observations lead Cullen and Jonson to the first of *three reasons* why they believe that RJ is an appealing theory of corrections (see also Cullen, Sundt, & Wozniak, 2001): *Everyone seems to benefit.* As noted, in the traditional system it seems that *everyone loses.* The victims are ignored and at times feel "twice victimized"—once by the offender, once by the way they are treated by prosecutors and the courts. Offenders are punished, but many Americans have a suspicion that prisons only delay the time when offenders will be back in the community wreaking havoc again.

In contrast, RJ's focus on *restoring harm* seems to help everyone out—to leave everyone better off. Thus, victims may receive the apology they have been seeking and may be compensated for their loss. The community might benefit from the offender's community service. And the offender is held accountable for his or her actions and then set on a path in which responsible behavior is possible (first by restoring the harm he or she has caused, and then by becoming an accepted member of the community again).

Unless you are irrational, how can anybody be against a system that has utility for everyone? Who can be against an approach to sentencing and corrections in which harm is lessened and victims, the community, and the offender are benefited?

Okay, now let's turn to the second reason why RJ has grown popular: *Both conservatives and liberals find something to support in restorative justice.* Everyone thus can like it! One premise (and a popular one at that!) of conservative approaches to crime is that the correctional system "pays too much attention to the offender" and "neglects the victim." Often, this view has led conservatives to favor "victim rights," which has translated into supporting harsher punishments for offenders. (It is questionable whether harsher punishments actually help victims, since rehabilitation might prevent more people from being victimized. But this is an issue for another time and place!)

RJ appeals to conservatives precisely because victims are placed center stage. Victims are given the option of confronting their victimizer. The harm suffered by victims is recognized, and they potentially benefit directly from the restorative action (e.g., restitution) of the offender. In short, conservatives like RJ because it extends victim rights and possibly serves the interests of victims.

Liberals, on the other hand, endorse restorative justice because they believe it benefits offenders. A central premise of the liberal approach to corrections is that prisons are overused, needlessly inflict pain on offenders (many of whom were born into the worst neighborhoods in the nation), and make offenders more likely to recidivate. As a result, they tend to favor *any policy that limits the use of imprisonment.* In this regard, RJ is a correctional intervention that mainly *takes place in the community.* It is a strategy that seeks to have offenders restore harm through their actions in the community. It also is an approach that sees offenders not as permanently stigmatized but as *restored to the community.* It is not an approach that seeks to inflict more pain or harm on offenders.

Of course, when conservatives and liberals support the *same* policy, this is "good news" and "bad news." The good news is that the policy—in this case RJ—is likely to enjoy bipartisan support and to have a chance of being implemented. The bad news is that each side—conservatives and liberals—might have a different vision of what RJ should look like and what its main value is. In such cases, conflict might ensue and one side's vision will not be realized. As discussed in Chapter 3, this is precisely what occurred with the movement to constrain state discretion through determinate sentencing. Liberals hoped to achieve just deserts but instead helped to usher in harsh legislations and, to their dismay, mass imprisonment (Cullen & Gilbert, 1982). Conservatives might not, in fact, misshape RJ, using it to add on punishments, for example, to offenders who might only have received a slap on the wrist. But liberals who wish to use RJ to reduce punishment—to send fewer offenders to prison—should beware of who they are sleeping with in this reform movement!

We have a third and final reason for restorative justice's appeal: *RJ is based on an accountability/social exchange model and not on a social welfare model.* If rehabilitation has a weakness, it is that it appears to be a case where those least deserving in society—criminals—are given social welfare services that many other people in society do not receive. As writers such as David Garland (1990, 2001) point out, the United States has been in the process of rejecting such a *welfare model* generally for more than two decades (see also Murray, 1984). Recall the movement away from welfare in the 1990s—a time described by Nicolaus Mills (1997) as marked by "the triumph of meanness."

Why don't Americans like welfare? Well, they do not like it when people are "given something for nothing." They do not mind helping out the "deserving poor"—those who work hard but still are in poverty—but they do not like giving "handouts" to the "undeserving poor"—those who "refuse to work" and still want money from hardworking citizens. This is not the place to debate the broader issue of welfare. It is highly complex and what makes someone "deserving" of our largesse—especially when kids are involved—is a complicated issue. Regardless, the issue here is not whether this way of thinking is good or bad, but simply to recognize it as part of what informs American social policy.

In this context, can you see why RJ might strike people as more in tune with the times? Well, the key is that restorative justice does not favor social welfare. It is not based on the idea that offenders are victimized by their disadvantaged circumstances and deserve our help *regardless of their behavior.* Instead, it *insists on offenders being held accountable for their actions.* Offenders are expected to *take responsibility* for the harm they have caused—to admit their guilt, to ask for forgiveness, and to make victims whole again.

In essence, it is these actions that transform the offender from an *undeserving* member of the community into a potentially *deserving* member of the community.

And as offenders make this transition into the *deserving category,* they become candidates for our acceptance. Reintegration can now be exchanged because the offender has shown accountability. In short, RJ coincides with core American values. This is one important reason why it seems to "make sense" to us or to "seem reasonable."

Three Problems

When put into practice, every theory of corrections will be misshaped in one way or the other (Cullen & Gilbert, 1982). The theory's conscience—its ideals—will be corrupted by convenience—the political, organizational, and practical realities that envelop and reign within the existing criminal justice system (Rothman, 1980). Of course, advocates of any fresh theory—such as RJ—have a stake in pointing out the problems with older theories and of ignoring or downplaying the potential ways in which their theory will be messed up when put into practice. The temptation to ignore possible difficulties is perhaps especially pronounced among those who have benevolent intentions and intend to help offenders—as do many RJ proponents. This good will, however, risks being transformed into hubris—a sense that their reforms, because they are rooted in benevolence, will somehow be uniquely immune to unanticipated consequences that might produce more harm than good.

Advocates of restorative justice thus must confront seriously the factors that might cause RJ's noble goals to be unrealized or only partially realized (Levrant, Cullen, Fulton, & Wozniak, 1999). In this section, we consider three problems that risk diminishing the luster of RJ. They are not necessarily insurmountable, but they are obstacles that must be fully understood if they are ever to be overcome.

THE JUSTICE PROBLEM

As discussed in Chapter 1 and elsewhere, theories of corrections tend to place an emphasis on *justice* (punishment as an end in and of itself) or on *utility* (using punishment to reduce crime). We will note soon that RJ started out as a theory of justice and then expanded into a theory of utility. Here, we are concerned with whether RJ will in fact achieve more just outcomes than the current sentencing process. Cullen and Jonson believe that, if implemented, the answer is almost certainly "yes," because many of the bad things that occur in the current system would be avoided. Nonetheless, this does not mean that RJ will be implemented as planned or be able to avoid areas where its pursuit of greater justice falls short.

In this regard, the noted feminist scholar Kathleen Daly (2008) has presented perhaps the most thoughtful assessment of the justice problems that RJ faces. She bases her commentary on the existing literature and on her analysis of data from her own research on an RJ intervention, the South Australia Juvenile Justice Program. She highlights a number of concerns, but we will focus on two of the most prominent.

First, RJ kicks into practice once offenders have consented to admit their guilt and to participate in a restorative process. But this fact means that RJ is largely silent on what occurs prior to the sanctioning process—and whether this part of the system will be just. As Daly (2008) notes, the reason why the front part of the system is adversarial is "that the adjudication process rests on a fundamental right of those accused to say they did not commit an offence" (p. 136). During this phase, the state investigates and builds a factual case against the accused. Meanwhile, citizens need to have the right "to defend themselves against the state's power to prosecute and punish alleged crime" (p. 136).

The tricky part is that an RJ program depends on persuading offenders to say they are guilty of their wrongdoing. Pressuring defendants to admit their guilt would be inappropriate for those who are innocent and perhaps even for those who, because the state has a weak case, might be found not guilty in a regular court. The risk also exists that RJ will become a preferable option only if it is seen by defense attorneys as offering less punishment—a form of plea bargaining rather than a genuine choice to seek restoration. And there is the related issue of what role victims will play in allowing an RJ process to move forward. What will occur if they prefer a traditional court sanction and refuse to participate in an RJ conference?

Cullen and Jonson do not have any data to suggest whether the uneven treatment and injustices that creep into RJ programs are extensive or approximate those found in today's justice system. But it would be equally naïve to ignore the stubborn reality that RJ does not extricate itself fully from the adversarial process or from inequalities that can permeate how its practice is accomplished.

Second, Daly (2008) cautions us to beware of the "nirvana story of RJ" (p. 142). Recall Braithwaite's (1998) account of Sam's encounter with restorative justice, which we presented above. This is an example of a nirvana story because the RJ conference ends well. But the reality is that at the conference's conclusion, Sam is not always hugged by forgiving, teary-eyed victims. As Daly (2008) observes, "RJ is limited by the abilities and interests of offenders and victims to think and act in ways we may define as restorative" (p. 143).

Thus, according to Daly (2008), "restorativeness requires a degree of empathetic concern and perspective-taking" (p. 138). But many offenders lack these qualities. In the South Australia project she studied, Daly found that half of the youths "had not thought *at all* about what they would say to the victim," and that most "did not think in terms of what they might *offer victims,* but what they would be *made to do by others*" (p. 139, emphasis in the original). Needless to say, many of these juveniles in the RJ conferences were not able to offer what is a core component of victim restoration—a sincere apology. A lot of the youngsters said that they apologized because they would get off more easily or to please their families. As for victims, "most believed that the youth's motives for apologizing were insincere" (p. 140).

Daly's other perceptive insight is that not all victims are equally prepared to be forgiving in and to be restored by an RJ conference. She notes that some victims are only "lightly touched" by crime but that "others experience many disabling effects such as health problems, sleeplessness, [and] loss of self-confidence" (p. 140). Victims experiencing this high distress did not respond well to the RJ intervention.

"After a conference ended," Daly (2008) observes, "the high distress victims were far more likely to remain angry and fearful of offenders, and to be negative toward them" (p. 141). Furthermore, a year after the conference, "71 percent of the high distress victims had *not* recovered" (p. 141, emphasis in the original). Daly offers the sobering conclusion that "for the most highly distressed victims, an RJ process may be of little help in recovering from crime" (p. 141).

Daly's research is important because, as she tells us, research on the restorative outcomes of RJ programs—on things like the sincerity of apologies and making victims feel restored—is in short supply. Her findings should not be taken as definitive, but they do prompt us to understand that *restoring victims, offenders, and the community* is a challenging task that will be imperfectly achieved (see also Bonta, Wallace-Capretta, Rooney, & McAnoy, 2002). Sam's heartwarming story and positive outcomes for all might occur at times. But RJ advocates have much more research to undertake to document the extent to which restoration to all involved is actually forthcoming.

Cullen and Jonson want readers to take special note of this last point. If offenders con the apology process and if victims are not made whole, then RJ is *not a source of justice but of injustice.* In such cases, offenders get off easily and victims receive little in return. Now, RJ advocates will certainly respond by citing statistics that far more participants in RJ proceedings express satisfaction than participants in traditional court proceedings. And this is, in fact, true. But as Daly (2008) warns, satisfaction with procedural justice (i.e., offenders and victims believe that they were treated fairly) is not the same thing as achieving restoration. For true justice to transpire, offenders must sincerely apologize and be forgiven, and victims must be improved by the process—not to mention that offenders must be successfully reintegrated into the community. A nirvana ending requires that restoration be accomplished. If not, then the process is, at best, an instrument of imperfect justice whose only claim is that it may not be as bad as what typically goes on in the court system.

THE PRISON PROBLEM

Perhaps the most daunting obstacle to RJ becoming the guiding theory of corrections is that it is an approach that wants to process nearly all offenders *in the community.* It is possible to imagine how aspects of restorative justice might be imported into the prison (see Cullen et al., 2001; Dhami, Mantle, & Fox, 2009; Johnstone, 2014; Presser, 2014). For example, victims and offenders might be encouraged to meet in prison as part of a reconciliation process. Offenders might devote some of their in-prison earnings to compensate victims for their harm or engage in service activities that benefit the community (e.g., training Seeing Eye dogs). Efforts might be made to work with offenders during their imprisonment to ensure their restoration upon release. Or perhaps restorative principles could be used to resolve conflicts and victimizations that occur within an institution. And so on. But having admitted this much, it remains the case that RJ is a program that attempts to remove offenders from the regular criminal justice system so that justice can be achieved in the community. As Braithwaite (1998) notes, RJ "concedes" only that "for a tiny fraction of the people in our prisons, it may actually be necessary to protect the community from them by incarceration" (p. 336).

The problem with this view, of course, is that it is nuts! Hello out there, our beloved RJ folks. Time for a reality check! We now have about 2.2 million people locked up. Even if the *tiny fraction thesis* were empirically correct—and it almost certainly is not—it is absurd to imagine that the nation's prison population will decline markedly (say, to under 1 million) in the foreseeable future. Okay, it is possible to let youthful offenders, first-time offenders, non-violent offenders, and even a few serious or violent offenders into RJ programs. In this instance, RJ functions as a sophisticated diversion program, getting low-risk offenders out of the system—where they do not belong. But for high-risk offenders—those who have committed serious crimes and/or have lengthy criminal records—putting them into RJ programs and onto the street *in large numbers* simply is not going to happen.

Indeed, doing so would place elected officials in jeopardy of political suicide. Imagine if a judge allowed a child molester into an RJ program. What would happen if that offender molested again? Or, God forbid, killed a child? The RJ program would be dismantled and the judge would be looking for a new line of work. To be sure, RJ advocates might argue that restorative programs are more effective with child molesters than simply warehousing them for a few years and, in the long run, would make society safer (McAlinden, 2008; see also Carich, Wilson, Carich, & Calder, 2010). And they may well be correct empirically. But this is beside the point. Sentencing practices might be moderated here and there, but serious, chronic offenders will be heading to prison for years to come.

Mass incarceration is thus a reality that RJ advocates cannot ignore. Saying that only a tiny fraction of the 2.2 million offenders behind bars needs to be locked up is beside the point. There are still more than a couple million people sitting in prison day in and day out. What do RJ advocates say we should do with these folks? Their virtual silence on this issue is a devastating weakness for the theory of restorative justice.

Again, the very essence of restorative justice is to remove the state from the justice process as soon as possible. The goal is to get out of the courts and into a more informal setting—albeit organized by a mediator or facilitator—in which everyone can get together and work out an agreement as to how the offender, the victim, and the community can be restored. The very nature of this process means that nobody will be heading to prison! The purpose is not to exclude the offender through incarceration but to reintegrate this person back into his or her family, school, and neighborhood. The difficulty is that a societal consensus exists that a lot of crimes (serious ones) deserve a harsh prison term and a lot of criminals (serious and chronic ones) should be placed behind bars. RJ proponents might not like this fact, but it is a fact nonetheless.

To conclude, preaching against the use of prisons is not a correctional policy but a correctional dream. Without a coherent answer for what to do with those locked up, RJ loses its relevance as a meaningful correctional theory.

THE CRIMINOLOGICAL PROBLEM

Restorative justice was originally conceived as a theory of justice, not a theory of utility. But needless to say, the issue of utility—of *crime control*—inevitably surfaced. In a way, of course, RJ sought to achieve justice *through utility:* by showing that restorative practices brought benefits to everyone, including justice to the victim. Again, it was a theory in which everyone could win! But here we are talking about the *big utility* question: *Does RJ reduce reoffending?*

We will address this issue in the next section on whether RJ works. But here we want to alert readers to Cullen and Jonson's insight—pretty brilliant we think!—that RJ has always been a *theory of justice in search of a theory of crime.* By this we mean that RJ advocates started out with a vision of what the justice process should look like. This new approach rejected traditional criminal justice in favor of practices in which the offender, victim, and community would figure out how to make everyone whole again. Again, despite some limitations, there is much to admire about this reform.

But having decided that RJ is what we should use to achieve justice, they then went to the next step and argued that it also would *reduce crime.* This assertion was essential because unless RJ had utility, it would be relegated to the dustbin of foolish correctional theories. But if restorative practices also advanced public safety, they would be hard to oppose: Everyone wins, including the public at large who is less at risk of criminal victimization!

One argument, not without some merit, is that RJ reduces crime because it does not do things—label, stigmatize, and exclude offenders—that the regular criminal justice system does daily and that research suggests may increase reoffending (see, e.g., Farrington & Murray, 2014). But eventually, of course, the argument was made that it was not simply the absence of harming offenders that reduced crime but the presence of good things: making offenders own up to their bad deeds and then enmeshing offenders in a web of social support. The challenge was to find a *criminological theory* that said that crime was caused by stigmatizing the wayward and reduced by not stigmatizing them. These ideas were generally consistent with Leftist views, especially feminist and peacemaking perspectives. Feminist and peacemaking scholars in general think that making peace, rather than war, on crime is a sensible thing to do. They are lovers, not haters!

But restorative justice received true legitimacy when advocates embraced John Braithwaite's (1989) brilliant book, *Crime, Shame and Reintegration.* In this volume, Braithwaite set forth the thesis that *stigmatizing shaming* would increase reoffending, whereas *reintegrative shaming* would decrease reoffending. According to Braithwaite, shaming a bad act was needed. Any community needs to establish moral boundaries and to let offenders know what behaviors will not be tolerated. But shaming that stigmatizes and excludes offenders, he proposed, would (much as labeling theory argued) push them away from prosocial relationships and into criminal subcultures. Criminality would thus be deepened. By contrast, if shaming communicated that bad acts were wrong but then expressed a willingness to accept a contrite offender back into the fold, then the sanction would knife off a person's criminal career. Hate the crime, love the criminal. Shame illegal acts, reintegrate the offender. Do this, urged Braithwaite, and recidivism is vanquished!

RJ advocates quickly recognized the power of Braithwaite's theory of reintegrative shaming and its capacity to provide criminological legitimacy to restorative justice. Braithwaite's perspective thus provided a clear reason why RJ would reduce recidivism: It was a form of reintegrative shaming. It also explained why traditional criminal justice was criminogenic: It was a form of stigmatizing shaming. Braithwaite (1998, 2002) similarly understood the policy implications of his work and became a reasonable and persuasive advocate for RJ.

Although not as popular to them as reintegrative shaming theory, another perspective that RJ folks find appealing is Tom Tyler's (2003, 2009) procedural justice theory. Along with Braithwaite, Tyler understands that criminal sanctioning can be done in a way that makes matters better (now not common) or worse (what is common). As noted at the beginning of the deterrence chapter, "sticking people's noses in it" is usually counterproductive. But what, then, is the alternative option? For Tyler, police officers, court personnel, and other state officials should use *procedural justice* when interacting with or sanctioning wayward individuals. Tyler's (2003) model is a bit complex, but it can be simply stated. Procedural justice involves two things. First, when dealing with criminal justice authorities, people want to be sure that the process used to make decisions about them (e.g., to arrest, to convict) is fair. Second, people want to be treated nicely, such as with "politeness and respect for rights" (Tyler, 2009, p. 324). They want to be able to tell their side of the story and to feel as though officials listen to them. When this does not occur—when they are treated with coercion and disrespect—they are likely to become defiant and more criminal (Sherman, 1993). By contrast, Tyler argues that procedural justice creates within individuals a belief that the process has been legitimate and, in turn, an obligation to "self-regulate" their conduct and to obey the law.

Maybe you can see the connection to RJ and holding conferences that bring victims, offenders, and people that care about them together. In these sessions, participation may not be fully voluntary (non-participation can lead to regular prosecution and family rejection), but it is not actively coerced. All those in attendance get to speak and to express their perspective. Respect and understanding are encouraged. And the endpoint is an agreement, signed onto by all parties, as to how mutual restoration will be achieved. Tyler (2003, p. 347) notes that the focus of "restorative justice models" is on building "relationships to others" and that the key "self-regulatory motivation" is "shame." By contrast, procedural justice focuses on increasing for offenders the "legitimacy of authority" and the key motivation is "obligation" to comply with laws. In reality, however, RJ conferences can be multimodal. Because they potentially involve reintegrating shaming and procedural justice, they can bring about a willingness to desist from crime—a new sense of self-regulation—through both shame and obligation.

All this is nice and not unimportant. Still, Cullen and Jonson worry that the criminological foundation underlying RJ remains weak—or not as strong as it could be. Sherman and colleagues point out that several theories, including reintegrative shaming and procedural justice, have strong "theoretical connections" to RJ.

Yet they also admit that there is "no causal theory that fully describes the manner in which [RJ] conferencing might affect repeat offending and victims' satisfaction" (Sherman, Strang, Mayo-Wilson, Woods, & Ariel, 2015, p. 3; see also Daly & Proietti-Scifoni, 2011). But Cullen and Jonson think it is worse than this. The problem is that RJ advocates treat criminology as though it is a store and they are going on a shopping trip. When they arrive at the mall and enter the Criminology Department Store, they look around for ideas that they fancy and then "buy" theories they like. Alas, they then leave behind theories and research not to their liking.

The problem with the RJ folks is that in purchasing theories they do like (such as Braithwaite's and Tyler's perspectives), they chose to ignore all other criminological data on predictors of recidivism. To be sure, sanctioning offenders in a crappy way is likely to make them, if anything, more criminal, not less so—as we noted in our discussion of deterrence. And reintegrative shaming may have some benefits in helping offenders start a new life. But the other reality is that offenders have a lot of deficits—such as antisocial values and low self-control—that if not fixed will lead them to recidivate. Unless these risk factors are targeted for change, an intervention is unlikely to be effective in reducing recidivism. This is the premise of rehabilitation scholars who have achieved success in lowering reoffending—a matter to which we return in the next chapter.

RJ advocates, however, do not like to see criminals as different from the rest of us. They do not seem to believe in what criminologists call *individual differences* that separate criminals from non-criminals. Ignoring such differences, however, is simply ignoring reality—it is stupid criminology (see Wright, Tibbetts, & Daigle, 2008). This view not only turns a blind eye to mountains of empirical data but also is manifestly illogical. Thus, many offenders arrive at the doors of the criminal justice system already deeply involved in crime; they are already high-risk, serious, chronic offenders. The state's reaction to them does not create their persistent criminal propensity (though we agree it can make matters worse). Rather, there are things about offenders—such as having learned antisocial values, hanging around with bad peers, and not possessing the capacity to control their anger—that get them into trouble, over and over again. Proponents of RJ, however, seem disinterested in measuring, knowing about, and rectifying these individual differences or risk factors that offenders must negotiate all the time. Rather, they optimistically assume that everyone is the same, that everyone can be saved, and that all we have to do is allow restorative processes to magically pull such life-course-persistent criminals out of their antisocial trajectory.

This is a nuanced point, so listen carefully to Cullen and Jonson here. RJ advocates believe that regardless of what caused someone to go into crime, the solution is to enmesh that person in a web of supportive social relationships. Again, as one of the founders of social support theory, Cullen (1994) agrees with this premise— up to a point. However, as scholars who have studied the rehabilitation and recidivism literature, Cullen and Jonson also know that individual differences exist and, if these deficits are not fixed, then offenders are likely to recidivate.

Cullen and Jonson are perplexed as to why RJ advocates do not like or ignore the rehabilitation literature. There is no inherent reason why restorative justice and rehabilitation cannot go together (Andrews & Bonta, 2010; Cullen et al., 2001; Raynor & Robinson, 2009). But there is a philosophical reason why RJ folks do not want to merge these two kind-hearted approaches to changing offenders.

Thus, RJ advocates believe that offender change should be primarily accomplished by *non-experts* and in *naturalistic settings.* That is, along with a facilitator, a bunch of community people—who know a lot about the offender *but nothing about the science of offender change*—should be able to come up with a plan to ensure that the offender stops his or her criminal involvement. The reason why this approach should work, say the RJ folks, is that these concerned relatives and friends will be with the offender, day in and day out, in the community. It is the strength of these supportive relationships between the offender and his or her family and neighbors that will allow the offender to be affirmed and reintegrated. In this naturalistic setting—that is, in this everyday, real-world setting—offenders will be helped by their new prosocial interactions to desist from crime (see also Brayford, Cowe, & Deering, 2010; Sampson & Laub, 1993; Veysey, Christian, & Martinez, 2009).

In contrast to their enthusiastic embrace of non-expert naturalistic reform, RJ advocates want to get not only state officials but also supposedly evil scientists out of offenders' lives! Thus, psychologists and social workers trained to use evidence-based interventions in a planned way to save wayward offenders are not to be trusted. Their interventions, it is said, are doomed to failure because those delivering them, who might know a whole bunch about offenders and how to change them, are not living with or near their clients. To be direct, Cullen and Jonson believe that this faith in naturalistic change rather than in planned evidence-based rehabilitation—this rejection of science and professional expertise—is loony. It is why, despite sympathies favorable to RJ, we think that this correctional theory rests on a weak scientific foundation. It also is why we prefer to reaffirm rehabilitation rather than RJ.

Does Restorative Justice Work?

In the end, it matters little what Cullen and Jonson believe or prefer! What does matter, then? As perceptive correctional scholars, readers now know the answer to this question: Show me the data! *It is the evidence that matters.* In the end, RJ programs either reduce recidivism or they do not.

Research on the effectiveness of RJ programs is not voluminous. But it has been growing and it does allow us to draw three conclusions (see Andrews & Bonta, 2010; Bonta, Jesseman, Rugge, & Cormier, 2006; Bonta et al., 2002; Bradshaw & Roseborough, 2005; Braithwaite, 2002; Jeong, McGarrell, & Hipple, 2012; Latimer, Dowden, & Muise, 2005; McGarrell & Hipple, 2007; Mills, Barocas, & Ariel, 2013; Rodriquez, 2005; Shapland et al., 2008; Sherman & Strang, 2007; Sherman et al., 2015; Strang & Sherman, 2006; Weatherburn, 2013). Let us hasten to say, however, that RJ advocates are likely to say that we are underplaying the prospects of RJ because—and we make no bones about this—Cullen and Jonson favor rehabilitation as the preferred theory of corrections. Readers, of course, can be the arbiters of this dispute. Go read the studies and see who is correct. In our defense, we must state that we have tried to collect the best reviews and studies available, and we attempt below to state their conclusions fairly. In the end, our commitment to science trumps any commitment to rehabilitation. So, here are the three main conclusions we draw from the research on RJ:

- Does RJ reduce recidivism? The answer is "yes" it does.

- How strong is the effect of RJ on recidivism? Although some programs achieve more promising results, the effects overall are modest and approximate those of human service interventions generally.

- Does RJ reduce recidivism as well as appropriate rehabilitation programs? The answer is "no" it does not.

We start by outlining four reasons why RJ's effects are not larger. This assessment reiterates and expands points made above in the discussion of the criminological problem facing RJ. We then present the findings of five studies that give a good picture of the effectiveness of RJ. This discussion starts with a long-term study of a well-known RJ program (Jeong et al., 2012). We next consider two systematic reviews undertaken by Lawrence Sherman and Heather Strang (Sherman & Strang, 2007; Sherman et al., 2015). Finally, we examine two others reviews of this literature—one conducted by Weatherburn (2013) and one by Andrews and Bonta (2010).

FOUR LIMITS

As we have stated, RJ likely starts with a huge advantage. By diverting offenders from the regular criminal justice system, it avoids a host of things that likely make them worse, including impersonal judicial proceedings, stigmatizing punishments, and imprisonment. What worries Cullen and Jonson, however, is RJ advocates' rejection of the knowledge about offending and effective intervention produced by scientific criminology. This knowledge is paid attention to in the best rehabilitation programs (which we like) but not in programs that typically prove ineffective (which we do not like). In our view, RJ programs risk being limited if they ignore what this knowledge has to teach us about recidivism and changing offenders. Four limits seem most salient to us:

- *RJ is based on a limited theory of crime.* In fact, the theory of crime informing any given RJ program is often left implicit and is not specifically stated. In general, though, there is some sense that crime occurs because of how offenders are treated once they are caught: stigmatized, rejected, and excluded from conventional roles. Although we agree that stigmatizing can deepen criminality, this is but one cause of recidivism. What about the other causes?

- *RJ does not target for change the known predictors of recidivism.* Interventions are not likely to be effective if they do not seek to change the factors known to cause recidivism (e.g., antisocial values). In many respects, RJ may focus on these factors, but if so, it does so *inadvertently, not systematically.* As a result, its effectiveness is limited.

- *RJ's dose of intervention is too weak to change serious offenders.* Sentencing conferences (or "circles") and restitution programs "sound good." But what would lead us to expect that these kinds of interventions are powerful enough to change deep-seated criminal impulses developed over 15 or 20 or 25 years? Do we really think that a couple of hours at a sentencing conference—even with an emotional meeting with a victim—are capable of transforming such offenders? Does this risk becoming much like a liberal scared straight program?

- *RJ ignores the principles of effective correctional intervention.* As we discuss in Chapter 7, research now shows empirically what things must be done in a treatment program to achieve significant reductions in recidivism. RJ does not rely on these principles to develop interventions with offenders. The result is that RJ limits its ability to change the behavior of offenders.

We should note that there is nothing to stop RJ advocates from taking these four points to heart—or to head!—and designing RJ programs to be more scientifically informed. There is nothing inherent in RJ that would prevent it from adding in a rehabilitation component in which part of the restorative process might involve participating in, say, a cognitive-behavioral treatment program. There is nothing inherent in RJ programs that prevents a risk assessment from being conducted so that more services might be directed toward high-risk offenders. And so on. To be honest, the failure to use rehabilitation knowledge and technology has less to do with practical problems (RJ and rehabilitation are too incompatible to be merged) and more to do with the ideology of RJ advocates. They tend to see RJ as an opponent of and alternative to traditional treatment approaches. The cost of this view, however, may well be that RJ programs are needlessly limited in the crime that they can prevent.

FIVE STUDIES

One Program Evaluation. We will begin our assessment of the research on the effectiveness of RJ in reducing recidivism by focusing on the Indianapolis Juvenile Restorative Justice Experiment (IJRJE). We might have selected another study to examine, but this seemed to be a well-run program and one that shows the potential benefits and limits of RJ as an intervention. In short order, we will turn our attention to works that have examined the research as a whole. These systematic reviews are more informative because they give us the big picture of the effectiveness of RJ across diverse contexts. Still, individual studies are valuable in giving us an up-close sense of the challenges restorative interventions face.

The IJRJE was one of the first restorative justice experiments, starting in September of 1997 (McGarrell & Hipple, 2007) in Marion County, Indiana, which includes Indianapolis. The RJ intervention was a traditional family group conference (FGC) developed to mirror FGCs used in Australia and, in particular, New South Wales. Participation criteria were set by the county's chief juvenile court judge and prosecutor: first-time offenders aged 14 or under who admitted their guilt and had been "charged with battery (or assault), trespass, mischief, conversion (shoplifting), and felony D theft" (Jeong et al., 2012, p. 371). After agreeing to join the study ($n = 782$), youths were randomly assigned to the FGC or to a diversion program. Rearrest was used as the measure of "failure" or recidivism.

As is typical of evaluation studies, the research team—led by Edmund McGarrell—examined recidivism for six months and then for two years. The findings were promising, revealing that "youths participating in FGC survive longer before being re-arrested over a 24-month period" and "had significantly lower incidence rates" (McGarrell & Hipple, 2007, p. 239). The results were "most pronounced during the period of 3–8 months following the initial arrest" (2007, p. 221). In short, the program worked! The research team could have declared victory and moved on to other things, but they did not. Unlike most evaluation studies, they subsequently conducted a 12-year follow-up (Jeong et al., 2012). Unfortunately, the program effects appeared to decay over time; there was no significant impact on recidivism over the long term.

It is not clear that this is all bad news for RJ. As Jeong, McGarrell, and Hipple note, it was a challenging test for RJ. Youths who participated in conferences were being compared to other kids who were diverted from the system—not kids in the regular juvenile justice system who experience "adversarial court processes" (2012, p. 383). Further, the positive results found at the beginning of the program (they were strongest at 3 to 8 months) might present a window for more permanent change were a more active aftercare intervention incorporated into the FGC intervention. After all, the conference itself lasted only about one hour, although youths typically still had to comply with an agreement in which they would make "good the harm that was caused by the offense" (Jeong et al., 2012, p. 373). The point of all this is that RJ likely was a better option for the youths than the traditional juvenile court, but its ability to diminish recidivism is likely modest.

Two Studies by Sherman and Strang. Lawrence Sherman and Heather Strang have conducted two systematic reviews of evaluations of restorative justice programs. Sherman and Strang are generally identified as proponents of RJ, having participated in evaluation studies and written favorably about restorative justice as an alternative to conventional criminal justice (see also Sherman, 1993). They also are solid scientists who read the data accurately. Accordingly, we can have confidence in their assessment of the evidence (see also Strang & Sherman, 2006).

To assess the ability of RJ to "reduce repeat offending," Sherman and Strang (2007) examined a number of experimental and quasi-experimental studies. Specifically, they were able to review the evidence regarding how RJ compared to "conventional" prosecution or criminal justice processing for violent crime

(11 comparisons), property crime (12 comparisons), and non-victim crimes such as shoplifting and drunk driving (3 comparisons). When counting up the votes—those instances in which it worked versus those in which it did not—RJ generally came out ahead. The tally of studies showed the following:

- For violent crimes, the count was: reductions of crime = 6, increases = 0, and no effect = 4.

- For property crimes, the count was: reductions of crime = 5 and increases = 2. In two comparisons with offenders given a custodial sanction, the RJ group was able to "match or beat" those incarcerated.

- For non-victim crimes, the count was: reduction of crime = 0, increase = 2, no effect = 1 (see Sherman & Strang, 2007, pp. 16–18).

What do these results tell us about RJ effectiveness? Well, this is a glass-half-full versus a glass-half-empty situation. Positively, the data can be interpreted as showing that RJ infrequently increases recidivism and about half the time actually decreases it. Negatively, the data can be interpreted as showing that about half the time RJ works better than conventional criminal justice processing and about half the time it does not. Advocates would see RJ as displaying promise as an alternative to current practices. Opponents would ask why folks are making such a big deal about an intervention that cannot consistently produce better results than what we are now doing.

Sherman and Strang (2007), however, make the important observation that "*RJ works differently on different kinds of people*" (p. 8, emphasis in the original). They add more detail in the following commentary:

> In general, *RJ seems to reduce crime more effectively with more rather than less serious crimes.* The results . . . suggest RJ works better with crimes involving personal victims than for crimes without them. They also suggest that it works with violent crimes more consistently than with property crimes. . . . These findings run counter to conventional wisdom, and could become the basis for substantial inroads in demarcating when it is "in the public interest" to seek RJ rather than CJ. (p. 8, emphasis in the original)

These findings prompt two comments from Cullen and Jonson. First, although perhaps not understood by most of the public or by most criminologists, the discovery that RJ works better with more serious crimes (and presumably offenders) is actually *not* surprising. As we will discuss in Chapter 7, rehabilitation scholars have known this fact for a while now. Indeed, one group of prominent scholars calls this the *risk principle,* which asserts that interventions should be targeted for high-risk offenders; low-risk offenders should be left alone and gotten out of the system as soon as possible (Andrews & Bonta, 2010).

In more practical terms, we can see why this occurs. Let's take medicine as an example. If someone is really sick, then seeing a doctor, taking prescription drugs, and going to the hospital is likely to help. It is hard to make a really sick person sicker, and there is a lot to fix. In a way, interventions cannot make matters much worse, but they have a chance to make the patient healthier. By contrast, if someone has an illness that will go away on its own, then seeing a doctor, taking drugs that are not needed, and being put in a hospital where infection is possible can only make the person sicker. With regard to offenders, the same logic applies. Interventions with high-risk offenders cannot make them much worse but might make them less criminal. Interventions with low-risk offenders who will desist on their own can only make them more criminogenic. They do not need any criminal justice medicine, including in particular a stay in prison where they might get "infected" with criminal values!

Second, the fact that RJ is more effective with serious crimes and criminals may not be good news. It is precisely these kinds of offenders that political and criminal justice officials are going to be least inclined to allow into RJ programs. It is one thing to convince a set of judges here and there to allow RJ to be given randomly to high-risk offenders in an experiment run by respected researchers. It is quite another to establish RJ as the standard intervention for offenders who seem quite likely to recidivate. In such cases, many judges will think twice, decline to use the kind-hearted RJ option, and conclude that they had better send this "loser" or "dangerous predator" to prison. In fact, many RJ programs already exclude serious, violent offenders.

Sherman and Strang essentially conducted a ballot-box or vote-counting study. Recall that a ballot-box review tells us how many studies show that a treatment intervention is effective versus those that do not show it reduces recidivism. It is like an election: If the treatment has more votes (more significant effects) than not, then it wins the election! It is declared to reduce recidivism. Their 2007 study, however, does not tell us how much recidivism was reduced (versus the comparison group) across all studies. This is what a meta-analysis does. To use baseball as an example, Sherman and Strang tell us how many times RJ got a "hit" (reduced crime) in the "games" (studies) in which it was tried. A meta-analysis tells s us what RJ's batting average is across all games (or studies). It takes into account how many times RJ comes up to the plate (sample size for each study) and how many hits it has in each game and then across all games (this is called the *effect size*). We will explain more about what meta-analysis entails in Chapter 7.

In the end, the meta-analysis gives us, like a batting average, a precise number that allows us to gain a sense of the *magnitude of an intervention's effect on reducing recidivism*. Notably, this avoids the glass-half-full versus glass-half-empty problem. Why? Because we get a number that either shows no effect (is around zero) or that shows that crime is reduced (positive or above zero) or is increased (negative or below zero). We will return to this pretty soon in the next chapter. As long as you get the gist of things, you will be fine for now. Trust us!

Importantly, however, Sherman and Strang, along with Evan Mayo-Wilson, Daniel J. Woods, and Barak Ariel, followed up their 2007 review by undertaking a meta-analysis of studies that conducted "randomized trials of face-to-face restorative justice conferences," had a two-year follow-up after subjects were randomly assigned, and measured recidivism by frequency of offending (2015, p. 1). They stipulated eight criteria that had to be met for an evaluation to be included in their assessment (p. 4). In essence, they used rigorous standards so as to minimize any potential impact of methodological biases on their conclusions. So, their selection of studies was like the selection of contestants on *American Idol*. They started out with a pool of 519 studies but ended up with only 10 studies in their meta-analysis—one from Indianapolis (described above), two from Canberra (which they evaluated), Australia, and seven from the United Kingdom (p. 8). Cullen and Jonson wonder who played the role of the criminological Simon Cowell on this project!

So what did Sherman, Strang, and their colleagues find? Let's start by noting that their findings are based only on 10 studies. By comparison, in his meta-analysis of effective interventions with juveniles, Lipsey (2009, p. 128) used "548 independent study samples"! We make this observation just to place the data on RJ programs in an appropriate context. To say that a zillion more studies are needed is an understatement.

Cullen and Jonson agree with the authors that the impact of participation in a restorative justice conference (RJC) on repeat offending is "modest" (Sherman et al., 2015, p. 1). In 9 of the 10 studies analyzed, the differences in offending between the RJC and controls groups were not statistically significant (and the confidence interval of their effects included zero). Only the Indianapolis study produced statistically significant results. As we know, these effects decayed over time to the point of non-significance (Jeong et al., 2012). Still, the batting average of RJCs across all the studies was positive (.155), statistically significant, and substantively meaningful. In practical terms, observe Sherman et al., the "percentage differences associated with the ten experiments range from 7 to 45% fewer repeat convictions or arrests" (p. 11). Based on a separate analysis, they also assert that RJCs are cost effective—essentially an inexpensive way to reduce crime.

Two More Reviews. Admittedly, it is easy to get lost in all the details of the empirical literature. Doing evidence-based corrections is not easy, and the data do not always produce clear-cut results. Still, as we can see so far, the evidence supports the conclusions we set forth above in the three bullet points. RJ programs almost certainly work better than traditional criminal justice processing but their effects tend to be modest. Two other reviews of the research lend further credence to Cullen and Jonson's interpretation of RJ's effectiveness.

First, Don Weatherburn (2013) focuses on evaluations published since 2007. He notes that studies prior to this time tended to show more positive results for RJ but were also more questionable in the methods they employed. So, he turns his attention instead to 10 evaluations conducted post-2007 that he judged to be the strongest methodologically. His analysis revealed that only 3 of 10 studies showed that RJ "reduces reoffending," with "seven finding no significant effect" (2013, p. 7). "This review," concludes Weatherburn (p. 1), "finds little reliable evidence that RJ reduces re-offending."

Second, Don Andrews and James Bonta (2010) have published a meta-analytic review in which they examined 46 studies that allowed for 67 comparisons of RJ versus another sanction across 25,771 offenders. The programs varied in the extent to which they employed restorative features. Some involved only restitution to victims and community service by offenders; others involved a victim–offender conference or reconciliation. We need to disclose that Andrews and Bonta are prominent advocates of rehabilitation. This scholarly predisposition, however, does not make them biased against RJ. In fact, the results from their meta-analysis should not be so surprising, given the findings reported in this section. Here is what they found:

- Across all comparisons, the effect size was .07, which means that the RJ group's recidivism rate was 7 percentage points lower. For FGCs specifically, the effect size was virtually the same ($r = .09$).

- According to Andrews and Bonta (2010), this overall effect size "is not a particularly impressive result" because it is "slightly smaller than providing any type of human service ($r = .10$)" (p. 456). This effect size is much lower than is achieved when rehabilitation programs conform to the principles of effective treatment—an issue we take up in Chapter 7.

- The programs that were more clearly restorative in nature "fared no better than programs that had the more mundane elements of restorative justice (restitution, community service)" (p. 456). For Andrews and Bonta (2010), this finding is significant, because it raises "the question of what restorative justice component contributes to reduced recidivism" (p. 456).

Consistent with other scholars, Andrews and Bonta believe that RJ might provide a very useful context in which to deliver quality rehabilitation programs (Raynor & Robinson, 2009; Weatherburn, 2013). The reasoning starts with the observation that RJ removes many of the stigmatizing and anti-treatment features of traditional criminal justice processing. In one meta-analysis that Andrews coauthored, it was found that the more RJ programs adhered to the principles of effective intervention, the higher the reduction in recidivism (see Andrews & Bonta, 2010, p. 457). Similarly, in a quasi-experimental evaluation undertaken by Bonta et al. (2002), an RJ program that delivered treatment services had an effect size of .31. This was based on a three-year follow-up using a matched sample of probationers. Cullen and Jonson think that this result—a recidivism rate that was 31 percentage points lower—is awfully impressive!

Importantly, Andrews and Bonta are *not* arguing, as some advocates of RJ do, that we should create treatment programs that are restorative in nature. Such interventions, which have been termed *relational rehabilitation,* would encourage offenders to do such things as work with mentors, participate in conservation or recycling projects, serve as tutors or peer counselors, and engage in positive conventional roles (Bazemore, 1999). This approach might help offenders with problems that interfere with them establishing healthy relationships (e.g., anger management), but the main focus would be on enmeshing offenders in activities that increase skills, foster positive self-concepts and public images, and deepen social bonds (see also Raynor & Robinson, 2009).

To be sure, Andrews and Bonta are not against such feel-good restorative practices. It is just that they do not believe that there is any convincing body of empirical evidence to show that this approach would work to reduce recidivism. As we discuss in the next chapter, the best rehabilitation programs use treatment strategies, such as cognitive-behavioral programs, that are capable of reducing the risk factors (e.g., antisocial attitudes) that are predictive of recidivism. Andrews and Bonta believe that individual deficits must be fixed before relationships will matter. Based on her extensive review of studies in her comprehensive *What Works in Corrections,* Doris MacKenzie (2006) has voiced a similar conclusion:

> When I compared the effective programs to the ineffective programs, I found an interesting difference. Almost all of the effective programs focused on individual-level change. In contrast, the ineffective programs frequently focused on developing opportunities. For example, the cognitive skills programs emphasized individual-level changes in thinking, reasoning, empathy, and problem solving. *In contrast, life skills and work programs, examples of ineffective programs, focus on giving offenders opportunities in the community.* Based on these observations, I propose that effective programs must focus on changing the individual. This change is required before the person will be able to take advantage of opportunities in the environment. (p. 355, emphasis in the original)

Lest Cullen and Jonson be guilty of hubris about rehabilitation and of being closed-minded, we must not rule out the possibility that relational rehabilitation programs capable of achieving positive effects might be developed. To do so, however, we believe that RJ advocates must not simply assert that restorative-oriented relationships will cure offenders. As Andrews and Bonta (2010) note, they must become far clearer regarding which predictors of recidivism their interventions are seeking to target for change (e.g., criminal thinking, lack of empathy, poor family relationships) (see Braithwaite, 2002, pp. 98–102). They must start to specify precisely which components of RJ will change which risk factors. Then, they must develop rigorous evaluation data to show that the effects of RJ and relational rehabilitation rival those achieved by programs following the principles of effective treatment. This challenge is daunting. But unless the task of rehabilitation is taken seriously, RJ-based interventions are likely to achieve, at best, modest results (see also Cullen, 2011).

Conclusion: The Limits of Harm

Cullen and Jonson hope that our trepidation about RJ as a correctional theory is misplaced, and that restorative justice shapes criminal justice policy in important ways. Our concerns about RJ as a guiding theory of corrections, however, are three-fold:

- First, as with any correctional theory, we doubt that RJ can be implemented on a large-scale basis. Its political viability in dealing with serious and violent offenders seems limited, especially when distressed victims resist meeting predators and demand that their victimizers not be allowed to "get off easily" through RJ. In short, we do not believe that RJ can become more than a limited sentencing option—a useful diversion program perhaps—in the vast majority of courts in the United States.

- Second, the strong community orientation of RJ means that it provides no persuasive answer for what to do with the millions of offenders who are sent to prison. Simply asserting that we should incarcerate only a tiny fraction of offenders is no answer at all. It avoids the stubborn reality that a viable correctional theory must have a clear plan for how to improve the lives of those who are destined to sit in our nation's prisons—at times for years on end.

- Third, RJ's rejection of scientific criminology and its blind faith in the power of quality relationships to transform the lawless into the law-abiding is a major barrier to improving the effectiveness of restorative interventions. We understand the reasoning behind this view—a belief in the power of non-expert, community-based justice to transform offenders' lives. Even so, we see little evidence that this approach, by itself, will achieve more than modest results in reducing recidivism.

At the same time, restorative justice has served as an indispensable counterpoint to the get tough rhetoric and call for mass incarceration that have gripped the United States for far too long. RJ advocates have spent years fighting gratuitously harsh policies and practices. They have articulated powerful reasons for why *harming offenders* is not the only way to achieve justice for victims or the only way to make society safer. In short, they have provided an invaluable service in showing the *limits of harm* in the correctional enterprise.

Paul Gendreau
University of New Brunswick at St. John
Scholar of Rehabilitation Theory and Research

7

Rehabilitation

What Works to Change Offenders

In 1982, Cullen published *Reaffirming Rehabilitation*. At the time, not many fellow criminologists—apart from his coauthor and friend Karen Gilbert—supported offender treatment. As discussed in previous chapters, Cullen's criminological compatriots thought that rehabilitation was a benevolent mask—an excuse—for treating offenders coercively. They did not like the discretion given to judges and parole boards that enabled them to decide who went to prison and who got out of prison. They preferred a justice model that would define in clear terms the punishment for each crime and ensure that everyone would receive the same sanction. Equal justice before the law! What criminologists did not realize was the danger of saying that the correctional system now had no obligation to provide social welfare services to offenders. Its only obligation was to do justice—to inflict pain, albeit in a supposedly fair way.

As it turns out, Cullen was a smart criminological pup. In *Reaffirming Rehabilitation,* he called one section "The Poverty of the Justice Model: The Corruption of Benevolence Revisited" and prognosticated that the justice model approach would backfire. Indeed, as reviewed earlier (in Chapter 3), this attack on rehabilitation, although not without merit, had the unanticipated consequence of facilitating the conservatives' takeover of corrections and of legitimating get tough rhetoric. Of course, few listened to Cullen. As his colleague Larry Travis noted upon publication of *Reaffirming Rehabilitation:* "Well, you are pissing in the wind."

Because most American criminologists thought that something was wrong with Cullen, he had to find like-minded associates wherever he could. Alas, Cullen was befriended by several Canadian psychologists, most notably Don Andrews, James

Bonta, and, in particular, Paul Gendreau. These remarkable scholars were strong advocates of offender treatment. It is instructive that, as Canadians, they were not enmeshed in America's social context that led criminologists to suspect the state's motives and power. They still embraced the belief that government should have a social welfare mission to support its citizens. And as psychologists, they were aware of a large scientific literature showing that behavior—from rats to humans—could be changed.

They were somewhat mystified by American criminologists' conviction that offenders could not be saved from a life in crime. They saw such a view as mere ideology and, still worse, as professionally unethical. Moreover, as the get tough movement swung into full force, they were disquieted by the simplistic belief, increasingly voiced by politicians, that offenders could be induced to conform by harsh punishment rather than by planned treatment based on scientific knowledge. The Canadians observed that this wild embrace of punishment was being made by people who knew absolutely nothing about the psychology of punishment. If they had read the available literature, the get tough crowd would have realized that much of their thinking was pretty stupid, eh?

Cullen (and Jonson) finds the Canadians' proclivity to say "eh" a rather cute cultural quirk, eh? It is said that Canada received its name when its founders were told they had to reach into a hat, pull out three letters of the alphabet, and call their country by what the luck of the draw revealed. They pulled out the three letters and, after each one, held it aloft in this way: C, eh?—N, eh?—D, eh?

Talk, especially criticism, is cheap. But Cullen's Canadian friends did more than complain about American criminologists and politicians! Instead, they devoted their careers to developing a paradigm that could demonstrate *what works* to change offenders. They undertook two interrelated tasks. First, they systematically compiled evidence on the characteristics of effective interventions with offenders. Second, they developed a coherent treatment theory that spelled out the *principles of effective correctional intervention* (see, e.g., Andrews & Bonta, 2010; Gendreau, 1996). Cullen and Jonson—who also now hangs around occasionally with the Canadians—believe that our northern neighbors' approach to rehabilitation comprises a powerful *paradigm* that should guide treatment interventions with offenders. We will return to this matter closer to the chapter's end, eh?

Let us provide a roadmap of the trip we will take in this chapter. After briefly reminding readers of the concept of rehabilitation, we will focus in detail on the *nothing works debate* that was at the heart of corrections for the last quarter of the 20th century and that continues to rear its ugly head even today (Cullen, Smith, Lowenkamp, & Latessa, 2009). You will hear again the name of Robert Martinson whose 1974 essay seemingly thrust an empirical dagger into the heart of rehabilitation, killing it off once and for all. But once Martinson made the legitimacy of offender treatment an *empirical issue,* this opened up an important avenue for rebuttal: If researchers showed that treatment does in fact work, then rehabilitation would have to be reaffirmed, not rejected. We will show how, to a large extent, this is what has occurred. Mounting evidence now exists that treatment interventions work—and, importantly, work better than punitive-oriented programs.

As will be seen, *meta-analysis* has been a key statistical procedure used to assess what works and what does not work to reduce reoffending. We will show how this novel technique shaped the debate over rehabilitation. Okay, do not recoil at the thought of more statistics and of some *novel* statistical technique (that sounds like trouble, eh?). Cullen and Jonson are not out to inflict more academic misery on you. We will keep the discussion simple. The take-away point is that meta-analysis is capable of detecting, in a more precise way, the effects treatments have on things like offender recidivism. Meta-analysis is neither liberal nor conservative. It is agnostic about what it finds. The fact that meta-analyses of interventions showed that the nothing works doctrine was incorrect was pretty momentous. This is why we focus on this issue in some detail below.

The chapter's punch line is that knowledge now exists as to what will and will not work to change offender behavior. Evidence-based corrections provides us with a fairly clear idea of what is a waste of time, energy, and public monies and what is the best bet for reforming offenders—and, in so doing, protecting public safety. Remember, correctional quackery—doing stupid things to offenders— not only does not save the wayward but also increases the likelihood that some innocent citizen will be victimized. Put another way: Effective corrections = public safety. Thus, we will devote the back third of the chapter to this issue, ending with a discussion of the Canadians' principles of effective correctional intervention.

The Concept of Rehabilitation

The concept of rehabilitation was discussed way back in Chapter 1. So, it behooves us to take a few moments to review the essence of this correctional theory. Various definitions of *rehabilitation* can be used. Here is an excellent one by Francis Allen (1981):

> One may begin by saying that the rehabilitative ideal is the notion that a primary purpose of penal treatment is to effect changes in the characters, attitudes, and behavior of convicted offenders, so as to strengthen the social defense against unwanted behavior, but also to contribute to the welfare and satisfaction of others. (p. 2)

This is the definition we developed and, as such, prefer:

> Rehabilitation is a planned correctional intervention that targets for change internal and/ or social criminogenic factors with the goal of reducing recidivism and, where possible, of improving other aspects of an offender's life. (Cullen & Jonson, 2011b, p. 295)

Our definition contains five components. Let's see what they are:

- The intervention is undertaken by the correctional system.
- The intervention is planned. It does not occur by chance but is designed to have specific features.

- The intervention targets for change the factors that are causing the offender's criminality. These factors may be internal or in the offender's social environment; regardless, the purpose of the intervention is to change them.

- The intervention's main goal is to reduce recidivism. This should help the offender, but it also is critical to protecting the public.

- The intervention may also help to improve the offender in other ways (e.g., making him or her more educated or psychologically healthier).

Remember, rehabilitation is a *utilitarian goal* of the criminal sanction. Why? Because it is justified largely by its utility or benefits. It does not seek to achieve justice simply for justice's own sake but also wishes to produce social good in terms of improving the offender, reducing recidivism, and increasing public safety. Rehabilitation also has a *social welfare* purpose. Similar to restorative justice but unlike just deserts, deterrence, and incapacitation, the goal is to use the correctional system to provide services to offenders that improve their lives. Finally, rehabilitation is the only correctional theory that embraces the *medical model* and *individualized treatment*. It argues that, through science, we can diagnose what is wrong with offenders and then prescribe correctional medicine (so to speak) to cure the underlying ailment.

As seen earlier in Chapter 2, rehabilitation also is a theory that has *mattered*—that has had *consequences*. In the first two decades of the 1900s, called the Progressive Era, the criminal justice system was reformed in hopes of achieving offender treatment. Francis Allen (1981) captures this fact:

> Perhaps the most tangible evidences of the dominance of the rehabilitative ideal are found in its legislative expressions. Almost all of the characteristic innovations in criminal justice in this century [the 20th century] are reflections of the rehabilitative ideal: the juvenile court, the indeterminate sentence, systems of probation and parole, the youth authority, and the promise (if not the reality) of therapeutic programs in prisons, juvenile institutions, and mental hospitals. (p. 6; see also Rothman, 1980)

Until the late 1960s and early 1970s, the hegemony (a fancy word for widespread acceptance) of rehabilitation was virtually complete. It was seen as a sign of a modern and civilized mind to embrace offender treatment as the goal of corrections. Vengeance was dismissed as a vestige of more barbaric times when, quite embarrassingly, public hangings, whippings, and brandings were still acceptable. Only yahoos and the socially dumb held onto such an outdated belief. Again, one more insight from Francis Allen (1981):

> Nevertheless, it is remarkable how widely the rehabilitative ideal was accepted in this century [the 20th] as a statement of aspirations for the penal system, a statement largely endorsed by the media, politicians, and ordinary citizens. It was in the universities, however, that the dominance of the rehabilitative ideal became most firmly established. . . . Yet even a brief glance at the college criminology textbooks in wide

use at midcentury clearly reveals the importance accorded penological treatment in criminological thought, and the *almost unchallenged sway of the rehabilitative ideal.* (pp. 6–7, emphasis added)

Why did rehabilitation lose its grip on the minds of Americans and on crime control policy? Again, we urge you to revisit Chapter 2 for the details. But for our purposes here, there were two types of criticisms that emerged. The first involved the criticism of *state use—or misuse—of discretion.* To individualize treatment, judges and corrections officials had to have the discretion—the freedom—to decide who went to prison, who was paroled from institutions, and what happened to those supervised in the community. But what if this discretion was not used for appropriate treatment goals but rather was abused? For conservatives, the abuse of discretion meant that dangerous predators were allowed to roam free and victimize. For liberals, the abuse of discretion meant that judges would discriminate in sentencing against the poor and people of color and that corrections officials could tell inmates to obey or face eternal incarceration. This is why people of all political orientations coalesced to attack rehabilitation by taking discretion away from judges and correctional officials. They did this mainly by implementing determinate sentencing (or sentencing guidelines) and by abolishing (or limiting) parole.

The attack on the abuse of discretion was a powerful one. It prompted liberals to embrace just deserts (see Chapter 3) and conservatives to embrace get tough policies (see Chapters 4 and 5). If rehabilitation were to guide correctional policy, then this potential abuse of discretion would be a vulnerability that advocates of offender treatment would have to address. But the debate on rehabilitation changed qualitatively in 1974 with the publication of Robert Martinson's essay, "What Works? Questions and Answers About Prison Reform." We discussed this study in Chapter 2, where we noted that the punch line to Martinson's review of the existing evaluation evidence was that *nothing works to rehabilitate offenders.* Martinson's work was quickly accepted by critics who were already prepared, due to their concern over state discretion, to believe his message. They now seemed to have science on their side. Even the data seemed to confirm that offenders were beyond redemption by any known correctional intervention.

Here is the key point: Martinson's work *reframed the debate about rehabilitation.* It once was about the quality with which state discretion was used. Now, it was transformed into a debate about the *effectiveness of treatment programs.* Critics of rehabilitation likely embraced the effectiveness argument because it seemed so simple to make and so damning in its implications. They could ask: How can you support something that does not work? People like Cullen and Jonson would have no real response to this kind of question. The most we could say would be something like: "Oh yeah? Well, yo momma!" Growing up in Boston, Cullen found this response, delivered with a bit of a swagger, an effective rebuttal to any challenge that he did not like but to which he had no coherent response. In fact, in the city streets, attacking the sanctity of an opponent's mother was a culturally valued, normative rejoinder. Unfortunately, much to Cullen's dismay, in criminological circles, this retort does not usually win arguments.

But by using the effectiveness issue, critics of rehabilitation ironically have ensured their own defeat—in two ways. First, they created the opportunity for treatment to regain its credibility *if its advocates could show empirically that rehabilitation worked to reduce recidivism.* Second, they placed the alternatives to rehabilitation—punishment-oriented correctional interventions (e.g., boot camps, intensive supervision programs)—in the advocates' methodological gun sights. If rehabilitation was fair game to evaluate, so too were these punishment-oriented interventions. If these programs were found wanting—as they were—then the tables could be turned: How can you support punishment when it does not work?

Science is thus a dangerous thing to use for ideological reasons. Science can be a cold partner. It can show you that your most cherished beliefs are wrong. It can turn on you and make you change your mind—if you are intellectually honest. In this case, science has indeed turned on rehabilitation's critics. In the end, it does appear that treatment works and punishment does not (Cullen, 2005).

Knowing What Works

Let's assume that you worked for an agency and the head administrator asked you, "Does rehabilitation work to reduce recidivism?" And then let's say that you answered, "Well, in my experience, I think that it does. Just last week, I had met an ex-offender I once had in a program and he turned his life around." Unfortunately, your boss responds, "I respect you and your experience. But I just read this article by Doris MacKenzie, and she said that what we need to do is to have an evidence-based corrections. So, what I am really asking you is whether the evidence shows that rehabilitation works. Or was that Martinson fellow right a long time ago?" Your boss then follows up: "What I want you to do is to write a report summarizing the research evidence on rehabilitation. Why don't you just review the evidence for me?"

Now, what the heck does it mean to review the evidence? Your boss probably thinks that this is a pretty straightforward request. But it is actually a complicated thing to do. And how you conduct the review can influence what answer you might give in your report to your boss. There are at least four steps in a review of the evidence:

- You must find or collect all the studies you can. Ideally, you would include not only published studies but also unpublished studies. If you do not, you may bias your results. (This is sometimes called the *file drawer problem;* many reviews do not include studies still in the file drawer and not published.)

- You must decide which of the studies you find are methodologically sound enough to include in your review. Ideally, you would like to include program evaluation studies that have used an experimental design (in which offenders are randomly assigned to the treatment and control groups). But not all evaluations are pure experimental designs (e.g., they might be quasi-experimental designs in which a control group but not random assignment is used). Among these studies, however, some are so flawed that to include them in your study would result in misleading findings. Accordingly, you have to know and use the appropriate methodological standards to decide which studies are (or are not) of sufficient quality to be included in the review.

- You must then decide what method or way you will use to convey the information. As we will see, one method is a narrative review; another is a meta-analysis. This selection of *method* is critical because it can lead to different conclusions being reached by the reviewer.

- You must then interpret the review you have conducted. After all this work, what do the studies mean? What do they tell us about, in this case, the effectiveness of rehabilitation?

For the longest time, we decided what the research *meant* by conducting a *narrative* review. If you have read literature reviews in the past, this is undoubtedly the style you have encountered. It also is likely to be what you may have used for papers you have written in college. In this type of review, the scholar essentially describes the studies he or she has collected and tells a story about what they mean—thus the term *narrative*.

For example, let's assume that 10 studies have been published on *therapeutic communities*. In a narrative review, the scholar would take each study—*one at a time*—and review how the study was conducted, who was in the sample, how recidivism was measured, how long the study was (i.e., the length of time the offenders were followed up), what the findings were, and so on. After going through the studies, the author also might count up how many times therapeutic communities reduced recidivism and how many times they did not. If there were 10 studies, the scholar might find that the intervention reduced recidivism half the time. The vote would be 5 to 5. Sometimes, this is called a *ballot-box approach* because the researcher is counting, in essence, *votes or ballots* for and against the treatment program's effectiveness.

After conducting this review, the scholar would then have to interpret what all this meant. This is precisely what Martinson did in his study of 231 programs. After examining all the evidence—a pretty large task—Martinson (1974) offered this widely cited conclusion: "*With few and isolated exceptions, the rehabilitative efforts that have been reported so far have had no appreciable effect on recidivism*" (p. 25; emphasis in the original). In short, nothing works!

Narrative reviews are very valuable. They help us to decide what the research on a topic says. But, at times, the evidence is of such a nature that there is disagreement about what the studies actually say. Why? Because a narrative review is mostly *qualitative* in nature. There may be some counting of studies—such as in *the ballot-box approach* where the number of studies showing that a program worked or did not work is tallied. But for the most part, a narrative review relies on the scholar to make sense of what the studies mean. In this case, the scholar must use his or her judgment. Of course, this is not just any judgment; it is a judgment informed by the standards of a field of study and often by years of training. Still, in the end, there is room for two scholars to read the same evidence and reach different conclusions.

A key problem is whether a scholar sees the glass as half full or as half empty. *Half-full reviewers* tend to emphasize what does work and will point to the promising programs that exist. *Half-empty reviewers* (such as Martinson) tend to emphasize what does not work and will conclude that treatment success in programs is like flipping a coin—it's a matter of chance. Thus, if, in evaluating an intervention, five studies show a reduction in recidivism and five do not, what should we conclude? Is the treatment glass half full or half empty? Is the program effective ("look at the five times it worked") or ineffective ("look at the five times it did not work")?

When it is a close call like this, all sorts of biases can creep into what should be an objective review of the evidence. Let's say that the scholar doing the review really likes the concept of developing therapeutic communities in prison. The scholar is likely to emphasize how this program has been used in at least five prisons success-fully. Alternatively, let's say that the scholar thinks that this idea is a crock. In this case, he or she is likely to say that these programs did not work in five prisons. In this researcher's mind, therapeutic communities fail as often as they work—and thus are unproven and a waste of the taxpayers' money.

Not all narrative reviews are a close call. In some cases—such as the effective-ness of boot camps—the evidence is so one-sided (they do not work) that even advocates of the program cannot dispute the data. But, again, there is a looseness to narrative reviews that makes them open to different interpretations and dispute. As will be noted later, the statistical technique of meta-analysis is an alternative way to assess what works. This approach is *quantitative* and less susceptible to the half-full versus half-empty kind of debate.

Below, we thus look at two different responses to Martinson's claim that nothing works in correctional treatment. The first response was presented by scholars using a narrative–ballot-box approach to reviewing the evidence on treatment effective-ness. The second response was presented by scholars using meta-analysis. Both responses reached the same conclusion that rehabilitation was an effective strategy to reform offenders.

Challenging Nothing Works: Narrative Reviews

STANDING UP TO MARTINSON: TED PALMER'S REBUTTAL

Unless one lives in a specific historical time, it is difficult to understand how ways of thinking can sweep across a field and reshape how nearly everyone thinks. Robert Martinson's 1974 essay was that kind of pathbreaking work. He was com-municating a message that, as noted, many people were prepared to hear. He was giving scientific legitimacy to a new way of thinking about corrections. For decades, the civilized or progressive view was that we should try to rehabilitate the wayward.

Now Martinson was telling everyone that this was a fool's errand. Our benevolence was misplaced. He cautioned that we were doing the objects of our assistance—offenders—no good and maybe even harming them and the society at large.

Martinson's ideas were powerful. He was interviewed on *60 Minutes,* which gave his views a national audience. Cullen was affected by his work, came to doubt rehabilitation (until he came to his senses!), and even was interviewed by Martinson for a job to do a follow-up on the 1974 article. (Cullen was distinctly unimpressive in his interview and never heard a word back from Martinson.) As Allen (1981) noted a short time after Martinson's article, "the rehabilitative ideal has declined in the United States; the decline has been substantial, and it has been precipitous" (p. 10). A true paradigm shift occurred. One day, it seemed, everyone believed in rehabilitation; the next day, nobody did. "What is most significant about the 1970s, and what distinguishes it from the past," observed Allen, "is the degree to which the rehabilitative ideal has suffered defections, not only from politicians, editorial writers, and the larger public, but also from scholars and professionals in criminology, penology, and the law" (pp. 8–9).

It took courage to stand up to Martinson. By Martinson, we do not really mean this one person. Rather, we mean that it took courage to stand up to all those who embraced Martinson's nothing works ideas, who would work to discredit anything positive about correctional treatment, and who were disparaging of anyone who would still suggest that offenders could be saved (Gottfredson, 1979). But one man did quickly stand up to the nothing works crowd: Ted Palmer.

At first glance, Palmer was an unlikely gladiator in the treatment battles. He is rather thin, short in stature, and very soft-spoken. Cullen admires him, whereas Jonson thinks he is grandfatherly and cute. But Palmer also is blessed with an abiding sense of integrity, a compassionate heart, and a sharp mind (see Palmer, 1978, 1992, 1994, 2002). When in his presence, he strikes one as a special human being. Trained as a psychologist—he earned his Ph.D. from the University of Southern California in 1963—he worked for years as a senior researcher for the California Youth Authority. By 1974, he had come to know delinquent youths and to see programs that worked to reform more than a few of them. Palmer was not naïve about offenders' criminality, but he was aware of the possibility of effective behavioral change—which, after all, is what psychologists do for a living. He also could read an article and, through diligent analysis, see that the treatment glass was, at the least, half full.

When Martinson's study appeared, Palmer knew something was amiss. Meta-analysis was not available at the time, so he could not critique the Martinson nothing works findings using this approach. But in what is now one of the classic rebuttals in the history of criminology, Palmer (1975) took the time to go back over Martinson's interpretation of what the evaluation studies actually found. What he discovered was rather remarkable.

In his 1974 article, Martinson cited 82 studies (of the 231 in his pool of studies), because these had recidivism data. Palmer reread these works. Based on Martinson's nothing works conclusion, one might have expected to find that none of these studies—or virtually none of these studies—showed that treatment reduced recidivism. But this is not what Palmer discovered. In fact, he calculated that 39 of the studies—*48% of the total*—could be categorized as reducing recidivism. Huh? How, then, could Martinson ever conclude that treatment programs had "few appreciable effects"? Was Martinson lying or just plain stupid?

Well, actually, Martinson's point was subtler—and not understood by the vast majority of readers who were anxious to believe that nothing works to reform offenders. Martinson, then, was saying this:

- First, there were various types of treatment programs (e.g., education, employment, counseling).

- Second, when considering the evidence, he found a consistent pattern across these treatment types or categories.

- Third, this pattern was that within any type of treatment, the program sometimes worked and sometimes did not work.

- Fourth, as a result, it was not possible to say, with any assurance, that any particular type of treatment program would consistently work to reduce offender recidivism.

- Fifth, therefore, nothing works—that is, no one specific type or category of correctional treatment works *consistently* or *reliably* to reduce offending recidivism.

Thus, let's suppose that in 1974, someone had come up to Martinson and said: "Okay, Robert, after everything you have studied, tell me what I can do to keep offenders from going back into crime. What kind of program should I set up?" His response would have been: "I don't know. Because treatment programs have inconsistent results, whatever I would tell you is likely to be as wrong as it is to be right." So, here then is the key point:

- Being *a half-empty reviewer,* Martinson concluded that since no one type (or modality) of program could be shown to work all or most of the time, *nothing works* in correctional treatment.

But what kind of reviewer do you think Ted Palmer was? Right, he was *a half-full reviewer!* So, his conclusion was exactly the opposite. For him, there was now a body of evidence showing that about half the time, treatment worked!

Where does this leave us? We have two criminological crowds. One is chanting "nothing works" and the other is chanting "something works." Does not work; does so! Does not, does so! Does not, does so. Does not, does so. Hmm. After a while, this does not seem to get us anywhere useful. Is there something else that might be done to resolve this criminological standoff? Well, actually, there is. Again, if we find that half the programs reduce recidivism and half do not, the next logical step would be to find out *whether those programs that worked differed in important ways from those programs that did not work.* There are two possibilities:

- *Success or failure in rehabilitation is a random process.* This, really, is Martinson's position. In this case, we will never find features that differentiate successful from unsuccessful programs. There is no underlying pattern of effective characteristics to discover. Whether programs work or do not work is like a flip of the coin; it is a chance event.

- *Success or failure in rehabilitation is patterned, not random.* This, really, is Palmer's position—and the position of the Canadian scholars (such as Paul Gendreau, James Bonta, Don Andrews) and (guess who?) of Cullen and Jonson. In this case, further study would find that there are features of programs that work that make them differ from programs that do not work. In turn, once these differences were detected, it would be possible to use them to develop principles or guidelines for conducting effective correctional interventions. Programs that follow the principles will reduce recidivism, whereas those that violate the principles will not reduce recidivism.

As it turns out, *the second position is correct.* Success and failure in rehabilitation is patterned and not random. *Some things work better than others.* We use fancy terms to describe this. We say that the effects of treatments on recidivism are not *homogeneous* but *heterogeneous.* Do not forget this fancy terminology. If you use it, it will make you seem quite erudite. Plus, we will return to these ideas shortly.

The second position here was important because it told scholars that, in the aftermath of Martinson's study, there was work to be done. It was not the case that nothing works, but it was the case that we needed to do a lot of analysis to establish the features of effective as opposed to ineffective rehabilitation programs. Unfortunately, the nothing works message caused many scholars to abandon the study of rehabilitation programs. After all, if one were convinced that nothing works, then why would one devote one's career to studying something that was a fruitless enterprise?

Fortunately, there was a small group of scholars who did continue to study rehabilitation (Cullen, 2005). As noted, the most prominent were Canadian scholars—Don Andrews, James Bonta, Paul Gendreau, and their colleagues. They were academics, researchers for the government, and people who set up treatment programs—and sometimes all three at various times in their careers. They really knew a great deal about programs and offenders. Eventually, the Canadians would derive the *principles of effective intervention,* which tell why some programs fail (they do not follow the principles) and others succeed (they follow the principles). Initially, however, the Canadian scholars saw poor Ted Palmer, like the sheriff in the movie *High Noon,* standing up as a lone figure facing down the nothing works crowd. They decided to protect Palmer's back.

Thus, they migrated across the border into United States' criminology, attending conferences and publishing in our journals. Their message was clear: Americans do not know what they are talking about. Their cynicism about treatment reigns because they are too lazy to go to the library and read the research. They are in need of *bibliotherapy for cynics.*

BIBLIOTHERAPY FOR CYNICS:
THE CANADIANS GET INVOLVED

"What was up with this Martinson guy and why were Americans snookered by him, eh?" So asked the bewildered Canadian psychologists. The Canadians had studied behavior change when still psychology graduate students (changing the behavior of a rat or two) and had changed the behavior of more than a few offenders in their careers. What did Martinson mean by suggesting that human conduct, including criminal conduct, could not be altered? Even more significant, when they searched the literature, they could find all sorts of evaluation studies showing that treatment interventions reduced recidivism (more generally, see Andrews & Bonta, 2010). Had someone ripped all these studies out of the academic journals south of their border or were Americans simply not looking for them any longer? Eh?

In this regard, Paul Gendreau and Robert Ross—two prominent Canadian scholars—compiled two of the more important and widely cited narrative reviews. One review, published in 1979, assessed 95 studies conducted between the years of 1973 and 1978. They titled this article "Effective Correctional Treatment: Bibliotherapy for Cynics." Cullen and Jonson love the subtitle "Bibliotherapy for Cynics" because it suggests that those who were then cynical about rehabilitation—who embraced the nothing works doctrine—needed some bibliotherapy; that is, they needed to read the available literature to cure themselves of their erroneous nothing works thinking. In 1987, Gendreau and Ross published a second massive review of the evidence in an article they titled "Revivification of Rehabilitation: Evidence From the 1980s." This was an update of their 1979 work. This second, updated review assessed 130 studies and covered the years from 1981 to 1987. Martinson's original study had surveyed evaluation studies appearing only up to 1967; the starting date for inclusion in his assessment was 1945.

In their two reviews, Gendreau and Ross uncovered literally scores of examples of treatment interventions that were successful in reducing recidivism. For Gendreau and Ross, Martinson's review had been incomplete and now was outdated. Indeed, the sheer number of these programs belied the idea that nothing works. In another critical conclusion, Gendreau and Ross revealed that behaviorally oriented programs (e.g., incentive systems, behavioral contracts) showed signs of being especially effective. This finding was important because Martinson's review did not contain a category on behavioral programs—a glaring omission caused by the lack of these studies in his sample of evaluations.

Further, Gendreau and Ross noted that successful programs targeted or focused on changing what they called *criminogenic needs*. As used by Gendreau and Ross, the term *criminogenic needs* referred to two things:

- Factors or predictors that the empirical research has shown are related to offender recidivism (e.g., antisocial attitudes).
- Factors or predictors that can be changed. For example, an attitude can be changed. In contrast, past record is a predictor of recidivism but it cannot be changed.

In short, if interventions focused on factors that were shown to cause recidivism and that could be changed, they were likely to be effective. By implication, this meant that if interventions focused on factors that were not related to recidivism (e.g., self-esteem) or could not be changed (e.g., past criminal record), they were unlikely to work.

Gendreau and Ross went on to make another point that we will revisit a bit later in the chapter. They started with the observation that offenders—like other humans—are marked by individual differences (recall our previous discussion of heterogeneity). Some of these differences pertain to their criminality; offenders differ in their level of risk for reoffending. And some differences relate to their personalities and their ability to learn. Gendreau and Ross presented evidence that the effectiveness of treatment programs can vary substantially to the extent that offenders' individual differences are measured and taken into account in the delivery of services. They suggested, for example, that high-risk offenders benefited the most from treatment interventions and that offenders with low intellectual abilities would benefit more from programs in structured learning situations. Here, they were making beginning steps at evolving principles or guidelines that, if followed, would increase the likelihood of treatment being effective.

Finally, Gendreau and Ross illuminated a major reason why correctional programs fail: They lack *therapeutic integrity.* For example, programs often had no underlying theory of crime, targeted for change factors that were unrelated to recidivism, used interventions that were too short or not intensive enough, employed staff that were untrained in the intervention being used, and so on. Indeed, how could rehabilitation programs ever hope to work in these circumstances? Think if medical interventions were conducted this way: no theory of why disease occurs, causes of the illness not targeted for change, hospital stays that were too short, doctors who were not trained in medical school, and so on. Again, we would call this quackery—in our case, *correctional quackery* (Latessa et al., 2002).

When examined objectively, the reviews of Gendreau and Ross were quite persuasive. And given the extensive evidence amassed, they should have transformed the thinking of those who endorsed the doctrinaire position that rehabilitation programs could not be effective. But, again, many criminologists, not to mention policy makers, already had made up their minds that treatment was ineffective. They were not good listeners to the empirical story being told.

Equally important, Gendreau and Ross had presented a narrative review. As advocates of rehabilitation, they could be accused of explicit or implicit bias. They could be accused of misreading the evidence—of seeing the glass as half full when it was really half empty. They could not point to any hard quantitative evidence showing definitively that correctional treatment worked. For many casual observers, this seemed like a loud argument in which it was the Canadians' word versus the critics' word. It would take another method for reviewing evaluation studies to make attacks on the effectiveness of rehabilitation more difficult to sustain. It is to this method—*meta-analysis*—that we now turn.

Challenging Nothing Works: Meta-Analytic Reviews

To get right to the point, a key strength of a meta-analysis is that it can take several hundred studies and tell you with one itty-bitty number what the effect of treatment is on recidivism. Martinson's full report on his review of the studies ran to 736 pages (Lipton, Martinson, & Wilks, 1975). Even his article was 32 pages long (Martinson, 1974). Gendreau and Ross's 1987 article extended to almost 60 pages. Whew! That is a lot of reading just to try to find out if rehabilitation works to reduce reoffending.

In many ways, going over study after study would be similar to watching a video of every at-bat a hitter had across every game of an entire season. Nobody would ever do that, of course. We would prefer to just look at the player's batting average. Hmm. The batter is hitting .325. Hall of Fame material. Hit .275. Not bad for a shortstop. Oh, no: .225. Send the player to the minors, likely never to be seen again. Of course, this one number does not tell us everything about a player's performance; also relevant are a player's runs batted in, on-base percentage, slugging percentage, prowess in the field, and so on. Still, a batting average is a parsimonious way to reduce several hundred trips to the plate to an understandable number. A high batting average is good; a low batting average is bad.

During the 1990s, scholars increasingly subjected the available treatment evaluation studies to meta-analysis. The Canadians conducted one of their own (Andrews et al., 1990), as did other reputable scholars (Lösel, 1995). But the most influential work was published by Mark Lipsey (1992, 1995, 1999a, 1999b, 2009; Lipsey & Cullen, 2007; Lipsey & Wilson, 1998). Lipsey is a rigorous scholar with an impeccable reputation. Although sympathetic to rehabilitation, he was not clearly identified with the pro-treatment crowd. As they say in Tennessee, where he works at Vanderbilt University, Lipsey had no dog in this hunt. Thus, given his impeccable methodological credentials and no agenda, any meta-analysis he conducted would have credibility. When he reported the batting average for rehabilitation, it would be believed! Overall, Lipsey argued that treatment's batting average was high enough to keep it in the correctional major leagues.

The other issue to keep in mind is that when correctional intervention programs were meta-analyzed, these included not only human services–oriented programs (those seeking to improve offenders in some way) but also punishment-oriented programs (those seeking to scare, inflict pain on, or discipline offenders in some way). We have already alluded to the results of the punishment-oriented programs in Chapter 4 on deterrence theory. But as we will see, it is important that, as predicted by the Canadians and others, these harsher interventions have proved decidedly ineffective. Remember, this is the *Bartlett Effect,* named after Cullen's late dog: Putting offenders' noses in *it* does not make them less likely to recidivate.

WHAT IS A META-ANALYSIS?

What is a meta-analysis? Well, you should have some idea, since in other chapters we have alluded to this method for making sense of a bunch of studies done on a particular intervention or topic. Here, we want to explain this approach in more detail because it proved to play a central role in rehabilitation's revitalization. So, to start with, it is another way of summarizing evaluation studies that have been done on treatment. In contrast to a narrative review, however, a meta-analysis is an attempt to use quantitative methods—or statistics—to synthesize all the studies that have been conducted. This is why the technique of meta-analysis is also referred to as a *quantitative synthesis* of the literature. It is not necessary to know the intricate details of this method (although readers certainly are free to learn them). Knowing the essence of what a meta-analysis involves is sufficient for our purposes.

In any evaluation study, there is a statistical relationship between (1) the treatment intervention and (2) the measure of recidivism. This statistical relationship can fall into one of three categories:

- The relationship is zero, which means that treatment has no effect on recidivism.

- The relationship is negative, which means that the treatment actually increases recidivism.

- The relationship is positive, which means that the treatment reduces recidivism.

Note that some authors reverse the meaning of the positive and negative in their studies (e.g., negative = lower recidivism whereas positive = higher recidivism). That really does not matter. The point is that a treatment can either increase or decrease recidivism—or have no effect.

The relationship between the treatment intervention and measure of recidivism is called the *effect size*. What a meta-analysis does is to compute the relationship between the treatment variable and recidivism for every study in the sample of studies being reviewed. When this is done, the researcher comes up with the *average or mean effect size*. This is treatment's batting average (so to speak). Moreover, this average effect size is a number, which is usually expressed as a correlation coefficient (Pearson's *r*).

So, what you get after reviewing tens, if not hundreds, of studies is essentially one number. It is more complicated than this, actually, because there are different ways of conveying this number (e.g., an effect size weighted by the sample sizes of the studies, presenting confidence intervals). But we are not going to bother you with this stuff. In the end, what you need to know is that there is a way to estimate what the magnitude of the relationship is between treatment interventions and recidivism. And here is a key point:

- Can you see the power or persuasiveness of this method? It's this: You have *one number* that shows whether rehabilitation works and, if so, by how much!

In this regard, what would Martinson and other nothing works critics have argued should be the relationship between treatment programs and recidivism? If you answered zero, then you are brilliant! Critics might even have predicted a negative number, which would show that treatment interventions increased recidivism. Such a number would show that treatment *really doesn't work.*

But what would happen if the effect size was *positive*? This would show that across all treatment programs, rehabilitation reduced recidivism. And what would happen if one analyzed different types of treatment programs and found that some program types really reduced recidivism while others did not? *Alas, this is precisely what the meta-analyses showed in the 1990s and continue to show today!*

Let's just touch on a few more points. Let's say that you are reading an article and the reviewer concludes that, overall, the effect size is +.20. That is, the *r* value is .20, which means that the correlation between treatment and recidivism is .20. What the heck does that mean?

In practical language, the *r* value (the effect size) can be seen as the difference in recidivism between the treatment group (the group that received the rehabilitation program) and the control group (the group that did not receive the rehabilitation program). One common approach is to assume that the average recidivism rate is 50%. If this were the case, then an effect size of +.20 would mean that the control group had a recidivism rate of 60% while the treatment group had a recidivism rate of 40%. This is a 20 percentage point difference. Similarly, a 10 percentage point difference would mean that the control group's recidivism rate was 55% and the treatment group's recidivism rate was 45%. As you can see, even a statistically modest effect size (e.g., +.10) can have practical policy effects. A 10% reduction in recidivism, for example, can save a lot of crime.

Although we are fans of meta-analyses as a way of synthesizing large bodies of research evidence, no method of analyzing or summarizing studies is without its weaknesses. Perhaps the largest problem is the *garbage in–garbage out* problem. No matter how sophisticated the statistical technique, the summary is only as good as the studies being analyzed. In practical terms, this means that if the studies available are too few in number or mostly are based on weak methodology, then the results reached in the meta-analysis are going to be open to question. Fortunately, in the rehabilitation area, the body of research studies is fairly extensive and allows for meta-analyses whose results are pretty believable.

We are now prepared to find out what the existing meta-analyses show about treatment effectiveness! We cover this research in two sections:

- What did the meta-analyses find was the *overall effect* of rehabilitation programs?
- What did the meta-analyses find was the effect of rehabilitation when different types of programs were assessed? Was there *homogeneity* or *heterogeneity* in the effect size?

THE OVERALL EFFECT SIZE

The first approach that researchers took when assessing rehabilitation programs was this: Let's take all the rigorous program evaluation studies we can find and see what the impact of rehabilitation is across all these studies (and programs). We will not make any distinctions by type of program. We just want to know whether rehabilitation works in general. We will include in this assessment punishment-oriented programs that advocates of rehabilitation would not see as treatment in the traditional sense of the word. Again, a meta-analysis is sort of like a batting average in baseball. It is not computed the same way, but what we are really asking here is how well treatment programs bat across all of the interventions that have been evaluated.

There have now been numerous meta-analyses conducted. In fact, McGuire (2013) has compiled a listing of 100 of these meta-analyses! They focus on different samples of evaluation studies and on offenders of different ages. Meta-analyses also have been undertaken by authors in other nations. Regardless, they seem to point to the same conclusion:

- *The overall effect size for rehabilitation across all interventions is approximately +.10.*

In layperson's language, this would mean that the recidivism rate for the control group would be 10 percentage points higher than for the treatment group. Thus, if the control group's recidivism was 55%, the treatment group's recidivism would be 45%.

This conclusion is quite significant. It immediately contradicts Martinson's nothing works view. That is, across all interventions, rehabilitation programs are effective in reducing recidivism. As McGuire (2013, p. 20) notes, "there are firm grounds for arguing that we can be more confident than ever that there is a range of methods which 'work.'" Their effects are modest but not inconsequential. McGuire provides a useful context for comparison, noting that "the mean effect for aspirin in reducing myocardial infarctions (heart attack) is 0.04; of chemotherapy for breast cancer it is 0.8–0.11; and of heart bypass surgery in reducing coronary thrombosis it is 0.15" (2013, p. 31). "Set against this background," he observes, "an average effect size of 0.10 cannot be dismissed as merely trivial" (p. 31).

Still, is a 10% reduction in recidivism the best that we can do? If so, then this means that rehabilitation will be a useful tool in corrections but not one that can be looked to for important savings in crime. Well, as it turns out, this is not the best we can do! It is to this issue that we now turn.

HETEROGENEITY OF EFFECT SIZES

Some correctional interventions work better than others. To return to language used above (we told you we would get back to this), the effects of treatment programs are *heterogeneous,* not homogeneous. Recall that Martinson contended that across various treatment types or categories, some things worked and some things did not work but that nothing worked consistently or better than any other modality. Again, this is a prediction of *homogeneity of effect sizes.* But this is just not what meta-analyses find.

In fact, meta-analyses suggest that some programs have no effect or are iatrogenic—they increase recidivism. By contrast, other types of programs work quite well. They have effect sizes of +.25 or higher. Recall that an effect size of +.25 would translate into the treatment group having a recidivism rate of 37.5% and the control group having a recidivism rate of 62.5%.

Of course, a key challenge is to discover what distinguishes programs that produce success—high effect sizes—and those that do not. In fact, this is what the Canadians—Paul Gendreau, Don Andrews, and James Bonta—have been doing for over two decades. As promised, we will review their theory of the principles of effective intervention up ahead. They contend, with some justification, that programs that follow their principles produce meaningful reductions in recidivism.

At this point, however, let us share one important finding. Across numerous studies, it now appears that one type of intervention is the most reliable in achieving high reductions in recidivism: *cognitive-behavioral programs* (see also MacKenzie, 2006; Wilson, Bouffard, & MacKenzie, 2005). If Cullen and Jonson were going to implement a program with high-risk/serious offenders, we would start with a cognitive-behavioral approach and then perhaps add in some other elements (e.g., work, training, education).

If you would like to learn more about cognitive-behavioral programs, some good books can be consulted (see, e.g., Spiegler & Guevremont, 1998; Van Voorhis, Braswell, & Lester, 2009). But we can give you a brief overview. Thus, cognitive-behavioral programs focus on doing two key things:

- They try to cognitively restructure the distorted or erroneous cognitions of an individual. These are sometimes called thinking errors.

- They try to assist the person to learn new adaptive cognitive skills.

In the case of offenders, existing cognitive distortions are thoughts and values that justify antisocial activities (e.g., aggression, stealing, substance abuse) and that denigrate conventional prosocial pursuits regarding education, work, and social relationships. Most offenders also have minimal cognitive skills as to how to behave in a prosocial fashion. In light of these deficits, effective cognitive-behavioral programs attempt to assist offenders (1) to define the problems that led them into conflict with authorities, (2) to select goals, (3) to generate new alternative prosocial solutions, and then (4) to implement these solutions.

Thus, a cognitive-behavioral program within corrections would involve the following steps:

- The predominant antisocial beliefs of the offender in question are identified.

- In a firm yet fair and respectful manner, it is pointed out to the offender that the beliefs in question are not acceptable.

- If the antisocial beliefs continue, emphatic disapproval (e.g., withdrawal of social reinforcers) always follows.

- Meanwhile, the offender is exposed to alternative prosocial ways of thinking and behaving by concrete modeling on the part of the therapist in one-on-one sessions or in structured group learning settings (e.g., courses in anger management).

- Gradually, with repeated practice, and always with the immediate application of reinforcers whenever the offender demonstrates prosocial beliefs and conduct, the offender's behavior is shaped to an appropriate level.

THE IMPACT OF META-ANALYSIS ON THE NOTHING WORKS DEBATE

The findings from the meta-analyses of treatment programs have been critically important in rebutting the nothing works doctrine. Again, once Martinson reframed the attack on rehabilitation as an issue of effectiveness (as opposed to state discretion), then the central issue was the status of the empirical data. At first, of course, rehabilitation's critics were in the position of citing Martinson's review and claiming that science was on their side. Ted Palmer and the Canadian psychologists muddied the water quite a bit, but not enough to swing the tide in the other direction.

The meta-analyses conducted by Lipsey and others, however, gave rehabilitation supporters a decided upper hand. With a quantitative analysis of a few hundred studies in tow, they could now show that overall (or across all interventions) treatment programs reduced recidivism and that some programs were quite effective. Of course, as discussed previously, what scholars and others believe or are ready to believe is not simply based on the data that are presented to them. There are still many scholars—especially criminologists—who simply fight the idea that correctional programming could possibly do any good.

Again, the meta-analyses are quite difficult to dismiss. Unlike narrative reviews, there is a clear number showing the effect size of rehabilitation overall and of specific types of intervention strategies in particular. It is possible to challenge the findings on methodological grounds, but the replication of the findings in meta-analysis after meta-analysis is hard to dispute. In fact, the onus now is on the critics to produce their own meta-analyses showing that rehabilitation programs have a zero effect size. They are free to go look at the existing research studies and show where the rehabilitation scholars have gotten it wrong! Of course, they have not done so, in large part because their findings likely would not differ from those published to date.

Before the rehabilitation crowd gets too big for their britches, it is important to realize that serious obstacles remain to making treatment a guiding correctional theory. Knowledge about what works is growing, but how to disseminate this information and to ensure the implementation of quality programs remain daunting challenges. This is a time for optimism, not hubris.

What Does Not Work

Now it is time to become a bit more specific about what works and does not work to reduce reoffending. In this section, we will briefly focus on what does not work. A weakness in all these approaches is that they are based on faulty criminology. They do not target for change the most important factors—again, which Gendreau and Ross (1987) called *criminogenic needs*—that underlie recidivism. Four types of programs merit special attention because they seem plausible but, alas, will never work (Andrews & Bonta, 2010):

- *Punishment-oriented programs.* Correctional interventions that are based on deterrence theory have not proven effective. *Scared straight programs,* where juveniles visit prison and are warned in an intimidating fashion about what life behind bars would entail, have either no impact or a slight criminogenic effect. As we saw in Chapter 4, control programs, such as *intensive supervision,* have produced dismal results.

- *Character-building programs.* This is really a subcategory of punishment-oriented interventions because they emphasize taking a tough and demanding approach with offenders. If a difference exists, it is that the underlying goal is not so much to scare offenders straight (as in traditional deterrence) but to break the offender down and then to rebuild him (or her). Exactly what breaking an offender down actually means is never specified, but it seems to imply stripping away the offender's defenses and seeming bravado to reach some inner core of vulnerability that will then make the offender open to a new way of life. In any case, such programs would include *boot camps* and *wilderness* programs. The research does not show that these approaches are effective.

- *Boosting self-esteem.* There is nothing wrong with boosting a youth's self-esteem, especially if it is based on realistic accomplishments. After all, we all like to feel good about ourselves! Still, self-esteem apparently has little to do with crime; it is a weak predictor of recidivism. Programs that focus exclusively on self-esteem are unlikely to work. In fact, they may risk creating confident criminals!

- *Client-centered, non-directive counseling.* When you read meta-analyses, they will often include a category called individual and/or group counseling. The problem with analyzing studies this way is that what is done in a counseling session can vary widely depending on the treatment approach taken by the counselor. In this context, it appears that one general approach to counseling does not work with offenders: counseling that is non-directive, allows inmates to set the agenda, and is not structured systematically to change antisocial values and ways of thinking. That is, if the approach is too client-centered and non-directive, the counseling sessions may be too poorly focused to change the factors central to recidivism.

What Does Work: Principles of Effective Intervention

If you were to read a meta-analysis by Lipsey and others (but not the Canadians), you would see variation in which treatment types or modalities work the best. You might be told, for example, that for youths in the community, individual counseling, interpersonal skills training, and behavioral programs reduce reoffending consistently whereas deterrence and vocational programs do not (Lipsey, 1999a, p. 150; see also MacKenzie, 2006). This guidance certainly is valuable and should be heeded. Its weakness, however, is that such advice is not a complete theory of correctional intervention. These data on effectiveness hint at which programs might work but they do not explain why and to whom they should be applied.

In this context, Cullen and Jonson believe that a better and more systematic approach is to implement programs based on the *principles of effective intervention* (Andrews, 1995; Andrews & Bonta, 2010; Gendreau, 1996). We alluded to core elements of these principles in our discussion of Gendreau and Ross's (1987) review of studies revealing effective treatment programs. Although some dispute exists (Porporino, 2010), there is now growing empirical evidence that the principles approach comprises the most powerful, empirically justified treatment paradigm available (Andrews & Bonta, 2010; Andrews et al., 1990; Gendreau, Smith, & French, 2006; McGuire, 2002; Ogloff & Davis, 2004; Smith, Gendreau, & Swartz, 2009).

Quite simply, for scholarship on correctional rehabilitation to move forward, it is essential that it go beyond the nothing works debate that is now more than four decades old and growing sterile. The dichotomous question—does or does not rehabilitation work?—is no longer productive. The terms of the debate, in short, have changed. We now know that certain kinds of programs have little prospect of ever working and we know that other kinds of programs achieve frequent success. When this occurs, the logical approach is to study systematically what it is about effective programs that is at the root of their success. Again, this is the approach taken by the Canadian psychologists, led most prominently by Don Andrews, James Bonta, and Paul Gendreau. Don Andrews passed away in 2010, but his ideas and contributions are enduring.

In developing their principles of effective intervention, the Canadian psychologists did not approach the topic from an armchair. Over the years, they had accumulated plenty of experience in the field with programs. They had established programs and evaluated many more. Still, they realized that personal experience is no substitute for data if one wishes to have a science of correctional treatment that is evidence-based. As a result, from the inception of their work, they rooted their understanding of criminal conduct and its change in the experimental research of psychology generally. They conducted meta-analyses on the main predictors of recidivism so as to know what to target for reform (Gendreau, Little, & Goggin, 1996). They examined what treatment interventions could change or be *responsive* to these risk factors. They developed instruments to classify offenders by risk level and to assess whether correctional agencies were capable of treatment integrity.

No one approach should be seen as sacrosanct—as so sacred that it is above criticism or above improvement. Cullen and Jonson believe that the Canadians' principles paradigm is awfully persuasive. We see it as the most criminologically sound, empirically based, and demonstrably effective treatment paradigm available (Cullen & Smith, 2011; Smith, 2013). But again, skepticism is a healthy part of science. Organized skepticism is the duty of any community of scholars (Merton, 1973). We should perhaps use the Canadians' approach but not be awed by it. Blind allegiance can be a dangerous thing (Cullen, 2012).

The RNR Model. So, what are these *principles of effective intervention*? The Canadians have listed them in various forms and numbers—an issue we return to below (see Andrews, 1995; Gendreau, 1996). However, three principles are at the core of the model: risk (R), need (N), and responsivity (R). Given the centrality of these principles, the perspective is now known by its acronym, the *RNR model*. Accordingly, we review each of the three principles in some detail. Note that this discussion is a bit out of order (need, responsivity, and risk or NRR rather than RNR) because it is easier to explain that way! We then add two more points at the end of this section.

- *The first principle is that interventions should target the known predictors of crime and recidivism for change. This is called the needs principle.*

This principle starts with the assumption that correctional treatments must be based on criminological knowledge—what the Canadian scholars call the *social psychology of criminal conduct*. They distinguish between two predictors that place offenders at-risk for crime:

- *Static predictors*—such as an offender's criminal history—that cannot be changed.
- *Dynamic predictors*—such as antisocial values—that can potentially be changed. In the Canadians' perspective, these dynamic predictors or risk factors are typically referred to as *criminogenic needs*. (We should warn that no one else uses this terminology in this specific way. This does not make the Canadians' usage faulty; it only means that other scholars have not read their work and/or adopted their terminology. This is really no big deal, except to the extent that you might get confused or use this terminology with the assumption that it is commonly understood.)

Importantly, when investigating risk factors or predictors of crime, it is possible that the research could have indicated that the major predictors are static. If so, then the prospects for rehabilitation would have been minimal (you cannot change something that is static and thus, by definition, unchangeable). But this did not turn out to be the case! Meta-analyses reveal that many of the most salient predictors are dynamic (they are criminogenic needs) and thus can be changed!

Again, this is a critical point. Let us assume that the only thing that predicted recidivism was the offender's past criminal record. If this were the case, what would this tell treatment scholars? It would mean that we could identify nothing that we could change at this time in an offender's life that could reduce recidivism. We cannot, after all, change a *past record,* since this is over and done with. It would be like telling a doctor that the only predictor of a patient's sickness is whether the person has been sick in the past. Without more knowledge of what could be changed about the patient here and now, the doctor would have no intervention to use.

But, as we have just said, there are dynamic risk factors that are closely associated with recidivism. According to Andrews and Bonta (2010), research reveals that four are most important. They call these the "Big Four" (2010, pp. 58–59). They explain them in this way (2010, p. 500):

- "History of antisocial behavior. Early and continuing involvement in the number and variety of antisocial acts in a variety of settings."
- "Antisocial personality pattern. Adventurous, pleasure-seeking, weak self-control, restlessly aggressive."
- "Antisocial cognition: Attitudes, values, beliefs, and rationalizations supportive of crime and cognitive and emotional states of anger, resentment, and defiance. Criminal/reformed criminal/anti-criminal identity."
- "Antisocial associates: Close association with criminal others and relative isolation from anti-criminal others, immediate social support for crime."

These factors should be given priority in any treatment intervention—again, because they are robustly related to offending and are amenable to alteration. Thus, if an offender is taught to embrace prosocial values, has antisocial friends replaced by "good people," and learns to think before acting, then this person is much less likely to return to crime. Obviously, it is not possible to change a history of antisocial behavior, but it is possible to "build up noncriminal alternative behavior in risky settings" (Andrews & Bonta, 2010, p. 500). Further, Andrews and Bonta (2010, p. 59) identify four other risks that they term the "Moderate Four." These include: "family/marital circumstances" (focus on quality of interpersonal relationships among family members); "school/work" (focus on relationships and on performance and accompanying rewards); "leisure/recreation" (low involvement and satisfaction); and "substance abuse." Together, the "Big Four" and "Moderate Four" are called the "Central Eight risk/need factors" (p. 58).

It is important to reemphasize a point made right above. Andrews and Bonta believe that treatment must be based on an accurate understanding of the causes of recidivism. This is why they devote so much attention to documenting the Big Four and Central Eight. They want to make sure that treatments are targeting the correct sources of crime ("criminogenic needs"). This insight would be commonsensical in medicine. When you go to the doctor, you expect the physicians to diagnose the cause of your illness. You know that if this is not the case, then the treatment you are given will not work. Effective medicine thus depends on an accurate scientific understanding of diseases. This reality also occurs in corrections. Alas, many interventions do not have a strong underlying criminological foundation. As a result, these programs focus on factors that their advocates believe cause crime, such as low self-esteem, which actually are unrelated or only weakly related to recidivism. Thus, targeting these factors for intervention will produce little, if any, change in an offender's conduct.

- *The second principle is that treatment services should be behavioral, social learning, and cognitive-behavioral in nature. This is called the responsivity principle.*

In general, behavioral or, as we have seen, cognitive-behavioral interventions are effective in changing an array of human behaviors. With regard to crime, they are well suited to altering the Big Four criminogenic needs—antisocial attitudes, cognitions, personality orientations, and associations—that underlie recidivism. Thus, Andrews (1995) notes that these interventions would "employ the cognitive behavioural and social learning techniques of modelling, graduated practice, role playing, reinforcement, extinction, resource provision, concrete verbal suggestions (symbolic modelling, giving reasons, prompting) and cognitive restructuring" (p. 56). Reinforcements in the program should be largely positive, not negative. And the services should be intensive, lasting three to nine months and occupying 40% to 70% of the offenders' time while they are in the program. Remember, the goal is to have offenders learn a set of behavioral and cognitive skills—such as how to think differently, how to control anger and impulsivity, how to avoid criminal associates, and how to respond in prosocial rather than antisocial ways when in risky situations (e.g., insulted in a bar, seeing an unguarded computer).

In contrast, many other interventions are ineffective not only because they do not address the factors that cause recidivism, but also because they are not delivered in a way that can change criminogenic needs; that is, they are not "responsive" to them. They are providing the "wrong medicine." Thus, Andrews and Hoge (1995) contend that less effective treatment "styles" have these characteristics: They "are less structured, self-reflective, verbally interactive and insight-oriented approaches" (p. 36). Punishment approaches also do not target criminogenic needs or target them responsively. Not surprisingly, they are among the most ineffective interventions with offenders (see Lipsey, 2009; McGuire, 2013).

- *Third, treatment interventions should be used primarily with higher-risk offenders, targeting their criminogenic needs (dynamic risk factors) for change. This is called the risk principle.*

It is often said that interventions should mainly be given to low-risk offenders because they are less hardened and thus open to change. Implicit in this view is that high-risk offenders are beyond redemption. As it turns out, however, higher-risk offenders are capable of change. And, more noteworthy, the most substantial savings and recidivism are acquired by providing them with treatment services. (Recall our discussion of this issue in Chapter 6.)

In part, this is because higher-risk offenders have more to change about them. Thus, when resources are scarce, it appears that it is this group of offenders that should be targeted for change. In fact, it appears that less hardened or lower-risk offenders generally do not require intervention because they are unlikely to recidivate. Subjecting them to structured, intrusive interventions is not a wise use of scarce resources and, under certain circumstances, may increase recidivism.

Note that the most effective strategy for assessing the risk level of offenders is to rely not on the clinical judgments of counselors (who they "think" are the worst cases). Clinical judgments should not be totally disregarded, but they are open to personal bias. Remember, they are a form of insider knowledge!

Not only in corrections but in other realms of human behavior, it appears that the best predictions are made through the use of actuarial-based assessment instruments (validated instruments that use largely quantitative scores to inform decisions) (Ayres, 2007). In corrections, one of the best instruments for classifying offenders—one that the Canadians developed to implement their treatment theory—is the Level of Service Inventory. Research has shown this instrument has strong predictive validity; that is, those offenders it says are high risk (i.e., score high on the LSI) are indeed more likely to offend (Smith, Gendreau, & Swartz, 2009; Vose, Cullen, & Smith, 2008; see also Andrews & Bonta, 2010).

Two More Points. We want to end this discussion with two further observations. First, the three principles just described form the core of the Canadians' perspective and are now widely known the field of corrections. "Everyone" in the field—including Andrews and Bonta (2010)—now uses the acronym *RNR* to refer to these three core principles. And as noted, "everyone" also refers to this correctional theory as the *Risk–Need–Responsivity model.*

However, the Andrews, Bonta, and their fellow compatriots north of the U.S. border have long understood that a range of other considerations can either boost or weaken the treatment gains achieved from the application of the core RNR principles. The Canadians thus developed a comprehensive treatment paradigm whose full statement requires 15 principles. These are laid out in the Canadians' correctional bible—Andrews and Bonta's (2010, pp. 46–47) *The Psychology of Criminal Conduct.* Here we will list a few of the major considerations that, if addressed, have the potential to increase treatment effectiveness.

- When possible, conduct an intervention in the community as opposed to an institutional setting.

- Ensure that the program uses staff who are well-trained, are interpersonally sensitive, are monitored, and know how to deliver the treatment service.

- Follow offenders after they have completed the program and give them structured relapse prevention (or aftercare).

- Specific responsivity: To the extent possible, match the way a treatment service is delivered to the learning styles of the offender. Factors that might be taken into account in service delivery are the offenders' lack of motivation to participate in the program, feelings of anxiety or depression, and neuropsychological deficits stemming from early childhood experiences (e.g., physical trauma). For example, offenders with low IQs might not respond as well to interventions that are verbal but would do better with interventions that emphasize more extensive use of tangible reinforcers and from repeated, graduated behavioral rehearsal and shaping of skills.

Second, the RNR model was invented to guide the delivery of treatment programs within correctional agencies, whether these are prisons, halfway houses, or community based facilities. More recently, however, James Bonta has been instrumental in developing a way to use RNR principles to guide the interactions of probation and parole officers with their supervisees. He came up with another clever acronym for this initiative—*STICS*, which stands for the "Strategic Training Initiative in Community Supervision" (Andrews & Bonta, 2010). The development of STICS made sense because his meta-analyses of existing studies found that traditional community supervision had very little impact on recidivism (Bonta, Rugge, Scott, Bourgon, & Yessine, 2008; see also Schaefer, Cullen, & Eck, 2016). This represents a colossal missed opportunity! On any given day, recall that 1 in 51 adults in the United States is under community supervision; the raw number exceeds 4.7 million (Herberman & Bonczar, 2014).

The challenge was whether RNR principles could be applied productively in a supervision meeting that may last less than a half hour. Bonta thought that it could be so used. Perhaps the key to the initiative was training officers how to recognize "expressions of antisocial attitudes in the clients, and how to use cognitive-behavioral techniques to replace these cognitions and attitudes with prosocial ones" (Andrews & Bonta, 2010, p. 415). During the office meeting, supervising officers would use about 15 minutes in the middle of the session to target risk factors for change, which might involve "teaching the cognitive-behavioral model or doing a role-playing exercise" (p. 416). Offenders might also be assigned homework—such as trying a new behavior (e.g., recognizing and replacing risky thinking)—that would then be discussed and reinforced in the next meeting.

Notably, a two-year evaluation found that compared with the control group, those receiving the RNR intervention had a recidivism rate that was 15 percentage points lower (Bonta et al., 2011). Promising evaluation results also have been reported from two similar programs conducted independently (Robinson et al., 2012; Smith, Schweitzer, Labrecque, & Latessa, 2012). More broadly, this research suggests the potential benefits of training all correctional personnel how to teach offenders prosocial cognitive-behavioral skills. Such a continuum of treatment—whether during probation or incarceration—would provide a consistent, integrated approach to offender rehabilitation.

What Else Might Work?

DESISTANCE-BASED REHABILITATION

Whenever you are the big dog, you are an inviting target. In this sense, Andrews, Bonta, Gendreau, and colleagues' RNR model is a victim of its own success. As the dominant paradigm in the field (Cullen, 2013), it is increasingly criticized either explicitly or implicitly. In general, Cullen and Jonson are not so enamored with these alternative perspectives (Cullen, 2012). Part of the problem is that they rarely start with a sound theory of criminal conduct that is based on the empirically established predictors of recidivism. They often sound plausible, but it is not always clear that their proposed treatment intervention would target the most important risk factors or be capable of changing them (i.e., be "responsive" to them). Just keep these ideas in mind as we proceed.

Perhaps the most important alternative to the RNR model is what might be called *desistance-based rehabilitation* (for examples, see Brayford et al., 2010; Veysey et al., 2009; see also Raynor & Robinson, 2009). As life-course theory and research has proliferated in criminology (Benson, 2013; Cullen, 2013)—an issue we return to when we discuss early intervention programs in Chapter 9—it became clear that, eventually, almost all offenders stop breaking the law (Laub & Sampson, 2003). We call this *desistance* from crime.

One possibility is that they just get old, and like old people (such as Cullen) just give up and retire. They may still be a jerk—argue a lot, get drunk a lot—but they stop burglarizing and robbing because it takes too much effort (see Gottfredson & Hirschi, 1990). Most criminologists, however, do not like this retirement theory, because they want to think that most things are caused. Explaining things is what makes them famous! One popular desistance theory is that offenders get lucky and meet, and then marry, a wonderful woman. Sampson and Laub (1993) describe this as acquiring a quality social bond. (Cullen, who is a father, is not so sure how many dads want their cherished daughter to be a social bond for some predator!) Another theory, this one by Maruna (2001), is that some offenders develop a "redemption script," sort of a new identity and story about their lives and its possibilities. They relinquish a "condemnation script" that tells them that they are "doomed to deviance" and instead redefine themselves as a fundamentally good person who can serve a higher purpose in life (2001, p. 74).

Okay, here is the link to corrections. Desistance is a form of rehabilitation, for these life-course-persistent offenders stop committing crimes. The key thing, though, is that reform is not due to a planned treatment program run by a professional but rather takes place in the real world. Offenders' desistance is called "naturalistic" because, again, it happens sort of "naturally" in the course of their lives. Notably, some scholars believe that important lessons can be learned from naturalistic desistance and imported into correctional treatment (Raynor & Robinson, 2009). One insight is that offenders often desist not because some deficit (or "criminogenic need") is fixed—as the RNR model contends—but rather because they draw on some *strength* that enables them to leave crime. This might be a new social bond (not Cullen's daughter) or a new prosocial identity or script. Another insight is that offenders who desist become *motivated* to change and exercise *human agency* through which they "will" their reformation. Desistance-based rehabilitation programs tend to emphasize these positives, arguing that correctional interventions should be strength based and prioritize efforts to inspire in offenders the motivation to change.

Cullen and Jonson suspect that desistance-based rehabilitation is popular because it is ideologically pleasing to a lot of criminologists. Rather than portray offenders as having deficits that make them predatory or at least chronically bothersome, a desistance perspective gets to see offenders as aspiring to "make good" and to live a "good life." This is a chance for everyone to feel good! The task of rehabilitation is now clear: help offenders to build upon their valued talents and traits—their strengths—which will also inspire them to become motivated to act like "the rest of us." Maybe this is true or true to a degree. But the other reality is that the research underlying desistance theories is limited in scope and far from definitive (see, e.g., Sullivan, 2013). For example, Skardhamar, Savolainen, Aase, and Lyngstad's (2015) recent review concludes that those who are married are less involved in crime. Good news for correctional desistance theory? Well, not really. A closer inspection of this literature leaves more questions about the effects of marriage unanswered than answered:

> Critical scrutiny of the evidence regarding the causal nature of the reported associations suggests, however, that claims about the restraining influence of marriage are overstated. None of the studies demonstrates evidence of direct (counterfactual) causality; no study has served a causal estimate unbiased by selection processes. Moreover, only a few studies address time ordering, and some of those show that desistance precedes rather than follows marriage. Evidence in support of the theoretical mechanisms responsible for the marriage effect is also mixed and insufficient. The criminological literature has been insensitive to the reality that entering a marital union is increasingly unlikely to signify the point at which a committed, high-quality relationship is formed. (Skardhamar et al., 2015, p. 385)

None of this is to say that desistance-based rehabilitation is fatally flawed. Rather, the point is just that those erecting rehabilitation models on the shaky foundation of desistance theories should exercise a lot of caution. As we have argued repeatedly, targeting for change factors unrelated or only weakly related to recidivism will consign a treatment modality to the dustbin of ineffectiveness. A major advantage of the RNR model is that Andrews and Bonta do not make this mistake. Just go and read their 672-page scientific tour de force, *The Psychology of Criminal Conduct*!

THE GOOD LIVES MODEL

Importantly, one rehabilitation theory has emerged from this general perspective that is gaining adherents cross-nationally: the *Good Lives Model*, also known by its acronym of the *GLM*. Cullen and Jonson must start with a confession: We are RNR model advocates and thus not terribly enamored with the Good Lives Model (GLM). That said, we are in the business of science, not religion; there is no correctional heresy! The weaknesses of the RNR model should be laid bare so, if possible, it can be improved. If we can develop a rival treatment technique with equal efficacy, that would be great! It would be like having two effective medicines that can treat the same disease (Cullen, 2012).

The GLM is a formidable opponent. Cullen and Jonson do not like the fact that the GLM has been put forth as a reaction to and critique of the RNR model. As a result, the advocates of these two perspectives have been in a bit of a tussle. It is sort of fun to watch academics fight it out, and we can learn from vigorous debate (see, e.g., Andrews, Bonta, & Wormith, 2011; Ward, Yates, & Willis, 2012). Still, at this point, Cullen and Jonson prefer to see each perspective as its own theory. For the GLM, criticizing the RNR perspective does not make the GLM more true. Only marshalling lots of data that demonstrates the perspective's effectiveness will do that.

The GLM was first developed by Tony Ward in a founding article published in 2002, and then was elaborated in an influential book coauthored with Shadd Maruna in 2007 and in numerous articles (see, e.g., Ward, Mann, & Gannon, 2007; Ward & Marshall, 2007; Whitehead, Ward, & Collie, 2007; Willis & Ward, 2013). Part of Cullen and Jonson's trepidation about the GLM is that it is based on a plausible but ultimately unverified theory of offending. For those familiar with strain theory, the GLM shares the assumption that people pursue goals and can achieve these through either legitimate or illegitimate means. There is an assumption that if legitimate means to cherished goals are blocked, individuals will likely turn to illegitimate means (see Cloward, 1959). Now, let's put things in their language.

The overarching goal of all humans is, or should be, to live a "good life"—ergo, the "good lives" model! You do this by achieving positive goals through positive means. In GLM language, goals are called "primary goods"—sort of an awkward phrase but then that's what the theory chooses to say! There are 11 categories of primary goods, which are listed in Willis and Ward (2013):

> (i) life (including healthy living and functioning); (ii) knowledge; (iii) excellence in play; (iv) excellence in work (including mastery experiences); (v) excellence in agency (i.e., autonomy and self-direction); (vi) inner peace (i.e., freedom from emotional turmoil and stress); (vii) friendship (including intimate, romantic, and family relationships); (viii) community; (ix) spirituality (in the broad sense of finding meaning and purpose in life); (x) happiness; and (xi) creativity. (p. 307)

People, including offenders, weigh or prioritize these goals or primary goods differently. In fact, what primary goods are desired define their "sense of who they are and what is really worth having in life" (Willis & Ward, 2013, p. 307). The challenge, however, is that not everyone can gain access to their most cherished primary goods through prosocial means. Such goal blockage is the major source of crime.

In the GLM model, means are given another odd name: "secondary goods." Secondary goods are the "concrete means of securing primary goods"; they are best seen as "the specific roles, practices and actions that provide the routes to primary goods" (Willis & Ward, 2013, p. 307). Criminogenic needs—the N in the RNR model—are seen as inappropriate secondary goods—the wrong way to achieve primary goods. Thus, antisocial peers might be a means to secure the goal of friendship and intimacy. Or antisocial attitudes might justify using violence as a means of displaying autonomy. Whereas Andrews and Bonta (2010) would see criminogenic needs as targets for treatment in and of themselves, Ward and his colleagues would see them in relation to the primary goods or goals that offenders hope to achieve.

Criminal behavior is caused directly or indirectly. "The direct route," note Willis and Ward (2013, p. 307), "is evident when primary good(s) are explicitly sought through offence-related actions." For example, an offender blocked from intimacy with an adult may seek this good through sexual victimization of a child; or a youth seeking happiness might steal a car for joyriding. Thus, in such cases, the offense is the illegitimate means used to reach the desired goals. By contrast, the "indirect route occurs when the pursuit of a good or set of goods creates a ripple effect in the person's personal circumstances and these unanticipated effects increase the chances" of offending (Ward et al., 2007, p. 92). In an example given by Willis and Ward (2013, p. 308), let us say that a husband so valued excellence at his job that he worked excessive hours, which in turn led to the deterioration in his relationship to his wife. This relationship, however, was the key means (secondary good) used by him to achieve another valued goal—intimacy. To cope with the emotional distress of a looming breakup of his marriage, the man might then use pornography—a decision that reflects an inability to adequately manage moods. Using "sexual arousal as a distraction" might then result "in the entrenchment of deviant sexual feelings and, ultimately, to his sexually assaulting a woman" (2013, p. 308).

All this makes Cullen and Jonson concerned—for two reasons. First and foremost, where is the empirical evidence that offenders commit crimes because they cannot reach primary goods? Andrews and Bonta link recidivism to the "Big Four" and "Central Eight" because of a wealth of meta-analytic data showing that these are the strongest dynamic predictors of offending. The criminological theory of the GLM is plausible but not demonstrated. Even by the advocates' own admission, much of the model is based on "assumptions." Thus, Ward and Maruna (2007, pp. 152–153) note that "the point of this evaluation is not to determine if various assumptions (e.g., that offenders are like everyone else and strive to live a good life) are 'right' or 'wrong,' but rather whether they are consistent, reasonable, and most importantly, therapeutically useful. We argue that they are all these things." The risk in relying on assumptions rather than on meta-analytic data, however, is that the underlying assumptions about causes of recidivism might be wrong, or only partially correct. If so, then the capacity of the GLM to target the correct factors for treatment would be compromised.

Second, even if the GLM has merit, it would seem that therapists would have to be quite skilled to implement it with offenders. In particular, they would have to be not only emotionally mature but also able to figure out for each individual what kind of good "lives" the offender wished to live (i.e., what was the person's set of most valued primary goods), what secondary goods were blocking the attainment of these goods, and then how to build capabilities so that the client could achieve goods through prosocial means. Whew! That's a lot to accomplish! We suspect that Tony Ward and his collaborators have the talent needed to be effective therapists. But can these complex skills really be taught to the average correctional worker?

There is one feature about the GLM that Cullen and Jonson find attractive. Ward and his buddies are concerned about the well-being of offenders. They not only want to reduce offenders' recidivism but also want them to live a good life. The two are inextricably mixed, because committing crimes will not produce a good life. But the goal of GLM treatment is not just to stop criminal behavior but also to leave the offender a better person capable of more personal fulfillment and better citizenship. Advocates of the RNR model do not buy this approach. They are focused like a laser on fixing criminogenic needs. They believe that attempting to improve offenders' general well-being is likely to result in an intervention targeting inappropriate, non-criminogenic needs that will lessen the effectiveness of the treatment.

From the GLM perspective, focusing on living a good life is crucial to the therapeutic enterprise because it is what inspires offenders to want to relinquish their criminal life course. Change is difficult, and it requires a lot of motivation. But how can we expect offenders to find a rehabilitation program worthwhile if it is imposed on them and they are largely told that they need to fix up a bunch of bad things about themselves? By contrast, the GLM involves offenders from the beginning of the intervention, trying to learn what their primary goods are—the goals that, if achieved, will make them fulfilled. Then, the trick is to build in them the capabilities to achieve their valued goals in a prosocial way. This involves developing with each offender an individualized Good Lives Plan. Willis and Ward (2013) describe the plan in this way:

> A key task of assessment involves mapping out an individual's good lives conceptualization by identifying the weightings given by the various primary goods. This is achieved through (i) asking increasingly detailed questions about an offender's core commitments in life and his or her valued activities and experiences, and (ii) identifying the goals and underlying values that were evident (either directly or indirectly) in an offender's offence-related actions. Once an individual's conceptualization of what constitutes a good life is understood, future-oriented secondary goods aimed at satisfying primary goods in socially acceptable ways are formulated collaboratively with the client and translated into a Good Lives (GL) treatment/intervention plan. (p. 308)

So, what then, should we make of the GLM? Remember, this book, *Correctional Theory*, is evidence based, so Cullen and Jonson would like to answer this question by consulting the existing studies assessing the GLM. Alas, research showing the effectiveness of this novel treatment theory is frustratingly limited. Some beginning data have been accumulated that are suggestive of the model's capacity to rehabilitate offenders (see Willis & Ward, 2013). But this research can be summarized in a few pages and pales in comparison to the case that Andrews and Bonta (2010) make for the vitality of the RNR model. For now, Cullen and Jonson would place our bets on the Canadians' treatment theory, although we welcome the further development and empirical testing of the GLM.

Conclusion: Reaffirming Rehabilitation

There is no panacea or cure-all for offender recidivism. Any intervention with offenders is likely to experience a fair amount of failure. Treating offenders is similar to treating cancer patients. There is no magic bullet—like a polio vaccine—that will wipe out the disease. Progress is slow. It takes painstaking research and experimentation to keep chipping away at the failure rate. Still, progress is important. Lives are at stake.

The critical question is what our best bet will be when placing offenders in correctional programs. At this stage, five conclusions can be drawn from the existing research:

- Punishment-oriented programs (deterrence, control, character building) have been extensively evaluated. There is no evidence that they work and some evidence that they increase recidivism. Of course, individual offenders might benefit from a program. But across all offenders, these programs are ineffective. As a policy, they can no longer be sustained.

- Across all programs, rehabilitation interventions (and these studies include the punishment-oriented programs) reduce recidivism about 10 percentage points.

- Programs that conform to the principles of effective intervention, including using cognitive-behavioral treatments, have the potential to reduce recidivism rates 20 to 25 percentage points (maybe more).

- The RNR model has the strongest claim to being evidence based. It should not be treated as the final word on rehabilitation; other interventions, such as the GLM, should be encouraged. However, for these perspectives to rival the RNR, far more empirical evidence demonstrating their efficacy will have to be accumulated. In the meantime, the RNR model is the safer choice to make in treating offenders.

- The special challenge for those advocating for rehabilitation is to transfer the what works knowledge to those in corrections (a process already under way) and to ensure that programs based on the principles of effective intervention are implemented appropriately (a daunting challenge).

The broader point is that when it comes to corrections, *the smart policy is to correct offenders*. Many offenders are within the grasp of the correctional system for years on end. If they leave our supervision with the same antisocial values, the same thinking errors, and the same social and psychological deficits, then shame on us. It is, one could argue, basic human decency to improve those under our power. If for no other reason, we have an obligation to reduce their propensity for crime so as to protect the public when these offenders are released into the community—as the vast majority will be within about two to three years. Again, hundreds of thousands of inmates—more than 600,000 annually—stroll through the prison gates and into someone's community. Releasing this mass of unreformed humanity into our midst without subjecting them to our best efforts at rehabilitation is irresponsible. The high cost of ignoring what works in corrections is often not seen but it is nonetheless quite real (Van Voorhis, 1987).

Some commentators worry that rehabilitation will rob the law of its sting. But if there is any deterrent effect at all, it most likely lies in the certainty of arrest and not in harsh sentences or a dreary, unproductive stay in prison. Rehabilitation does not undermine arrest whatsoever. Indeed, *the certainty of rehabilitation* depends on it! Unless offenders are caught, they cannot be treated. Similarly, even under a treatment regime, high-risk offenders would likely be sent to prison. Accordingly, much of the incapacitation effect achieved by locking up high-risk offenders would be preserved under a system guided by rehabilitation. The difference perhaps would be that low-risk offenders would not be needlessly imprisoned.

These observations are important because they suggest that were rehabilitation reaffirmed and allowed to guide the nation's correctional system, there would likely be little lost in terms of deterrence or incapacitation. But what would be gained? Much, Cullen and Jonson think. Most important, there would be a renewed effort to ensure that our correctional system is not designed to fail (Reiman, 1984). There would be a clear mandate not to allow offenders to sit idle in their cells or to emerge from years behind bars worse off than when they first entered prison. There would be a strong imperative to use science to evaluate all of our practices so as to root out the harmful and keep the beneficial. And above all, there would be a renewed social purpose in corrections—originally articulated by the founders of the American penitentiary—to forfeit the easy policy of warehousing the wicked in favor of the more difficult but noble policy of saving the wayward.

PART IV

Extending the Vision of Corrections

8

Reentry

Saving Offenders From a Life in Crime

Joan Petersilia
Stanford University
Author of *When Prisoners Come Home*

> *I cannot fully describe the feelings that I had as I stepped out of the House of Corruption. . . . The prison clerk had given me seven cents for carfare. Walking along the street to the street-car line, I studied the seven cents in my hand, and cynically and silently sneered at the city's benevolent generosity toward its forsaken wards. After a year of idleness and monotony in that stagnant cesspool I was now supposed to make good on seven cents. A fine start, I'll say, with not one word of advice from anyone. They just kick you out of the place, and to hell with you.*
>
> —Stanley, "the jack-roller" (Shaw, 1930/1966, p. 167)

W ho is Stanley—the "jack-roller"? Well, we will get to that shortly. Cullen and Jonson think that Clifford Shaw was one of the great criminologists of all time. If there was a Criminology Hall of Fame, he would be in it. Along with Henry McKay, he did groundbreaking studies of delinquency in Chicago. Originally published in 1942, Shaw and McKay's (1972) classic *Juvenile Delinquency and Urban Areas* mapped crime by neighborhoods, showing that delinquents were concentrated in inner-city communities. They argued that these areas were marked by the crime-inducing condition of "social disorganization." Not much has changed since that time. Published 70 years later, Robert Sampson's (2012) book, *Great American City*, carries the subtitle of *Chicago and the Enduring Neighborhood Effect*. Sampson uses slightly different language to describe these delinquency areas—"concentrated disadvantage" and "lack of collective efficacy"—but he is talking about much the same thing. As his analysis shows—based on a lot of fancy statistics—growing up in a really poor Chicago neighborhood where social institutions have broken down is still a recipe for being involved in crime.

However, Shaw wanted to do more than just compile official records and put dots on a large map of Chicago noting where each delinquent lived. To really know what induced kids to become embedded in crime, Shaw decided that he needed to talk to them. Today, we would say he used "mixed methods," supplementing quantitative data with qualitative data. In any case, based on extensive interviews with delinquent youths, Shaw collected a number of life histories, a few of which he published. The most famous was a life history of Stanley, captured in Shaw's (1930/1966) *The Jack-Roller: A Delinquent Boy's Own Story*.

Back then, few delinquents were African American, in part because only 2% of Chicago's population was Black in 1910 (Bulmer, 1984), three years after Stanley was born (Snodgrass, 1982). This meant that nearly all inner-city delinquents were White kids, most from the array of European ethnic groups that immigrated to the United States and chose to settle in Chicago. Like youths in slums today, they were often seen as incorrigible and as part of the dangerous class. Upstanding citizens would wonder "what was wrong with those Germans, Irish, Italians, Scandinavians, and so on." Perhaps they even wondered if the United States "should build a fence along the nation's eastern seaboard to keep these undesirables out." This historical perspective may make us less prone to embracing stereotypes about crime today! Regardless, it is perhaps not surprising that Shaw interviewed a delinquent, Stanley, born into a family of Polish immigrants. In 1907, and including the newly arrived Stanley, Chicago's Polish population reached the 360,000 mark, making the city (after Warsaw and Łódz) "the third largest Polish center in the world" (Bulmer, 1984, p. 50). Many of their descendants would come to root for "Da Bears!"

Like a lot of other delinquents of his day, Stanley came from an impoverished neighborhood located next to the stockyards—"the jungle" as Upton Sinclair (1906/1960) would memorably call it (Snodgrass, 1982). He lived in a dysfunctional family (he bitterly disliked his stepmother), ran free on the streets most of the time, and was educated in crime by older kids, including his brother William. He engaged in many offenses, including jack-rolling, which involved mugging mostly helpless men who typically were either drunk or sleeping (Snodgrass, 1982). Eventually, with the help of Shaw, Stanley would escape a life in crime, though he had a rocky existence as an adult, holding many different jobs and being confined in a mental hospital (Snodgrass, 1982). When Shaw interviewed him, he was in the middle of an active delinquent career; he had amassed 38 arrests (Snodgrass, 1982). As might be expected, he was no stranger to correctional facilities. And this brings us back to the quote at the beginning of this chapter!

As revealed in *The Jack-Roller*, Stanley entered crime early in life and would be imprisoned several times, including in the city's House of Correction (Shaw, 1930/1966; see also Snodgrass, 1982). Stanley could see that imprisonment created a fundamental challenge. It was a house not of "Correction" but of "Corruption"—as he put it. Stanley thus was being failed in two ways—inside prison where idleness and criminal education prevailed, and outside prison where his release was of little concern to anyone. He was sent on his way with just 7 cents—the equivalent of $1.00 today according to U.S. Inflation Calculator (you can look it up on Google). He was forced to wear "the same old suit" that he had on when entering the facility a year before. It had been "crumpled into a ball for a year, and was now dirty, moldy, wrinkled, and much too small" (Shaw, 1930/1966, p. 167). The angst of "humiliation came back" as he "felt the stares of other people burning through" him (p. 167). He was not in good condition. "Physically," he said, "I was broken and felt weak. Mentally I was confused and uncertain about the proper course" (p. 168). He had no support from his family: "I hadn't heard from any of my relations and didn't care to see them" (p. 168).

Stanley was describing the experience of *reentry*. We might think that things are a lot better for prisoners released nearly a century later. In too many instances, however, the truth is that we do little more. Okay, we usually give returning inmates a set of clean clothes and more than 7 cents (or its inflated $1.00 equivalent today). But our generosity has embarrassing limits; gate money of $20 to $100 is typical. Corrections officials and scholars have long understood these issues, of course, and often urged that they be given more attention. Still, even as tens of thousands and then hundreds of thousands of inmates marched back into society year after year, the issue never quite became a salient policy concern. Instead, the task of ensuring community reintegration was allocated to parole and largely ignored. Alas, all this changed in the early to middle part of the 2000s when *the problem of prisoner reentry* was discovered—and this is the focus of the current chapter.

We do need to finish the rest of Stanley's reentry story, however. In his "desperation," Stanley went to see "Mr. Shaw," as he called him. Clifford Shaw must have been a great person. Shaw had promised to help him upon his release, though Stanley "viewed this plan half-heartedly" (Shaw, 1930/1966, p. 268). Shaw gave him some money and then helped to arrange for a job and a place to live—with "Mrs. Smith" and her family. Stanley was in a "new world," having been "transferred so suddenly from the prison, with the scum of the earth as my companions, into this refined family" (p. 269). He often lost jobs—we would say due to lack self-control and externalization of blame—but Mrs. Smith would remain supportive and counsel him "that there were other ways to settle these things, by using diplomacy and tact" (p. 180)—perhaps a form of cognitive-behavioral therapy! Within four years of his release from the House of Correction, Stanley had his own home and a wife and child. He was able to provide sage advice about how best to foster successful reentry. "Society can force children into correctional institutions," observed Stanley, "but it cannot force them to reform" (p. 182). Something else was needed: "In order to reform a boy you have to change his spirit, not break it, and only sympathetic treatment will do that" (p. 182).

Let us give brief roadmap of what is to come; it comes in five parts. The first section briefly shows that prison release was transformed from an issue of parole to an issue or reentry. The second sections tells why prisoner reentry is a serious problem and then how it was "discovered" around 2005—give or take a few years. The third section reviews what reentry programs generally look like. The fourth section gives some sad news: Most reentry programs probably have limited effectiveness in reducing recidivism, which is a nice way of saying that they tend not to work. This discussion tries to show why programs often fail and how their effectiveness might be improved. Finally, the fifth section identifies two other issues that prisoner reentry must address: the fact that failure often occurs sooner rather than later following release and collateral consequences remain a major barrier to reintegration that must be removed.

From Parole to Reentry

What should be done with prisoners when they are released and "come back home"? If they have served their full sentence, one option is just to let them out and send them on their merry way. But the Progressive designers of the rehabilitative ideal (remember them?) had another idea: If a parole board judges that an inmate is reformed, then return that person to the community under the supervision of a parole officer (Rothman, 1980). This sounds simple, but it can be done in different ways. Indeed, Jonathan Simon (1993) wrote a great book—*Poor Discipline: Parole and the Social Control of the Underclass, 1890–1990*—in which he documented how parole changed across the 20th century. He shows that the parole enterprise over time has been guided by distinct organizing models. Although these models were never fully all-encompassing and when superseded never fully vanished, certain ways of thinking about parole were preeminent during given periods.

Thus, before World War II and especially thereafter, "disciplinary" or "industrial" parole was normative. Building on the cultural belief that the discipline of routine work instills moral fiber, states required parolees to have a job to secure release and to keep a job to avoid reincarceration. Fluctuations in the economy and high unemployment among minority offenders increasingly made the work requirement less tenable. According to Simon (1993), beginning in the 1950s, a "clinical" model rose in prominence in which parole agents were tasked with normalizing offenders by building close relationships and delivering treatment services. In the 1960s, the treatment approach encouraged the implementation of halfway houses and of efforts at "community reintegration" (Latessa & Smith, 2011). Concern for parolees' welfare increased but would soon be severely curtailed.

By the mid-1970s—and as discussed in Chapter 2—a coalition of liberals and conservatives attacked the rehabilitative ideal (Cullen, 2013; Cullen & Gilbert, 1982). They took special aim at the indeterminate sentence and parole release—and, by default, showed little confidence in the value of the delivery of treatment during parole supervision. For liberals, parole boards lacked the expertise and political insularity to make legitimate decisions on who should, or should not, be released from prison. Their discretion was seen as unfettered, inequitable, and an invitation for racial and class bias. For conservatives, parole boards were a source of unwarranted leniency, allowing dangerous offenders serving long sentences to "con" board members into returning them to the community prematurely. This revolving door of justice was held to rob the legal system of its deterrent powers by teaching that crime pays and of its capacity to incapacitate by allowing predators to roam free on neighborhood streets (Cullen & Gilbert, 1982; Tonry, 1999).

In response to this attack on the discretionary powers inherent in individualized treatment, more than 20 states moved to some form of determinate sentencing and abolished parole release, although Colorado, Connecticut, and Mississippi later restored the practice (Rhine, 2011; see also Caplan & Kinnevy, 2010; Petersilia, 1999). Even in states that retained parole, certain types of crimes (e.g., violent, multiple felonies) often rendered offenders ineligible for release, leading Rhine (2011, p. 612) to conclude that "regardless of sentencing structures . . . parole boards have experienced a pronounced contraction in their releasing authority." Eventually, all states constrained sentencing discretion in some way, such as by passing laws stipulating mandatory minimum sentences, truth in sentencing, and/or life or lengthy sentences for those convicted of "three strikes" (Tonry, 1996, 2013; Johnson, 2011). The result was what Tonry (2013, p. 141) has called a "crazy quilt" of sentencing policies that mix, across and often within states, elements of determinacy and indeterminacy (see also Reitz, 2011). Notably, one outcome of these changes is that as of 2012, one in five inmates now "maxes" out (serves a full sentence) and is then subjected to no post-release supervision (Pew Charitable Trusts, 2014a). In states lacking parole, it is typical for offenders to be given some period of post-release supervision (e.g., one to three years).

Taken together, these various changes helped to usher in a new model of parole supervision—what Simon (1993) terms "managerial parole" (see also Rhine, 2011). As the label implies, this model emphasized the close surveillance of offenders to curtail their potential misconduct. This could involve risk assessment to know who to intensively supervise, drug testing, electronic monitoring, and revocation for the non-compliant. Simon (1993) uses the metaphor of "waste management" to describe the purpose of this parole model. He argues that this is not simply a "polemical label" (p. 259). Rather, the term's use is simply an "acknowledgement that many of the young men who encounter the criminal justice system will likely become lifetime clients" (p. 259). As in any waste management system, "it follows that methods must be deployed to allow this population"—this waste—"to be maintained securely at the lowest possible cost" (p. 259). Importantly, this parole model legitimated the denial of attempts to invest in or enrich the lives of offenders; in short, it attenuated the rationale for the delivery of treatment services. The use of such "expensive techniques," notes Simon (p. 259), is "not warranted if the basic assumption is that there is no realistic potential to alter the offenders' status as toxic waste."

Then, rather unexpectedly, things changed! First, the attack on parole lost steam. Since 2000, observes Rhine (2011, p. 632), "no parole board was abolished or lost a significant amount of authority relative to its discretionary release decision making. In fact, one state (Mississippi) recently restored the parole granting function." Second, and more significant, the term *reentry* entered the correctional and public-policy lexicon. Policy makers, academics, and any sentient creature that looked at American corrections started to use the term reentry and to remind anyone with earshot that "they all come back" (Petersilia, 2003; Travis, 2005). Duh! Regardless of sentencing structure, it suddenly seemed indefensible to ignore the stubborn reality that 95% of the prison population—more than 600,000 inmates annually—were reentering society, many of whom would recidivate and be reincarcerated. The so-called waste management system was failing. It became "obvious" that mere surveillance was not sufficient to allow offenders to negotiate the barriers and burdens of reentry. Programs would have to be developed that helped offenders to make the difficult transition between prison and citizenship. In fact, Rhine and Thompson (2011) document the rise over the past decade of "the reentry movement in corrections" (see also Garland & Wodahl, 2014; Petersilia, 2009).

A key feature of the reentry movement is its focus on developing *programs* to facilitate the successful return of prisoners to the community. This emphasis on programs for offenders is important because it ties reentry to the rehabilitative ideal. Implicit in the very idea of programming—whether conducted inside or outside the prison—is that offenders face personal and situational risk factors that, if left unaddressed, will likely lead them back into crime. Reentering prisoners are thus seen as being at risk for recidivating—but not destined to this fate. The challenge is thus to develop programs that work—that is, interventions that are effective and can earn the status of being evidence based.

Conceptually, the term reentry can also be employed to describe the *process* of an inmate's movement from custody into society. In a sense, this usage is overly amorphous because it potentially includes virtually any experience that offenders have had during and following their incarceration. Other than describing the obvious—the fact that prisoners become non-prisoners—it is not clear what the term, as employed in this way, substantively adds. Perhaps its one advantage, however, is that it reminds us that reentry covers not only inmates who are paroled but also those released without supervision.

We use the term reentry in a way related to the purpose of our book: as the name of a *theory of corrections*. This theory has a *normative* and *prescriptive* side. The normative side defines what reentry *should* accomplish. Reentry is thus envisioned as a social welfare enterprise in which efforts should be made to help offenders make the transition from prison to society without any further criminal involvement. The prescriptive side involves how to accomplish this noble purpose of saving prisoners from a life in crime. As noted previously (see Chapter 1), the prevention of recidivism is held to have two components. The first is the *correctional component*, which is the delivery of rehabilitative services to offenders; the second is the *reintegration component*, which involves helping offenders to acquire employment, housing, and medical assistance and working to remove barriers (collateral consequences) that inhibit their participation as full citizens and functioning adults.

The Reentry Problem

When Cullen was in graduate school a long time ago, it became popular to distinguish between objective reality and how people thought about it. In a famous book, Berger and Luckmann (1966) called this "the social construction of reality." In essence, something could be a problem for a long time but not be viewed as a problem—until suddenly it was. Then, it is usually given a name that seems to capture its essence, and a lot of people pay attention to it. "Date rape" and "bullying" are two examples of serious problems that were neglected but then named and publicized. Well, you probably know the punch line here: Prisoner reentry has experienced this fate. Inmates had a lot of difficulty returning to society for many years, but this fact was mostly ignored. Then, it was socially constructed as the "reentry problem," and most everyone in corrections paid attention to it. So, this section is about why reentry truly is a problem and then why, not too long ago, it was "discovered" and socially constructed as a major policy concern.

NATURE OF THE PROBLEM

Social problems thus have two features: first, whether the issue is by objective standards a problem; and, second, whether an objective problem is recognized or "socially constructed" as a "problem" (Spector & Kitsuse, 1977). This section initially discusses why prisoner reentry is objectively a public-policy concern due to four considerations. Please bear with us: We present a lot of statistics to make this case. But unless we can substantiate that there truly is a reentry problem, Cullen and Jonson have wasted their time writing this chapter! Then, the section argues that a confluence of events in the first part of the current century worked to define reentry as a social problem (not many statistics—this is more of a story). This social construction of reality has been instrumental in elevating reentry from a neglected to a central correctional issue (for good overviews, see Gunnison & Helfgott, 2013; Mears & Cochran, 2015).

First, the problem of reentry is inextricably tied to the problem of mass imprisonment. The numbers are now stated with numbing regularity—including in this book!—almost to the point of banality: On any given day in the United States, more than 1.5 million offenders are incarcerated in state and federal prisons, with the count exceeding 2.2 million when jail inmates are included (Glaze & Herberman, 2013). As state and prison populations rose intractably—from around 200,000 in the early 1970s to over 1.6 million in 2008—the "iron law" of incarceration that the "they all come back" remained in effect (Travis, 2005). Growing prison inputs produced growing prison outputs.

Just look at Table 8.1. By 1978, the number of offenders released each year from state and federal prisons stood at 142,033 inmates. A little more than a decade later in 1990, however, the impact of mass incarceration could be seen: The number of prison releases had more than doubled to over 400,000. By the turn of the century, the count had jumped another 230,000 releases annually. Five years later

Table 8.1   Number of Prisoners Released From State and Federal Prisons, 1978–2013

Year	Inmates Released	Year	Inmates Released
1978	142,033	1996	488,748
1979	154,277	1997	514,322
1980	157,604	1998	546,616
1981	162.294	1999	574,624
1982	174,808	2000	635,094
1983	212,302	2001	628,626
1984	208,608	2002	633,947
1985	219,310	2003	656,574
1986	247,619	2004	672,202
1987	288,781	2005	701,632
1988	318,889	2006	709,874
1989	367,388	2007	721,161
1990	404,000	2008	734,144
1991	420,000	2009	729,749
1992	428,300	2010	708,877
1993	434,082	2011	691,072
1994	434,766	2012	637,411
1995	474,296	2013	623,337

SOURCE: Carson and Golinelli (2013, p. 4). Data for 2013 from Carson (2014, p. 10).

in 2005, such releases broke the 700,000 inmate barrier. This number slipped under the 700,000 mark in 2011 and then more steeply the year thereafter (Carson & Golinelli, 2013). Still, as of 2013, prison releases in the United States still stood at 623,337 (Carson, 2014).

As an aside, these figures do not include the number of offenders cycled through local jails each year. After reaching a high of 13.6 million offenders admitted to a jail during 2008, the yearly population of admissions has stabilized since 2011 at about 11.8 million. This number is roughly 15 times larger than the average daily jail population of about 740,000 individuals (Minton & Golinelli, 2014; Minton & Zeng, 2015; see also Applegate, 2011). Even considering the jailed inmates awaiting trial who later will be sent to state prisons, it is likely that jails release upwards of 10 million offenders annually. Further, 38% of the jail population was serving sentences due to a conviction, meaning that when released these offenders might well experience many of the same reentry challenges as those returning from prison (Minton & Golinelli, 2014; Minton & Zeng, 2015).

Second, prisons do not seem to reduce the criminality of inmates, making offenders' return to the community problematic. As we saw in Chapter 4 on deterrence, mounting evidence now exists that the effects of imprisonment on reoffending is likely null or criminogenic (see Cullen, Jonson, & Nagin, 2011). In fact, recidivism rates remain at high levels. In their classic study of the recidivism of released prisoners, Langan and Levin (2002) traced the recidivism of 272,111 discharged inmates in 15 states. These offenders comprised two thirds of the nation's reentering offenders in that year. They reported that within three years, 67.5% of the sample had been rearrested for a new offense, 46% had been reconvicted, and 25.4% had been resentenced to prison. Including technical violations, over half (51.8%) had been returned to prison. During this period, these released inmates had been charged with 744,480 new offenses, including more than 100,000 violent crimes and 2,871 homicides. Notably, failure following reentry into society was pronounced in the first six months to a year. The cumulative percentage of rearrest thus was 29.9% for six months and 44.1% for one year; the percentage then climbed more slowly to 59.2% for two years and 67.5% for three years.

More recent research by Durose, Cooper, and Snyder (2014) presents similar data on the risk of reoffending faced by reentering inmates. Durose et al. (2014) examined the experiences of 404,638 prisoners released in 30 states from 2005 to 2010. The percentage of former inmates arrested for a new crime in three years— 67.8%—was virtually identical to the 67.5% figure reported in the Langan and Levin (2002) study. The five-year statistic for arrests was more than three fourths of the sample (76.6%). For those ages 24 or younger, this figure reached 84.1%. Again, failure was highest in the time shortly following release, with about one third (36.8%) of released inmates arrested within six months and more than half (56.7%) arrested by the end of the first year. Data available on 23 states revealed that about half (49.7%) of the offenders were returned to prison in three years and 55.1% in five years.

So, what do these two studies tell us? Well, the following:

- Inmate reentry into society is marked by widespread failure.
- High proportions of released offenders have contact with the law, often soon after reentry, and about half are reincarcerated.
- For those concerned with both public safety and inmate welfare, the current system of reentry is difficult to justify. A problem exists that warrants a solution.

Third, reentry is hampered by the lack of treatment services available to prisoners prior to release—and then after release. A particularly stark example is California. As noted in Chapter 3, the state's correctional system turned decidedly away from rehabilitation with the passage of determinate sentencing in 1976 (Cullen & Gilbert, 2013; see also Kruttschnitt & Gartner, 2005; Page, 2011). Petersilia (2008, p. 236) reports that based on 1997 data, only 2.5% of the state's inmates in "high need of drug treatment received professionally run treatment." Further, for California offenders released in 2006, almost half sat idle during their entire prison sentence, participating in no work or treatment program. The negative consequence of this lack of services is palpable. "They return to communities unprepared for reentry," observes Petersilia (2008, p. 211), "and two-thirds are returned to prison within 3 years, nearly twice the national rate."

National statistics reveal a similarly bleak picture. Based on 1997 data, Lynch and Sabol (2000) found that the proportion of "soon-to-be released" inmates who had participated in treatment was only 27% for vocational programs, 35% for educational programs, and 13% for prerelease programs. More recently, Taxman, Pattavina, and Caudy (2014) have shown that although the prevalence of treatment services in prisons is high, the proportion of inmates participating in such programs is low (see also Taxman, Perdoni, & Caudy, 2013; Taxman et al., 2007). Drawing on the National Criminal Justice Treatment Practices survey, Taxman and her colleagues (2014, p. 56, Table 2) report that 74% of prisons have outpatient substance abuse programs available. On closer inspection, however, only 13.3% of inmates participate in the program during their incarceration, and 4.7% of offenders with a specific need for such treatment can gain access to these appropriate services. The pattern of high prevalence (many prisons have an array of programs) but low inmate usage appears to occur for a variety of treatment services. For example, most prisons offer educational/GED and vocational training/job readiness programs. But on any given day, only 7% to 8% of the adult inmate population is involved in such educational and employment treatments. The implications of these findings are clear to Taxman et al. (2014):

> In other words, a routine regime of treatment and programming is more likely to produce positive outcomes than programming that is rare or offered to few individuals within a prison or correctional setting. Essentially, what happens inside prison will affect what happens in the community; the result being that mass incarceration will have a long-term impact on offenders, their families, and communities. (p. 51)

The difficulty of inmate reentry is further exacerbated by offenders' limited access to appropriate rehabilitation services while under parole supervision. For example, among all those in community corrections (probation and parole), Taxman et al. (2013, p. 82) report that 7 in 10 have "some type of substance abuse disorder." On any given day, however, only 5% receive appropriate clinical treatment services. Most of these offenders complete only "low intensity" treatment, such as "infrequent counseling and some type of pharmacological medications" (2013, pp. 78, 82). Similarly, data provided by agencies in 17 states found that only 9% of parolees "were enrolled in a mental health treatment program operated by a formally trained mental health professional" (Bonczar, 2008, p. 6). By contrast, it is estimated that 16% of those under correctional supervision in the United States have a serious mental disorder, such as major depression, bipolar disorder, or schizophrenia (Manchak & Cullen, 2014).

Fourth, a final component of the reentry problem consists of the array of barriers that prisoners face upon release that parole authorities and state policy makers more generally are ill-prepared to address. Many offenders likely share the sentiment of Stanley, *The Jack-Roller*, who (as we have noted) upon reentering society stated that, "They just kick you out of the place, and to hell with you" (Shaw, 1930/1966, p. 167). Beyond funds accumulated in personal accounts, most states release prisoners with little concern for their material welfare. Inmates are typically given $20 to $100 in gate money, a bus ticket to an in-state location, a single set of clothes worn on their backs, and prescription medicine that will expire in one week to 60 days (*Corrections Compendium,* 2011; Rukus & Lane, 2014).

Prisoners must depend on family members or, in some instances, other relatives or friends to house them with no compensation from the government. An unknown number of these inmates—one study in New York State placed the two-year percentage at 11.4%—will become homeless (Travis, 2005). Those with a criminal record can be barred under federal law from public housing (Alexander, 2010; Travis, 2005). Private rental housing, which is often in short supply in the impoverished communities to which prisoners return, also may request and check criminal record information on rental applications. A 2006 survey found that 60% of the state parole supervising agencies had no housing assistance programs (Bonczar, 2008).

With limited vocational training, literacy capacity, and educational degrees, securing living-wage employment can be challenging, especially in a recession-period labor market with a declining use for unskilled workers (Bushway, Stoll, & Weiman, 2007). Many offenders lack a stable work history prior to incarceration to fall back upon, with one third unemployed at the time of their most recent arrest (Petersilia, 2011). Other barriers exist as well. A major collateral consequence of a criminal conviction is being barred from work in the "fields of child care, education, security, nursing, and home health care—exactly the types of jobs that are expanding" (Petersilia, 2011, p. 940). Occupations requiring licensure either automatically exclude or limit those with criminal records. As Alexander (2010, p. 146) notes, this can even include self-employment as a "barber, manicurist, gardener, or counselor," even if the offenders' crimes "have nothing at all to do with their ability to perform well in their chosen profession."

Beyond legally mandated exclusion, employers are reluctant to hire released inmates. In 2001, Holzer, Raphael, and Stoll (2007, p. 120) polled 619 establishments in Los Angeles about their willingness to "accept an applicant with a criminal record for the last noncollege job filled." They discovered that more than 40% answered "probably not" (24.1%) or "definitely not" (18.5%); another 36.4% stated that it "depends on the crime" (2007, p. 124). A 2011 survey of 69 of the largest employers in the Pensacola, Florida, SMSA produced comparable results, with 40.6% of the respondents stating that their company does not "hire people who are formerly convicted felons" (Swanson, Schnippert, & Tryling, 2014, p. 213).

Experimental studies have probed this issue by submitting employment applications from matched pairs identical except for the admission of a criminal record and seeing whether the fictitious job-seekers receive a call back for an interview. In a study of newspaper-advertised openings for entry-level jobs located within a 25-mile radius of Milwaukee, Pager (2007) discovered that Whites with a criminal record were half as likely to receive a call back as those with no criminal record (17% vs. 34%). For Blacks, the call-back ratio was about one in three (5% vs. 14%). Pager (2007, p. 146) notes that the low probability of African Americans with a criminal record receiving a call back suggests a case of "a 'two strikes and you're out' mentality among employers, who appear to view the combination of blackness and criminal record as an indicator of serious trouble" (see also Pager, Western, & Bonikowski, 2009). Similar findings have been reported from a 2011–2012 study in Phoenix, Arizona, that included the submission of both online and in-person job applications (Decker, Spohn, Ortiz, & Hedberg, 2014; see also Pager et al., 2009).

DISCOVERY OF THE PROBLEM

If you wanted returning inmates to commit a lot of crimes, what would you do? Well, you would not give them much rehabilitation inside or outside the prison. You would not give them much money to get started, a job, or a place to live. You would then erect barriers that make it hard for them to land jobs or be regular citizens. If they had mental health problems, you would hope that they could find some help when their medication ran out. Hmm. Sounds nuts. But this is what reentry has been like in the United States since Stanley was complaining about getting only 7 cents almost a century ago!

An objective disquieting condition does not become a social problem, however, unless it is "discovered"—the point we made above. Spector and Kitsuse (1977) illuminated that social problems are "constructed" through a definitional process. This process of persuading others that a problem exists involves "claims-making" activities in which the negative consequences of an issue are highlighted and ameliorative steps requested. But the other part of this process involves attaching a specific label to the condition that is pregnant with meaning and policy implications. For example, calling erratic emotional conduct "mental illness" implies that troubled people should be seen as patients suffering from a disease that merits clinical treatment by professional experts either in an office visit or a psychiatric hospital (Szasz, 1970).

In this context, the challenges posed by offenders returning to society following their incarceration had existed since the invention of prisons. Until the beginning years of the current century, however, this condition had not been defined or "framed" in a way that made it a "social problem" salient to policy makers and thus central to the correctional enterprise. The issue of released inmates was subsumed under the umbrella of parole, which was criticized by liberals as being inequitable and by conservatives as being overly lenient. At times, the issue was seen as a matter of offender reintegration, which was part of the rehabilitative model embraced by the Left but not the Right. Perhaps because they were enmeshed in ideological debates, "parole" and "reintegration" failed to emerge as labels capable of inspiring concrete actions to address the problem of prisoners released into society. Even when the number of released inmates surpassed the 600,000 mark in 2000, discussions of reentry were just beginning and no movement was yet on the horizon to address this objective problem.

Soon thereafter, however, the term reentry galvanized attention to this annual mass release of prisoners. With stunning alacrity, *reentry* entered the correctional lexicon as the now-accepted way of defining the inmate release process. This concept had two distinct advantages. First, it had no apparent ideological preference.

Unlike parole, reentry was not attached to any existing correctional practice or organization that had been the object of political dispute. Unlike reintegration, it did not mandate any particular practices. It was not a construct of the Left or the Right, but a mere description of an empirical fact. Second, use of the term reentry thus had a sobering quality to it. Reentry was an "iron law"—they all come home (Travis, 2005). To ignore this stubborn reality was manifestly irrational and, from a correctional policy standpoint, irresponsible. In short, framing the issue as a problem of reentry made it easier for claims-makers to argue that action should be taken to address the yearly exodus of offenders from the nation's prisons.

Despite its useful qualities, there is nothing inherent in the word reentry that, in and of itself, would have inspired a policy movement. Might not "return" have sufficed just as well? Rather, it was the use of this reentry in two influential books that gave the term currency and encouraged its embrace in academic, policy-making, and practitioner circles. These books had similar titles and both linked the inescapable fact of prisoners "coming home or back" to the term "reentry." Thus, in 2003, Joan Petersilia published *When Prisoners Come Home: Parole and Prisoner Reentry*. Two years later, Jeremy Travis authored *But They All Come Back: Facing the Challenges of Prisoner Reentry*.

Importantly, there was nothing inevitable in Petersilia's and Travis's use of the term reentry. Historical contingency, not unavoidable discovery, led each of these scholars independently to adopt the concept at virtually the same time (see also Cullen, 2005). According to Petersilia (2009), she was originally scheduled to write a chapter titled "Parole in the United States," which was to be included in a volume in *Prisons* of the *Crime and Justice* series she was co-editing with Michael Tonry (Tonry & Petersilia, 1999). Here is where a turning point in correctional history occurred:

> [Tonry] changed the title to read, "Parole and *Prisoner Reentry* in the United States," observing that my chapter not only described the parole system but also the individual-level experiences of prisoners returning home—what we now think of as prisoner reentry. Writing that chapter was the starting point for what became my professional absorption and ultimately resulted in this book, *When Prisoners Come Home: Parole and Prisoner Reentry* (2003). (Petersilia, 2009, p. 249, emphasis in the original)

Once sensitized to the issue and concept of reentry, Petersilia sought to use this book "to gain attention for what I believed was one of the most significant *social problems* of our time: the challenges posed by the more than 600,000 adults who leave prison and return home each year" (2009, pp. 249–250, emphasis added). Her goal as a prominent claims-maker was "to deliver a national prisoner reentry 'wake-up call,' spurring progressive prison reform" (p. 250).

Jeremy Travis's interest in prison reentry was perhaps more serendipitous. While serving as the Director of the National Institute of Justice in 1999, he was asked by then-U.S. Attorney General Janet Reno, "What are we doing about all the people coming out of prison?" (Travis, 2005, p. xi). The answer was that virtually nothing was being done, which prompted Travis, with the assistance of Laurie Robinson, to delve into the issue in more detail. Because many inmates were being released unsupervised, they decided that they could not focus only on parole. At this point, Travis (2005) made a crucial contribution:

> I suggested we use the word "reentry" to capture the experience of being released from custody, and the word quickly became a convenient shorthand for our inquiry. An examination of "prisoner reentry," we hoped, would allow us to set aside debates over sentencing policy and avoid the pitfalls of defending or critiquing parole. We hoped that the topic of "prisoner reentry" would be broad enough to allow conservatives and liberals, pro- and antiprison advocates to come together with pragmatic answers to Janet Reno's question. (p. xii)

It would be inaccurate to suggest that the mere celebrated use of the word reentry was in and of itself transformative. Importantly, in his position as NIJ director, Travis (2005, p. xii) took steps to translate the concept into reality. He was able to sponsor funding for eight communities to develop "reentry courts" and for "the first Reentry Partnerships in another five sites, bringing together police, corrections agencies, and community leaders to improve reentry planning." When he moved in 2000 to the Urban Institute as a senior fellow, he established a diverse study group (the "Reentry Roundtable") and published an NIJ Research in Brief that he called *But They All Come Back: Rethinking Prisoner Reentry* (2000). He then was invited by the Urban Institute to write his book carrying the similar title, *But They All Come Home: Facing the Challenges of Prisoner Reentry*. Perhaps the most prominent corrections scholar, Petersilia's focus on reentry drew attention. And together, Travis's and Petersilia's books provided a thorough account of the objective nature of the problem and made a persuasive claim for a series of policy reforms.

Still, what might have occurred if they had not employed the term reentry? Assessing this counterfactual situation is speculative, but consider, for example, if Petersilia had subtitled her book *The Problem of Parole* and had not used reentry as the organizing concept of her analysis. In all likelihood, *When Prisoners Come Home* would be been seen as a valuable critique of parole but not much more. And if Travis's book had not used the term reentry—or if he had never been asked by Janet Reno to think about the issue and written it—then his role in defining mass prisoner release as a problem of "reentry" would not have taken place.

In short, much as the construct of mental illness was "invented," so too was prisoner "reentry." Both Petersilia and Travis defined prisoner release as reentry and then, as claims-makers argued, that this was a social problem in need of attention. It helped, of course, that their claims were not false but true. Indeed, there was a constituency ready to join a reentry movement. When asked, virtually every correctional leader and academic analyst knew that the current system of prisoner release was designed to fail and in need of reform.

WHAT'S GOING ON TODAY

Here is the key reason why Cullen and Jonson added a brand new chapter on prisoner reentry for the second edition of our book: Reentry shows few signs of being a correctional fad that is losing its luster and will soon vanish. "Interest in prisoner re-entry over the last decade," notes Petersilia (2011, p. 945), "has fueled the development of hundreds of programs across the United States." Although this movement was boosted by a number of developments (see Rhine & Thompson, 2011), two events were especially important in lending legitimacy to the idea of prisoner reentry.

First, in 2003, the federal government allocated more than $110 million to fund the Serious and Violent Offender Reentry Initiative (SVORI). Located in all 50 states, 69 agencies received between $500,000 and $2 million over a three-year period. In all, 89 programs were implemented that focused not only on reducing recidivism but also on improving "employment, health (including substance use and mental health), and housing outcomes" (Lattimore & Visher, 2009, p. ES-1; see also Petersilia, 2011). We will get to this important project later.

Second, on January 20, 2004, George Bush delivered his State of the Union Address. His remarks proceeded predictably. Citing 9/11, he noted that "our greatest responsibility is the active defense of the American people," a goal enhanced by actions ranging from the Patriot Act to the pursuit of freedom in Iraq and the Middle East (Bush, 2004, p. 1). On the domestic front, he touted tax relief, the No Child Left Behind Act, policies advancing free and fair trade, the defense of traditional marriage against "activist judges," and his support for immigration reform. Toward the end of his address, however, President Bush turned his attention to the nation's imprisoned population. And then he did something pretty amazing for a conservative politician—something decent that perhaps showed where his heart really stood: He asked Americans to give a "second chance" to prisoners reentering society:

> In the past, we've worked together to bring mentors to the children of prisoners and provide treatment for the addicted and help for the homeless. Tonight I ask you to consider another group of Americans in need of help.
>
> This year, some 600,000 inmates will be released from prison back into society. We know from long experience that if they can't find work or a home or help, they are much more likely to commit crime and return to prison.
>
> So tonight, I propose a four-year, $300 million Prisoner Re-Entry Initiative to expand job training and placement services, to provide transitional housing and to help newly released prisoners get mentoring, including from faith-based groups. (Applause)
>
> America is the land of second chance, and when the gates of the prison open, the path ahead should lead to a better life. (Applause) (Bush, 2004, pp. 9–10)

President Bush's support eventually led to the passage of the Second Chance Act (signed into law on April 8, 2008) and to millions of dollars in annual funding for reentry services. Perhaps more important, his remarks were a clear departure from the punitive rhetoric that had long fused crime-related commentary among conservative political elites (Hagan, 2010; Simon, 2007). At least to a degree, they signaled that prisoner reentry was a policy issue open to bipartisan support. And that, indeed, has proven to be the case.

So, when it comes to reentry, the genie is clearly out of the bottle—and isn't going to be put back in! Now that prisoner release has been socially constructed as a problem and given an identifiable name—*reentry*—it is difficult to imagine how ignoring the annual return of hundreds of thousands of offenders to society could be justified. As Petersilia (2009, p. 255) notes, reentry may have "staying power" because it "makes good sense, plain and simple." Put another way, reentry has become part of the culture of American corrections, with the term "reentry" now an accepted part of the field's lexicon. Reflecting this fact, beyond the early works of Petersilia (2003) and Travis (2005), books with reentry in the title are appearing with some regularity (see, e.g., Crow & Smykla, 2014; Gideon & Sung, 2011; Gunnison & Helfgott, 2013; Mears & Cochran, 2015). A number of websites also have been created to promote offender reentry, including the National Reentry Resource Center's *What Works in Reentry Clearinghouse* and Reentry Central News Headlines (for a full list, see Mears & Cochran, 2015, p. 234).

Notably, reentry is being institutionalized as a standard practice across state correctional and/or parole agencies. It is difficult to find a state correctional agency that has not institutionalized some form of reentry into its organization. A survey of 42 correctional systems in the United States (eight did not respond) found that all but three states offered inmates planned release programs. In 14 states, these were mandatory (*Corrections Compendium*, 2011). Numerous reentry programs also now exist in states, counties, and communities across the nation. Further, as Rhine and Thompson (2011, p. 203) observe, a "sizable cluster" of states have actively participated in reentry initiatives (e.g., Transition to Community Initiative, Prisoner Reentry Policy Academy). In fact, "state departments of corrections are found exercising leadership across these initiatives, deploying high level executive staff to stimulate and engage in such efforts" (2011, p. 204). Further, the policy of reentry is consistent with this bipartisan interest in restraining prison growth—of returning more offenders to the community while not jeopardizing public safety. For example, the deep Red State of Mississippi enacted reform legislation in 2014 intended to stave off prison growth and to save $266 million. Part of this package was the implementation of "comprehensive reentry planning for all offenders returning to the community" (Pew Charitable Trusts, 2014b, p. 9).

Finally, the public strongly favors prisoner reentry programs. This sentiment is part of something we have already mentioned: Americans' broader, long-standing support of rehabilitation (Cullen et al., 2000; Jonson, Cullen, & Lux, 2013). For example, in a 2001 national survey, Cullen, Pealer, Fisher, Appelgate, and Santana (2002, p. 137) found that 92% of the respondents agreed that "it is a good idea to provide treatment for offenders who are in prison." Similarly, 88% agreed with the same item that asked about providing "treatment for offenders who are supervised by the court and live in the community." A bunch of polls show similar endorsements of providing reentry services, including both state and national surveys (see, e.g., Krisberg, 2006). We will give just three examples of public support for reentry whose findings are representative of other studies:

- The 2007–2008 New York City and Tri-State Region (New York, New Jersey, and Connecticut) survey found that 84.8% of the respondents were "concerned" about "the fact that about 700,000 prisoners will be released from prison to their home communities." Further, 83.1% expressed support for the Second Chance Act (Gideon & Loveland, 2011).

- A 2010 poll of Oregon residents found that a high percentage—about 9 in 10—were in favor of providing reentry support to offenders, such as help finding housing (88.9%), education (91.3%), job training (92,8%), drug treatment (91.7%), and mental health services (94.2%) (Sundt, Cullen, Thielo, & Jonson, 2015).

- A 2012 national poll revealed that 87% of the sample agreed with the following: "Ninety-five percent of people in prison will be released. If we are serious about public safety, we must increase access to treatment and job training programs so they can become productive citizens once they are back in the community" (Public Opinion Strategies and The Mellman Group, 2012, p. 4).

The point of all this: Elected officials will not lose their jobs if they endorse and implement policies facilitating prisoner reentry! The public's support for any policy is not unconditional, and its embrace of reentry might be tempered if tight budgets are used to give services to returning offenders that are denied to "upstanding citizens" (see Garland, Wodahl, & Schuhmann, 2013). That said, citizens understand the irrationality of throwing inmates back into society with no regard for what happens thereafter. For most Americans, a planned reentry that addresses the obvious criminogenic and reintegration needs of offenders seems a better path to follow. Cullen and Jonson agree. But the challenge is undertaking a "planned reentry" that is effective. We review the kinds of programs that have been implemented. Alas, most have fallen short of what they have hoped to achieve.

Reentry Programs

A lot of programs have been developed to assist returning offenders make the transition from a life behind bars to a life on the street. These programs focus on the variety of risk factors that incarcerated individuals face, including substance abuse, deficits in behavioral/cognitive behavioral skills, and issues surrounding housing, employment, mental health, family, health, and mentoring. Some of these initiatives are limited to a single reentry issue (e.g., drug abuse, employment), whereas others are multi-modal and address several factors believed to underlie recidivism. Reentry programs also differ in their setting, with some undertaken while offenders are institutionalized and others following their release into the community. Finally, some programs are more correctional in orientation, seeking to deal with recidivism, whereas others are more reintegrative, seeking to deal with the basic adjustment of inmates to the shock of release (e.g., finding a place to live).

In this context, this section tries to capture the nature of reentry programs. Our interest is in formal interventions, but we need to note that many programs exist that are staffed by volunteers and run by non-profit organizations, faith-based groups, ex-offenders, and so on (Frazier, 2011; Petersilia, 2011). Because most treatment interventions, especially those in prison, can be said to be preparing offenders for a return to society, we do not review standard treatment programs in such areas as employment, education, substance abuse, and mental health (for such a review, see Cullen & Jonson, 2011b). Instead, we highlight programs that have a distinctive focus on reentry.

INSTITUTIONAL PROGRAMS

We begin by describing two examples of broad-based programs. We then discuss reentry programs created to address specific offender needs: substance abuse, mental health, and the maintenance of family bonds during incarceration.

One of the most creative institutional reentry programs can be found in Missouri's Parallel Universe program (Schriro, 2000; Schriro & Clements, 2001). This program attempted to make the prison environment approximate life outside of prison; hence, the prison environment should "parallel" the community where offenders would eventually find themselves living. Four main components provided the basis of the Parallel Universe program. First, offenders engaged in behaviors during the day that were similar to what those in free society do on a regular basis. Thus, during the day, offenders had a job, attended school, and/or undertook treatment. During evening hours and weekends, individuals participated in community service, religious programming, or recreation (Schriro & Clements, 2001). Second, offenders worked toward sobriety and were provided with relapse prevention education to reduce their likelihood of using drugs upon release. Third, inmates made and were held accountable for their decisions. Prisoners were encouraged to participate in the prison's governance by serving on councils and committees. Fourth, offenders were recognized for positive conduct. For example, when individuals achieved higher education levels while incarcerated, they were eligible to be assigned higher paying jobs. Furthermore, positive reinforcements, such as better housing and additional visits, were given when the inmates made progress in their treatment (Schriro & Clements, 2001). This program sought not only to teach inmates the skills needed to be productive and law-abiding citizens, but also to give them the opportunity to practice and refine these skills before being returned to society.

Another well-known institutional reentry program was created by the Vera Institute and implemented in New York State (Wilson, 2007; Wilson, Bouffard, & MacKenzie, 2005; Wilson & Davis, 2006). Project Greenlight was a multimodal, 60-day program. During the two months of intervention, a variety of risk factors were targeted, including substance abuse, short- and long-term housing upon release, employment, family counseling, practical life skills (e.g., managing bank accounts, how to use public transportation), and cognitive-skills training while providing a reentry plan for the offender to follow once released. This program, based upon the "What Works" literature, sought to provide a comprehensive transition of care from the institution to the street to increase the offenders' chance at success in the reentry process. The program proved ineffective—an issue we return to later. Still, this program is similar to many of the comprehensive programs provided in correctional institutions seeking to prepare incarcerated individuals for their journey back home (Wilson, 2007).

Beyond more general initiatives, specialized interventions have been developed that focus on offender needs seen as major barriers to successful reentry. Thus, with upwards of 75% of offenders having a history of substance abuse or addiction, it has become commonplace for reentry programs to concentrate on the delivery of substance abuse treatment (Council of State Governments [CSG] Justice Center, 2012). A majority of inmates possess drug and/or alcohol problems, and they often report that their addiction was a major contributing factor to their criminal behavior as well as other life problems (e.g., loss of relationships, loss of jobs) (Visher & Kachnowski, 2005; Visher, Kachnowski, La Vigne, & Travis, 2004). However, only 61% of prisons offer substance abuse treatment (Mears, Moore, Travis, & Winterfield, 2003; Petersilia, 2003; Travis, 2005), with most of the programs taking the form of self-help programs such as Alcoholics and/or Narcotics Anonymous or educational programs (Mears et al., 2003). By contrast, therapeutic communities, known by their acronym of "TCs," offer a unique reentry intervention. These programs emphasize the provision of treatment in phases, beginning during incarceration and then continuing as offenders move into the community (Inciardi, Martin, Butzin, Hooper, & Harrison, 1997; Mears et al., 2003; Robbins, Martin, & Surrat, 2009).

The Delaware KEY/Crest Substance Abuse Program is one of the most well-known TCs (Inciardi, Martin, & Butzin, 2004; Martin, Butzin, Saum, & Inciardi, 1999). The first phase of this program, KEY, begins 12–18 months prior to release when individuals in the program are removed from the general prison population and placed in an environment with only other KEY participants. Phase one requires participants to engage in programming every day, with the ultimate goal to alter the criminogenic attitudes, beliefs, and thinking that results in the offender's desire to use (Delaware Department of Corrections, 2014).

Phase two, Crest, which lasts roughly six months, occurs when the offenders are moved to a community-based residential center. During this phase, offenders engage in self-help groups, substance abuse education, cognitive restructuring, stress and anger management, life skills, communication skills, problem solving, and relapse prevention training. Furthermore, the participants in the program are presented with job-skills training, enroll in education programs or seek employment through work release, have intensive treatment, attend mandatory groups, develop a relapse prevention and recovery plan, create a sober network of people on the outside, find housing in which to live upon release, and set up aftercare programming (Delaware Department of Corrections, 2014).

The final phase of the program is the aftercare component. This phase begins when the offender is released from Crest and is placed on community supervision. As part of their conditional release, the participants are required to attend weekly meetings for group counseling. Furthermore, they are subjected to mandatory random drug testing (Delaware Department of Corrections, 2014). Continuity of care thus is central to the KEY/Crest Substance Abuse Program; treatment and the reentry process do not end when offenders are released from prison. Rather, treatment is an ongoing process that must be cultivated consistently if sobriety and law-abiding behavior are to be maintained over the long term.

Notably, the TC model is increasingly being expanded to include substance abusing offenders with co-occurring mental disorders. The Modified Therapeutic Community for Offenders with Mental Illness and Chemical Abuse (MICA) Disorders is one such program (Sacks, Sacks, & Stommel, 2003; Sullivan, McKendrick, Sacks, & Banks, 2007). Similar to TC programs for substance abusers, the MICA program begins 12 months before inmates are released from prison. Here, the individuals in the program are separated from non-participants and engage in intensive treatment based on peer self-help. During this phase, offenders are educated on how the unique interaction of their mental illness and substance abuse contributes to their criminal behavior. This phase also includes medication and therapeutic interventions addressing the individuals' mental health needs as well as psycho-educational courses and cognitive-behavioral treatment. Upon completion of this phase and the drafting of aftercare plan, the offender is released and maintains a treatment component in the community. During this aftercare phase, the participants engage in mental health and substance abuse treatment, work in the community, obtain housing, learn basic skills such as budgeting, understand relapse prevention and mental health symptom management, and develop mental and emotional coping skills.

Reentry programs have also been developed to address the maintenance of familial bonds (CSG Justice Center, 2012; Petersilia, 2003; Travis, 2005). Research suggests that familial support plays an important role in offender reentry. Such support can be integral in helping released offenders obtain housing and employment as well as providing social and financial assistance (diZerega & Villabos Agudelo, 2011; Hairston, 1988; La Vigne, Visher, & Castro, 2004). However, relatively few inmates are visited on a regular basis, with over 60% not receiving a single visit in the past 30 days (Hairston, Rollin, & Jo, 2004). As the distance between the offenders' homes and the prison increases, the frequency of contact decreases substantially. Offenders must rely on collect calls and letters sent through the mail to stay in touch with friends and family (Hairston et al., 2004). Given these challenges, maintaining contact with family members has become a focus of some reentry plans.

The Council of State Governments Justice Center (2012) identified a unique familial program found to assist in the reentry process of offenders. The Private Family Visiting (PFV) program involves a conjugal visit for up to 72 hours, once every two months (Derkzen, Gobeil, & Gileno, 2009). These visits can be made by a parent, significant other, child, friend, or any other relative. The goal of this program is to cultivate, maintain, and possibly renew relationships in order to ease the offenders' transitions back to society. The PFV program differs from traditional visitation programs found in many prisons by both its private setting and the frequency in which these conjugal visits are allowed (Derkzen et al., 2009).

COMMUNITY PROGRAMS

Okay, as is obvious, reentry involves the jump from prison to the community. So, it makes sense to have programs for offenders both during and after their incarceration. A review of some of the more common community-based reentry programs follows.

Halfway Houses. Halfway houses are one of the most long-standing community-based reentry programs. They seek to provide a gradual rather than an abrupt transitional process back into society for offenders. When used for transitional purposes, halfway houses are literally residential facilities that house offenders who are "half way" between prison and the community (Latessa & Allen, 1982; Latessa & Smith, 2011). These facilities traditionally supply offenders with food, shelter, and clothing while they search to find permanent housing and employment. Halfway houses are continuing to evolve and increase the number of services they provide.

Notably, in March 2014, then-Attorney General Eric Holder and the Department of Justice announced that federal halfway houses were required to further enhance the treatment services that were being currently offered (U.S. Department of Justice, 2014). These new requirements mandated that all federal halfway houses must deliver standardized cognitive-behavioral programming, provide public transportation vouchers or transportation assistance to assist offenders in finding work, and allow the use of cell phones to help obtain employment and to maintain familial contact. These new requirements are in addition to the services that were already being provided, such as substance abuse and mental health treatment, housing and employment assistance, medical care, and financial management assistance (Federal Bureau of Prisons, 2014).

Various locally run halfway houses also provide a multitude of services. For example, one halfway house in Ohio, Volunteers of America, offers over a dozen transitional services to those who are being released from prison (Handwerk & Peterson, 2012). Some of the interventions offered to offenders include: life skills, anger management, health awareness and education, victim awareness, medication monitoring, employment assistance, relapse prevention, financial support, housing assistance, crisis intervention, and sex offender treatment, if applicable.

Mentoring. As a component area of the *Second Chance Act*, the mentoring of returning offenders was deemed an important aspect of offenders' reentry process (McDonald & Jonson, 2013). Mentoring is intended to link those returning from prison with law-abiding role models in society. The assistance provided by mentors ranges from aiding in finding and maintaining employment and housing, to serving as a source of encouragement and support, to acting as a positive role model, to assisting in the development of life skills, to providing opportunities for engagement in prosocial activities (Jolliffe & Farrington, 2007).

One example of a mentoring program is the FOCUS: Offender Re-entry Mentoring Project (FOCUS, 2014). Initiated in 2005 in Boulder, Colorado, FOCUS seeks to facilitate reentry by providing assistance in finding a place to live and work, by helping offenders seek professionals and appointments needed to maintain any medical and/or mental health care they may have been receiving while incarcerated, and by being a source of emotional support. The mentors in the program receive 12 hours of training outside the institution in addition to the one-and-a-half hours of training in the jail prior to meeting their mentee. Furthermore, mentors are required to attend monthly mandatory workshops on topics such as substance abuse, domestic abuse, and anger management. After training is complete and the mentor is matched with a mentee, the mentors are expected to spend one to two hours per week for one year with the reentering offender. However, mentors often spend more than the required number of hours per week with their mentee, with any time above the minimum determined at their discretion (FOCUS, 2014).

Employment. Many community-based employment programs for reentering offenders are short in duration. These transitional job programs often provide temporary employment while an offender searches for a more permanent position. Furthermore, these programs offer assistance in obtaining employment through job readiness classes, mock interviews, job coaching, and résumé writing (CSG Justice Center, 2012; Ndrecka, 2014; Redcross, Millenky, Rudd, & Levshin, 2012).

An example of a transitional job placement program is the Center for Employment Opportunities (CEO) in New York City (CSG Justice Center, 2012; Ndrecka, 2014; Redcross et al., 2012). The CEO program serves parolees by giving minimum-wage paid work immediately upon their release. Offenders complete a five-day class and then are assigned to paid positions doing maintenance, janitorial, and repair work for local and state agencies. The participants are required to work a four-day work week, where they are to paid each afternoon after completion of their shift. On the fifth day, the offenders go to the CEO office where they receive additional treatment such as parenting classes and child support assistance programming (Redcross et al., 2012).

The CEO program offers additional treatment beyond temporary job placement and parenting courses. While offenders are employed in their transitional work assignment, they are continuously assessed and monitored by their supervisor. The supervisor reports any workplace issues that must be addressed. Once all issues are addressed, the CEO program assists offenders in finding permanent employment. After permanent employment is secured, CEO staff members maintain contact with offenders for at least a year, and offenders are given incentives (e.g., store gift cards) for set retention milestones and a year of continuous employment (Redcross et al., 2012).

Mental Health. Returning offenders often have mental health needs. They may have received little or no effective services in prison. Many times a medication regimen is the only treatment provided during incarceration; offenders often lack the ability and resources to maintain their prescriptions once released (Petersilia, 2003; Travis, 2005). In response, mental health reentry initiatives in the community have emerged, such as the *Connections* program located in San Diego County (Burke & Keaton, 2004; CSG Justice Center, 2012). The program's overarching goal is to provide offenders with mental health interventions for nine to 12 months after release from jail (Burke & Keaton, 2004). The *Connections* programs offers pre-release services planning that identifies treatment needs upon release, possible courses of action to secure housing, and obtaining signatures on consent forms (mainly medical and mental health consent forms) to help continue any treatment that may have begun in the prison once released. However, this portion of the program, the pre-release screening, is not mandatory (Burke & Keaton, 2004).

During the first month of release, offenders must meet daily with *Connections* staff and complete an LSI risk assessment. In the following two months, contact is reduced to weekly meetings. During these meetings, various needs are addressed (e.g., housing, transportation, employment, substance abuse testing), but the major focus is on mental health treatment and the obtainment of medical resources (Burke & Keaton, 2004). During months three through six, contact with the staff remains on a weekly basis. The program continues to dispense needed services provided earlier but also long-term goals are developed. Finally, crisis prevention training is introduced. Months six through nine begin the transfer of care stage where continued support is given. However, post-program plans are made in order to continue the mental health treatment that has been, hopefully shown by this time, to be effective for the offender. After nine months, the *Connections* team determines if the participant is ready to leave the program. If so, offenders are discharged; if not, they can remain in the program for another three months to overcome any obstacles they still face (Burton & Keaton, 2004).

Substance Abuse. Although the most effective institutional-based substance abuse programming includes an aftercare component, some programs begin treatment only following an inmate's release (Hanlon, Nurco, Bateman, & O'Grady, 1999). Offenders, especially those who have histories of heroin or cocaine use, are at a high risk of relapsing (Hanlon et al., 1999; Wexler, Lipton, & Johnson, 1988). They often return to the neighborhoods, associates, and activities that led to the onset and continued use of the substance. These offenders are in need of reentry services.

For example, a program located in Baltimore targets recently released parolees with a history of narcotic addiction (Hanlon et al., 1999). This intervention—deemed a "social support with drug testing" program by the Council of State Governments Justice Center (2012)—enhances traditional parole and urine monitoring with support and services given by a counselor (Hanlon et al., 1999). Participants in the program receive weekly substance abuse testing as well as counseling sessions that address their underlying dispositions and reasons for use. Furthermore, social supports in the offenders' lives and in the larger community are identified for each participant, and offenders are linked with any available services judged to be needed (Hanlon et al., 1999). Finally, relapse prevention strategies are taught to parolees in order to assist with their reintegration back into society.

Housing. Many obstacles stand in the way of returning offenders when they attempt to secure housing. These barriers can include private landlords refusing to rent to those who have served time in prison, families who will not allow their returning family member to live with them, and eligibility restrictions for federal subsidized housing (CSG Justice Center, 2012; Scally, 2005; Travis, 2005). Another obstacle is that upwards of one in ten offenders are homeless when entering prison and thus lack housing to return to upon release (Metraux & Culhane, 2004).

Although helpful, halfway houses offer only temporary housing in which offenders reside for a brief time. Other reentry programs, however, have been created to assist offenders in finding more permanent residences, such as The Fortune Academy located in New York City. To be eligible, offenders must agree to be employed, or in treatment or school, for 35 hours a week and not pose a danger to society (Scally, 2005). Offenders are placed in emergency housing (ranging from days to several months) and then have the option of being allocated more permanent housing. The more permanent housing consists of single- or dual-occupancy units, with the length of stay usually ranging from six to 18 months depending on how soon housing is secured in the community. In addition to housing assistance, The Fortune Academy provides services to its participants to help ease their transition back into the free world. These services include substance abuse treatment, medical care (especially for HIV/AIDS clients), independent-living skills training, family services, and education and career development (Scally, 2005).

The Effectiveness Problem

When Cullen and Jonson start out by calling something a "problem," that is not a good thing. Alas, that is where we stand with prisoner reentry. Thus, the main challenge for the reentry movement is to avoid the trap of developing programs that ultimately prove to be ineffective. In fact, the movement's creation of numerous programs is far outstripping knowledge about "what works" in reentry. Given their human services orientation, it is likely that many programs are providing prisoners before and after release with needed social support and, overall, tend to decrease criminal involvement (Ndrecka, 2014; Seiter & Kadela, 2003). However, little evidence exists to confirm that most reentry programs are capable of reducing offender recidivism consistently and substantially.

In this section, we first explore why we do not know a lot about "what works" to keep released offenders away from crime. We call these barriers to reentry effectiveness and identify four of them: the diversity of programs; the lack of programs based on a credible theory of recidivism; the lack of treatment fidelity in the implementations of programs; and the inability of the major reentry evaluation study to date (SVORI) to produce a clear blueprint for how best to deal with released offenders. We then try to tell what we know so far about what likely works in reentry to reduce recidivism.

FOUR BARRIERS TO EFFECTIVENESS

Diversity of Programs. Deciding "what works" is difficult enough when studies evaluate a single treatment modality, such as boot camps or cognitive-behavioral therapy. But assessing how best to facilitate prisoner reentry is especially daunting because of the heterogeneity of interventions that fall under this category (Gunnison & Helfgott, 2013; Mears & Cochran, 2015). Thus, reentry programs vary along several dimensions: (1) existing rehabilitation programs relabeled as "reentry" versus programs created specifically to facilitate reentry; (2) the setting of the program—in prison, in the community, in between, or across all three phases of reentry; (3) programs that are multi-modal versus those that focus on specific criminogenic or life needs, such as deficits in behavioral/cognitive behavioral skills, mental health, substance abuse, and problems surrounding housing, employment, family bonds, and physical health; (4) formal programs administered by correctional agencies versus programs staffed by volunteers and run by non-profit organizations, faith-based groups, ex-offenders, and so on.

Given that most programs are not evaluated (Mears & Cochran, 2015), it is difficult to build a large body of studies that assesses each variant of reentry programs. As we will discuss below, this reality means that reentry programs—including those that appear promising—are rarely evaluated by more than one or two studies. With this level of empirical support, it is unclear whether such programs should be touted as evidence-based models to be implemented in other contexts.

Lack of Credible Theory Informing Programs. As Mears and Cochran (2015, p. 209) observe, most "reentry efforts . . . rest on little to no coherent or credible theoretical foundation" (see also Garland & Wodahl, 2014). Most often, program inventors do not rely on scientific criminology when implementing an intervention. Instead, most programs are developed to address the readily observable problems that offenders face. If offenders are mentally ill or addicted to drugs, does it not make sense to have programs to address these needs? If offenders lack job skills and are unemployed, are homeless, or have lost ties to family members, does it not make sense to have programs to address these needs? To improve offenders' quality of life—if not on sheer humanitarian grounds—the answer is "yes." But what is not clear is whether such programs, if not rooted in a credible treatment theory, have any chance of reducing recidivism. Thus, interventions will likely fail or have only modest results when targeting weak predictors of recidivism or targeting them in the wrong way (Listwan, Cullen, & Latessa, 2006).

Employment is a useful example, because it is difficult to imagine any person—offender or not—having a structured, prosocial, fulfilling life without having a job. Here, it is assumed that the reintegration component of reentry (getting a job) contributes to the correctional component of reentry (getting out of crime). Alas, employment reentry programs may have, at best, a modest impact on recidivism—for three reasons. First, Andrews and Bonta (2010) identify work (and school) as a risk factor meriting intervention. However, employment is a moderate risk factor and not among the four most important sources of recidivism (which they call the "Big Four"). If these other factors are not addressed in the intervention, they may continue to exert a criminogenic influence on offenders.

Second, merely having a job may not be enough to stop offenders from recidivating straight upon release. It may be that recidivism is reduced only if quality employment is secured, a point made by Sampson and Laub (1993). Similarly, Andrews and Bonta (2010, p. 59) emphasize that work or school are conduits for diminishing criminal propensity mainly because they provide "quality interpersonal relationships." These activities can be used as "intermediate targets for change" if steps are taken to "enhance performance, involvement, and rewards and satisfactions" (p. 59).

Third, recent research by Skardhamar and Savolainen (2014, pp. 270–271) is fascinating because it is a chicken-versus-egg study: Which comes first—getting a job (employment) or getting out of crime (desistance)? They examined a sample of Norwegian "crime-prone offenders" (at least five felonies) with an "unstable work history who managed to get stable jobs." They found that employment fostered desistance but only for fewer than 2% of the sample! For most offenders, the causal ordering was in the opposite direction: First they desisted from crime and then they secured stable employment. This finding suggests that for offenders to take advantage of employment—sometimes called a "hook for change"—it might first be necessary to have a cognitive transformation that reduces their criminal propensity and allows them to take advantage of a new life chance (see Giordano, Cernkovich, & Rudolph, 2002; Maruna, 2001). In concluding her comprehensive review presented in *What Works in Corrections*, MacKenzie (2006) makes this same point:

> When I compared the effective programs to the ineffective programs I noticed an interesting difference. Almost all of the effective programs focused on individual-level change. In contrast, the ineffective programs frequently focused on developing opportunities. For example, the cognitive skills programs emphasize individual-level changes in thinking, reasoning, empathy, and problem solving. In contrast, life skills and work programs, examples of ineffective programs, focus on giving offenders opportunities in the community. Based on these observations, I propose that effective programs must focus on changing the individual. This change is required before the person will be able to take advantage of opportunities in the environment. (p. 335)

We can give one more example of targeting questionable risk factors. Recall the Parallel Universe program—used in Missouri and then later in Arizona (Schriro, 2000, 2009; Schriro & Clements, 2001). Recall as well that the word "parallel" is used because the program attempted to make life inside prison approximate life outside of prison. The underlying theory is plausible: Living a structured prosocial life inside prison will lead offenders to live the same way upon release. Still, the theory's appeal rests more on common sense than on an empirically validated criminological theory linking compliant behavior inside institutions to law-abiding behavior in the community. An evaluation based on limited qualitative observations and non-experimental quantitative data suggested that Arizona's Parallel Universe program (called "Getting Ready") improved the quality of institutional life but, at best, had a small effect on recidivism (Gaes, 2009). Although a well-known reentry program, it is thus not clear that creating "parallel universes" in prison is the best option for producing meaningful savings in recidivism.

From Chapter 7, you should be able to guess what Cullen and Jonson would think is a better way to approach this whole issue: Develop reentry programs based on a scientifically validated correctional theory such as the risk-need-responsivity (RNR) model invented by Andrews, Bonta, Gendreau, and other Canadian scholars (Listwan et al., 2006). Although not often informed explicitly by the principles of effective interventions, programs that adhere to the components of the RNR model tend to be more effective (see also Petersilia, 2011; Mears & Cochran, 2015; Turner & Petersilia, 2012). The RNR model, which is the leading treatment approach in corrections, has been explained in Chapter 7. But since that was a whole chapter ago—who can remember things from that far back!—we will briefly revisit it here. Recall that this perspective argues that rehabilitation interventions, including reentry programs, will be most effective if they do the following: (1) focus on high-risk offenders (the risk principle); (2) target for change predictors of recidivism that can change, such as antisocial attitudes and low self-control (the need principle); and (3) use treatment modalities that are "responsive to" and thus capable of reducing the risk factors that lead to reoffending, such as cognitive-behavioral therapy (the responsivity principle).

The value of following the RNR model is demonstrated by Lowenkamp and Latessa's (2002) now-classic study of the impact of halfway houses on recidivism. Using a two-year follow up, they compared rearrests and reincarceration for 3,737 offenders released in 1999 from 37 halfway houses versus a comparison group of 3,058 offenders. The analysis revealed considerable heterogeneity or variation in effects, with some halfway houses reducing recidivism more than 30% and others increasing it by more than 35%. Using the RNR model as their guide, Lowenkamp and Latessa discovered that this heterogeneity was explained by the risk principle. According to Andrews and Bonta (2010, p. 47, emphasis in original), "the risk principle involves the idea of *matching levels of treatment services to the risk level of the offender.*" Specifically, to reduce their recidivism, "higher-risk offenders need more intensive and extensive services"; by contrast, for "low-risk offenders, minimal or even no intervention is sufficient" (2010, p. 48). Consistent with this principle, halfway houses serving low-risk offenders were associated with increased rearrest and reincarceration, whereas programs targeting high-risk offenders resulted in lower recidivism rates. A follow-up evaluation largely replicated the earlier study (Lowenkamp et al., 2006). Lowenkamp and Latessa concluded that failure to comply with the risk principle can have criminogenic effects, especially for low-risk offenders (see also Andrews et al., 1990).

Lack of Integrity in Program Implementation. Rhine, Mawhorr, and Parks (2006, p. 347) argue that implementation problems are "the bane of correctional programs." Andrews and Bonta (2010, p. 395) argue that correctional programs that fail to adhere to the "principles of RNR clinical practice, staffing and management, core practices and program integrity" are ineffective, if not criminogenic. Such failure, however, is commonplace, especially in real-world programs as opposed to demonstration projects designed by researchers. Given that most reentry programs fall into this category, their effectiveness is likely limited.

The challenge of implementation is illuminated by Project Greenlight, another program described previously in this chapter. Project Greenlight was "an institution-based transitional services demonstration program that was piloted in New York State's Queensboro correctional facility" (Wilson, Cheryachukin, et al., 2005, p. 8; see also Wilson, 2007; Wilson & Davis, 2006). Developed and largely run by the Vera Institute of Justice, the program was based on the "what works" literature, employing a form of cognitive-behavior treatment ("Reasoning and Rehabilitation"; see Ross, 1995; Ross & Fabiano, 1985). As noted, the program lasted two months and targeted for change a bunch of risk factors (e.g., housing, life skills, substance abuse, antisocial behavior and thinking). Offenders even received a reentry plan to follow upon release. Given all these good practices, the intervention had to work. Right? Unfortunately, the evaluation results were disappointing, with the recidivism rates of Project Greenlight participants exceeding those of two control groups (Wilson, Cheryachukin, et al., 2005; Wilson & Davis, 2006).

But good intentions do not always produce good results. In this case, implementation problems likely account for the program's ineffectiveness. Thus, the dosage (60 days) may have been too brief for high-risk offenders; the treatment groups were at least twice as large as recommended by the inventors of Reasoning and Rehabilitation; and offenders received no systematic aftercare once released (Wilson & Davis, 2006). Commenting on the program, Andrews and Bonta (2010, p. 399) note that "even programs that were designed with reference to 'what works' are often not well implemented." As they observed:

> A few points are striking. The inmates, without any discussion or consent, were taken abruptly from their prison and transferred to the program site. Many "clients" experienced program participation as the equivalent of being mistreated by the system. No reference is made to the employment of risk/need assessment instruments. Indeed, participation in the substance abuse program was mandatory, even for inmates who did not have a substance abuse problem. The selection of program staff explicitly did not follow the recommendations of the creators of the program. The negative outcomes associated with two of the four workers totally accounted for the program failure. (2010, p. 399)

Inability of SVORI to Guide Program Development. Implemented in 2003, the Serious and Violent Offender Reentry Initiative (SVORI) was a collaborative effort by the U.S. Departments of Justice, Labor, Education, Housing and Urban Development, and Health and Human Services. These agencies awarded $100 million in federal funds to 89 adult and juvenile programs attempting to increase the likelihood of successful offender reentry in five areas: criminal justice, housing, health, employment, and education (National Institute of Justice, 2011). Given its scope, SVORI had the potential to establish a clear blueprint for effective reentry programming. But things did not turn out this way. In fact, on the U.S. Department of Justice's own website—CrimeSolutions.gov—the program is categorized as having "no effects."

The research on SVORI was undertaken by Lattimore and her colleagues, who conducted a systematic, high-quality assessment (Lattimore, Steffey, & Visher, 2009; Lattimore & Visher, 2009; Lindquist, Lattimore, Barrick, & Visher, 2009; Lattimore et al., 2012). The evaluation included 1,618 adult males, 348 adult females, and 337 juvenile males drawn from 12 adult and 4 juveniles programs "diverse in approach and geographically distributed" (Lattimore et al., 2012, p. 7; for a list of programs, see Lattimore & Visher, 2009, p. 23). Because random assignment was not possible for all programs, propensity-score matching and multivariate analysis were used to compare SVORI participants and non-participants.

Even though the 16 programs were selected from among SVORI grantees because they were "deemed most promising as impact candidates" (Lattimore et al., 2012, p. 7), the effect of SVORI participation on recidivism and other life outcomes was inconsistent. In their 2009 "summary and synthesis" of the "multi-site evaluation," Lattimore and Visher reported that as the follow-up progressed, SVORI participation had no effect of juvenile self-reported crime. Among adults, SVORI women, but not men, had lower arrests than the comparison group. However, by 24 months, both male and female SVORI participants had higher reincarceration rates. Similarly, an analysis of rearrest and nine other self-reported outcomes (i.e., housing, employment, job pay and benefits, drug use, committed any crime) at 15 months showed that SVORI participation had mostly "beneficial but non-significant" effects (Lattimore et al., 2012, p. ES-10). In a subsequent follow-up at 56 months or more for adults and 22 months for juveniles, more promising findings were reported (Lattimore et al., 2012). All groups were found to have a longer time to rearrest and fewer arrests following release. Adult males also had a longer time to reincarceration and fewer reincarcerations (but this latter effect was not statistically significant). No statistically significant findings on reincarceration were reported for adult females or juvenile males.

In the end, the federal government spent $100 million to fund 89 programs and sponsored a long-term, careful evaluation by respected researchers. But the stubborn reality is that this investment did not yield a clear blueprint for how to conduct an effective reentry program. Participation in SVORI had only "limited effects . . . on intermediate outcomes" (such as housing and employment) and, over the long term, seemed to reduce arrests but have mixed effects on reincarceration (Lattimore et al., 2012, p. 148). Unfortunately, it is not clear why SVORI had these effects or which specific SVORI programs should serve as evidence-based models for future program development. Perhaps the best that can be said is that a well-intentioned reentry program that seems promising on the surface generally is better than doing nothing, but its impact is likely to be mixed and modest.

TAKING STOCK OF EFFECTIVENESS

Okay, Cullen and Jonson are going to keep this brief and tell you what we think the existing research tells us about what works in prisoner reentry. So, here it goes.

The ability to develop reentry programs informed by evidence-based corrections is limited. Existing evaluations are spread across a diversity of programs (typically one evaluation per program), rarely use high-quality experimental designs, and at times yield inconsistent results. Systematic reviews, including meta-analyses, suggest that, overall, reentry services tend to reduce recidivism (see, e.g., Ndrecka, 2014; Seiter & Kadela, 2003). But here is the rub: The effects of programs are heterogeneous. They vary in their effectiveness—some high and some low, and even some criminogenic. Promising programs have been identified and are listed on a government website (CrimeSolutions.gov). They might be used as models for specific correctional populations (e.g., offenders with substance abuse problems, violence prevention among high-risk juvenile detainees). Doing so, however, must be undertaken with caution because of the risk that positive findings might not replicate across different contexts.

Finally, several conclusions from the evaluation literature, most of which are consistent with the RNR model, can be drawn that might inform reentry program development:

- Programs that provided a continuity of care, beginning in the prison and continuing once prisoners were released into the community, were found to be more effective.

- Programs lacking treatment fidelity often showed no appreciable effects on recidivism.

- Programs targeting high-risk offenders and their criminogenic needs were found to be more effective.

- Programs that employed therapeutic communities were found to be effective.

Two Things to Keep in Mind

Our discussion of reentry is just about wrapped up. But we wanted to cover two more issues that must be given attention in any attempt to understand reentry and, in turn, to develop an effective strategy. These issues are the following: (1) Reentry failure—recidivism—tends to occur soon after prisoners are released. And (2) policy makers must do something about collateral consequences, since they mostly make no sense and can make offender reintegration needlessly difficult.

TAKE COMING HOME SERIOUSLY

Much of the failure experienced by reentering offenders occurs in the first six months to a year following their release. More than two in five of these offenders (just under 45%) are arrested by the end of their first year, with that percentage climbing only to two thirds in three years (Durose et al., 2014; Langan & Levin, 2002). It thus appears that it is critical that the period in which offenders first "come home" following reentry must be taken seriously. Not surprisingly, a common recommendation is to concentrate services during this time period rather than spread them evenly across all offenders under supervision (Turner & Petersilia, 2012). As Petersilia (2003, p. 153) notes, the recidivism data "suggest that the most intensive services and surveillance should begin immediately upon release and be front-loaded in the first six months to the first year."

But here is where much of our knowledge about reentry is lacking. Why does failure occur so soon after release? Two alternative explanations are possible—both plausible and both potentially true to a degree.

First is the "reintegration" explanation, which provides the most obvious answer for why so many reentering prisoners fail so rapidly: The strain and difficulty of adjusting to society after life in a total institution, combined with joblessness and unstable living arrangements, undermine integration into prosocial roles. Research also indicates that returning to a neighborhood where criminogenic influences are ubiquitous and quality treatment providers are limited can increase the chances of recidivating (Wright & Cesar, 2013).

Second is the "propensity" explanation. Here, released offenders' rapid failure is attributed to the fact that they are, after all, criminals! So, what would we expect? In this view, prisoners are sort of itching to get back to what they do—commit crimes. More academically, the argument is that recidivism ensues because moderate-risk to high-risk offenders return to crime as soon as the opportunity presents itself upon release. This thesis is consistent with the research showing that imprisonment's effect on reoffending is null or even slightly criminogenic (see Chapter 4 on deterrence). Neither scared straight nor given effective treatment, many inmates do not improve while incarcerated; instead, they are "put on ice" in a "behavioral deep freeze" (Gendreau & Goggin, 2014). Thus, they return to society unchanged—just as criminal, if not more so, as they were when they first entered the institution. Although prisoners' criminogenic propensities are blocked during their incarceration, they reappear as soon as they are back on the streets. High rates of immediate recidivism are the result.

As this discussion shows, the sources of early reentry failure remain largely unknown, with understanding remaining at the pre-scientific level of informed speculation. Closing this knowledge gap has obvious, important implications for effective reentry programming. Although front-loading services appears imperative, it is difficult to know what is causing prisoners' high rates of recidivism upon release and thus which specific services should be given priority. At present, programs tend to take a "shotgun" approach, spraying services at the reentry program in hopes that something will hit the appropriate mark. This strategy may produce some promising results, but it will likely be of limited value until research unpacks the factors producing early failure in reentry.

CONFRONT COLLATERAL CONSEQUENCES

One of the more disquieting policy developments in corrections has been the steady expansion of the collateral consequences attached to a criminal conviction (Alexander, 2010). These legislated mandates deprive ex-offenders of an array of employment, housing, government, family, and civil rights. The courts have defined these consequences not for what they clearly are—added on punishments. Instead, the courts say that these statutes are used to regulate ex-offenders' behavior (Chin, 2012). To make this claim, all the government has to do is to show that the regulation (e.g., restrictions on voting, being a doctor) has some reason—some iota of "rational basis." This is all mythology—and everyone knows it. There are some collateral consequences that do make sense, of course—such as not letting pedophiles teach kids. But it is increasingly apparent that statutes passed to deny offenders rights and privileges are gratuitous and have little plausible relationship to protecting public safety.

The good news is that elected officials on the political Left and Right—such as Senators Cory Booker and Rand Paul in their recently proposed "Redeem Act" (Terkel, 2014)—are seeing these collateral consequences as a matter of *overregulation*. Indeed, if subjected to the same cost-benefit analysis given to other government regulations, it is unclear how many of these statutes would survive such scrutiny. Efforts are being made to bring more standardization and fairness to this area, such as through the Uniform Collateral Consequences of Convictions Act proposed by the National Conference of Commissioners on Uniform State Laws (2010). Further, we would argue that all statutes imposing collateral consequences should be "sunset laws" that expire within a specified period (e.g., five years) unless reinstated by legislative vote. This step would ensure that only collateral consequences that have an enduring rationale would remain operative. At present, collateral consequences instituted over many years accumulate, leading to "literally hundreds of collateral sanctions and disqualifications on the books" (National Conference of Commissioners on Uniform State Laws, 2010, p. 3).

What remains to be determined, however, is whether collateral consequences are related to offender recidivism. With the exception of deportation, such consequences—since they are not legally punishments—do not have to be conveyed to offenders during a plea bargain or at the time of sentencing (Chin, 2012). It is not clear that most of those working with offenders are informed about such consequences and communicate these potential disabilities to their offender clients (Burton, Fisher, Jonson, & Cullen, 2014). How to secure an expungement of a criminal record also is not discussed or planned for (since applying to have a record cleansed might occur three to five years later). In terms of reentry, there is a knowledge gap about how much offenders are aware of collateral consequences and how such legal discrimination potentially hinders successful reintegration (for a broader discussion, see Jacobs, 2015).

More generally, there is a lack of research on the stigma faced by reentering offenders. This is in marked contrast to research on mental patients where theory and research is extensive and where stigma has been shown to have deleterious effects (see, e.g., Link, Cullen, Struening, Shrout, & Dohrenwend, 1989; Link & Phelan, 2001). Studies that do exist show variation in how much hope and optimism offenders display about their future prospects (Benson, Alarid, Burton, & Cullen, 2011; LeBel, Burnett, Maruna, & Bushway, 2008; Maruna, 2001). Evidence also is consistent with the view that the stigma from official labels will lead offenders to lose conventional bonds and be exposed to criminal influences, thus increasing the risk of recidivism (Krohn, Lopes, & Ward, 2014; Raphael, 2014). However, given the social stigma and legal consequences associated with being an "ex-offender," a clear need remains for sustained analysis of how these factors affect the reentry prospects of released offenders.

Conclusion: Saving Offenders From a Life in Crime

Context matters, which is a core theme of this book. Since the early part of this century, policy makers across the nation finally awoke to the irrationality of releasing hundreds of thousands of prisoners into society with no clear idea of how to reduce their reoffending. The yearly figure is bad enough (which we have now told you a zillion times is more than 620,000!), but compute this out over 5 years (3 million) or 10 years (6 million). It just boggles the mind that for decades those whose get tough policies put a mass of people into prison took no responsibility for the mass of people coming out of prison. How could they not do everything in their power to ensure that inmates returning to society did not recidivate? Remember, as advocates of restorative justice (Chapter 6) remind us, crime is harmful to all involved—to the offender, whose life is put on a path of social difficulties, and to victims, who suffer financial, physical, and psychological costs. Reentry failure is not inevitable—as the story of Stanley, the jack-roller, reveals. Although deeply embedded in a criminal life course, Stanley was saved from a life in crime by Clifford Shaw and his friends.

A bunch of commentators are giving sage advice on how to make reentry work (see, e.g., Garland & Wodahl, 2014; Gunnison & Helfgott, 2013; Mears & Cochran, 2015; Taxman, Young, & Byrne, 2004; Turner & Petersilia, 2012; Wright & Cesar, 2013). We will join this conversation by adding our two cents—actually we will add our two final points! Saving offenders, we suggest, involves the heart and the mind.

First, good will—such as that shown by Shaw—is an essential ingredient. Cullen and Jonson wish they could have met Clifford Shaw. He was a Hall-of-Fame criminologist, as we noted, but he also must have had an enormous heart. What a guy! A lot of corrections involves caring about people who often are not too easy to care about. We understand why religious clerics forgive sinners, since without sinners they would not have much of a job (just as criminologists depend on criminals for our livelihood). The rest of us, however, have a seven-letter word beginning with "A" that we use to describe such annoying people. But as we have tried to show in this book, having a collective big heart often gets us further than having a collective mean heart. And one thing is clear from studying reentry: Returning prisoners do not need more punishment but rather a helping hand—a social welfare response.

Second, a good heart is not enough. We also need a smart mind. Here is another central message of this book. Offenders do not get better if given the wrong correctional medicine! Changing inmate behavior, especially in the context of a transition from a total institution into a community where offenders face an array of barriers, is a daunting prospect. Part of taking this challenge more seriously is recognizing the difficulty of the task and of the need to use science to direct rehabilitative efforts (Cullen, 2012). Thus, those inventing and implementing reentry programs need to consult the existing knowledge on treatment. Relying on common sense—liberal or otherwise—is no longer justified (Latessa et al., 2002).

Put another way, *a criminology of reentry* is sorely needed to produce the kind of detailed scientific insights required to direct program development. Although meaningful advances in the science of offender treatment have been made (see Chapter 7), serious knowledge gaps in the area of reentry continue to exist. Basic facts about the reentry experience and how they affect post-prison adjustment remain to be identified and systematically studied. The criminology of reentry thus is in its beginning stages. Given the mass of inmates who will be released now and in the future, this seems to be an area of theory, research, and practice that warrants concentrated and sustained attention.

9

Early Intervention

Saving Children From a Life in Crime

David P. Farrington
Cambridge University
Author of *Saving Children From a Life in Crime*

Fat Katie. There was a crisis in the Cullen household. Jordan, Cullen's daughter, had a birthday on the immediate horizon. It was thus time to invite all the children in Jordan's kindergarten class to this celebratory gathering. Jordan dutifully compiled her roster of invitees. Everyone was on the list except Fat Katie. When queried about this glaring omission, Jordan said that Fat Katie pushed her and other kids down and that nobody much liked her.

Cullen was about to lecture his typically kind-hearted daughter about the inappropriateness of calling anyone Fat Katie—especially since as a child he had been tormented with the taunt of Fat Franky by his older brother. But a larger issue beckoned. In the Cullen household, Jordan was told, nobody—not even Fat Katie—would be excluded from a class event. Either Fat Katie was invited or there would be no birthday party. With the prospect of treats, attention, and gifts of 13 Barbie dolls hanging in the balance, Jordan allowed her nicer sentiments to guide her to the compassionate decision: Fat Katie was invited. Somewhat sadly, she did not show up.

Fat Katie. As early as kindergarten—age 5 to 6—Jordan and her classmates had identified one child, Fat Katie, who was different. She was big, pushed kids down, and was rejected by her classmates. She manifested developmental problems, at least in this setting. By the next year, she had departed the school. In all likelihood, she has since blossomed into a wonderful young adult. A change in context—a place where other kids did not label her as Fat Katie—might have been all that was needed. If any real problems had existed, Fat Katie's affluent parents undoubtedly would have noticed them, had them diagnosed by professionals, and ensured that an appropriate intervention took place.

But not all Fat Katies will be this fortunate. They will be born into more disadvantaged settings—perhaps to homes headed by young, single, impoverished mothers with substance abuse addictions. When they manifest behavioral problems in early childhood, everyone will know they exist. Fellow classmates, teachers, and parents—all those interacting daily with these Fat Katies—will experience and thus know that trouble is brewing. Nothing, however, will be done. There will be no change in school or expert professionals called in to save these Fat Katies. As their lives develop, they will not blossom into wonderful young adults. Too many of them will endure repeated peer rejection, fail at school, flock together with other wayward Fat Katies, and confront a life of increasing *cumulative disadvantage*. One bad thing after another—one more *criminogenic risk factor* after another will pile up; one on top of another, on top of another, on top of another. These Fat Katies—or Fat Frankys—will move steadily away from a conventional life course and become trapped on a developmental trajectory headed straight into crime. The train will have left the station, with prison as its destination.

When these Fat Katies and Fat Frankys are age 6 or perhaps age 10 or 11, we—the good and decent people of the world—will look at them and shake our heads. We will see that these kids, through no choice of their own, are destined for a life of hardship and crime. We will feel fortunate that our children do not face the array of personal and social pathologies that these children face. We will see them as victims of being born with the wrong traits and in the wrong place. We will lament their horrible luck of the draw—they have won the lottery for a life in crime—and we will feel sorry for them. But by the time they reach age 16 or perhaps 21, our language will change. We will see *these very same children*—now larger and stronger and meaner—as *super-predators* to be feared. We will experience a sense of relief when they are locked away. "Get the dangerous off the street. Incapacitate them," we will chant. "Hold them responsible for the choices they make. After all, they are adults, aren't they?"

We will forget that today's super-predator was yesterday's wayward child. Today, we see choice, harm, and accountability. Yesterday, we saw no choice, a child being harmed, and an inevitable future in crime. As Gustave de Beaumont and Alexis de Tocqueville reminded us long ago, those who become delinquent "have been unfortunate before they became guilty" (as cited in Allen, 1981, p. 12). Somehow, however, we disconnect these links in the developmental chain into crime. Doing so allows us to focus, undistracted by sympathy, on the very real threat posed by the adult offender standing before us. It also allows us to absolve ourselves for why none of us cared enough to redirect these offenders, while they were still helpless youngsters, into a more productive and civil life.

The great lesson of *life-course criminology*, which we will discuss in a moment, teaches us that *criminals come from somewhere*. Most often, children develop in predictable ways into juvenile delinquents and then into adult criminals. Such a simple insight, huh? But it is an insight pregnant with important policy implications. What we now know is that the vast majority of serious, violent offenders do not suddenly spring into action in the teenage or adult years. Some do, of course, and we call them *late onset offenders*. If they commit a heinous offense, they end up in the front page of the newspaper, with all of us wondering how such a bad thing could have been done by such a good person. But the prototypical pathway into serious, violent criminality starts in childhood—perhaps in the womb where the brain develops and temperament is acquired. Again, most criminals are not late bloomers. The seeds of their criminality were planted and nurtured in the beginning stages of life.

If the origins of crime start early in life, then what lesson should we draw? At present, it is largely to do nothing until a wayward child turned super-predator is standing before the court and before us—society. Cullen and Jonson think that is tragic—stupidity and neglect run amok. We see the failure to *intervene early in life* as needlessly consigning many youngsters to a life in crime and—in what is often forgotten—as needlessly consigning many innocent citizens a few years hence to a preventable victimization. Any sensible approach to crime control would make *early intervention with at-risk children* a high priority (Farrington & Welsh, 2007).

Saving wayward children from a life in crime is really a policy that extends correctional rehabilitation to the earlier years in life. It is based on the sound criminological insight that we should not sit by and wait for troubled youths to commit illegal acts that place them behind prison bars. Crime has causes, and we should knife them off as early as possible. Thus, corrections should be implemented as part of a seamless set of interventions that seeks, from birth into adulthood, to prevent further criminality. As Friedrich Lösel (2007) notes, it is *never too early and never too late to intervene*. Put a different way, the stuff in the last chapter and in this chapter are part of the same paradigm.

Fortunately, there is an increasing recognition of the wisdom of this view. In this chapter we thus will reveal the case for expanding early intervention programs. We will show that such a policy would be based on sound criminology. We will show that there is a range of programs available that have proven, at least in some instances, to be effective in preventing youngsters from developing into offenders. These programs are also cost effective. And we will show that the American public is virtually unanimous in supporting efforts to save children from a life in crime.

Lessons From Child Criminology

THE DISCOVERY OF CHILDHOOD

Students majoring in psychology typically are required or encouraged to take a course in *Child Psychology* (Cullen did so a few decades ago when he was an undergraduate studying psychology). Criminal justice majors, however, do not enroll in *Child Criminology* because, alas, this course does not exist! In retrospect, this curricular omission is rather odd. After all, psychologists have known for ages—even for decades before Cullen, old as he is, went to college!—that humans *develop*. They study childhood because this is where—you guessed it!—that human development begins. Until recently, criminologists have pretty much ignored this reality. Instead, they skipped childhood and created courses in *Juvenile Delinquency*.

Did criminologists skip childhood because they were stupid? Well, in a way they were. They would not come out and say that the first stages of life were inconsequential; rather, they simply ignored what occurred prior to adolescence. In all fairness, they had two good reasons for doing so—even if these justifications do not obviate the fact that ignoring childhood led to stupid criminology.

First, as criminologists, they were interested in *crime*. With rare exceptions, children are not seen as able to form criminal intent and do not do things that get them arrested. Yet, in a way, kids are quite "criminal." From very early in life, they hit, bite, kick, and shove one another down—and do so a lot (Nagin & Tremblay, 2005; Tremblay, 2006; Tremblay et al., 1999). This is why parenting can be exhausting; children always seem to be doing something that requires correction or discipline. But even when our children bloody someone's nose or knock another kid down, we do not interpret this act as an assault, call the police, and seek to give them a prolonged time out behind prison bars. In short, children are not seen as law-breakers and thus it is easy to dismiss them as falling outside the subject matter of criminology.

Second and related, there is something called the *age–crime curve*. You likely know what a bell curve is: a curve, shaped like a bell, that is low at its left and right tails and high in the middle. The bell curve is typically used to show the normal distribution of IQ scores, but much human behavior can be plotted on such a curve. When it comes to crime, the bell curve's tail is low in childhood whereas the peak of the curve is around age 17 or 18 (a bit later for violent crimes like homicide). The curve then gradually descends on a downward slope, showing that crime decreases with age.

Practically speaking, this age–crime curve conveys the view—correct in some ways—that crime is low in childhood, rises to a peak in the teenage years, and then decreases as youths move into adulthood. Importantly, the age–crime curve thus suggests that something peculiar must occur during adolescence that transforms youngsters from cherubic children into juvenile delinquents. And when this storm of criminal influences subsides, these same teenagers move into the adult roles of work, spouse, and parent and stop offending. This process is sometimes called *maturational reform* (see Matza, 1964).

As might be anticipated, criminologists focused on this transitional, turbulent stage in life. Albert Cohen (1955) and Richard Cloward and Lloyd Ohlin (1960) wrote famous books on the origins and nature of gang delinquency. In *Causes of Delinquency*, Travis Hirschi (1969) showed how self-report data from junior high and high school students could be used to test competing delinquency theories, including his own classic social bond perspective. Following in Hirschi's large footsteps, scholars have conducted hundreds of studies on juveniles, all with the goal of deciphering the criminogenic features of adolescent life.

Terrie Moffitt (1993) perhaps has done the most to challenge this brand of research. In her developmental theory of antisocial behavior, Moffitt observed—consistent with traditional criminology—that most youths engage in a lot of crime only during the teenage years. She called this group *adolescence-limited offenders* (also known to criminological insiders as the *ALs*). In essence, she was arguing that the standard developmental pathway for youths obeys the age–crime curve: okay until adolescence, run haywire for a while, then back on a prosocial track as adulthood beckons. Many readers might well be on this pathway. Not too long ago, some of you might have done some deviant things—knocking down mailboxes, shoplifting, needless fights, even trying to tip over cows—that now you would not do. If so, your delinquency was *adolescence-limited*. You were an AL!

But Moffitt was brilliant enough to understand that the age–crime curve masked a second developmental pathway: *life-course-persistent offenders* (known as *LCPs*). When the age–crime curve was disaggregated—a fancy word for broken down more carefully—it was apparent that a smaller group of youngsters also existed who were hidden by the bell curve pathway that most kids—the ALs—followed. This second group, the LCPs, started to manifest conduct problems very early in childhood. Remember Fat Katie? Well, these kids fall into the Fat Katie category. Both in the preschool years and in the primary grades, they have lots of difficulties. Parents, teachers, and other students all know that "something is wrong with them." These youngsters graduate from conduct problems to delinquent acts and then to adult criminality.

Their age–crime (or age-antisocial behavior) curve is more like a line that jumps up in very early childhood and stays high for years to come. Admittedly, few actually are holding up banks at age 80. Feel relieved that you do not have to ask grandma and grandpa if they are packing guns and scoring some crack today! However, these offenders remain entrenched in a criminal career deep into adult life (e.g., into their late 30s and 40s). This is why Moffitt called them *life-course-persistent offenders* (Moffitt, 2006).

Cullen and Jonson like Moffitt's theory because it is simple: two groups with names and acronyms that are easy to remember because they make intuitive sense. Adolescence-limited offenders' crimes are limited to adolescence. Life-course-persistent offenders persist in crime across the life course. Brilliant! Alas, criminologists cannot resist complicating things! They have used fancy statistical techniques to map out developmental trajectories. They find that there may be another two or three groups of offenders whose trajectories in crime are variants of the two groups (ALs and LCPs) identified by Moffitt (see, e.g., Nagin & Tremblay, 2005; Piquero, Farrington, & Blumstein, 2007). But we can put this more sophisticated stuff aside for another time. The main point to grasp here is that the source of serious, life-course offending typically does not start in the teenage years but *in childhood*. Yes, it looks like we need a course in *Child Criminology* after all!

BEYOND ADOLESCENCE-LIMITED CRIMINOLOGY

Moffitt's work had profound implications (see also Sampson & Laub, 1993). It made clear that scholars could no longer practice *adolescence-limited criminology* (Cullen, 2011)! For if the origins of serious criminality can be traced to childhood, then we must explore what it is about the early years of life that place a youngster on one developmental pathway rather than another.

A dramatic revelation advanced by Moffitt is that the fork in the road—one path leading to crime and the other to conformity—may start *in the womb* (see also Wright et al., 2008). Traditionally, criminologists have been skeptical about biological explanations of crime. They worry that they are a mask for blaming crime on individuals when the true fault lies in the awful life conditions into which too many future inmates are born. But the science is now irrefutable that pre-natal experiences affect brain development and that everyone enters the world with a disposition rather than as a blank slate. Indeed, think of your siblings. Do you ever wonder how you came from the same parents? Biology matters.

When Moffitt made this point, criminologists surprisingly did not dispute it—as they normally would any other biosocial theory of crime. Why not? Well, we suspect that it was because everyone liked her and knew that she was smarter than the rest of us. But it also was because Moffitt was shrewd enough not to claim, as Cesare Lombroso did long ago, that offenders were *born criminals*. Rather, she said that these unfortunate kids suffered from *neuropsychological deficits*. Scholars assume that inborn traits are immutable and cannot be changed; deficits, however, sound like they can be replenished and taken away. In short, Moffitt's theory did not seem to consign those with biosocial pathology to a life in crime. She was pointing to a deficit that might be amenable to intervention. She was a biosocial theorist with a hopeful message.

As Alper and Beckwith (1993) point out, it is common for people to erroneously believe in *genetic fatalism,* which is the fallacious view that traits or behavior rooted in biology cannot be changed. But the notion that biology is destiny is simply false. Eyesight is inherited but it can be adjusted through the use of glasses. Attention Deficit Hyperactivity Disorder (ADHD) has a high heritability component, but its impact on behavior—including crime—can be modified through medicine (e.g., Ritalin) and cognitive-behavioral therapy. And so on.

For Moffitt, neural or brain development can be compromised during the pre-natal period due, for example, to mothers' drug use or poor nutrition. These problems in turn affect psychological traits such as executive functioning (e.g., self-control or impulsivity) and verbal development. These neuropsychological deficits do not automatically lead to antisocial conduct. But children with deficits tend to be difficult to handle, and they can evoke harsh and erratic discipline from parents who may share similar deficits from their own childhood. When they enter school, they are likely to fail and be rejected by other children. In response, their antisocial propensity deepens, provoking more harsh reactions and failure. Over time, these individuals experience the *cumulative continuity* of these criminogenic conditions, causing them to become increasingly entrenched in an antisocial life course. They become, in short, life-course-persistent offenders.

In any event, criminologists' warm acceptance of Moffitt's theory was important because it legitimated two views about crime. The first view, as mentioned, was that the roots of chronic offending extend to the earliest moments of life. *Child development* thus was essential to understanding *criminal development*. The second view was that, as Moffitt (1993) put it, "continuity is the hallmark of the small group of life-course-persistent antisocial persons" (p. 697). Unlike adolescence-limited offenders, this group does not change by jumping into and out of crime. Rather, the lives of LCPs are marked by stability of behavior across the life course. Thus, they bite and hit others at four years of age, they skip school and pilfer from stores at age 10, they sell drugs and steal cars at age 16, they rape and rob at age 20, and they engage in fraud and child abuse at age 30 (p. 695).

This is not the place to evaluate the merits of every aspect of Moffitt's theory (see Moffitt, 2006; Sampson & Laub, 2005). However, it is essential to note that there is considerable support for Moffitt's claim that among those who become the most serious and chronic offenders, a high proportion manifest conduct problems early in life (Farrington, 2003; Murray & Farrington, 2010; Wright et al., 2008). Early antisocial behavior is the strongest predictor of involvement in delinquency (Lipsey & Derzon, 1998). Not all problem children become criminals, but the risk for future difficulties is clearly elevated. This is especially the case among youngsters who (1) engage in high rates of misbehavior, (2) are in trouble across social settings (e.g., home, school), (3) are involved in many different types of antisocial behavior, and (4) show a particularly early onset of problems (Wright et al., 2008, p. 27). Although late onset into crime occurs—some individuals turn to crime later in life—most of those found in prison for serious offenses experienced troubled childhoods and lives. According to Lee Robins (1978), "adult antisocial behaviour virtually *requires* childhood antisocial behaviour" (p. 611, emphasis in the original; see also Robins, 1966).

To summarize:

- Having early childhood conduct problems does not inevitably lead to a life in crime.

- However, there is considerable stability in behavior, so that troubled kids are likely to be troubled teens.

- Further, adults who are antisocial and are imprisoned typically are drawn from the pool of children who manifest strong antisocial propensities early in life. Again, these are Moffitt's life-course-persistent offenders.

What does all this discussion of stability in behavior have to do with early intervention? Well, we suspect that readers already have anticipated the punch line: *If many serious offenders start their criminal development early in life, then it is logical that efforts to knife off a life of persistent offending should occur early in life.* Child criminology thus provides the rationale for—indeed, it demands— early intervention (see also Farrington & Welsh, 2007).

The Need for Early Intervention

Child criminology is really part of a broader attempt to study offenders from *womb to tomb*. This theoretical and research paradigm is called *life-course or developmental criminology*. As might be expected, to follow offenders across their lives, it is necessary to employ a particular kind of study design. Do you know what that is? Yes, it is a *longitudinal study*. A *cross-sectional study* examines people at one point in time—often with the advantage of great depth but with the disadvantage of not being able to measure developmental processes. Longitudinal studies are expensive because they necessitate keeping tabs on people over many years and interviewing them multiple times. Even so, this is the only way to capture how criminal careers unfold over time, including revealing how what occurs in childhood matters later in life.

Much has been learned from longitudinal studies, but too many suffer from an odd omission: They do not measure whether the sample members have received a treatment intervention for their antisocial problems. Efforts are at times made to record whether people have been in prison and, if so, for how long. But few studies have reliable data on whether at-risk youngsters receive any early intervention or simply are allowed to develop into criminals. Why have researchers not incorporated this potentially important source of behavioral change into their investigations? Cullen and Jonson believe that the most likely answer is that they simply did not think about it. When most of the great longitudinal studies were initiated, early intervention was not on most scholars' radar screen. And you cannot measure what you are not thinking about.

One notable exception to this rather remarkable omission is the Pittsburgh Youth Study, known by its acronym PYS (do not sound this out!). Under the direction of Rolf Loeber and Magda Stouthamer-Loeber, this longitudinal project followed three samples of boys attending Pittsburgh public schools who, at the beginning of the study, were in Grades 1, 4, and 7. For each grade, 500 boys were selected, 250 of whom were assessed by the researchers to be at high risk of wayward conduct. Many studies have been published using PYS data. We are interested in two studies that examined the neglected topic of whether troubled youngsters in the PYS received quality intervention. The focus was on the help-seeking behavior of the boys' "caretakers," who in over 90% of the cases were their mothers.

In the first study, Stouthamer-Loeber, Loeber, and Thomas (1992, p. 161) explored all three groups of boys (called, you guessed it, "youngest, middle, and oldest samples"). The PYS addressed the issue of whether youngsters, by age group, received help for their problem behaviors. We will focus mainly on whether they received help—intervention—for their delinquencies. Here are the study's main findings:

- Younger or "early onset" youths who manifested a problem were less likely to receive help than older youths who manifested the problem.

- Caretakers were more likely to seek help for aggression and oppositional behaviors—especially Disruptive Behavior Disorder—than anything else. This may have been because they had to "deal" with this behavior at home on a regular basis.

- However, especially for younger children, many caretakers (almost 50%) did not seek help. "This suggests that a substantial portion of caretakers struggle unaided with serious child behavior problems" (Stouthamer-Loeber et al., 1992, p. 175).

- Seeking help for delinquents—even serious delinquents—was less common. "Between 50% and 70% of the caretakers of the most seriously delinquent boys had never sought help [for various problems], and only about a quarter had ever sought help from a mental health professional" (p. 173).

- When caretakers did seek help, about a quarter of the time they had only one or two contacts.

- Bottom line: A substantial proportion of delinquent youths did not receive adequate intervention.

Now on to the second study, authored by Stouthamer-Loeber, Loeber, van Kammen, and Zhang (1995). This work focused only on the oldest sample and attempted to see how interventions may have differed for delinquent youths who had contact with the juvenile court versus those who did not. Again, here are the major findings:

- Compared to delinquents who did not go to court, youngsters who appeared in juvenile court had similar histories of offending (onset, frequency) but they were involved in more serious delinquent acts.

- For court delinquents—who were only in the eighth grade when surveyed—the average interval or time between the onset or beginning of problem behaviors and court contact was *four years*; more than half of this group exhibited problems for more than *five years*. The interval between serious problem behaviors and court contact was *two years*.

- Those who had not had contact with the court also exhibited delinquent problems for a similar length of time. The point: Youngsters can be involved in delinquency for some time before coming into contact with the court.

- Despite having "careers of disruptive problems of many years' standing . . . only 41% of the caretakers had ever sought help for the boys' problems" (p. 248).

- Those delinquents who received help tended to show problems for a longer period of time and that were more serious. Those delinquents who did not receive help, however, "were not without problems; on average they had exhibited problems for 5.75 years" (p. 248).

- Bottom line: "Thus, the disruptive problem careers of many of the delinquent boys were left unchecked" (p. 248).

It is possible, of course, that the findings from the PYS are somehow biased. But in all likelihood, any "Steeler . . . er . . . Pittsburgh" effect on the findings is not great. A similar longitudinal study conducted in Denver reported comparable results. The Denver Youth Survey (DYS) was comprised of 1,527 youngsters (806 boys and 721 girls) drawn from at-risk, socially disorganized, high-crime neighborhoods in—you guessed it—Denver! The DYS participants were purposely sampled at ages 7, 9, 11, 13, or 15. As Huizinga, Weiher, Espiritu, and Esbensen (2003) discovered, the percentage of parents who sought help for their kids was only 20% for children and

30% for adolescents—though the percentages increased as their offspring's delinquency and psychological problems grew more serious. As Huizinga et al. (2003) concluded, "for the majority of delinquent and serious delinquent youth, help has not been sought" (p. 84; for more details, see Espiritu, 1994).

This state of affairs bothers Cullen and Jonson. Year after year, children are manifesting psychological, behavioral, and criminological problems. Their careers in crime are blossoming, and nothing is being done. Part of the problem, of course, falls on the shoulders of parents. But the reality is that many parents of at-risk youngsters are at risk themselves. They lack the health insurance, money, education, transportation, and ability to take time off work to haul a resistant child off to a help provider on a weekly basis. They also are living in at-risk neighborhoods where effective services may not be close at hand (Guerra, 1997). In this context, the real culprit is that we lack an overarching agency whose job it is to identify troubled youths and to coordinate a coherent intervention (see also Farrington & Welsh, 2007). Meanwhile, the *future super-predators of America* are allowed to fall between the cracks—until they victimize, earn an arrest, and eventually are sent off to prison. Based on the PYS, Loeber and colleagues (2003) leave us with this sobering reality that we ignore at our own peril:

> In summary, the development of disruptive and delinquent behaviors was largely left unchecked by parents and helping agencies. These findings have important implications for planners of preventative interventions and policy makers. Preventative interventions should take place in the *relatively long time window* between the onset of early problem behaviors of a minor kind and the first contact with the juvenile court. Policy makers should realize that eventual index [or serious] offenders have often had the *unchecked opportunity to commit delinquent acts for many years*. (p. 127, emphasis added)

Five Programs That Work—At Least When Done Right

Okay, there is a need to intervene with at-risk youths. But do any programs exist that *work*, that are effective in knifing off their criminal development? Fortunately, the answer to this question is a resounding "yes." Based on rigorous, experimental evaluations, the evidence is clear that we have a growing repertoire of interventions that can save children from a life in crime (Farrington & Coid, 2003; Farrington & Welsh, 2007; Greenwood, 2006; Morizot & Kazemian, 2015; Welsh & Farrington, 2012). In this section, we review five famous interventions. They are exemplars for how to design an effective system of early intervention.

Still, this is not a time for hubris—for getting so overconfident or giddy that we assume that child saving is an easy task. The most daunting challenge is what is known as *technology transfer*, which is how to take knowledge about what works and spread it into new settings (see Becker, David, & Soucy, 1995). As Welsh, Sullivan, and Olds (2010, p. 115) point out, this involves "going to scale." To use an analogy, companies develop products all the time and then test them in a limited way. But in the end, they must move from achieving positive results in the test market to selling the product profitably nationwide. In the same way, once an effective program is designed, it remains to be seen if it can "go to scale" and be used successfully across diverse contexts. In this dissemination process, some "discounting" or drop in the overall success rate is virtually inevitable (Welsh et al., 2010). The key is anticipating this possibility and taking steps to minimize it.

Remember that the original programs are typically invented and implemented by researchers. These folks are bright, well funded, and devoted to ensuring that their program is effective. As a result, the founding program works to reduce problem behavior. But when others try to transfer this intervention technology to another setting, the same positive results may not be forthcoming. This sometimes is called a *researcher or investigator effect*. This reality does not mean that the interventions that researchers design cannot be used effectively by other people. But it does mean that unless those who borrow the program do what the researcher did—unless they achieve *therapeutic integrity*—then the intervention is unlikely to be effective. Showing *fidelity to the original program design* can be difficult for a host of reasons: lack of resources, lack of organizational talent, hostile judges, a resistant staff, and so on. Even so, these are obstacles and not insurmountable barriers. Programs can be established effectively in multiple settings; it just is a challenge to do so. In short, we know what works—*if it is done the right way*.

Beyond the issue of ensuring fidelity to the program design when implementation occurs, Cullen and Jonson are going to tell you something else about why certain early intervention programs work: *They adhere to the principles of effective treatment*. Wait a minute! Didn't we cover that in Chapter 7 on rehabilitation when we talked about the Canadians, eh? Yes, but Cullen and Jonson have realized that the principles that guide effective correctional interventions also guide effective early intervention. To be sure, those who invented the exemplary early intervention programs had no idea that they were obeying principles made up by a bunch of Canadians. Nonetheless, in order to change human behavior—especially problem human behavior—programs sort of have to follow the same principles.

The Canadians' approach is sometimes referred to as the *RNR paradigm*. Each letter stands for a core principle: R = risk principle; N = need principle; R = responsivity principle. Let us reiterate the key points:

- The *risk principle* says that interventions should be focused on high-risk individuals. This is because there is more to change and more future problems to prevent.

- The *need principle* says that interventions should target the known predictors of the problem behavior. These should be dynamic risk factors (also called criminogenic needs) in that they must be changeable. This also means that we must know what the risk factors are if we are to target them for change.

- The *responsivity principle* says that we should use interventions that are capable of changing the risk factors causing the problem behavior.

Guess what? Virtually all effective early intervention programs adhere to the RNR paradigm. They focus on high-risk cases; they identify risk factors and target them for change; and they use interventions that are responsive to—capable of altering—the risk factors that they have identified. This approach seems to make sense, doesn't it? It is like medicine: Focus on people who are really sick and will not get better on their own; know what it is you are trying to cure; and then select medicine or surgery that can fix the problem. The RNR paradigm is thus a powerful strategy for saving adults and kids from a life in crime.

Now it is time to turn to five programs that have rightly earned national attention for their effectiveness. As we take a tour across these programs, keep an eye out for how they typically, if implicitly, employ the RNR paradigm. Also keep in mind what it might take to transfer these programs to settings across the nation and have them be effective.

NURSE HOME VISITATION PROGRAM

After graduating from Johns Hopkins University in 1970, David Olds started working in a day care center in West Baltimore for underprivileged children. Despite his best efforts, Olds felt that some of the youngsters were so troubled that it was too late—even by ages four and five—to reverse the damage. In a common story, Olds discovered that one "boy's speech was so severely delayed because his mother was a drug addict and alcoholic, and had been using throughout her pregnancy" (Goodman, 2006, p. 7). Frustrated, Olds decided to learn more about children and to pursue a doctorate in developmental psychology at Cornell University. His mentor was the famous scholar Urie Bronfenbrenner.

Olds was anxious to make a difference in the lives of children. In 1975, he jumped into a part-time job at an organization—located in Elmira, New York—that "conducted programs intended to prevent health and developmental problems in young children" (Goodman, 2006, p. 8). Under the auspices of this organization, Olds had the opportunity to try to save the kind of kids he could not impact in West Baltimore. He understood that youngsters' problems could be traced back to the earliest time in life—to the pre-natal and post-natal periods. This was especially the case for those born to at-risk mothers. A pressing need thus existed to intervene at this stage in life. But how? Who could establish trust and work with these moms? Olds had a remarkable insight: nurses!

Nurses were an ingenious choice for two main reasons. First, nurses are not threatening, judgmental figures. Rather, they are part of a helping profession that would legitimately provide expectant moms something they would like to have: health care. Second, given this inroad into the lives of at-risk women, nurses have the skills to do things that could change early predictors of crime and other wayward behaviors. In his blueprint, the nurses would work with first-time mothers, go to the moms' homes, and start visiting early in pregnancy (hopefully in the first trimester). The intervention was intended to improve the health of the mothers' pregnancy, to teach them how to parent a newborn, and to help them to envision a future that involved few pregnancies, schooling, and employment.

From a criminological standpoint, Olds's approach is important because he was targeting for change pre-natal and post-natal *criminogenic risk factors among high-risk mothers* (Olds, 1998, 2007; Olds, Hill, & Rumsey, 1998). According to Olds et al. (1998), "to prevent youth crime and delinquency, it is important to understand how antisocial behavior develops and to design programs to interrupt that developmental pathway" (p. 1). He wished to impact "three important risk factors associated with early development of antisocial behavior" (p. 1). In his words, this is what those factors are:

- Adverse maternal health-related behaviors during pregnancy associated with children's neuropsychological deficits.
- Child abuse and neglect.
- Troubled maternal life course.

The gist of his thinking was that one challenge was *pre-natal:* to get mothers to do healthy things (e.g., eat correctly) and to stop mothers from doing unhealthy things (e.g., smoking, taking drugs). This would mean that a child would have a better chance of being born without neuropsychological deficits. The next challenge was *post-natal*—after the child was born—and involved two parts. First, it would be essential to teach mothers how to parent newborns and toddlers so that they would be more caring and not react to their offspring by hitting or ignoring them. Second, mothers would be more likely to remain effective parents and good role models if they could improve their lives through schooling and/or employment. They needed to be helped to make this transition.

The key was to develop an intervention that was *responsive* to—that is, that could change—these risk factors experienced by high-risk moms and their children. Again, here is where the nurses came in! Pregnancy is a crisis for many women. The nurses would see the expectant mothers once a week to build up a bond of trust so that the moms would follow their advice to take steps to ensure a healthy pregnancy. As Olds (2007) notes:

> During pregnancy, the nurses helped women complete 24-hour diet histories on a regular basis and plot weight gains at every visit; they assessed the women's cigarette smoking and use of alcohol and illegal drugs and facilitated a reduction in the use of these substances through behavioral change strategies. They taught women to identify the signs and symptoms of pregnancy complications, encouraged women to inform the office-based staff about those conditions, and facilitated compliance with treatment. They gave particular attention to urinary tract infections, sexually transmitted diseases, and hypertensive disorders of pregnancy (conditions associated with poor birth outcomes). They coordinated care with physicians and nurses in the office and measured blood pressure when needed. (pp. 212–213)

The nurses would continue seeing the moms every other week until the baby's birth when they would resume weekly visits for six weeks. Eventually, the visits would be spread out to every other week and then to once a month. They would end at the baby's second birthday (Goodman, 2006). Overall, then, the program would last about two and a half years. During this time, the home visiting nurses "would focus simultaneously on the mother's personal health and development, environmental health, and quality of caregiving for the infant and toddler" (Olds et al., 1998, p. 2). Put more simply, the nurse would help the mother to stay healthy, to give the right kind of care to her child, and to make good choices in her life.

The name of *Prenatal and Early Childhood Nurse Home Visitation Program*— that is a mouthful!—has since been shortened by Olds to the *Nurse-Family Partnership* or *NFP*. Programs based on the Olds model are now operating in 250 counties nationwide and serve over 20,000 mothers (Goodman, 2006; Olds, 2007). Many other variants of this home visitation program, not specifically designed by Olds but based on the same general idea, are in operation as well. By one estimate, "as many as 200,000 children and their families" are currently involved in home visiting programs (Gomby, Culross, & Behrman, 1999, p. 1). Cullen and Jonson think that this attempt to save children is pretty amazing! But with so many lives at stake, the next question only increases in its significance: Does this model actually work to improve the health and lives of mothers and, in particular, to reduce future antisocial behavior, including crime, among the children?

Based on reviews of the evidence, the answer appears to be "yes" (Farrington & Welsh, 2007; Greenwood, 2006; Piquero, Farrington, Welsh, Tremblay, & Jennings, 2009). Greenwood and Turner (2009) include the NFP in their list of "preferred programs," which earn this designation because the extant research suggests that they are "proven, effective models" (p. 369). Still, we say *appears to be "yes"* because Gomby et al. (1999) have concluded that the effects of home visitation programs are mixed and modest. Part of the problem may be that many programs do not follow the Olds model fully. To save money, some interventions have visitations conducted not by nurses but by paraprofessionals—often high school graduates trained to intervene with the at-risk mothers. But lack of fidelity to the original design has a steep price: Evidence exists that nurses are an essential ingredient in program effectiveness (Goodman, 2006; Olds, 2007). Another issue to consider is that mothers and kids who finish the visitation programs do not receive any aftercare that builds on gains made early in life. More work needs to be done to explore how early gains can be sustained as at-risk youngsters negotiate at-risk environments.

With these qualifications, Olds has provided experimental evidence across three sites—Elmira, Memphis, and Denver—that his intervention is effective with mothers and with their children (Olds, 1998, 2007; Olds et al., 1998). Let us take as one example the evidence from Olds's initial program in Elmira, New York. This evaluation included 400 pregnant mothers—200 randomly assigned to the treatment condition and 200 randomly assigned to the control condition (who also received some pregnancy services but no nurse visitations). In most areas examined, the mothers engaged in healthier behavior and more nurturing parenting. Most important, when evaluated at 15, the children who were visited by nurses— especially those of mothers who were poor and were unmarried—had fewer arrests, convictions, and violations of probation (Olds, 2007).

We want to mention one other program outcome recently re~
his colleagues (2014): the impact of nurse visit ~
ity. Yes, we are talking about death de~
merits investigation. "Mortality," they as~
prevention aligns with the goals of the~
(p. 804). They note further that "nurses a~
child health by helping activate and supp~
dren and themselves" (p. 804). Based on a t~
do indeed find that nurse home visitations~
what they call "preventable deaths" among c~
death syndrome, unintentional injuries, an~
these findings capture one of the importan~
grams: They can have diverse, often-unantici~
well-being across the life course.

HIGH/SCOPE PERRY PRESCHOOL PROGRAM

In the early 1960s, David Weikart was the director of special education in the Ypsilanti, Michigan, school district. Weikart and his colleagues were concerned that many youngsters experienced academic failure upon first entering the educational system. It seemed obvious that the need existed to enrich these children's intellectual functioning. Trying to achieve reform across the school district seemed too complex. Instead, they decided to try to intervene before at-risk youngsters would enter the formal system. To do so, they selected youngsters who would eventually attend Perry Elementary School to participate in a preschool program (Schweinhart, 2007). The Perry Preschool is no longer in existence. In 1970, however, Weikart established the High/Scope Educational Research Foundation, which continued to follow children in the program for nearly 40 years (Parks, 1998; Schweinhart, 2007). This is how this intervention became known as the *High/Scope Perry Preschool Program*.

Weikart wanted to break the cycle of poverty. When underprivileged children experienced educational failure, they were less likely to complete high school and be economically successful. This poverty would then be transmitted to their offspring, who would enter the cycle of school failure, economic failure, and poverty. To knife off this intergenerational cycle of poverty, it thus was essential to ensure that children do well in elementary school, complete high school, and move into decent paying jobs (Schweinhart, 2007).

But what should be the components of an effective preschool intervention? Weikart and his buddies were really bright. They created a program that adhered to the RNR principles years before these ideas were set forth by the Canadians (Andrews & Bonta, 2010). First, they selected for the program African American preschool children ages three and four who were from low socioeconomic families and who had IQ scores "between 70 and 85, the range for borderline mental impairment" (Parks, 1998, p. 2). In short, the children were at high risk of educational failure. Second, they targeted for change the youngsters' intellectual development. Of course, this leads to the third component: developing a responsive intervention. What did they come up with?

Well, from what Cullen and Jonson can determine, Weikart realized that the intervention had to be intensive. Similar to curing a serious disease, treating a serious human deficit needs high-dose treatment. A few flimsy tutoring sessions or some happy playgroup meetings would not do the trick. Weikart thus devised the following intervention (Parks, 1998; Schweinhart, 2007):

- Children would be in the program for two years.

- Five mornings a week, the kids would attend preschool for two and a half hours.

- The teachers would visit each child's parents in the families' homes one afternoon a week for one and a half hours.

- Parents were required to attend a monthly group meeting of parents that the staff facilitated.

- There was a teacher–student ratio of between 5 and 6.5—or four teachers assigned to every 20 to 25 children.

The next issue is the nature of the treatment. In various places, the program is described as being "based on an active learning model that emphasizes participants' intellectual and social development" (Parks, 1998, p. 2). Okay, but what the heck does that mean? Part of the process is that teachers try to develop the kids' "intellectual and social skills through individualized teaching and learning" (Schweinhart, 2007, p. 147). They do this, it seems, through a process that guides the children to internalize the ability to learn on their own. Schweinhart (2007) has done a nice job of explaining the program's educational approach, noting that it is based on:

> the natural development of young children. It emphasizes the idea that children are intentional learners, who learn best from activities that they themselves plan, carry out, and review afterward. Adults introduce new ideas to children through adult-initiated small- and large-group activities. Adults observe, support, and extend the children's play as appropriate. Adults arrange interest areas in the learning environment; maintain a daily routine that permits children to plan, carry out, and review their own activities; and join in children's activities, asking appropriate questions that extend their plans and help them think about their activities. They add complex language to the discussion to expand the children's vocabulary. Using key developmental indicators derived from child development theory as a framework, adults encourage children to make choices, solve problems, and engage in activities that contribute to their intellectual, social, and physical development. (pp. 148–149)

This all sounds wonderful, but Weikart and the Perry Preschool Program would have lapsed into historical oblivion if not for one consideration: data! Weikart did not intend simply to build *a program* but rather wanted to develop a *program that worked*. Having confidence in his ideas, he decided to test his program and get good data through an experimental design. To do this, he and his staff recruited

128 African American male and female children to participate in the study. Half were randomly assigned to the treatment or preschool group and half to the control group. Due to attrition, the study lost five cases. Remember that folks like Weikart who put their ideas to the test have, well, guts. Data are dangerous; they can show that one's ideas are pretty stupid and that years of well-intentioned child-saving efforts were a waste of time.

Of course, Cullen and Jonson would not be discussing Weikart and his intervention if the data had shown that the Perry Preschool Program was a bust! In fact, the outcomes were amazingly positive. Compared to the control group, program participants were less likely to be placed in a special education program and were more likely to graduate from high school. They had lower rates of births out of wedlock and of welfare assistance. And they earned more money and were more likely to own a home (Parks, 1998; Schweinhart, 2007). Still, from our perspective, the key consideration is whether any of these is relevant to crime. Again, as you may have imagined, the answer is "yes."

Human beings tend not to be very compartmentalized. If they do well in one area of their development, they tend to do well in other areas. Unfortunately, if they tend to have problems, these difficulties tend to pervade their lives. This is what criminologists call *the generality of deviance* or the *co-morbidity of problems*. Thus, those who hit and steal from others also tend to smoke, abuse drugs and alcohol, become sick, be accident prone, get a lot of tattoos, fail at school, lose jobs, and experience unstable relationships. The important insight here is that if intervention programs succeed in fixing kids so that the youngsters succeed at school and thereupon in other domains of their lives, then they also tend to have the *collateral effect of reducing involvement in juvenile delinquency and adult crime*. Alas, although not intended as a crime prevention strategy, the Perry Preschool Program diverted a lot of participants from criminal activities across their life course (Parks, 1998; Schweinhart, 2007).

Schweinhart (2007) has presented data based on a follow-up of the Perry Preschool kids at age 40. All readers should stop and realize, as Cullen and Jonson have done, how darn amazing this is. Can you imagine keeping track of study participants for nearly four decades (the kids started the program at age 2 or 4)? Such a follow-up is the gold standard of a *longitudinal study*. It does not get much more longitudinal than this!

In any event, by age 40, the program participants had experienced a lot fewer legal entanglements (Schweinhart, 2007, p. 150). This is not meant to imply they were free from system contact. As we know, for a host of reasons, disadvantaged African Americans—such as those in the Perry Preschool Program—are prone to justice system processing. In fact, in the preschool treatment group, only 29% had never been arrested. Even so, compared to non-participants who were assigned to the control group, their odds of an arrest over their lifetime were 46% lower. And if arrested, they experienced fewer numbers of arrests. Further, the percentage never arrested for major crime categories was consistently higher for those from the program: violent offenses (67% vs. 52% for the control group), property offenses (64% vs. 42%), and drug offenses (86% vs. 66%). Only 28% of the preschool kids ended up spending time in jail or prison; the statistic for the control-group kids was 52%. Finally, the difference in criminal participation between the preschool and control groups became wider as the sample aged. This finding is surprising because in most instances program effects tend to weaken as time passes and participants are farther away from the original intervention.

Beyond intellectual development (IQ is a predictor of criminal involvement), Schweinhart (2007) offers the interesting thesis that the Perry Preschool Program may also have lowered the participants' impulsivity. Recall the description of the program presented above. It may be that the program's focus on kids' planning, decision making, and cognitive awareness instilled (much like a cognitive-behavioral program) more self-control. Impulsivity or a lack of self-control (including ADHD) is an empirically established predictor of crime, largely, it is believed, because this trait prompts people to act before they think—in particular, before they think of the consequences of what they are about to do (Farrington & Welsh, 2007; Gottfredson & Hirschi, 1990). As Schweinhart (2007) suggests, if inculcated with the capacity to handle impulsivity, those in the program group may have been "more purposeful in avoiding" criminal choices (p. 157).

There is general agreement that the High/Scope Perry Preschool Program is an effective intervention and that similar early enrichment programs have shown success (Farrington & Welsh, 2007; Greenwood, 2006; Greenwood & Turner, 2009; Reynolds, Temple, Ou, Arteaga, & White, 2011; Schindler & Yoshikawa, 2012). In fact, high-quality findings tend to have "robust" effects across a variety of outcomes (Farrington & Welsh, 2007, p. 119). Again, however, the key qualification here is that the programs must be *high quality*. Do things the right way, and it seems that prosocial development will be promoted and meaningful savings in criminal involvement will be achieved (Schweinhart, 2007).

Cullen and Jonson find two other aspects of the Perry Preschool Program and similar enrichment programs noteworthy. First, James Heckman, a Nobel Prize-winning economist from the University of Chicago, has become a prominent advocate of early intervention programs, including his book, *Giving Kids a Fair Chance* (2013). Using sophisticated statistical techniques (something that economists do for a living!), Heckman and colleagues examined the "rate of return" of the Perry Preschool Program (Heckman, Moon, Pinto, Savelyev, & Yavitz, 2010a, 2010b). They noted that the cost-benefit ratios were not as high as those found by previous analyses using less rigorous statistical controls. That said, they reported that the results remained statistically significant in favor of program participants. In more concrete language, they noted that the annual return for the program was between 7% and 10%. This figure surpassed the post-World War II "annual return to equity" in the stock market, which is "estimated to be 5.8 percent before the 2008 meltdown" (Heckman, 2011, p. 35). Based on these findings, Heckman (2013, p. 31) now touts early childhood education as a means of addressing the "economics of inequality." In particular, he argues for what he calls "*predistribution*—improving the early lives of disadvantaged children"—rather than trying to redistribute incomes for people later in life (Heckman, 2012, p. 11; emphasis in the original). "Predistribution policies," he argues, "are both fair and economically efficient" (2012, p. 11).

Second, the early enrichment interventions—such as the Perry Preschool Program and Head Start—hoped to boost at-risk kids' IQ and standardized test scores. As Duncan and Magnuson (2013) report, the initial gains achieved by these programs tend to decay gradually and to disappear after 10 years. But here is the catch—actually, here is the good news. While these intended intellectual consequences peter out, the programs have a lot of unintended consequences in various aspects of participants' lives that seem to persist deep into adulthood! Duncan and Magnuson (2013, p. 120) call this "the puzzle—academic fade-out, but long-term benefits." These include "beneficial impacts on a broad set of later-life outcomes like high school graduation rates, teen pregnancy, and criminality" (p. 120). Understanding why this occurs is challenging. One possibility is cumulative advantage: Program kids enter school and succeed, which in turn leads them to eventually graduate from high school and avoid drugs and crime. Another possibility is that the intervention inadvertently builds other personal skills—such as self-efficacy, the capacity to pay attention, and emotional intelligence—that are needed to succeed in various life domains. Regardless, one reason why early intervention programs are valuable—and cost effective—is that they have the potential to improve kids in ways that have multiple and cascading benefits.

FUNCTIONAL FAMILY THERAPY

It is commonly believed that if you grow up in a troubled family, you are likely to live a troubled life. To a large extent, this wisdom turns out to be, well, wisdom. Scholars have reviewed many studies, and they tend to agree that family factors are consistent predictors of early misconduct and of subsequent offending. It also appears that the more bad family factors children are exposed to, the more likely they are to be wayward. This effect is called *cumulative risk* (Farrington & Welsh, 2007). As Farrington and Welsh (2007) conclude with regard to families and offending, "the strongest predictor is usually criminal or antisocial parents. Other quite strong and replicable predictors are large family size, poor parental supervision, parental conflict, and disrupted families" (p. 74; see also Lipsey & Derzon, 1998; Petrosino, Derzon, & Lavenberg, 2009).

These findings point to a potential avenue for early intervention. How about if we teach parents to be better parents? Will that make a difference? One complication is that some research suggests that *parenting style*—how kids are parented—is not a strong predictor of conduct problems and offending (Wright et al., 2008). Scholars thus challenge the *nurture assumption*—the idea that kids enter the world as a blank slate and that their destiny is determined by how their parents socialize them. Instead, they argue that it is mainly through *nature* or genetics that parents really transmit advantages—and problems—to kids (Harris, 1998). For example, impulsive parents with ADHD may raise their children in a lousy way. When their kids then get into trouble, why is this? Is it because of the lousy parenting they have received or because their parents' ADHD and impulsivity have been inherited, which then causes them to act waywardly?

This is not the place to disentangle this hotly debated issue, but we can make an important point: Even if bad parenting is not the cause of problem behavior, this does not mean that good parenting is not the solution to decreasing such conduct. Recall from earlier in the chapter the idea of *genetic fatalism*. Let us assume, again, that a child has ADHD and gets into trouble by acting impulsively. If mom and dad are taught how to parent in a way that helps the child to cope more effectively with impulsivity, then the child may develop increased impulse control and avoid making bad decisions. That is, parents may learn how to employ cognitive-behavioral techniques to manage their youngsters in a way that curbs criminal propensities—regardless of whether these propensities are due to social or biological causes. In fact, there is now fairly substantial evidence that interventions that teach *parental management* of children work to reduce offending (Farrington & Welsh, 2003, 2007; Greenwood, 2006; Greenwood & Turner, 2009; Petrosino et al., 2009; Piquero et al., 2009). Thus, in their meta-analysis of the impact of parental management training programs on antisocial behavior and delinquency, Farrington and Welsh (2003) reported a mean effect size of .395. This meant that the programs achieved a "20% reduction in antisocial behavior/delinquency (e.g., from 50% in a control group to 30% in an experimental group)" (Farrington & Welsh, 2007, p. 127).

Teaching parents how to manage their children more effectively is important because, as Farrington and Welsh (2007) state, "crime runs in families" (p. 57). To be sure, there are families where there is the so-called black sheep—the single bad child in an otherwise good family. In fact, those asserting that parenting has no effect on any youngster's behavior use this empirical reality as evidence in support of their perspective. After all, if two kids share the same family environment yet one turns out good and the other bad, how can parenting be said to cause both outcomes? Cullen and Jonson have no insightful response to that conundrum. But the other reality is that in *at-risk families*, as opposed to families from across the spectrum, it is often the case that *crime is highly concentrated*—it runs in families. That is, most of the family members—parents, child, siblings—are all troubled. An important implication of this fact is that families such as these are inviting targets for early intervention.

As is likely apparent, in this chapter we often make a statement and then cite some research by David Farrington. This is because he is very bright and publishes a zillion articles—all of them good ones! Google him or go look him up on the website of Cambridge University—the one in England! Well, here we go again. In this area, Farrington and his colleagues conducted two studies that show the extent to which offending is concentrated in at-risk families—one based on his Cambridge Study in Delinquent Development and the other on the PYS (Pittsburgh Youth Study) data. Both studies show virtually the same thing, which gives us confidence that the results hold across social context (London and Pittsburgh) and types of samples (mostly White and a majority African American).

The Cambridge Study in Delinquent Development is a longitudinal study of 411 males born in the working-class section of South London. They were drawn from 397 families. Most of the sample members were born in 1953, and then first contacted by a research team led by David West in 1961 or 1962. (David Farrington joined the research team in 1969 and has been director of the Cambridge Study since 1981.) These lads were followed from as young as age 8 to the age of 32, during which time they were interviewed on multiple occasions. Data from records were collected on them from ages 10 to 40 (Farrington, 2003; Piquero et al., 2007). In the study of interest, Farrington, Barnes, and Lambert (1996) examined how the convictions of these males "relates to the convictions of their biological fathers and mothers, full brothers and sisters, and wives" (p. 47).

The key issue is whether offending is spread evenly across families or is concentrated in a subset. To start with, nearly two thirds of the families (64%) had some family member convicted of a crime. But here is the key finding: Only 5.8% of the families accounted for 49.9%—or about half—of all the convictions experienced by the study's families. Further, just over one tenth of the families (10.3%) accounted for 64.3% of the convictions. To hit the point home a bit more, here are other findings quoted from Farrington et al. (1996, p. 47):

- Convictions of one family member were strongly related to convictions of every other family member.

- About three quarters of convicted fathers and mothers had a convicted child.

- In both generations, the majority of convicted mothers mated with convicted fathers. (Note from Cullen and Jonson: This is called *assortive mating*—or birds of a feather flocking together!)

Well, it could be that there was something screwy about males born in 1953 in South London. Maybe if they drank water with fluoride, as we do in the United States, crime would be dispersed and not so concentrated—and they would have healthier teeth! Maybe if they rooted for Manchester United and not Chelsea, their lives would be more in order. Just some thoughts from Cullen and Jonson! But, alas, this is not the case. When Farrington, Jolliffe, Loeber, Stouthamer-Loeber, and Kalb (2001) examined data from the PYS—a Pittsburgh sample first contacted in 1987–1988—similar results were found. In fact, they discovered that the "concentration of offenders was greater in Pittsburgh than in London" (p. 586).

Cullen and Jonson think that these findings are immensely important. If such at-risk families are targeted for intervention, it might be possible to reduce the offending of multiple children in the household. It also might be possible to channel these youngsters along a life course where they would eventually select prosocial mates, which in turn would block the intergenerational transmission of criminality. Let us put it another way. The concentration of offending means that some families are really messed up and pose a daunting threat to society. But if an intervention were to work, then it could do a great deal of good—for the families and for public safety.

In this regard, we again reiterate that parental management interventions have been found to be effective. Here, we want to focus on one with a good track record:

Functional Family Therapy, also known by its acronym *FFT*. Cullen and Jonson think that it should have been called Dysfunctional Family Therapy since, after all, the families getting fixed are dysfunctional! But those in the treatment business are an optimistic bunch and prefer to give their programs nice-sounding names. In this case, the program inventor is James Alexander. He founded the program in 1969 at the University of Utah where the Department of Psychology had a Family Clinic. He chose the name *family* because this was the *core unit* or focus of the intervention. He chose the name *functional*—positive guy that he is!—because of "the overriding allegiance to positive outcome" (Alexander, Pugh, & Parsons, 1998, p. 7). Today, FFT is in 220 sites, including Europe, New Zealand, and nearly every state in America (*FFT,* 2010).

Alexander and his colleagues were quite shrewd in how they developed FFT. They realized that a viable program had to be practical. In this regard, they decided—as all good programs do!—to focus on at-risk antisocial youths. In this case, they targeted youngsters ages 11 to 18 who were *at risk of institutionalization.* They also understood that lengthy psychotherapy was a non-starter when funding was coming from the public treasury. Freud might not be happy, but nobody wants to pay for troubled families to spend a couple of years in psychoanalysis trying to figure out who is envious of what. Rather, they designed the program to be completed in three months. Staff would meet with families in one-hour sessions that numbered from 8 to 12 for "mild cases" and from 26 to 30 for youths in family situations that were "severely dysfunctional" (Alexander et al., 1998, p. 8; see also Onedera, 2006).

FFT is extremely well planned. It is divided into five stages (Alexander et al., 1998). The first two, *engagement* and *motivation,* are designed to ensure that at-risk families will enter and develop favorable views about the intervention. In the *engagement* stage, the therapist's job is to engage the family and the antisocial youth and to take steps to retain them in the program. The main strategy is to create a belief that positive change can occur. This occurs in the first session. In the *motivation* stage, the special challenge is to focus on things like negativity, hopelessness, and blaming within the family. If strides can be made, this shows everyone involved that change is possible. If so, then these positive experiences may increase the desire to stay in the program and make a commitment to further change. As Alexander has pointed out in an interview, without "engagement and motivation, all the rest of the phases, even if they are done perfectly, are basically almost doomed to failure" (Onedera, 2006, p. 308). Put simply, before you can fix people, you gotta get them involved!

The third stage, *assessment,* is when the therapist tries to understand what the heck is going on in the family. In figuring this out, the therapist does not look aimlessly but uses the program's conceptual framework; this is like putting on FFT glasses that channel the therapist's vision to look for some things but not others. The challenge here is to determine what needs to be targeted for change. Based on the empirical literature, FFT has identified a range of child, intrafamilial, and contextual risk and protective factors that are likely to affect outcomes (Alexander et al., 1998, pp. 16–17). As an intervention based on crime-producing family dynamics, the main focus is on detecting poor parenting skills and negative (or belittling and blaming) communication or, conversely, on detecting any positive parenting skills and communication that might exist and can be built upon. Based on this assessment, a plan for change individualized to the needs of the family and child is developed.

Getting back to the RNR model, FFT is meant for high-risk families and youths (one R) and focuses on sources of criminality (the N). But what about the second R—responsivity? Well, this is undertaken in the fourth stage of FFT, which Alexander calls *behavior change*. So, what do you think Alexander came up with? If the sources of problem behavior involve the inability of parents to communicate effectively and to parent their child, what should the intervention do? What would be a treatment that would be *responsive*? You got it! The FFT therapist works with the family to train them to communicate in a positive way (e.g., how to listen and to interact in a direct, concrete, and optimistic way) and to train adults in effective parental management strategies (e.g., how to use praise, to ignore irrelevant acts, to set limits, to monitor, and to set up behavioral contracts where rewards are tied to achievable good conduct).

In essence, FFT employs a cognitive-behavioral approach, which as you know from Chapter 7 is pretty darn effective in addressing problem behavior. As Alexander notes, "people have belief systems, and they have ways of thinking. They also have behavior patterns. They also have emotional reactions. You need to address all of those, and you need to address them differently based on different people" (Onedera, 2006, p. 309). FFT is oriented toward giving people the "tools" to transform how they think, behave, and feel. According to Alexander, "these include emotional tools, cognitive tools, and behavioral tools to initiate and maintain the short-term and then long-term behavior changes that are necessary for them to be more adaptive within the family and outside the family" (p. 309).

By following the sequence from stages 1 to 4, FFT hopefully has achieved effective change *within the family*. But as the intervention—again, which lasts three months—starts to wind down, the therapist must enable the family and problem youth to negotiate the context in which they live. Alexander calls this the *generalization* stage. Some risk factors in this context cannot be altered, such as the presence of gangs in the neighborhood. Still, this is a time when the therapist can collaborate with community systems to undercut potential risk factors and to take advantage of opportunities for support. For example, the therapist might work with teachers to address learning deficits, direct a youth to participate in prosocial community recreational centers, or actively assist family members to secure treatment in self-help groups for substance abuse problems.

Most noteworthy, FFT has been shown to reduce a range of problem behaviors. Across 13 experimental or quasi-experimental studies, with outcomes ranging from offending to foster care placement, consistent positive effects have been reported. Compared to control groups (random or matched samples), problematic outcomes have been reduced between 25% and 60%. One study also discovered that positive effects extended to siblings. More studies are ongoing (Alexander et al., 1998; *FFT*, 2010).

SEATTLE SOCIAL DEVELOPMENT PROJECT

To be effective, early interventions need to operate in those social domains or systems where kids reside. One of these is the school. It is estimated that from Grades 1 to 12, youngsters spend 18% of their waking hours within educational institutions (Gottfredson, Wilson, & Najaka, 2002). The other reality is that for youths, a "disproportionate amount of crime occurs in or around school buildings" (Gottfredson et al., 2002, p. 149). Bullying is another form of student victimizing behavior that can have damaging physical and psychological consequences.

When kids have trouble at school, it can cause them to have trouble outside of school. Put another way, some important risk factors for crime include academic failure and weak bonds to the school (Gottfredson et al., 2002). Further, it appears that certain kinds of schools—those marked by poor classroom management, distrust between teachers and students, and inconsistently enforced rules—produce higher rates of misconduct inside and outside the school grounds (Farrington & Welsh, 2007).

Fortunately, there is mounting evidence regarding the effectiveness of school-based interventions to reduce kids' antisocial conduct. Some do not work particularly well (such as the D.A.R.E. program), but others do work well (Baldry & Farrington, 2007; Catalano, Arthur, Hawkins, Berglund, & Olson, 1998; Catalano, Loeber, & McKinney, 1999; Farrington & Welsh, 2007; Gottfredson et al., 2002; LeMarquand & Tremblay, 2001; Mytton, DiGuiseppi, Gough, Taylor, & Logan, 2002; Najaka, Gottfredson, & Wilson, 2001; Wilson, Gottfredson, & Najaka, 2001; Wilson & Lipsey, 2007; Wilson, Lipsey, & Derzon, 2003; see also Gottfredson, 2001). Consistent with the risk principle, evidence exists that the program achieves greater reductions with higher-risk youth (Wilson et al., 2003). Importantly, Gottfredson et al. (2002, pp. 176–182) have highlighted programs that seem to be most effective:

- *Programs that improve school and discipline management.* These can be multifaceted, involving efforts to bolster school climate, to increase achievement, to target at-risk students for special assistance to avoid academic failure and behavioral problems, and to enhance the consistency of student discipline.

- *Programs that attempt to establish norms and expectations about acceptable behavior.* This might include instructing students that bullying will not be tolerated and supervising students to ensure that this victimizing conduct does not occur. Or it might include correcting misconceptions that substance abuse among classmates is widespread (when the silent majority does not engage in serious abuse) and teaching students how to resist peer pressure to consume alcohol and drugs.

- *Programs that use instructional strategies or cognitive-behavioral interventions to improve students' coping and decision-making skills.* This might involve teaching students how to exercise self-control, to manage their anger, to consider alternatives to deviant ways of solving problems, to think about possible consequences that actions might have, and to be more sensitive to their classmates.

One exemplary school-based intervention strategy is the *Seattle Social Development Project,* also known by its acronym *SSDP* (Hawkins, Smith, Hill, Kosterman, & Catalano, 2007; Hawkins et al., 2003). The SSDP is directed by J. David Hawkins, with Richard F. Catalano serving as the project's associate director. As with all effective programs, the inventors are smart people. Or, to put it another way, they are really good criminologists.

Hawkins and Catalano realized two things early on. First, they knew that "to be effective in stopping crime before it happens, crime prevention efforts must address factors that predict crime" (Hawkins et al., 2003, p. 270). Duh! Of course! But until the 1980s—about the time they started the SSDP—this knowledge did not exist, programs were largely blind in what they targeted for change, and thus few school-based interventions were found to be effective (Hawkins et al., 2007). Second, Hawkins and Catalano knew that schools are invaluable settings in which to locate a prevention project. They comprise the one place that gives nearly universal access to youngsters in a community. Further, things done in and through schools can change students' lives. According to Hawkins et al. (2007), "many of the factors that predict problem outcomes are accessible through schools" (p. 162).

The SSDP started as an intervention with first graders in five Seattle public schools in 1981 and then was expanded into a longitudinal study four years later. The sample included 808 students, who were age 10 and in the fifth grade in 1985. They attended 18 Seattle elementary schools that served high-crime neighborhoods. The sample members were followed into early adulthood and beyond (Hawkins et al., 2007; Hawkins et al., 2003).

Cullen and Jonson think that the neat thing about the SSDP is that it was based on a coherent theoretical model. Hawkins and Catalano did not just go out and start intervening aimlessly. Rather, they built their program around what they believed were the two most empirically verified theories of their day: differential association/social learning theory and social bond theory. Many readers will recognize these theories; you probably have gotten multiple-choice questions correct on these perspectives in your introduction to criminology course! The first theory, popularized by Edwin Sutherland and Ronald Akers, says that crime is learned through interaction with others and is repeated when reinforced. The second theory, popularized by Travis Hirschi, says that the more closely bonded to society individuals are, the less likely they are to break the law (for summaries, see Lilly et al., 2015). These theories are typically seen as rivals, but Hawkins and Catalano understood that learning and bonding can happen at the same time. Duh! What's more, they added four important twists to create what they called the *social development model.*

First, in advancing one of the earliest life-course theories, they noted that differential association/social learning and social bond theories had a common weakness: They ignored childhood and were, in essence, adolescence-limited. But Hawkins and Catalano asserted something that, while obvious today, was not obvious back in the 1980s: That these perspectives had to be extended back into childhood and placed within a *developmental* framework. Ergo, the name they gave to their theory: the *social development model*. Second, they knew that kids did not begin a developmental pathway as blank slates. Accordingly, they identified three sets of factors that affect whether children's social development gets off on the right or wrong foot: (1) individual constitutional factors or traits; (2) a child's location in the social structure (e.g., race, class); and (3) something called *external constraints,* which seems to mean how prosocial or antisocial their parents and peers are.

Third, they then said that youngsters were likely to leave the train station of childhood on one of two developmental tracks: *prosocial* or *antisocial*. Their constitutional, social structural, and external constraint factors increased their opportunities to begin life with an abundance of either prosocial or antisocial interactions. These interactions would shape children's involvement in activities, social bonds, and moral beliefs. Importantly, if kids could be directed early in life into prosocial activities, they would likely develop prosocial bonds and prosocial moral beliefs and, voilà, we have a prosocial life course! Of course, the opposite pathway had the same components, except that they were antisocial in nature and led to criminological hell rather than to prosocial heaven. Thus, one pathway brought exposure to protective factors, whereas the other brought exposure to risk factors.

Fourth, Hawkins and Catalano had one final crucial insight. In order to keep on a prosocial pathway, youngsters had to find the experience rewarding; that is, they had to be positively reinforced. But in order to receive reinforcements, they had to have the appropriate *skills for interaction*. If they had deficits and ended up failing at school or aggravating and being rejected by other kids, they might decide that all this prosocial stuff is worthless and decide to flock over to the dark side with the antisocial birds, so to speak; here they could be successful messing up and be accepted for it. Most theories of crime simply do not talk about the kinds of skills needed to take advantage of prosocial opportunities; Hawkins and Catalano's did. Perhaps not surprisingly, subsequent empirical tests of their model have been mostly favorable (Hawkins et al., 2003).

Now on to the SSDP intervention! Given their theory, Hawkins and Catalano decided to save kids in three ways—again, all of which were school-based. First, parents who volunteered were given classes to increase their skills in behavior management, in supporting their children's academic performance, and in helping their kids to exercise self-control and to contribute to the family. Second, for the children, efforts were made to enhance their social and emotional skills, including communication, problem solving, conflict resolution, and learning how to refuse to do bad things. This was accomplished through a cognitive and social skills curriculum. Third, teachers were trained in classroom management techniques, how to engage in more interactive instruction with students, and how to encourage cooperative learning among their youngsters (Hawkins et al., 2007, p. 171; Hawkins et al., 2003).

Again, these programs were oriented toward undercutting risk factors and increasing the likelihood that kids would find prosocial activities and relationships rewarding. Phrased differently, Hawkins and Catalano carefully designed interventions that were *responsive* to *criminogenic needs* (or risk factors)—then delivered to kids attending elementary schools in *high-risk* neighborhoods (although, due to integration, not all kids were from the local area). RNR sort of revisited, once again.

The youngsters finished the program by the sixth grade. Some had been receiving the intervention since the first grade, some only in the fifth and sixth grades (and some of those only the parenting part). The control group, of course, received no intervention. The key issue is whether any of this would do any good many years later. Well, the gist of the findings is as follows: For those who received the *full intervention*—first through sixth grade—the results were pretty impressive. Here are some key accomplishments for the full intervention group at age 18 (Hawkins et al., 2007, pp. 176–177):

- Greater school attachment and commitment. Higher grades and less misbehavior at school.

- Less reported violent behavior in their lifetime and less heavy alcohol use in the past year.

- Less sexual activity and sexual partners.

By age 21, the treatment group still achieved "broad significant effects on functioning in school and work, on emotional and mental health, and on risky sexual practices and adverse health outcomes" (p. 177). Differences in crime and substance use narrowed by age 21, "although those in the full intervention group were significantly less likely than the controls to be involved in a variety of crimes, to have sold drugs in the past year, or to have received an official court charge in their lifetime" (p. 177).

MULTISYSTEMIC THERAPY

Multisystemic therapy—also known by its acronym *MST*—is one of the most popular early intervention strategies. It is estimated that MST programs serve approximately 10,000 youngsters in 30 U.S. states and in 11 nations (Jonson & Cullen, 2011). That's a lot of kids in a lot of places! Where did MST come from? What does it involve? And does it work? Each of these questions is addressed below.

MST is the invention of Scott Henggeler. The ideas first coalesced in 1978 when Henggeler and his psychology students at Memphis State University developed a juvenile diversion program. (He is now at the Medical University of South Carolina in Charleston.) Recall that this was not long after Martinson's (1974) nothing works doctrine emerged and was dominating thinking about corrections. However, Henggeler was a psychologist, not a criminologist, so he was not about to believe that kids were beyond redemption. After all, a lot of psychologists would be out of jobs if they agreed that therapy didn't work!

Indeed, Henggeler thought that he knew the real nature of the problem. It was not that antisocial youngsters could not change but rather that they were being treated with the wrong medicine, so to speak (Cullen, 2005). At the time, the traditional psychotherapeutic model required troubled youths, and perhaps their parents, to come weekly to an office for an individual session lasting an hour. The length of treatment was open ended and could last months, if not years, on end. Recalcitrant youngsters were candidates for placement in a residential facility. This approach often proved costly, was ineffective in reducing antisocial conduct, and often failed to reach inner-city youths.

This individual psychotherapeutic model typically had a psychodynamic, rather than a sociological, orientation. It tended to look inside a youth's mind to unravel what was wrong with him or her. But most kids in the justice system not only were personally troubled but also were drawn from troubled contexts or *systems*. As part of a community psychology movement, Henggeler was aware of these realities and was convinced that these *multiple systems* had to be addressed if kids were to be effectively treated. More specifically, he embraced the *social-ecological model*, which "depicts the process of human development as a reciprocal interchange between the individual and 'nested concentric structures' that mutually influence one another" (Henggeler, 1999, p. 2). That is, youths not only have individual traits but also are affected by such social systems as families, peers, schools, and community. In short, they live in *multiple systems*. Cullen and Jonson hope readers are getting the point! The concept of multiple systems has been italicized twice because it is the core of *multisystemic therapy*. If the risks for crime come from multiple systems, the intervention darned well better take that into account!

Empirical research has demonstrated that along with individual traits, each of these systems can expose a child or adolescent to criminogenic risk factors that increase the likelihood of law-breaking conduct. For example, a family risk factor might include ineffective parental discipline; a peer risk factor might involve contact with antisocial friends; and a school risk factor might be low achievement. For each troubled youth, the particular set of risk factors underlying his or her misconduct is likely to be unique. The intervention thus must be aware of this fact and be flexible enough to address risk factors drawn from different social systems.

So far, so good. But what exactly does MST involve? Similar to other inventors of classic intervention programs, Henggeler is a really clever guy—with *clever* being used in the best sense of the word! It makes little sense to ask, for example, a single mother—who might be a working mom—to try to get her at-risk son (or daughter) and perhaps a couple of siblings to board a bus and travel downtown to some psychotherapist's office where, like Cullen (but fortunately not Jonson), the therapist can stroke his beard and say, "Do I hear you saying you want to beat someone up? Do you want to go with those feelings?" Instead, Henggeler understood that he would bring the intervention to the troubled youngster. Go to the home—or, on occasion, to some close-by community setting, such as the kid's school.

To provide meaningful therapy, each MST clinician has a small caseload that is limited to about five families, each of which receives 2 to 15 hours of intervention each week. Recognizing the uncertain timing of crises, clinicians are available 24 hours a day, seven days a week. The MST intervention is intended to be intensive but also time limited (about four to six months), a factor that contributes to its cost effectiveness (Henggeler, 1997, 1998, 1999).

Cullen and Jonson again believe that, as with other successful early intervention programs, the RNR model implicitly informs Henggeler's MST. His intervention focuses on high-risk kids (ages 12 to 17). In his words, these youths possess "serious behavior disorders," and include those who are "violent and chronic juvenile offenders" (1997, pp. 1, 6) and who are "at high risk of out-of-home placement" (1998, p. 3). Clients are assessed individually, with the focus on their criminogenic needs or with an "emphasis on addressing the known causes of delinquency" (p. 6). Finally, treatment interventions are selected that are responsive to—or capable of changing—these targeted risk factors. In Henggeler's (1999) words, "MST addresses the known determinants of clinical problems" using services "with high ecological validity" and "targeting processes directly in home, school, and neighbourhood contexts that are linked with identified problems and that can serve as protective factors" (p. 4).

In more concrete language, when initiating the intervention, the MST clinician and supervisor take the responsibility to engage or hook the youth and family into the treatment. (This is similar to the engagement and motivation stages of Alexander's FFT.) An important task is to diagnose the risk factors or problematic relations that are contributing to the youngster's misbehavior. This might involve persistent conflict with parents, drinking with friends, and truancy. The intervention attempts to build on individual (e.g., high IQ) and system (e.g., a supportive teacher or coach) strengths in a positive way. Services are individualized to meet the unique needs of each troubled youngster. The specific interventions used are adapted from "pragmatic, problem-focused treatments that have at least some empirical support. These include strategic family therapy, structural family therapy, behavioural parent training, and cognitive behaviour therapies" (Henggeler, 1999, p. 3).

Henggeler (1997, 1998, 1999, 2011, 2015) has amassed a fair amount of experimental evidence showing that MST is effective in reducing antisocial behavior. We should note that Julia Littell (2005) stirred up some controversy when she published a meta-analysis suggesting that the effects of MST were suspect when complex methodological issues were taken into account. However, other scholars have reported more favorable results. Thus, in their meta-analysis, Farrington and Welsh (2007) concluded that MST was "the most effective family-based approach" (p. 135). The mean effect size was .414 (p. 107). Drake, Aos, and Miller (2009) assessed 10 MST studies that focused on offenders in the juvenile justice system. They calculated a shrinkage in crime recidivism of 7.7%. Further, in a meta-analysis of 11 studies conducted by Curtis, Ronan, and Borduin (2004), MST was found to significantly lower criminal behaviors. MST was associated with a reduction in the number of arrests for all crimes, the number of arrests for substance abuse crimes, seriousness of arrests, number of days incarcerated, and self-reported delinquency and drug use. Similarly, Borduin and his colleagues (1995) explored whether MST would have long-term (four years) preventative effects on crime, including violent offending. When comparing juvenile offenders placed in MST versus individual therapy, Borduin et al. determined that MST was more effective in reducing rearrrests. Specifically, 71.4% of the individual therapy youths were rearrested within four years, whereas only 26.1% of the MST youths were rearrested. Finally, van der Stouwe, Asscher, Stams, Deković, and van der Laan (2014) recently published perhaps the most sophisticated meta-analysis, including 22 independent studies. The results fell in between Littell's (2005) assessment and those reaching more promising conclusions. The effects of MST on general delinquency were modest but meaningful (d = .233). Several variables moderated the effect. For example, MST effects were larger for youths who were offenders and under 15 and when the control group received a "single and non-multimodal control treatment type" (van der Stouwe et al., 2014, p. 472).

Cullen and Jonson decided to find out for themselves how well MST worked. We realized that obtaining all evaluation studies on MST—published and unpublished—would be a lot of work. So, we got Jennifer Lux to take on this task, guiding her efforts along the way (i.e., she did all the work and we rode her coattails!). Lux's (2010) results are mostly good news for MST. Lux analyzed 21 studies that had delinquency or problem behaviors as the dependent variable; 16 of the studies used a random experimental design. The control groups typically received the usual services given to kids in trouble. This is important, because MST is not often compared to *doing nothing*. Although not all differences were statistically significant, the general pattern was that MST consistently outperformed the control group in manifesting less antisocial behavior. Further, when Lux assessed a larger group of 45 studies, MST evidenced positive effects on a range of other outcomes (e.g., mental health, family functioning, diabetes, and HIV/AIDS measures) (see also Cullen, Lux, & Jonson, 2012).

Two More Reasons to Support Early Intervention

Let's pretend that you are a policy maker—maybe a governor, mayor, city council member, or director of a social services agency. If asked by a constituent whether you intend to expand early intervention programs, what would you say? Well, Cullen and Jonson have already given you two good reasons for supporting child-saving programs. The first reason, based on life-course criminology, is that today's highly troubled kids are tomorrow's serious delinquents and life-course-persistent offenders. If we do not intervene early—which we typically do not—then the future will be dismal for these children and hazardous for those whose property they will steal and bodies they will victimize. It is simply irrational to sit back and let criminal lives unfold.

The second reason, based on the section just concluded, is that we know how to divert kids either off of, or from ever entering, this antisocial developmental pathway. The knowledge now exists to intervene in the womb, in the post-natal period, in pre-kindergarten, in families, in schools, and across multiple systems. Cullen and Jonson are not naïve. We already have said that transferring intervention technology from program inventors to real-world settings administered by typical people is daunting—and will not always be successful (Welsh et al., 2010). Still, regardless of these challenges, the fact remains (1) that non-intervention, or doing nothing, is a guaranteed recipe for failure and (2) that treatment programs—based on rigorous experimental evaluations—have been shown to achieve meaningful reductions in future criminal behavior and enhancements in life outcomes (e.g., education, employment, health).

So, to be direct, we now know that early intervention is needed and that it works! But here we give to you, Mr. or Ms. Policymaker, two more reasons to support early intervention: These programs are *cost effective* and the *American public supports child saving.*

COST EFFECTIVENESS

These days, any attempt to use public money to help someone might get you accused of being one of those Obama socialists who want to take money from good people (us) and give it to bad people (them). In fact, attempts to save kids could be the first step down the slippery slope to death panels to decide which kids live and which will die. You can never be too careful! Not to worry, our fellow Americans: Capitalism is on the side of early intervention! As it turns out, investing in programs can actually save money. *Early intervention is cost effective.*

Americans really love it when you can say that something is *cost effective.* It appeals to three of our central, if unspoken, values:

- *Rationality:* We should do things that have utility.

- *Accountability:* "Cost effective" implies that we have a standard—that we will keep doing what *pays* and not do what *does not* pay.

- *Commodification:* The idea that anything in American society can be reduced to a *price*—to a matter of dollars and cents.

Now, Cullen and Jonson are a bit skeptical of cost-benefit analysis. No, we are not in favor of cost *ineffective* policies! We are not that stupid or un-American. Rather, the problem is two-fold. First, money has a way of crowding out other considerations. However, should we base all public policy decisions on money? Can we commodify everything? What about doing what is right? Should other values play a role? Such as justice? Humaneness? Let us assume, for example, that keeping very old people alive on life support in the intensive care unit, where they have virtually no quality of existence, is not cost effective (which it is not). Should we simply euthanize them or forbid doctors to prolong their time on earth? Or are you willing to say that life trumps money on this occasion? Well, with a child destined to a life in crime, money should never be the sole consideration.

Second, cost-benefit analysis is predicated on the assumption that it is feasible to measure accurately all possible costs and benefits. However, it is almost impossible to get such precise and complete information. For example:

- How do you measure how much crime is saved? What if only official data (e.g., arrests) are available? We know that if self-report data were used—which reveal all the offenses not detected by the police—then the count of crimes saved would be much higher. Ergo, the estimated benefits might sky-rocket. Based on evaluation data from the Stop Now and Plan program for boys ages 6 to 11, Farrington and Koegel (2015, p. 263) computed what this difference would be. They found that for every dollar invested, the benefits based on convictions ranged from $2.05 to $3.75. But when the estimates were scaled up to include "undetected offenses," the savings jumped to between $17.33 and $31.77.

- What costs of crime do you measure? Do you include only things that are tangible, such as the medical bills or court expenses that flow from a specific crime? What about more intangible savings, such as victim suffering? (We will return to this shortly.)

- What range of factors needs to be included when trying to compute an intervention's benefits? How many years are sample members followed? What areas of a person's life are taken into account? Only crime? Or education, employment, marriage, and health? Are impacts on siblings or on the next generation considered?

Our point here is not that cost-benefit analysis is worthless and should not be conducted (Greenwood, 2006). If the assumptions on which the analysis is based are specified, then the meaning of what has been computed can be considered in its appropriate context. What Cullen and Jonson most fear, however, is that that cost effectiveness will be granted sacred status and be accepted uncritically. As often occurs in capitalism, when it comes to claims of cost effectiveness, it is buyer beware!

Except in this instance, because, as it turns out, quality early intervention programs are cost effective (Aos, Phipps, Barnoski, & Lieb, 2001; Cohen, Piquero, & Jennings, 2010; Drake et al., 2009; Farrington & Welsh, 2007; Greenwood, 2006; Greenwood et al., 2001; Welsh, 2003; Welsh, Farrington, & Gowar, 2015)! Cullen and Jonson like this finding, so forget what we said about treating such data with caution. Trust us. The data we like are sacred and should not be questioned! We are, of course, only kidding. Skepticism is the hallmark of a quality scientific mind.

Still, for most major early interventions, the inventors or their followers are very conscientious to present cost-benefit data. They take this step because they realize that it is a powerful way to convince policy makers to implement their programs (see, e.g., Henggeler, 1997; Olds, 2007; Schweinhart, 2007). More independent evidence on the cost effectiveness of the programs reviewed in the previous section—the *five programs that work*—has been presented by Steve Aos et al. (2001; see also Drake et al., 2009; Greenwood et al., 2001; Welsh, 2003).

Aos et al. (2001), who are located at the Washington State Institute for Public Policy, were mandated by the Washington state legislature to conduct a cost-benefit analysis of a range of programs, from those focused on adult offenders to those focused on early intervention with young and future offenders. In essence, they were engaged in an evidence-based approach to assist legislators in allocating resources (see also Drake et al., 2009). The results of their cost-benefit analysis for the five programs are presented in Table 9.1.

A few explanatory comments about the columns in Table 9.1 are in order. Column 1 presents the cost (in dollars) of the program for each participant. Column 2 presents how much money Aos et al. (2001) estimated would be saved by taxpayers because of lower criminal justice expenditures (e.g., costs not incurred by the police, courts, corrections). Column 3 is simply column 2 divided by column 1. The goal is to determine how many benefits are realized for every dollar spent. In concrete terms, if the dollar amount in column 1 exceeds the dollar amount in column 2, the program is not cost effective; the number in column 3 will be below $1.00, which is the break-even point. So, if I spend $4,000 on a program participant (column 1) and save an average of $2,000 per participant (column 2), I lose money. For every dollar I spend, I save only 50 cents (column 3). Of course, a program is cost effective if I save more than I spend. Thus, if I spend $2,000 (column 1) and save $4,000 (column 2), then for every dollar I spend, I save 2 dollars (column 3).

Now things get a touch complicated. When a crime occurs, a victim has monetary costs (e.g., medical expenses, property loss, wages not earned) and quality of life costs (e.g., pain and suffering) (Drake et al., 2009, p. 179). These are sometimes called *tangible* and *intangible* costs, respectively. Tangible costs are more easily measured

Table 9.1   Cost Effectiveness of Five Early Intervention Programs That Work (in dollars)

Programs	Column 1 Cost to Run Program	Column 2 Criminal Justice Costs Saved	Column 3 Cost-Benefit Ratio	Column 4 All Costs Saved (CJ and Victim)	Column 5 Full Cost-Benefit Ratio
Nurse Home Visitation	$7,403	$6,155	$0.83	$11,369	$1.54
High/Scope Perry Preschool	13,938	9,237	0.66	20,954	1.50
Functional Family Therapy	2,068	14,167	6.85	22,739	10.99
Seattle Social Development Project	3,017	2,704	0.90	5,399	1.79
Multisystemic Therapy	4,540	38,047	8.38	61,068	13.45

SOURCE: Adapted from Aos, Phipps, Barnoski, and Lieb (2001, pp. 154–155).

NOTE: Cost-benefit estimates made per participant in each program.

because they affect physical things—such as your car is gone or court costs go up. Intangible costs are fuzzier, because they involve pain and suffering. The pain and suffering are real—especially if you are the one in pain and the one suffering! The trick, however, is to figure out what dollar amount to assign to such things. How much compensation is due to someone who is forced to hurt—or, alternatively, what would it be worth to you not to feel such things? Importantly, scholars have estimated intangible or quality of life costs based on the awards given to victims by juries in civil cases for pain and suffering. All this is complex, and there are debates over the best way to measure victims' costs (for a helpful discussion, see Greenwood, 2006). In any event, Aos et al. (2001) use a standard estimate of this sort to assess, when a crime does not occur, how much savings to victims are realized.

Okay, back to Table 9.1. Here, column 4 adds together the savings or benefits per participant that come from the (1) criminal justice costs and (2) victim costs that are not incurred because a given intervention has prevented offenses from occurring. Finally, column 5 divides column 4 (total benefits per participant) by column 1 (total costs per participant). The result is the cost-benefit ratio. If more money is saved than spent, then the figure in column 5 exceeds 1 dollar. So, column 5 is where we see what programs are cost effective.

Whew, that was a mouthful, huh? Our eyes glazed over just writing this. But the gist of the matter is this: When a program is effective, it prevents crime. Each crime that is prevented lowers criminal justice and victim costs. Programs that prevent a lot of crime—that work—thus save a lot of costs. The money that is saved is, in other words, *the program's benefits*. But programs also cost money to deliver, especially high-quality ones. The money it takes to run the intervention is the *program's cost*. To be *cost effective*, the program's benefits must be higher than the program's costs.

Perhaps you can understand why designers of interventions want to target high-risk kids and to treat them in programs that last a limited time (e.g., three months). Thus, if a program is successful with a high-risk kid, a lot of crime will be saved and the program will have lots of benefits (see Cohen, 1998). Indeed, a recent sophisticated analysis estimates that the "costs imposed by a career criminal" range from $2.1 to $3.7 million (Cohen et al., 2010; see also Cohen & Piquero, 2009). And if the program can be delivered in a shorter rather than a longer time period, it will not cost as much. So, treating high-risk kids keeps benefits up, whereas a time-limited program keeps costs down. Of course, none of this matters if the intervention does not work. Only if crime is saved can something be cost effective.

So, now to the punch line; let's look at Table 9.1. Three conclusions are apparent:

- MST and FFT seem to be really cost effective.

- Just based on criminal justice expenses saved, three of the programs are not cost effective (see column 3).

- However, when victim costs are added in, *all five of the programs are cost effective* (see column 5). Again, the issue of victim costs is somewhat controversial because pain and suffering are intangible. But to the extent that crime control policy is supposed to be victim-oriented, such benefits cannot be dismissed.

A few final considerations are important. First, we would caution not to treat the cost-benefit estimates reviewed here as though they were sacrosanct. Second, we have chosen to focus on five major programs because they are well researched and an abundance of information about them is available. However, the five programs reviewed are a subset of a wide array of interventions that have been found to be both effective in reducing antisocial behavior and cost effective (Aos et al., 2001; Drake et al., 2009; Farrington & Welsh, 2007; Greenwood, 2006; Welsh et al., 2015). Policy makers thus now have available a rich menu of successful interventions from which to choose.

Third and perhaps most important, do not fall into the trap of assuming that the only standard for judging cost effectiveness is if 1 dollar invested in a program yields more than 1 dollar in benefits. The crucial issue with programs is *effectiveness*, not cost effectiveness—that is, whether children are saved and crime is reduced. Who is to say that one dollar in crime benefits—given what is at stake—is not worth a two-dollar investment? Of course, it certainly makes sense to allocate dollars to those interventions that yield the highest returns. Nonetheless, lack of complete cost effectiveness should not be used as an excuse *for doing nothing*. If no intervention takes place, taxpayers may have a few more dollars, or cents, in their pockets. But the cost will be that a lot of kids will remain entrenched in an antisocial pathway. And their future victims will await, unsuspecting, these youngsters' inevitable criminal maturation.

PUBLIC SUPPORT

Okay, early intervention is needed, it is effective in reducing crime, and it is cost effective. But will the American public ever support this loony, bleeding-heart idea of trying to save kids from a life in crime? Well, as it turns out, the answer is *"yes"—overwhelmingly so*. Every opinion poll—including those conducted by Cullen—has reached this conclusion.

Americans, it seems, are softies when it comes to their wayward youngsters. Why is this so? Cullen and Jonson think it is because child saving meshes with three core beliefs that Americans embrace:

- The belief that youths are malleable and can change.
- The belief that youths are less responsible for the choices they make.
- The belief that children are victims of their circumstances.

And we might add in one more: *rationality*. Again, it makes no sense to let a troubled youngster grow up into a serious offender when we could intervene with a proven program and stop that from happening. After all, not to do so is a form of child neglect. Who would be in favor of allowing kids that we know are on an antisocial developmental pathway to reach a deviant destination? Only a fool, say Cullen and Jonson!

Now let's get on to the data! We have claimed that there is a bunch of evidence that child saving is as American as apple pie and, as was once the case, General Motors! We can start, therefore, with surveys on whether the justice system should mainly punish or try to rehabilitate juvenile offenders. The research is clear in showing that the public embraces rehabilitation (Cullen et al., 2000; Moon, Cullen, & Wright, 2003; Moon, Sundt, Cullen, & Wright, 2000; Nagin, Piquero, Scott, & Steinberg, 2006). For example, in a 2001 national study, 80.1% of the sample said that *rehabilitation* should be the main emphasis of prisons that hold juveniles. The comparable figures for the other options were 8.3% for *punishment,* 7.7% for *protect society,* and 3.8% for *not sure.* When asked how important rehabilitation is as a goal of juvenile prisons, over 97% said that it was either *very important* (72.6%) or *important* (24.5%). Only 2.2% selected *a little important* or *not important at all* (0.6%) (Cullen, Pealer, et al., 2002, pp. 137–138). Similarly, in a 2005 statewide survey in Pennsylvania, nearly three in four respondents (74.2%) answered that it was *true* that "juvenile offenders are more likely to become adult criminals if they are sent to jail than if they get rehabilitation in juvenile facilities" (Piquero, Cullen, Unnever, Piquero, & Gordon, 2010, p. 195; see also Piquero & Steinberg, 2010).

But now let's go to surveys that deal directly with the issue of early intervention—of the kinds of community-based programs we have been talking about in this chapter. Well, public support is, if anything, even stronger (Cullen, Vose, Jonson, & Unnever, 2007; Cullen et al., 1998; Moon et al., 2003). One question, which always gets the same results in surveys, is to ask respondents whether they would rather use their tax dollars to control crime (1) by building more prisons "so that more criminals can be locked up for longer periods of crime" or (2) by expanding early intervention programs "that try to prevent crime by identifying delinquent youths early in life and rehabilitating them so that they do not grow up to be criminals" (Cullen, Pealer, et al., 2002, p. 139). In our 2001 national survey, 86% of the sample chose the *early intervention option* compared to 14% that favored *the prison option* (Cullen, Pealer, et al., 2002).

In other research, Cullen and his associates have asked people about the extent to which they supported a range of specific early intervention programs even if that might mean raising taxes (Cullen, Pealer, et al., 2002; Cullen et al., 1998; Moon et al., 2003). In all surveys, large majorities of the public embraced a diverse range of programs aimed at improving parental management, early intellectual development, conduct disorders, school retention, and school after-care. In the national study by Cullen, Pealer, et al. (2002), the level of support for seven programs ranged from a low of 89% to a high of 95%. What other social policy in today's political climate—a time of Red States and Blue States, of culture wars between Right and Left—would enjoy such universal support? Based on these and a wealth of similar findings, Cullen et al. (2007) have thus concluded that child saving is a "habit of the heart"—a fundamental, unshakable cultural belief that we Americans should do whatever we can to rescue troubled youngsters and to place them on a healthy developmental pathway (see Bellah, Madsen, Sullivan, Swidler, & Tipton, 1985).

Conclusion: Beyond Adult-Limited Corrections

Books on corrections do not typically include a discussion of early intervention. This omission is understandable. Works on corrections are focused mainly on adults, with perhaps a chapter on institutionalized juveniles as a special population. This adult-limited orientation makes sense because it is mainly adults that enter the correctional system and that we lock up in our jails and prisons. By contrast, many of those served by early intervention are in the beginning stages in life, well before they would fall into the clutches of the legal system.

Still, just because something is *understandable* does not make it *intelligent*. In fact, Cullen and Jonson think that it is pretty stupid for corrections to be adult-limited. As we have seen, most individuals involved in crime do not suddenly awaken one day at age 25 and say, "Oh, I think I'll become a super-predator. It should be more fun than being a teacher." Instead, as we have seen, they enter the gates of our correctional institutions only after embarking on a life course, at times while still in the womb, in which they are exposed to multiple and accumulating criminogenic risk factors. To ignore this stubborn criminological fact requires an ostrich-like capacity to stick our heads in the sand.

As a field, then, corrections needs to broaden its subject matter to include the study of youngsters who are destined to replenish prison populations a decade or two down the road. Corrections must transform itself—much as policing is doing by embracing problem-oriented approaches—from a field that is reactive and into a field that is proactive. That is, corrections should see itself not only as a system that processes those sent by the courts to its doors but also as a system that should advocate for the prevention of offending. Knifing off criminal careers can occur among adult offenders through effective rehabilitation programs. But prevention must be early as well, seeking to head off the development of troubled youths into incarcerated felons (Howell, 2003).

Put another way, corrections must consider the wisdom of becoming a profession that is involved in preventing crime from womb to tomb. The goal should be to develop a range of interventions that are age-graded—that is, that are capable of attacking the unique criminogenic factors that arise at each stage in the life course. If this daunting challenge is undertaken, it might be possible to create a continuum of care in which multiple attempts are made to redirect at-risk individuals—when they are children, juveniles, and then adults—from life-course-persistent antisocial and criminal conduct. Corrections thus would truly embrace the mission that it is *never too early and never too late* to use criminological knowledge and evidence-based interventions to save the wayward among us (Lösel, 2007).

10

Francis T. Cullen
University of Cincinnati

Cheryl Lero Jonson
Xavier University

Authors of *Correctional Theory*

Six Correctional Lessons

Choosing Our Future

F or readers who have made it this far, Cullen and Jonson extend our congratulations! *Correctional Theory* is not an easy book. To be sure, we have tried to use plain language and even silly stories to make your journey through the volume's pages as pleasant as possible. But you have traveled over some rocky scholarly terrain. We have asked you to trudge through complex ideas, lots of data, and sticky methodological points. Your trip has been lengthy as well, traversing both historical periods and a variety of theoretical perspectives. Of course, we trust that taking this correctional expedition with us as your guides has proven rewarding. By now, readers should know quite a lot about corrections and, indeed, have formulated their own ideas on what theory they favor to guide the nation's correctional system.

Still, before we say goodbye—before we bid you adieu—Cullen and Jonson want to leave you with what we see as the key *take away points* of *Correctional Theory*. We promise to keep this discussion short and simple. We ask you to focus on *three themes* and *six lessons*. Together, that makes only nine things to remember. That's fewer points than fingers on most people's hands!

Three Themes

Across *Correctional Theory*, Cullen and Jonson's analysis has been informed by three themes or organizing ideas: Theory has consequences; the social context has consequences; and ignoring the evidence has consequences. Our subject matter is corrections, but these themes are applicable for criminal justice generally and for other public policy disciplines. They are meant to help readers make sense of the world in a more coherent way—to understand how and why they and others see the world, in this case the correctional world, as they do. They also are cognitive resources to allow readers to escape the blinders that often cause people to think narrowly and stupidly. And Cullen and Jonson know that you want to engage in intelligent corrections! So, we are here to help with our insights, set forth below.

THEORY HAS CONSEQUENCES

The first theme to remember is that *theory has consequences.* Correctional theories sometimes are voiced by non-academics in populist language, such as this statement of the theory of incapacitation: "I think we should lock 'em all up and throw away the key; then they won't hurt anyone again." On other occasions, theories are laid out in book-length manuscripts. Either way, these ideas give credence to one kind of correctional system while debunking others.

Correctional theories, in fact, have a *trinity of components.* To start with, they contain *ideas about crime.* For example, deterrence theorists think that people commit crime when it pays—that the decision to offend is rational. Rehabilitation advocates often believe that criminals have clear individual differences—with roots extending from the womb into adulthood—that keep them on an antisocial pathway. Next, with a particular view of crime in mind, each theory has a *logically consistent recommendation for how to prevent such unlawful conduct.* Thus, deterrence proponents urge more punishment so as to raise the cost of offending, whereas rehabilitation proponents urge us to fix the deficits that fuel criminal propensity. Finally, given ideas on what causes and how to prevent crime, each theory tells us *how the correctional system should be organized—what policies it should implement, what practices it should follow, and even what kinds of people it should hire.* Advocates of deterrence thus would favor determinate sentences, intensive supervision of offenders in the community, and employees who wish to carry guns and police offenders. Advocates of rehabilitation would favor indeterminate sentences, community reintegration, and employees who wish to carry a treatment manual and save offenders.

The point is to be aware that each theory—once you are inside of it—has a powerful logic that makes its views on the nature of the correctional system seem compelling. To deconstruct a theory—to escape its clutches—it is necessary to be able to know what is happening! Equipped with this perspective, someone—yes, even you!—can take a step back and attack a theory's weak points. For example, with deterrence theory, the shaky part is that, as criminology teaches us, crime has causes other than rational choice. How can these empirically established predictors of recidivism be ignored? Obviously, they cannot.

THE SOCIAL CONTEXT HAS CONSEQUENCES

The second theme is that *the social context has consequences.* The prevailing social context influences *whether a correctional theory is accepted or rejected.* Because Cullen lived through the 1960s, he thinks that all public policies can be traced back to this period (Jonson looks at Cullen quizzically but says she takes his word for it). This statement about the sixties causing everything is an obvious exaggeration, but not much of one. Because of the intersection in a relatively short time period of huge events—think about having five Hurricane Katrina–like events one right after the other—the United States experienced a dramatic shift in how Americans came to see the world. Think of the assassination of Martin Luther King Jr. and the Kennedy brothers, civil rights advocates murdered in the South, riots in inner cities, Kent State, Attica, Watergate, the Vietnam War, and on and on. The nation just got all shook up! Today, we speak of a *culture war* and of *Red and Blue States.* When did the cultural consensus break down into two warring views of the world? You got it; it was right after the sixties!

Put simply, Cullen and Jonson have argued in earlier chapters that the consensus in support of rehabilitation and the embrace of get tough, law-and-order policies occurred in response to the turmoil of the 1960s and early 1970s. As trust in the state withered, so too did trust in the ability of correctional officials to reform offenders. Of course, Martinson's (1974) nothing works article drove another nail into rehabilitation's coffin. But his conclusion was readily accepted precisely because he was telling folks what they already believed. In a different social context, similar articles had been ignored or interpreted as meaning that more work needed to be done to develop successful treatment programs (Cullen & Gendreau, 2000).

The message, then, is that theories of corrections are not embraced primarily based on the data. In fact, if they were, then this book would not be needed—a point we turn to shortly. But these observations also have implications for the readers and for Cullen and Jonson. All of us are creatures of *our social context.* It is easy to see how people in a distant time embraced stupid ideas because of *their social context.* And it is easy to see how other people in our own time believe idiotic things because of *their social context.* But it would be hubris to think that we are the only ones not affected by our location in society and the experiences we have had.

As Alvin Gouldner (1970) points out, scholars need to develop a *reflexive* sense—that is, a capacity to reflect on how their views of the world are shaped by their experiences and interests. Developing this perspective means that a scholar "must surrender the assumption, as wrongheaded as it is human, that others believe out of need while we believe—only or primarily—because of the dictates of logic and evidence" (p. 490). Equipped with reflexivity, people can increase their freedom of thought. They no longer are prisoners of their context—unaware of how their context colors their view of the world.

As we noted in Chapter 1, a persistent danger in criminal justice is the over-reliance on *insider knowledge*—the sense that someone's personal experience trumps other views, including those based on science. Such criminal justice insiders fail to see how occupational socialization (hanging around with people like themselves) might narrow and bias how they view crime and its correction. It is not a coincidence that police officers and prosecutors typically see the world differently than probation officers and group counselors. Part of this is self-selection—certain kinds of folks are attracted to certain kinds of jobs—but part of it is that those working in different jobs are socialized by coworkers to think alike. Again, social context has consequences.

In short, being open to seeing the world as it truly is—to allowing one's cherished beliefs to be tested by empirical data—depends on understanding that we are social participants whose reality has been socially constructed not just by us but for us (see Berger & Luckmann, 1966). Too often in corrections, we have clung to ineffective, if not harmful, ideas because, based on our *personal experiences,* we *just knew* that a program would work (again, boot camps come quickly to mind). A dose of reflexivity is thus healthy. It reminds us that in forming our beliefs, we should not trade passion—a good thing because it motivates action—for certitude. In the end, we must remain sufficiently humble to know that we too might occasionally be wrong.

IGNORING THE EVIDENCE HAS CONSEQUENCES

The third theme is that *ignoring the evidence has consequences.* As we have argued, the movement toward evidence-based practices is increasingly shaping decision making in numerous social domains—from medicine and education to investments and baseball (Ayres, 2007). In corrections, there have been explicit calls for evidence-based practice (see, e.g., Cullen & Gendreau, 2000; MacKenzie, 2000), and discussions of the need to do *what works* are now commonplace. Perhaps the most telling sign that data now matter is the appearance in *The New Yorker* of a cartoon in which three men are sitting at a bar and one comments: "Are you just pissing and moaning, or can you verify what you're saying with data?"

In corrections, paying attention to the evidence is essential for three reasons. First, it tells us what does not work and thus what we should not do with offenders. Second, it tells us what does work and thus what we should do with offenders. Please understand the cost of embracing failure and of ignoring success (Van Voorhis, 1987). When we subject offenders to ineffective interventions, we place them at risk of recidivating. This means that they will needlessly remain ensnared in a life-course trajectory of persistent offending. But even if one has little sympathy for such criminals, there is no excuse not to care about their future victims. To be blunt, to stubbornly use failed interventions when effective ones are available risks jeopardizing public safety. In a very real sense, the culpability for the losses and pains victims suffer rests, in important ways, with those who choose to ignore the data and to engage in correctional quackery (Latessa et al., 2002).

The third reason for paying attention to the evidence is more subtle but no less important. The hallmark of any profession is expertise and ethics. Imagine physicians who are proud that they refuse to read the medical journals and can make diagnoses on gut-level instincts. Unless they are House, you would not want to enter their offices! Or imagine a group of physicians who rejected the Hippocratic Oath and, in particular, its core mandate to always "prescribe regimens for the good of my patients according to my ability and my judgment and never do harm to anyone." Again, you would not want to walk into their offices!

If corrections is to be a profession, those working within the field can no longer afford to remain purposefully ignorant of best practices (Rhine, 1998). Why would anyone want to employ worst practices? Or practices shown to be ineffective? Or practices for which not a shred of evidence exists that they are capable of changing offender behavior? To be sure, the nature of corrections and the complexity of human conduct mean that ambiguity will often surround the degree to which any intervention is known to be effective. But simply to ignore the evidence is, in the end, stupid—and unprofessional.

Still worse, it opens up policy makers and practitioners to the charge of being unethical. The Hippocratic Oath is powerful in its mandate to physicians *to do no harm* to patients. In corrections, the fact that offenders are being punished—and thus, to this extent, purposefully harmed—is no excuse to heap needless, unwarranted harm upon them. A democratic, ethical state has every right to exact just deserts but has no right to inflict harm outside the law. But this is precisely what we do when we ignore the evidence and place offenders in correctional programs that are ineffective. In these cases, we are giving correctional medicine that will not cure them and likely will make them worse. In these cases, we are also withholding correctional medicine capable of saving them from future criminality. When lives are at stake, ignoring the evidence—engaging in such quackery—is simply unethical and undermines any claim of professionalism (see Latessa et al., 2002). We can do better. We can do less harm and avoid much needless harm. Pay attention to the empirical evidence and allow it to help guide what we do to those under our control.

Six Lessons

Now Cullen and Jonson want to get more specific. The three themes covered above are big picture items—cognitive tools to guide readers in how to see the world. But *Correctional Theory* also has reviewed mountains of evidence and thus has some concrete lessons to teach about how best to proceed in the corrections enterprise. In drawing these lessons, we attempt to be—as we have been throughout this volume—fair in our reading of the data. We have endeavored not to overreach in what we recommend.

Still, after sifting through and trying to make sense of existing studies, Cullen and Jonson would be pretty mindless scholars if we had no conclusions to offer about correctional policy and practice. Indeed, imagine if you asked us what should be done in the correctional system and we replied: "Hmm. Duh. We don't know!" Alas, we do have clear ideas of the best course for corrections to follow. We share these in the six lessons to follow.

PUNISHMENT DOES NOT WORK WELL

Once they have children, most parents quickly learn the limits of punishment. This is why they yell so much, even though they pledge they will not. This is why they say stupid things like: "I'll give you something to cry about" and "So long as you live under my roof, you will obey my rules." Such outbursts occur when a child, who is smaller than parents and to whom they can apply swift, certain, and severe punishment, simply does not obey. In the end, parents learn that getting children to do the right things involves the judicious use of punishment, not its overuse. In the end, they learn that things like love, modeling good habits, and placing their children in the right situations and with the right friends are what keep them on the straight and narrow path away from jail. Phrased differently, parents—or at least good parents—come to understand the limits of whacking kids. They come to understand that behavior is complex and must be dealt with in a nuanced way. They practice rehabilitation, not pure deterrence, with their offspring.

Of course, if we eliminated the criminal justice system, chaos would eventually ensue, and we might be hiring warlords to protect us. So, the presence of a legal structure undoubtedly is essential to law and order. But in the realm of corrections, we are not discussing such a silly scenario. Rather, we are trying to determine if harsh punishments make offenders less likely to recidivate than more lenient punishments. The issue is one of *specific deterrence*. Thus, if offenders are placed on intensive supervision, does this make them less likely to recidivate than if placed on regular probation? Are offenders sent to prison less likely to recidivate than those not incarcerated? To be sure, there are some cases where this undoubtedly occurs. Across all offenders, however, the specific deterrence thesis is not supported. Harsher punishment simply does not reap many rewards. It does not make offenders less likely to break the law and does not make society safer.

So, why do we engage in the fruitless practice of getting tough with offenders? Part of the reason is that some crimes simply deserve a good whacking. Do really bad things and just deserts—or retribution—demands that we do bad things to you. But Cullen and Jonson suspect that the other reason we impose overly stiff punishments is that those who run the legal system—from legislators to judges to correctional officials—simply believe in specific deterrence. They are, in short, stupid about crime. They choose to be willfully ignorant—to not take the time to read the studies and understand the limits of punishment. Hopefully, these stupid folks are reading *Correctional Theory*. If so, they will no longer be stupid and will start to implement smarter punishment policies.

PRISONS WORK SOMEWHAT

Criminologists do not like prisons. And as criminologists, Cullen and Jonson share this predilection to keep people out of prison whenever feasible. We take this position because correctional institutions are not particularly nice places. We also take this position because the evidence shows that prisons do not specifically deter. Jonson, in particular, knows this because she has read every available study on this topic (Jonson, 2010; Nagin et al., 2009).

Criminologists, however, face two sticky problems that make abolishing prisons impossible and that make lessening the use of incarceration as a sanction difficult.

The first problem is that most people in prison deserve to be there. By "deserve," we do not mean that they have to be there—that prison would be the only way to punish them. In fact, for a lot of offenders, we expect that a non-prison intervention, which includes treatment, would not only be less expensive but also make them less criminal and society safer. But by "deserve," we do mean that they have broken laws for which a sentence of imprisonment is legal and, in many cases, not something weird. That is, most offenders end up in prison because they do bad things repeatedly.

The other sticky problem for criminologists is that when offenders are in prison, they are not on the street committing crimes. The public thinks this is a good idea: not allowing predators to be where they can be predators—in the public's neighborhoods! As readers know, the amount of crime prevented simply by caging offenders is called *incapacitation.*

Sounds good? But, of course, incapacitation has some troubling weaknesses— four of which we will recount here. First, as a correctional theory, it does not tell us what should be done with those not placed in prison. Second, because it has no plausible plan for offenders in the community, it encourages us to lock up as many people as possible. It makes us risk averse. Given that any offender placed on probation *might* offend, the inclination is to take no chances and put everyone behind bars. In short, it encourages over-incarceration. Third, it does not tell us what to do with those in prison, other than to warehouse them. Although they ignore or hide this fact, proponents of incapacitation are willing to let offenders leave prison just as criminally disposed as they were the day they entered prison. Of course, this makes no sense whatsoever.

The fourth concern is that we have to wonder why we use incarceration more in the United States than in other advanced Western nations. Are we just smarter? Are we simply richer so that we can afford to do so? Well, times are now changing. As financial difficulties have placed many states on the verge of bankruptcy and, in any case, in the position of deeply cutting support for education and other social services, handing out prison sentences is becoming an expensive luxury that is difficult to justify. We have reached the point where an increasing number of elected officials are opening their minds to correctional policies that can provide public protection but not necessitate lengthy stays behind bars.

In the end, the problem with *mass incarceration* is, well, that it is *mass.* It would be foolish to suggest that prisons should be emptied; Cullen and Jonson do not want all those criminals moving in next door to them! But as with any other governmental resource, prisons must be used *judiciously.* Similar to binge drinking, it is not good for our societal health to engage in binge imprisonment! Beyond serious, chronic offenders—especially those who are violent—we do not need to hand out 10-year or 20-year prison terms. These sentences are just plain nuts. More than this, we need to find ways to intervene with offenders earlier and more effectively in their criminal careers—before the time when locking them up seems the only plausible alternative. We return to this point immediately below.

There is thus an emerging literature that is asking us to be smarter about how we control crime in the United States—and elsewhere. There is a general consensus that while *prisons work somewhat* to help control crime, they are a blunt instrument that proves way too costly and, at times, makes those brought within their walls more, rather than less, criminal. Within criminology, in fact, thoughtful scholars are now calling for us to think quite differently. The title of Mark Kleiman's (2009) book captures this line of inquiry—*When Brute Force Fails: How to Have Less Crime and Less Punishment* (see also Durlauf & Nagin, 2011; Jacobson, 2005; Waller, 2006). We will leave it to readers to consult these works to get the full story. But the gist of the message is that crime is best addressed through a mixture of efforts aimed at community crime prevention, alternatives to incarceration, and the use of prison as a sanction of last—rather than of first—resort.

REAFFIRM REHABILITATION

Cullen and Jonson are unabashed advocates of rehabilitation (see Cullen, 2007; Cullen & Jonson, 2011b). We make no bones about it. In fact, we are proud to be bleeding hearts. But we also are evidence-based criminologists who believe that a correctional system devoid of treatment services not only risks descending into inhumanity but also needlessly endangers public safety. Thus, beyond what was conveyed in Chapter 7, we defend *rehabilitation as our preferred correctional theory* on three key grounds.

- *First, rehabilitation has virtually all the benefits of punishment-oriented theories of corrections.*

Huh? Yes, that is correct! After all, in a rehabilitation system, offenders are not hugged, let go, and told to have a nice day. They are not sent to country clubs where they wear Ralph Lauren Polo shirts with collars turned up, Dockers, and boat shoes. In fact, most of the bad things that happen to offenders happen to them even when the correctional system seeks to rehabilitate them. Thus, offenders are still arrested, brought to court, sentenced, and at times sent to prison. There may be less severity of punishment, but not of certainty—and, if anything, it is the certainty of the sanction that matters in reducing recidivism. Furthermore, dangerous offenders will remain locked up. Perhaps the only difference would be that low-risk offenders will not be needlessly kept behind bars—as they too often are now.

- *Second, rehabilitation makes us safer.*

The punishment crowd wants us to believe that the best and only way to change behavior is through the threat or infliction of pain. Unfortunately for them, science is simply not on their side—as the research reviewed in this book has shown (see also Andrews & Bonta, 2010; Cullen, Pratt, et al., 2002).

Put more concretely, Cullen and Jonson start with the criminological reality that crime, including recidivism, has causes. If interventions do not use techniques capable of changing these risk factors—if the interventions are not *responsive to these factors*—then offenders will continue on their way, merrily committing crime after crime. Importantly, inflicting pain is not responsive to the causes of recidivism, which is why specific deterrence has such a lousy success rate. In contrast, rehabilitation programs—especially those that adhere to the principles of effective treatment—do things that are capable of reducing such risk factors (e.g., cognitive-behavior programs). This is why rehabilitation is far more effective than get tough programs in lowering recidivism and thus in making society safer from crime (Andrews & Bonta, 2010).

A key point here is that rehabilitation makes offenders think more prosocially, develop skills to resist going into crime, and acquire human capital (such as education and job training). In short, it tends to make them *better people and members of society.* In the aftermath of punishment, offenders might be afraid to break the law (though there is little evidence of this), but they are not better off. Punishment does not invest in offenders, and thus we spend a whole bunch of money and get little in return. Beyond maybe feeling a touch more afraid of getting caught and punished, they are the same schmucks they were when we first arrested them.

Our point is that rehabilitation allows us to have our cake and eat it too! We get to improve offenders—albeit within the context of a system that is inherently discomforting to them—and to improve public safety. Cullen and Jonson think that this two-fer is too good to pass up. Make offenders into better people and, in doing so, make the community safer. We just do not see the payoff in punishment. Indeed, a correctional system based exclusively on inflicting punishment seems, ironically, *not a rational choice!*

- *Third, it would be un-American not to rehabilitate offenders.*

In this regard, Cullen and Jonson wish to remind readers that since the invention of the *penitentiary system* in the 1820s, the reformation of offenders has been a core goal of the correctional system. Indeed, it is instructive that we do not use the term *punishment system.* The word *corrections* embodies our collective belief that we are a people of second chances—a people who, whether for religious or humanistic reasons, believe in the redemption of the wayward.

For much of the 1900s, faith in the treatment enterprise was pervasive. As Allen (1981) notes, "it is remarkable how widely rehabilitation was accepted in this century as a statement of aspirations for the penal system, a statement largely endorsed by the media, politicians, and ordinary citizens" (p. 6). To be sure, the hegemony of rehabilitation was challenged in the aftermath of the 1960s and during the ascendancy of conservative politics and the policy of mass incarceration. Still, even during this mean season in corrections, opinion polls revealed that faith in offender rehabilitation remained high (Cullen, Pealer, et al., 2002). Indeed, the tenacity of the rehabilitative ideal suggests that this aspiration is deeply ingrained in American culture—in who we are as a people.

This observation does not mean that the public is prepared to rise up against get tough policies or to lament the lengthy imprisonment, if not execution, of heinous criminals. But it does mean that there is a genuine openness to reasonable, effective efforts to rehabilitate offenders. The challenge for treatment advocates is to continue their concerted efforts to develop interventions that not only work in ideal settings but also can be transferred and implemented with sound results across the correctional landscape.

REENTRY MATTERS

Cullen and Jonson are dismayed that elected officials can lock up 2.2 million people—folks they claim are sufficiently dangerous or criminal to be placed in a cage—and then *take no responsibility for making them less criminal*. Huh? Excuse me? How can such officials look at themselves in the mirror?

So, let's repeat Jeremy Travis's (2005, p. xxi), "iron law of imprisonment: they all come back." Each year, this means more than 620,000 inmates are released. Is it responsible public policy to allow these offenders to reenter society no better off and prone to reoffend? Is it responsible to allow them to reenter society without the cognitive, emotional, and social skills that they will need to surmount the daunting obstacles that make staying out of crime a challenge (see Gideon, 2010; Petersilia, 2003; Travis, 2005)? In short, the failure to make a systematic effort to cure these offenders is no different from sending thousands of people to hospitals and then withholding treatment. Imagine if physicians were to say: "Let's just hope they get better and do not infect others!" Such quackery would never be tolerated in medicine; it should not be tolerated in corrections either. What's worse, of course, is that released inmates not only harm themselves by returning to crime—and perhaps to prison—but also the people they victimize. To just let this happen is mind-boggling.

The good news is that more policy makers are paying attention to reentry; they, too, have gotten the message that *reentry matters*. The bad news is that not enough is being done to address the challenge of bringing back hundreds of thousands of prisoners annually and that much of what is being done is probably not working or working very well. The evidence-based revolution in corrections is just beginning to influence reentry interventions. Solid knowledge needs to inform two crucial components of reentry. First and foremost, reentry must be correctional and rely on the "what works" rehabilitation literature. Unless criminogenic needs are adequately addressed, offenders' propensity to break the law will not change much. Second, reentry must be reintegrative and thus help offenders to assume a normal life. Positively, this means helping them have things like a place to live, a job to support themselves, and medical care. Negatively (so to speak), it means taking steps to get rid of all the irrational collateral consequences that the state and federal statutes now place on ex-offenders that inhibit their genuine efforts to go straight (see Jonson & Cullen, 2015; Mears & Cochran, 2015).

SAVE THE CHILDREN

We will keep this brief. Let us imagine a room—perhaps a classroom filled with students, a church filled with worshipers, or a hall filled with legislators.

Now, we ask this question: "Will all those in the room who are against saving children from a life in crime raise your hands?" As we scan these crowds, we will see only one bozo in the corner with his hand up. Enough said. Everyone wants to save the children!

The accompanying criminological reality is that we need to do so. Exceptions exist, but serious, chronic offenders disproportionately start on a pathway to prison very early in life. They are exposed to and accumulate risk factors one after another. They manifest antisocial conduct early enough that *everyone knows that they are troubled*. The point is that people do not mystically become criminal when they first break the law; the seeds of their propensity for crime exist prior to this time and have been displayed in the bad conduct in which they have repeatedly engaged.

The sad fact is that despite knowing that at-risk youngsters are headed into crime and into prison, most are never helped before they enter the criminal justice system. This neglect of their criminality is shameful. It also is irrational, given the existence of evidence-based models for quality early intervention programs. The difficulty is that unlike the criminal justice system, there is no single early intervention system whose job it is to save kids from crime and other misery. Creating such a system and seamlessly linking it to corrections would be no easy task. But however daunting, it is a challenge that is worth taking up. In fact, it is long overdue (Farrington & Welsh, 2007).

THINGS CAN CHANGE

In 1991, John DiIulio predicted that "over the next two decades" there would be "no escape" from rising numbers of people in prison and under community supervision (p. 3). DiIulio was certainly prescient, but his message of *no escape* was accurate only in the sense that few policy makers were prepared to stand up and call for corrections to move in a decidedly different direction. This is no longer the case (Cullen, Jonson, & Stohr, 2014).

We have reached in corrections what Malcolm Gladwell (2000) calls a "tipping point." In his scenario, there are times when ideas seem to spread like viruses and when change can occur "not gradually but at one dramatic moment" (p. 9). In the final chapter of the first edition of this book (finished by us in 2011), we wrote the following: "Cullen and Jonson are not prepared to predict that a Gladwell-like transformation in American corrections is happening next week!" (2012, p. 215). But we did say that something important was afoot—that change was in the air. We stated that we detected the emergence of "a broad-based realization that mass incarceration as a crime control policy is bankrupt. It is too costly, reaps too few savings in crime, and disproportionately is focused on the poor and on people of color." Alas, Cullen and Jonson proved to be really good correctional prognosticators.

So, what has changed? Well, two things. First, on a policy level, the era of mass imprisonment is over. Obviously, no claim is being made that states are opening up the prison gates and emptying their institutions. It took the U.S. Supreme Court, for example, to force California to achieve a major reduction in its inmate population

(Simon, 2014). Admittedly, New York and New Jersey lowered their prison counts 26% between 1999 and 2012, but they remain the exception (The Sentencing Project, 2014). In all likelihood, most states will sort of stumble forward, hoping to limit the number of offenders they are locking up. Some will succeed; others will not. Unlike past times, however, it is now virtually unimaginable that the governor of any state will proudly announce bold new initiatives to incarcerate a bunch more wicked people. The United States has now moved from the era of mass imprisonment to the era of prison downsizing (Petersilia & Cullen, 2015).

Correctional policy and practices thus have a certain inertia about them. They are like a big barge loaded up with cargo traveling down a river; they do not change directions quickly. Ways of thinking about corrections—what Cullen and Jonson call "theories"—are more mutable. More mutable does not mean unstable! Indeed, theories are persistent and resistant to challenge. But when they change, they can change rapidly. Such a transformation occurs in the mind; it does not require, for example, finding the political will and votes to close prisons and create community alternatives.

As we have discussed, changing social contexts tend to produce or permit new perspectives on the world, including on how offenders should be treated. Now is one of those important turning points in the history of corrections. Policy makers are now thinking differently about offenders and what to do with them (Simon, 2014). So, the second change is this: The *correctional theory of meanness* has been replaced by the *correctional theory of social welfare*.

The theory of meanness is an amalgamation of retribution, deterrence, and incapacitation. In this view, prisons are an essential correctional tool. Prisons allow for true retribution (anything else is not really punishment), for true deterrence (nobody is going to be scared straight by probation), and for true incapacitation (caging is needed to keep the predatory at bay). The meanness enters in because offenders are portrayed as "the other" (Garland, 2001) or as "waste" to be managed (Simon, 1993). This depersonalization and degradation implies that the wayward merit no concern and that their humanity and dignity can be ignored (Simon, 2014). Being mean to them allows us to get even and may cause them to avoid crime in the future. If not, then that's okay too. We do not care if offenders suffer.

The theory of social welfare is really the trusted rehabilitative ideal with the newer ideas of reentry and early intervention thrown in. But there is also an emotional content to this theory. It involves a dislike and distrust of the punishment response to crime and the meanness it involves. Its advocates do not deny that criminals do bad things and must therefore have some bad things done to them. But those embracing this theory cannot get it out of their minds that offenders are, after all, people and thus have value. If we can rescue them from a life in crime, we should do so. A fancy way of capturing this reaction is to say that the social welfare crowd has "empathetic identification" with offenders. Alas, it is hard to be mean toward someone you have empathy for (Unnever & Cullen, 2009).

Such thinking is clearly manifest in the pronouncements of President Obama and Pope Francis. Barack Obama became the first sitting president to visit a maximum security prison. He noted that "many people face years in prison because they made foolish, youthful mistakes—many of them similar to the mistakes he and others made as kids" (Jackson & Davis, 2015, p. 2B). He noted that "There but for the grace of god. . . . And that is something that we all have to think about" (p. 2B). Hmm. Lots of empathetic identification there! In his remarks on "penal law," Pope Francis (2014) strikes a similar chord. His letter is worth reading in its entirety. The Pope argues against "restraining, dissuading and isolating" those who have caused evil. "The church," he asserts, "proposes a humanizing, genuinely reconciling justice, a justice that leads the criminal, through educational development and brave atonement, to rehabilitation and reintegration into the community." A change in "mentality," Pope Francis (2014) advises, will allow us to avoid "unnecessary suffering, most of all among the most defenseless."

We suppose that such empathy might be expected from a Kenyan socialist. We might say from an "Argentine socialist" as well, but our Catholic roots stop us from casting Pope Francis in such a light. But you get the point. The punch line in all this, however, is that advocacy of the theory of social welfare, replete with empathetic identification, is no longer restricted to bleeding-heart liberals and those whose mission in life is to forgive and save sinners. Yes, things have changed that much! Indeed, similar remarks can be found in the video message to the *Bipartisan Summit on Criminal Justice Reform* by John Kasich (2014), the governor of Ohio. In his address, Governor Kasich highlights his administration's efforts in sentencing reform so that "offenders have the opportunity to receive intensive rehabilitation in the community." He notes his desire to remove collateral sanctions and to "take a comprehensive, common sense approach to restoring our citizens who have made a mistake in their past and who are eager to live their lives anew." In the end, he urges empathy:

> Think about that woman when she has that little baby in her arms and she has such hopes and dreams for that little baby about what the possibility is for that human being, her child. And somehow those folks can get off track. But you know they do have a God given mission. And sometimes it isn't easy to get them to see it, to understand it, to search for it. Look we're all in this together restoring a human being's hope, opportunity, and purpose. It changes the world. And that's why we're doing what we're doing out here. And we'll keep doing it—even with a very conservative legislature that has seen the need to value all human life.

Conclusion: Choosing Our Future

Whether as policy makers or as citizens, we face a continuing challenge: We must *choose for ourselves as a nation a better correctional future* (see Cullen & Wright, 1996). We understand that such talk sounds a touch naïve—an uplifting, but ultimately disingenuous, message used to end a book on a high note. But we are persuaded that no-escape thinking—the idea that change is impossible—consigns us to a future that will merely replicate an unhappy past. In fact, every day, choices are made across the nation regarding the laws that will govern corrections, whether offenders will be locked up, and whether those in the system will receive treatment. The issue thus is not whether a future will be chosen, but rather *which future we will choose and whether this choice will be made thoughtlessly or with a social purpose in mind.*

Perhaps because we have lived and/or worked in Cincinnati for a long time, Cullen and Jonson cannot help but think back to a time when leading correctional figures came together in Cincinnati to articulate—yes, to choose!—a different correctional future. Readers may recall from Chapter 2 the discussion of the Cincinnati Congress of 1870. Again, what strikes us is that this was a period when dreary realities could have led these reformers to expect little from corrections. Prisons had grown crowded, filled largely with the urban poor and immigrants who were depicted as defective members of the dangerous classes. But in the face of these difficulties, the Congress's participants were not disillusioned but resolved to identify the principles of a new penology that would allow corrections to realize greater aspirations. In a thoroughly American way, they called out for a system that rejected "the infliction of vindictive suffering" in favor of the "reformation of criminals" (Wines, 1870/1910, p. 39).

To this day, their words and the conviction underlying them are moving. Cullen and Jonson hope that, as with our predecessors, we have the wisdom and courage to see corrections as a conduit for bringing light and hope to a realm where darkness and despair typically reign. Attempting to choose such a future does not guarantee the emergence of a new era of correctional reform, but it is an essential first step away from a recent past that too often has cultivated our meanness, exploited our fears, and encouraged us to see our fellow citizens as little more than irredeemable super-predators. Cullen and Jonson know that as a just and generous people, the desire exists among us to create a correctional system that reflects the best, not the least, we have to offer. Let us envision a better, more hopeful future. And then let the work begin to make it our reality!

References

Abramsky, S. (2007). *American furies: Crime, punishment, and vengeance in the age of mass imprisonment.* Boston, MA: Beacon.

Alexander, J., Pugh, C., & Parsons, B. (1998*). Functional family therapy: Blueprints in violence prevention* (Book 3). Boulder: Institute of Behavioral Science, University of Colorado at Boulder.

Alexander, M. (2010). *The new Jim Crow: Mass incarceration in the age of colorblindness.* New York, NY: The New Press.

Allen, F. A. (1981). *The decline of the rehabilitative ideal: Penal policy and social purpose.* New Haven, CT: Yale University Press.

Alper, J. S., & Beckwith, J. (1993). Genetic fatalism and social policy: The implications of behavior genetic research. *Yale Journal of Biology and Medicine, 66,* 511–526.

American Friends Service Committee Working Party. (1971). *Struggle for justice: A report on crime and punishment in America.* New York, NY: Hill and Wang.

Andrews, D. A. (1995). The psychology of criminal conduct and effective treatment. In J. McGuire (Ed.), *What works: Reducing reoffending—Guidelines from research and practice* (pp. 35–62). New York, NY: John Wiley.

Andrews, D. A., & Bonta, J. (2010). *The psychology of criminal conduct* (5th ed.). New Providence, NJ: Anderson/LexisNexis.

Andrews, D. A., Bonta, J., & Wormith, J. S. (2011). The risk-need-responsibility (RNR) model: Does adding the Good Lives Model contribute to effective crime prevention? *Criminal Justice and Behavior, 38,* 735–755.

Andrews, D. A., & Hoge, R. D. (1995). The psychology of criminal conduct and principles of effective prevention and rehabilitation. *Forum on Corrections Research, 7*(1), 34–36.

Andrews, D. A., Zinger, I., Hoge, R. D., Bonta, J., Gendreau, P., & Cullen, F. T. (1990). Does correctional treatment work? A clinically relevant and psychologically informed meta-analysis. *Criminology, 28,* 369–404.

Aos, S., Phipps, P., Barnoski, R., & Lieb, R. (2001). The comparative costs and benefits of programs to reduce crime: A review of research findings with implications for Washington state. In B. C. Welsh, D. P. Farrington, & L. W. Sherman (Eds.), *Costs and benefits of preventing crime* (pp. 149–175). Boulder, CO: Westview Press.

Apel, R., & Nagin, D. S. (2011). General deterrence: A review of recent evidence. In J. Q. Wilson & J. Petersilia (Eds.), *Crime and public policy* (pp. 411–436). New York, NY: Oxford University Press.

Applegate, B. K. (2011). Jails and pretrial release. In M. Tonry (Ed.), *The Oxford handbook of crime and criminal justice* (pp. 795–824). New York, NY: Oxford University Press.

Arpaio, J., & Sherman, L. (1996). *America's toughest sheriff: How we can win the war against crime.* Ottawa, ON: Summit Publishing Group.

Arpaio, J., & Sherman, L. (2008). *Joe's law: America's toughest sheriff takes on illegal immigration, drugs, and everything else that threatens America.* New York, NY: AMACOM.

Aviram, H. (2015). *Cheap on crime: Recession-era politics and the transformation of American punishment.* Berkeley: University of California Press.

Ayres, I. (2007). *Super crunchers: Why thinking-by-numbers is the new way to be smart.* New York, NY: Bantam Books.

Baldry, A. C., & Farrington, D. P. (2007). Effectiveness of programs to prevent school bullying. *Victims and Offenders, 2,* 183–204.

Barnes, J. C. (2014). Catching the really bad guys: An assessment of the efficacy of the U.S. criminal justice system. *Journal of Criminal Justice, 42,* 338–346.

Bazemore, G. (1999). After shaming, whither reintegration: Restorative justice and relational rehabilitation. In G. Bazemore & L. Walgrave (Eds.), *Restorative juvenile justice: Repairing the harm of youth crime* (pp. 155–194). Monsey, NY: Criminal Justice Press.

Becker, T. E., David, S. L., & Soucy, G. (1995). *Reviewing the behavioral science knowledge base on technology transfer.* Rockville, MD: National Institute on Drug Abuse.

Beckett, K. (1997). *Making crime pay: Law and order in contemporary American politics.* New York, NY: Oxford University Press.

Bellah, R. N., Madsen, R., Sullivan, W. M., Swidler, A., & Tipton, S. M. (1985). *Habits of the heart: Individualism and commitment in American life.* Berkeley: University of California Press.

Bennett, W. J., DiIulio, J. J., Jr., & Walters, J. P. (1996). *Body count: Moral poverty and how to win America's war against crime and drugs.* New York, NY: Simon & Shuster.

Benson, M. L. (2013). *Crime and the life course: An introduction.* New York, NY: Routledge.

Benson, M. L., Alarid, L. F., Burton, V. S., & Cullen, F. T. (2011). Reintegration or stigmatization: Offenders' expectations of community re-entry. *Journal of Criminal Justice, 39,* 385–393.

Berger, P. L., & Luckmann, T. (1966). *The social construction of reality: A treatise in the sociology of knowledge.* Garden City, NY: Anchor.

Bernburg, J. G., & Krohn, M. D. (2003). Labeling, life chances, and adult crime: The direct and indirect effects of official intervention in adolescence on crime in early adulthood. *Criminology, 41,* 1287–1318.

Bernburg, J. G., Krohn, M. D., & Rivera, C. J. (2006). Official labeling, criminal embeddedness, and subsequent delinquency: A longitudinal test of labeling theory. *Journal of Research in Crime and Delinquency, 43,* 67–88.

Bewley-Taylor, D., Hallam, C., & Allen, R. (2009). *The incarceration of drug offenders: An overview.* London, UK: International Centre for Prison Studies, King's College London.

Bhati, A. S. (2007). Estimating the number of crimes averted by incapacitation: An information theoretic approach. *Journal of Quantitative Criminology, 23,* 355–375.

Blokland, A. A. J., & Nieuwbeerta, P. (2007). Selectively incapacitating frequent offenders: Costs and benefits of various penal sanctions. *Journal of Quantitative Criminology, 23,* 327–353.

Blumstein, A., & Cohen, J. (1973). A theory of the stability of punishment. *Journal of Criminal Law and Criminology, 64,* 198–206.

Blumstein, A., Tonry, M., & Van Ness, A. (2005). Cross-national measures of punitiveness. In M. Tonry (Ed.), *Crime and punishment in Western countries, 1980–1999* (Crime and Justice: A Review of Research, Vol. 33, pp. 347–377). Chicago, IL: University of Chicago Press.

Blumstein, A., & Wallman, J. (Eds.). (2000). *The crime drop in America.* New York, NY: Cambridge University Press.

Bonczar, T. P. (2008). *Characteristics of state parole supervising agencies, 2006.* Washington, DC: Bureau of Justice Statistics, U.S. Department of Justice.

Bonta, J., Bourgon, G., Rugge, T., Scott, T.-L., Yessine, A. K., Gutierrez, L., & Li, J. (2011). An experimental demonstration of training probation officers in evidence-based community supervision. *Criminal Justice and Behavior, 11,* 1127–1148.

Bonta, J., Jesseman, R., Rugge, T., & Cormier, R. (2006). Restorative justice and recidivism: Promises made, promises kept? In D. Sullivan & L. Tifft (Eds.), *Handbook of restorative justice* (pp. 108–120). New York, NY: Routledge.

Bonta, J., Rugge, T., Scott, T.-L., Bourgon, G., & Yessine, A. K. (2008). Exploring the black box of community supervision. *Journal of Offender Rehabilitation, 47,* 248–270.

Bonta, J., Wallace-Capretta, S., & Rooney, J. (2000). A quasi-experimental evaluation of an intensive rehabilitation supervision program. *Criminal Justice and Behavior, 27,* 312–329.

Bonta, J., Wallace-Capretta, S., Rooney, J., & McAnoy, K. (2002). An outcome evaluation of a restorative justice alternative to incarceration. *Contemporary Justice Review, 5,* 319–338.

Borduin, C. M., Mann, B. J., Cone, L. T., Henggeler, S. W., Fucci, B. R., Blaske, D. M., & Williams, R. A. (1995). Multisystemic treatment of serious juvenile offenders: Long-term prevention of criminality and violence. *Journal of Consulting and Clinical Psychology, 63,* 569–578.

Bradshaw, W., & Roseborough, D. (2005). Restorative justice dialogue: The impact of mediation and conferencing on juvenile recidivism. *Federal Probation, 69*(2), 15–21.

Braithwaite, J. (1989). *Crime, shame and reintegration.* Cambridge, UK: Cambridge University Press.

Braithwaite, J. (1998). Restorative justice. In M. Tonry (Ed.), *The handbook of crime and punishment* (pp. 323–344). New York, NY: Oxford University Press.

Braithwaite, J. (2002). *Restorative justice and responsive regulation.* New York, NY: Oxford University Press.

Braithwaite, J., & Pettit, P. (1990). *Not just deserts: A republican theory of criminal justice.* Oxford, UK: Oxford University Press.

Brayford, J., Cowe, F., & Deering, J. (Eds.). (2010). *What else works? Creative work with offenders.* Cullompton, Devon, UK: Willan Publishing.

Brodeur, J.-P. (2007). Comparative penology in perspective. In M. Tonry (Ed.), *Crime, punishment, and politics in comparative perspective* (Crime and Justice: A Review of Research, Vol. 36, pp. 49–92). Chicago, IL: University of Chicago Press.

Bruinsma, G. J. N. (in press). The emergence of deterrence theory in the Age of Enlightenment. In D. S. Nagin, F. T. Cullen, & C. L. Jonson (Eds.), *Deterrence, choice, and crime: Contemporary perspectives* (Advances in Criminological Theory). New Brunswick, NJ: Transaction.

Bulmer, M. (1984). *The Chicago school of sociology: Institutionalization, diversity, and the rise of sociological research.* Chicago, IL: University of Chicago Press.

Burke, C., & Keaton S. (2004). *San Diego County's Connections program: Board of Corrections final report.* San Diego, CA: San Diego Association of Governments.

Burton, V. S., Jr., Fisher, C., Jonson, C. L., & Cullen, F. T. (2014). Confronting the collateral consequences of a criminal conviction: A special challenge for social work with offenders. *Journal of Forensic Social Work, 4,* 80–103.

Bush, G. W. (2004, January 20). Text of President Bush's 2004 State of the Union Address. *Washington Post,* pp. 1–10. Retrieved from http://www.washingtonpost.com/wp-srv/politics/transcripts/bushtext_012004.html

Bushway, S., Stoll, M. A., & Weiman, D. F. (Eds.). (2007). *Barriers to reentry? The labor market for released prisoners in post-industrial America.* New York, NY: Russell Sage.

Bushway, S. D., & Paternoster, R. (2009). The impact of prison on crime. In S. Raphael & M. A. Stoll (Eds.), *Do prisons make us safer? The benefits and costs of the prison boom* (pp. 119–150). New York, NY: Russell Sage.

Byrne, J. M., & Pattavina, A. (1992). The effectiveness issue: Assessing what works in the adult community corrections system. In J. M. Byrne, A. J. Lurigio, & J. Petersilia (Eds.), *Smart sentencing: The emergence of intermediate sanctions* (pp. 281–303). Newbury Park, CA: Sage.

Caplan, J. M., & Kinnevy, S. C. (2010). National surveys of state paroling authorities: Models of service delivery. *Federal Probation, 74*(1), 34–42.

Caputo, G. A. (2004). *Intermediate sanctions in corrections.* Denton: University of North Texas Press.

Carich, M. S., Wilson, C., Carich, P. A., & Calder, M. C. (2010). Contemporary sex offender treatment: Incorporating circles of support and the Good Lives Model. In J. Brayford, F. Cowe, & J. Deering (Eds.), *What else works? Creative work with offenders* (pp. 188–210). Cullompton, Devon, UK: Willan Publishing.

Carson, E. A. (2014). *Prisoners in 2013.* Washington, DC: Bureau of Justice Statistics, U.S. Department of Justice.

Carson, E. A., & Golinelli, D. (2013). *Prisoners in 2012: Trends in admissions and releases, 1991–2012.* Washington, DC: Bureau of Justice Statistics, U.S. Department of Justice.

Catalano, R. F., Arthur, M. W., Hawkins, J. D., Berglund, L., & Olson, J. J. (1998). Comprehensive community- and school-based interventions to prevent antisocial behavior. In R. Loeber & D. P. Farrington (Eds.), *Serious and violent juvenile offenders: Risk factors and successful interventions* (pp. 248–283). Thousand Oaks, CA: Sage.

Catalano, R. F., Loeber, R., & McKinney, K. C. (1999). *School and community interventions to prevent serious and violent offending*. Washington, DC: Office of Juvenile Justice and Delinquency Prevention, U.S. Department of Justice.

Chen, M. K., & Shapiro, J. M. (2007). Do harsher prison conditions reduce recidivism? A discontinuity-based approach. *American Law and Economic Review, 9,* 1–29.

Chin, G. J. (2012). The new civil death: Rethinking punishment in the era of mass conviction. *University of Pennsylvania Law Review, 160,* 1789–1833.

Chiricos, T., Barrick, K., Bales, W., & Bontrager, S. (2007). The labeling of convicted felons and its consequences for recidivism. *Criminology, 45,* 547–581.

Cid, J. (2009). Is imprisonment criminogenic? A comparative study of recidivism rates between prison and suspended prison sanctions. *European Journal of Criminology, 6,* 459–480.

Clear, T. R. (1994). *Harm in American penology: Offenders, victims, and their communities.* Albany: State University of New York Press.

Clear, T. R. (2007). *Imprisoning communities: How mass incarceration makes disadvantaged neighborhoods worse.* New York, NY: Oxford University Press.

Clear, T. R., & Frost, N. A. (2014). *The punishment imperative: The rise and failure of mass incarceration in America.* New York: New York University Press.

Cloward, R. A. (1959). Illegitimate means, anomie, and deviant behavior. *American Sociological Review, 24,* 164–176.

Cloward, R. A., & Ohlin, L. E. (1960). *Delinquency and opportunity: A theory of delinquent gangs.* New York, NY: Free Press.

Cohen, A. K. (1955). *Delinquent boys: The culture of the gang.* New York, NY: Free Press.

Cohen, M. A. (1998). The monetary value of saving a high-risk youth. *Journal of Quantitative Criminology, 14,* 5–32.

Cohen, M. A., & Piquero, A. R. (2009). New evidence on the monetary value of saving a high-risk youth. *Journal of Quantitative Criminology, 42,* 89–109.

Cohen, M. A., Piquero, A. R., & Jennings, W. G. (2010). Estimating the costs of bad outcomes for at-risk youth and the benefits of early interventions to reduce them. *Criminal Justice Policy Review, 21,* 391–434.

Conrad, J. (1973). Corrections and simple justice. *Journal of Criminal Law and Criminology, 64,* 208–217.

Coolidge, S. (2009, November 22). County probation program assailed: Intensive supervision often less effective than none. *Cincinnati Enquirer,* pp. A1, A10.

Corrections Compendium. (2011). Reentry: Survey summary. *Corrections Compendium, 36*(4), 12–32.

Council of State Governments (CSG) Justice Center. (2012). *What works in reentry clearinghouse.* Lexington, KY: Author.

Crow, M. S., & Smykla, J. O. (Eds.). (2014). *Offender reentry: Rethinking criminology and criminal justice.* Burlington, MA: Jones and Bartlett Learning.

Cullen, F. T. (1994). Social support as an organizing concept for criminology: Presidential address to the Academy of Criminal Justice Sciences. *Justice Quarterly, 11,* 527–559.

Cullen, F. T. (2005). The twelve people who saved rehabilitation: How the science of criminology made a difference—The American Society of Criminology 2004 presidential address. *Criminology, 43,* 1–42.

Cullen, F. T. (2007). Make rehabilitation corrections' guiding paradigm. *Criminology and Public Policy, 6,* 717–728.

Cullen, F. T. (2011). Beyond adolescence-limited criminology: Choosing our future—The American Society of Criminology 2010 Sutherland Address. *Criminology, 49,* 287–330.

Cullen, F. T. (2012). Taking rehabilitation seriously: Creativity, science, and the challenge of offender change. *Punishment and Society, 14,* 94–114.

Cullen, F. T. (2013). Rehabilitation: Beyond nothing works. In M. Tonry (Ed.), *Crime and justice in America, 1975–2025* (Crime and Justice: A Review of Research, Vol. 42, pp. 299–376). Chicago, IL: University of Chicago Press.

Cullen, F. T., Blevins, K. R., Trager, J. S., & Gendreau, P. (2005). The rise and fall of boot camps: A case study in common-sense corrections. *Journal of Offender Rehabilitation, 40*(3–4), 53–70.

Cullen, F. T., Cavender, G., Maakestad, W. J., & Benson, M. L. (2006). *Corporate crime under attack: The fight to criminalize business violence* (2nd ed.). Cincinnati, OH: Anderson/LexisNexis.

Cullen, F. T., Fisher, B. S., & Applegate, B. K. (2000). Public opinion about punishment and corrections. In M. Tonry (Ed.), *Crime and justice: A review of research* (Vol. 14, pp. 1–79). Chicago, IL: University of Chicago Press.

Cullen, F. T., & Gendreau, P. (2000). Assessing correctional rehabilitation: Policy, practice, and prospects. In J. Horney (Ed.), *Policies, processes, and decisions of the criminal justice system*: *Criminal justice 2000* (Vol. 3, pp. 109–175). Washington, DC: National Institute of Justice, U.S. Department of Justice.

Cullen, F. T., & Gendreau, P. (2001). From nothing works to what works: Changing professional ideology in the 21st century. *Prison Journal, 81,* 313–338.

Cullen, F. T., & Gilbert, K. E. (1982). *Reaffirming rehabilitation*. Cincinnati, OH: Anderson.

Cullen, F. T., & Gilbert, K. E. (2013). *Reaffirming rehabilitation* (2nd ed.). Waltham, MA: Anderson.

Cullen, F. T., & Jonson, C. L. (2011a). Labeling theory and correctional rehabilitation: Beyond unanticipated consequences. In D. P. Farrington & J. Murray (Eds.), *Empirical tests of labeling theory* (Advances in Criminological Theory, Vol. 17, pp. 63–85). New Brunswick, NJ: Transaction.

Cullen, F. T., & Jonson, C. L. (2011b). Rehabilitation and treatment. In J. Q. Wilson & J. Petersilia (Eds.), *Crime and public policy* (pp. 293–344). New York, NY: Oxford University Press.

Cullen, F. T., & Jonson, C. L. (2012). *Correctional theory: Context and consequences*. Thousand Oaks, CA: Sage.

Cullen, F. T., Jonson, C. L., & Chouhy, C. (2015). *The Saints and the Roughnecks revisited: How labeling kids creates criminals*. Unpublished manuscript, University of Cincinnati.

Cullen, F. T., Jonson, C. L., & Nagin, D. S. (2011). Prisons do not reduce recidivism: The high cost of ignoring science. *Prison Journal, 91,* 48S–65S.

Cullen, F. T., Jonson, C. L., & Stohr, M. K. (Eds.). (2014). *The American prison: Imagining a different future*. Thousand Oaks, CA: Sage.

Cullen, F. T., Link, B. G., & Polanzi, C. W. (1982). The seriousness of crime revisited: Are attitudes toward white-collar crime changing? *Criminology, 20,* 83–102.

Cullen, F. T., Lux, J. L., & Jonson, C. L. (2012). Assessing the effectiveness of multisystemic therapy: A case study in evidence-based corrections. In E. W. Plywaczewski (Ed.), *The current problems of the penal law and criminology* (pp. 65–84). Warszawa, Poland: Wolters Kluwver Polska.

Cullen, F. T., Manchak, S. M., & Duriez, S. A. (2014). Before adopting Project HOPE, read the warning label: A rejoinder to Kleiman, Kilmer, and Fisher's comment. *Federal Probation, 78*(2), 75–77.

Cullen, F. T., Myer, A. J., & Latessa, E. J. (2009). Eight lessons learned from *Moneyball:* The high cost of ignoring evidence-based corrections. *Victims and Offenders, 4,* 197–213.

Cullen, F. T., Pealer, J. A., Fisher, B. S., Applegate, B. K., & Santana, S. A. (2002). Public support for correctional rehabilitation in America: Change or consistency? In J. V. Roberts & M. Hough (Eds.), *Changing attitudes to punishment: Public opinion, crime and justice* (pp. 128–147). Cullompton, Devon, UK: Willan Publishing.

Cullen, F. T., Pratt, T. C., Micelli, S. L., & Moon, M. M. (2002). Dangerous liaison? Rational choice theory as the basis for correctional intervention. In A. R. Piquero & S. G. Tibbetts (Eds.), *Rational choice and criminal behavior: Recent research and future challenges* (pp. 279–296). New York, NY: Routledge.

Cullen, F. T., & Smith, P. (2011). Treatment and rehabilitation. In M. Tonry (Ed.), *The Oxford handbook of crime and criminology* (pp. 156–178). New York, NY: Oxford University Press.

Cullen, F. T., Smith, P., Lowenkamp, C. T., & Latessa, E. J. (2009). Nothing works revisited: Deconstructing Farabee's *Rethinking Rehabilitation*. *Victims and Offenders, 4,* 101–123.

Cullen, F. T., Sundt, J. L., & Wozniak, J. F. (2001). The virtuous prison: Toward a restorative rehabilitation. In H. N. Pontell & D. Shichor (Eds.), *Contemporary issues in crime and criminal justice: Essays in honor of Gilbert Geis* (pp. 265–286). Upper Saddle River, NJ: Prentice Hall.

Cullen, F. T., Vose, B. A., Jonson, C. N. L., & Unnever, J. D. (2007). Public support for early intervention: Is child saving a "habit of the heart"? *Victims and Offenders, 2,* 109–124.

Cullen, F. T., & Wright, J. P. (1996). Two futures of American corrections. In B. Maguire & P. Radosh (Eds.), *The past, present, and future of American corrections* (pp. 198–219). New York, NY: General Hall.

Cullen, F. T., Wright, J. P., & Applegate, B. K. (1996). Control in the community: The limits of reform? In A. T. Harland (Ed.), *Choosing correctional interventions that work: Defining the demand and evaluating the supply* (pp. 69–116). Newbury Park, CA: Sage.

Cullen, F. T., Wright, J. P., Brown, S., Moon, M. M., Blankenship, M. B., & Applegate, B. K. (1998). Public support for early intervention programs: Implications for a progressive policy agenda. *Crime and Delinquency, 44,* 187–204.

Currie, E. (1998). *Crime and punishment in America.* New York, NY: Metropolitan Books.

Curtis, N. M., Ronan, K. R., & Borduin, C. M. (2004). Multisystemic treatment: A meta-analysis of outcome studies. *Journal of Family Psychology, 8,* 411–419.

Daly, K. (2008). The limits of restorative justice. In D. Sullivan & L. Tifft (Eds.), *Handbook of restorative justice: A global perspective* (pp. 134–145). New York, NY: Routledge.

Daly, K., & Proietti-Scifoni, G. (2011). Reparation and restoration. In M. Tonry (Ed.), *The Oxford handbook of crime and criminal justice* (pp. 207–253). New York, NY: Oxford University Press.

Davies, P. (1999). What is evidence-based education? *British Journal of Educational Studies, 47,* 108–121.

Decker, S. H., Spohn, C., Ortiz, N. R., & Hedberg, E. (2014). *Criminal stigma, race, gender and employment: An expanded assessment of the consequences of imprisonment for employment.* Report Submitted to the U.S. Department of Justice. Phoenix: School of Criminology and Criminal Justice, Arizona State University.

Delaware Department of Corrections. (2014). *Treatment services.* Dover, DE: Department of Corrections.

Derkzen, D., Gobeil, R., & Gileno, J. (2009). *Visitation and post-release outcome among federally-sentenced offenders.* Ottawa, ON: Correctional Service Canada.

Dhami, M. K., Mantle, G., & Fox, D. (2009). Restorative justice in prison. *Contemporary Justice Review, 12,* 433–448.

DiIulio, J. J., Jr. (1987). *Governing prisons: A comparative study of correctional management.* New York, NY: Free Press.

DiIulio, J. J., Jr. (1991). *No escape: The future of American corrections.* New York, NY: Basic Books.

DiIulio, J. J., Jr. (1994). The question of Black crime. *The Public Interest, 117*(Fall), 3–32.

DiIulio, J. J., Jr., & Piehl, A. M. (1991). Does prison pay? *The Brookings Review, 9*(Fall), 28–35.

Di Tella, R., & Schargrodsky, E. (2013). Criminal recidivism after prison and electronic monitoring. *Journal of Political Economy, 121,* 26–73.

diZerega, M., & Villabos Agudelo, S. (2011). *Piloting a tool for reentry: A promising approach to engaging family members.* New York, NY: Vera Institute.

Doherty, E. E., Cwick, J. M., Green, K. M., & Ensminger, M. E. (2015). Examining the consequences of the "prevalent life events" of arrest and incarceration among an urban African-American cohort. *Justice Quarterly.* Advance online publication.

Doob, A. N., & Webster, C. M. (2003). Sentence severity and crime: Accepting the null hypothesis. In M. Tonry (Ed.), *Crime and justice: A review of research* (Vol. 30, pp. 141–195). Chicago, IL: University of Chicago Press.

Drago, F., Galbiati, R., & Vertova, P. (2008). *Prison conditions and recidivism* (Discussion Paper No. 3395). Bonn, Germany: IZA.

Drake, E. K., Aos, S., & Miller, M. G. (2009). Evidence-based public policy options to reduce crime and criminal justice costs: Implications from Washington state. *Victims and Offenders, 4,* 170–196.

Duncan, G. J., & Magnuson, K. (2013). Investing in preschool programs. *Journal of Economic Perspectives, 27,* 109–132.

Duriez, S. A., Cullen, F. T., & Manchak, S. M. (2014). Is Project HOPE creating a false sense of hope? A case study in correctional popularity. *Federal Probation, 78*(2), 57–70.

Durlauf, S. N., & Nagin, D. S. (2011). Imprisonment and crime: Can both be reduced? *Criminology and Public Policy, 10,* 13–54.

Durose, M. R., Cooper, A. D., & Snyder, H. N. (2014). *Recidivism of prisoners released in 30 states in 2005: Patterns from 2005 to 2010.* Washington,

DC: Bureau of Justice Statistics, U.S. Department of Justice.

Espiritu, R. C. (1994). *Help-seeking patterns of parents of high-risk youth.* Unpublished manuscript, Department of Psychology, University of Colorado at Boulder.

Farrington, D. P. (2003). Key results from the first forty years of the Cambridge Study in Delinquent Development. In T. P. Thornberry & M. D. Krohn (Eds.), *Taking stock of delinquency: An overview of findings from contemporary longitudinal studies* (pp. 137–183). New York, NY: Kluwer Academic/Plenum.

Farrington, D. P., Barnes, G. C., & Lambert, S. (1996). The concentration of offending in families. *Legal and Criminological Psychology, 1,* 47–63.

Farrington, D. P., & Coid, J. W. (Eds.). (2003). *Early prevention of adult antisocial behaviour.* Cambridge, UK: Cambridge University Press.

Farrington, D. P., Jolliffe, D., Loeber, R., & Homish, D. L. (2007). How many offenses are really committed per juvenile court offender? *Victims and Offenders, 2,* 227–249.

Farrington, D. P., Jolliffe, D., Loeber, R., Stouthamer-Loeber, M., & Kalb, L. M. (2001). The concentration of offenders in families, and family criminality in the prediction of boys' delinquency. *Journal of Adolescence, 24,* 579–596.

Farrington, D. P., & Koegl, C. J. (2015). Monetary benefits and costs of the Stop Now And Plan Program for boys aged 6–11, based on the prevention of later offending. *Journal of Quantitative Criminology, 15,* 263–287.

Farrington, D. P., & Murray, J. (Eds.). (2014). *Labeling theory: Empirical tests* (Advances in Criminological Theory, Vol. 18). New Brunswick, NJ: Transaction.

Farrington, D. P., & Welsh, B. C. (2003). Family-based prevention of offending: A meta-analysis. *Australian and New Zealand Journal of Criminology, 36,* 127–151.

Farrington, D. P., & Welsh, B. C. (2007). *Saving children from a life in crime: Early risk factors and effective interventions.* New York, NY: Oxford University Press.

Federal Bureau of Prisons. (2014). *Completing the transition.* Washington, DC: Author. Retrieved from http://www.bop.gov/about/facilities/residential_reentry_management_centers.jsp

Feld, B. (1999). *Bad kids: Race and the transformation of the juvenile court.* New York, NY: Oxford University Press.

Felson, M. (2002). *Crime in everyday life* (3rd ed.). Thousand Oaks, CA: Sage.

FFT: Functional Family Therapy. (2010). Retrieved from http://www.fftinc.com/index.html

FOCUS. (2014). *FOCUS: Offender re-entry mentoring project.* Boulder, CO: Restoring the Soul. Retrieved from http://restoringthesoul.org/collaborations/focus

Fogel, D. (1979). *"We are the living proof": The justice model for corrections* (2nd ed.). Cincinnati, OH: Anderson.

Fogel, D., & Hudson, J. (Eds.). (1981). *Justice as fairness: Perspectives on the justice model.* Cincinnati, OH: Anderson.

Forst, B. (2011). Prosecution. In J. Q. Wilson & J. Petersilia (Eds.), *Crime and public policy* (pp. 437–466). New York, NY: Oxford University Press.

Frazier, B. D. (2011). Faith-based prisoner reentry. In L. Gideon & H. E. Sung (Eds.). *Rethinking corrections: Rehabilitation, reentry, and reintegration* (pp. 279–306). Thousand Oaks, CA: Sage.

Gaes, G. (2009). Evaluation of getting ready. *NIJ Journal, 263,* 1, 9.

Gaes, G. G., & Camp, S. D. (2009). Unintended consequences: Experimental evidence for the criminogenic effect of prison security level placement on post-release recidivism. *Journal of Experimental Criminology, 5,* 139–162.

Garland, B., & Wodahl, E. (2014). Coming to a crossroads: A critical look at the sustainability of the prisoner reentry movement. In M. S. Crow & J. O. Smykla (Eds.), *Offender reentry: Rethinking criminology and criminal justice* (pp. 399–422). Burlington, MA: Jones and Bartlett Learning.

Garland, B., Wodahl, E., & Schuhmann, R. (2013). Value conflict and public opinion toward prisoner reentry initiatives. *Criminal Justice Policy Review, 24,* 27–48.

Garland, D. (1990). *Punishment and modern society: A study in social theory.* Chicago, IL: University of Chicago Press.

Garland, D. (2001). *The culture of control: Crime and social order in contemporary society.* Chicago, IL: University of Chicago Press.

Gatti, U., Tremblay, R. E., & Vitaro, F. (2009). Iatrogenic effect of juvenile justice. *Journal of Child Psychology and Psychiatry, 50,* 991–998.

Gawande, A. (2009). *The checklist manifesto: How to get things right.* New York, NY: Metropolitan Books.

Gaylin, W., Glasser, I., Marcus, S., & Rothman, D. (Eds.). (1978). *Doing good: The limits of benevolence.* New York, NY: Pantheon.

Geis, G. (1972). Jeremy Bentham. In H. Mannheim (Ed.), *Pioneers in criminology* (2nd ed., pp. 51–68). Montclair, NJ: Patterson Smith.

Gendreau, P. (1996). The principles of effective intervention with offenders. In A. T. Harland (Ed.), *Choosing correctional options that work: Defining the demand and evaluating the supply* (pp. 117–130). Thousand Oaks, CA: Sage.

Gendreau, P., Cullen, F. T., & Bonta, J. (1994). Intensive rehabilitation supervision: The next generation in community corrections? *Federal Probation, 58*(1), 72–78.

Gendreau, P., & Goggin, C. (2014). Practicing psychology in correctional settings. In I. B. Weiner & R. K. Otto (Eds.), *The handbook of forensic psychology* (4th ed., pp. 759–793). Hoboken, NJ: John Wiley.

Gendreau, P., Goggin, C., Cullen, F. T., & Andrews, D. A. (2000). The effects of community sanctions and incarceration on recidivism. *Forum on Corrections Research, 12*(May), 10–13.

Gendreau, P., Little, T., & Goggin, C. (1996). A meta-analysis of the predictors of adult offender recidivism: What works! *Criminology, 34,* 575–607.

Gendreau, P., & Ross, R. R. (1979). Effective correctional treatment: Bibliotherapy for cynics. *Crime and Delinquency, 25,* 463–489.

Gendreau, P., & Ross, R. R. (1987). Revivification of rehabilitation: Evidence from the 1980s. *Justice Quarterly, 4,* 349–407.

Gendreau, P., Smith, P., & French, S. A. (2006). The theory of effective correctional intervention: Empirical status and future directions. In F. T. Cullen, J. P. Wright, & K. R. Blevins (Eds.), *Taking stock: The status of criminological theory* (Advances in Criminological Theory, Vol. 15, pp. 419–446). New Brunswick, NJ: Transaction.

Gideon, L. (2010). *Substance abusing inmates: Experiences of recovering drug addicts on their way back home.* New York, NY: Springer.

Gideon, L., & Loveland, N. (2011). Public attitudes toward rehabilitation and reintegration: How supportive are people of getting-tough-on-crime policies and the Second Chance Act? In L. Gideon & H. E. Sung (Eds.), *Rethinking corrections: Rehabilitation, reentry, and reintegration* (pp. 19–36). Thousand Oaks, CA: Sage.

Gideon, L., & Sung, H.-E. (Eds.). (2011). *Rethinking corrections: Rehabilitation, reentry, and reintegration.* Thousand Oaks, CA: Sage.

Gill, C. E. (2010). *The effects of sanction intensity on criminal conduct: A randomized low-intensity probation experiment.* Unpublished doctoral dissertation, University of Pennsylvania.

Giordano, P. C., Cernkovich, S. A., & Rudolph, J. L. (2002). Gender, crime, and desistance: Toward a theory of cognitive transformation. *American Journal of Sociology, 107,* 990–1064.

Gladwell, M. (2000). *The tipping point: How little things can make a big difference.* Boston, MA: Little, Brown.

Glaze, L. E., & Herberman, E. J. (2013). *Correctional populations in the United States, 2012.* Washington, DC: Bureau of Justice Statistics, U.S. Department of Justice.

Glaze, L. E., & Kaeble, D. (2014). *Correctional populations in the United States, 2013.* Washington, DC: Bureau of Justice Statistics, U.S. Department of Justice.

Gomby, D. S., Culross, P. L., & Behrman, R. E. (1999). Home visiting: Recent program evaluations: Analysis and recommendations. *Future of Children, 9,* 195–223.

Goodman, A. (2006). *The story of David Olds and the nurse home visiting program.* Princeton, NJ: Robert Wood Johnson Foundation.

Gordon, D. R. (1994). *The return of the dangerous class: Drug prohibition and policy politics.* New York, NY: W. W. Norton.

Gottfredson, D. C. (2001). *Schools and delinquency.* New York, NY: Cambridge University Press.

Gottfredson, D. C., Wilson, D. B., & Najaka, S. S. (2002). The schools. In J. Q. Wilson & J. Petersilia (Eds.), *Crime: Public policies for crime control* (2nd ed., pp. 149–189). Oakland, CA: ICS Press.

Gottfredson, M. R. (1979). Treatment destruction techniques. *Journal of Research in Crime and Delinquency, 16,* 39–54.

Gottfredson, M. R., & Hirschi, T. (1990). *A general theory of crime*. Stanford, CA: Stanford University Press.

Gottschalk, M. (2006). *The prison and the gallows: The politics of mass incarceration in America*. New York, NY: Cambridge University Press.

Gottschalk, M. (2015). *Caught: The prison state and the lockdown of American politics*. Princeton, NJ: Princeton University Press.

Gouldner, A. W. (1970). *The coming crisis of Western sociology*. New York, NY: Avon Books.

Grattet, R., Petersilia, J., Lin, J., & Beckman, M. (2009). Parole violations and revocations in California: Analysis and suggestions for action. *Federal Probation, 73*(1), 2–11.

Gray, S. (2006). *The mind of Bill James: How a complete outsider changed baseball*. New York, NY: Doubleday.

Greenwood, P. W. (2006). *Changing lives: Delinquency prevention as crime-control policy*. Chicago, IL: University of Chicago Press.

Greenwood, P. W., Karoly, L. A., Everingham, S. S., Houbé, J., Kilburn, M. R., Rydell, C. P., Sanders, M., & Chiesa, J. (2001). Estimating the costs and benefits of early childhood interventions. In B. C. Welsh, D. P. Farrington, & L. W. Sherman (Eds.), *Costs and benefits of preventing crime* (pp. 123–148). Boulder, CO: Westview Press.

Greenwood, P. W., & Turner, S. (2009). An overview of prevention and intervention programs for juvenile offenders. *Victims and Offenders, 4,* 365–374.

Griggs, R. A. (2014). Coverage of the Stanford Prison Experiment in introductory psychology textbooks. *Teaching Psychology, 41,* 195–203.

Griset, P. L. (1991). *Determinate sentencing: The promise and the reality of retributive justice*. Albany: State University of New York Press.

Guerra, N. G. (1997). Intervening to prevent childhood aggression in the inner city. In J. McCord (Ed.), *Violence and childhood in the inner city* (pp. 256–312). Cambridge, UK: Cambridge University Press.

Gunnison, E., & Helfgott, J. B. (2013). *Offender reentry: Beyond crime and punishment*. Boulder, CO: Lynne Rienner

Hagan, J. (2010). *Who are the criminals? The politics of crime policy from the age of Roosevelt to the age of Reagan*. Princeton, NJ: Princeton University Press.

Hairston, C. F. (1988). Family ties during imprisonment: Do they influence future criminal activity? *Federal Probation, 52*(1), 48–52.

Hairston, C. F., Rollin, J., & Jo, H.-j. (2004). *Children, families, and the criminal justice system*. Chicago, IL: University of Chicago Press.

Hakes, J. K., & Sauer, R. D. (2006). An economic evaluation of the *Moneyball* hypothesis. *Journal of Economic Perspectives, 20,* 173–185.

Handwerk, A. M., & Peterson, K. (2012). *Halfway house program overview*. Columbus, OH: Reentry Resource Center.

Hanlon, T. E., Nurco, D. N., Bateman, R. W., & O'Grady, K. E. (1999). The relative effects of three approaches to the parole supervision of narcotic addicts and cocaine abusers. *Prison Journal, 79,* 163–181.

Harland, A. T. (Ed.). (1996). *Choosing correctional interventions that work: Defining the demand and evaluating the supply*. Newbury Park, CA: Sage.

Harris, J. R. (1998). *The nurture assumption: Why children turn out the way they do*. New York, NY: Free Press.

Harrison, P. M., & Beck, A. J. (2006). *Prison and jail inmates at midyear 2005*. Washington, DC: Bureau of Justice Statistics, U.S. Department of Justice.

Hawken, A., & Kleiman, M. (2009). *Managing drug involved probationers with swift and certain sanctions: Evaluating Hawaii's HOPE*. Unpublished evaluation report, Pepperdine University.

Hawkins, G. (1976). *The prison: Policy and practice*. Chicago, IL: University of Chicago Press.

Hawkins, J. D., Smith, B. H., Hill, K. G., Kosterman, R., & Catalano, R. F. (2007). Promoting social development and preventing health and behavior problems during the elementary grades: Results from the Seattle Social Development Project. *Victims and Offenders, 2,* 161–181.

Hawkins, J. D., Smith, B. H., Hill, K. G., Kosterman, R., Catalano, R. F., & Abbott, R. D. (2003). Understanding and preventing crime and violence: Findings from the Seattle Social Development Project. In T. P. Thornberry & M. D. Krohn (Eds.), *Taking stock of delinquency:*

An overview of findings from contemporary longitudinal studies (pp. 255–312). New York, NY: Kluwer Academic/Plenum.

Heckman, J. A. (2011). The economics of inequality: The value of early childhood education. *American Educator,* (Spring), 31–35, 47.

Heckman, J. A. (2012, September 1). Promoting social mobility. *Boston Review*, pp. 1–12. Retrieved from http://www.bostonreview.net/forum/promoting-social-mobility-james-heckman

Heckman, J. A. (2013). *Giving kids a fair chance: A strategy that works*. Cambridge, MA: MIT Press.

Heckman, J. A., Moon, S. H., Pinto, R., Savelyev, P. A., & Yavitz, A. (2010a). Analyzing social experiments as implemented: A reexamination of the evidence from the HighScope Perry Preschool Program. *Quantitative Economics, 1,* 1–46.

Heckman, J. A., Moon, S. H., Pinto, R., Savelyev, P. A., & Yavitz, A. (2010b). The rate of return to the HighScope Perry Preschool Program. *Journal of Public Economics, 94,* 114–128.

Henggeler, S. W. (1997). *Treating serious anti-social behavior in youth: The MST approach*. Washington, DC: Office of Juvenile Justice and Delinquency Prevention, U.S. Department of Justice.

Henggeler, S. W. (1998). *Blueprints for violence prevention: Multisystemic therapy*. Boulder: Institute of Behavioral Science, University of Colorado.

Henggeler, S. W. (1999). Multisystemic therapy: An overview of clinical procedures, outcomes, and policy implications. *Child Psychology and Psychiatry Review, 4,* 2–10.

Henggeler, S. W. (2011). Efficacy studies to large-scale transport: The development and validation of MST programs. *Annual Review of Clinical Psychology, 7, 351–381.*

Henggeler, S. W. (2015). Effective family-based treatments for adolescents with serious anti-social behavior. In J. Morizot & L. Kazemian (Eds.), *The development of criminal and anti-social behavior: Theory, research and practical applications* (pp. 461–475). New York, NY: Springer.

Hepburn, J. R., & Griffin, M. L. (1998). *Jail recidivism in Maricopa County: A report submitted to the Maricopa County Sheriff's Office*. Tempe: Arizona State University.

Herberman, E. J., & Bonczar, T. P. (2014). *Probation and parole in the United States, 2013.* Washington, DC: Bureau of Justice Statistics, U.S. Department of Justice.

Hickey, J. E., & Scharf, P. L. (1980). *Toward a just correctional system*. San Francisco, CA: Jossey-Bass.

Hirschi, T. (1969). *Causes of delinquency.* Berkeley: University of California Press.

Holzer, H. J., Raphael, S., & Stoll, M. A. (2007). The effect of an applicant's criminal history on employer hiring decisions and screening practices: Evidence from Los Angeles. In S. Bushway, M. A. Stoll, & D. F. Weiman (Eds.), *Barriers to reentry? The labor market for released prisoners in post-industrial America* (pp. 117–150). New York, NY: Russell Sage.

Howell, J. C. (2003). *Preventing and reducing juvenile delinquency: A comprehensive framework*. Thousand Oaks, CA: Sage.

Huizinga, D., Weiher, A. W., Espiritu, R., & Esbensen, F. (2003). Delinquency and crime: Some highlights from the Denver Youth Survey. In T. P. Thornberry & M. D. Krohn (Eds.), *Taking stock of delinquency: An overview of findings from contemporary longitudinal studies* (pp. 47–91). New York, NY: Kluwer Academic/Plenum.

Hunt, K. S., & Peterson, A. (2014). *Recidivism among offenders receiving retroactive sentence reductions: The 2007 crack cocaine amendment*. Washington, DC: United States Sentencing Commission.

Hyatt, J. M., & Barnes, G. C. (2014). An experimental evaluation of the impact of intensive supervision on the recidivism of high-risk probationers. *Crime and Delinquency*. Advance online publication.

Inciardi, J. A., Martin, S. S., & Butzin, C. A. (2004). Five-year outcomes of therapeutic community treatment of drug-involved offenders after release from prison. *Crime and Delinquency, 50,* 88–107.

Inciardi, J. A., Martin, S. S., Butzin, C. A., Hooper, R. M., & Harrison, L. D. (1997). An effective model of prison-based treatment for drug-involved offenders. *Journal of Drug Issues, 27,* 261–278.

Irwin, J. (2005). *The warehouse prison: Disposal of the new dangerous class*. Los Angeles, CA: Roxbury.

Irwin, J., & Austin, J. (1994). *It's about time: America's imprisonment binge.* Belmont, CA: Wadsworth.

Jackson, D., & Davis, S. (2015, July 17). Obama promotes his criminal justice plans: President visits federal prison as he takes steps for overhaul of system, with bipartisan support. *Cincinnati Enquirer* (*USA Today Section*), p. 2B.

Jacobs, J. B. (2015). *The eternal criminal record.* Cambridge, MA: Harvard University Press.

Jacobson, M. (2005). *Downsizing prisons: How to reduce crime and end mass incarceration.* New York: New York University Press.

Jacoby, J. E., & Cullen, F. T. (1998). The structure of punishment norms: Applying the Rossi-Berk model. *Journal of Criminal Law and Criminology, 89,* 245–312.

Jeong, S., McGarrell, E. F., & Hipple, N. K. (2012). Long-term impact of family group conferences on re-offending: The Indianapolis Restorative Justice Experiment. *Journal of Experimental Criminology, 8,* 369–385.

Johnson, B. D. (2011). Sentencing. In M. Tonry (Ed.), *The Oxford handbook of crime and criminal justice* (pp. 696–729). New York, NY: Oxford University Press.

Johnson, D. T. (2007). Crime and punishment in contemporary Japan. In M. Tonry (Ed.), *Crime, punishment, and politics in comparative perspective* (Crime and Justice: A Review of Research, Vol. 36, pp. 371–424). Chicago, IL: University of Chicago Press.

Johnson, R. (2014). Kant's moral philosophy. In E. N. Zalta (Ed.), *The Stanford encyclopedia of philosophy* (Electronic edition, Summer 2014). Retrieved from http://plato.stanford.edu/archives/sum2014/entries/kant-moral/

Johnstone, J. G. (2014). *Restorative justice in prisons: Methods, models, and effectiveness.* Strasburg, France: European Committee on Crime Problems, Council of Europe.

Jolliffe, D., & Farrington, D. P. (2007). *A rapid assessment of the impact of mentoring on re-offending: A summary.* London, UK: Home Office.

Jonson, C. L. (2010). *The impact of imprisonment on reoffending: A meta-analysis.* Unpublished doctoral dissertation, University of Cincinnati.

Jonson, C. L. (2013). The effects of imprisonment. In F. T. Cullen, & P. Wilcox (Eds.), *The Oxford hand-book of criminological theory* (pp. 672–690). New York, NY: Oxford University Press.

Jonson, C. L., & Cullen, F. T. (2011). Multisystemic therapy. In B. S. Fisher & S. P. Lab (Eds.), *Encyclopedia of victimology and crime prevention* (pp. 571–574). Thousand Oaks, CA: Sage.

Jonson, C. L., & Cullen, F. T. (2015). Prisoner reentry programs. In M. Tonry (Ed.), *Crime and justice: A review of research* (Vol. 44, pp. 517–575). Chicago, IL: University of Chicago Press.

Jonson, C. L., Cullen, F. T., & Lux, J. L. (2013). Creating ideological space: Why public support for rehabilitation matters. In L. Craig, L. Dixon, & T. Gannon (Eds.), *What works in offender rehabilitation: An evidence-based approach to assessment and treatment* (pp. 50–68). London, UK: Wiley-Blackwell.

Kahneman, D. (2011). *Thinking fast and slow.* New York, NY: Farrar, Straus and Giroux.

Kasich, J. (2014). *Bipartisan Summit: Video message from John Kasich, Governor of Ohio.* Address to the Bipartisan Summit on Criminal Justice Reform, Washington, DC, March 26. Available at https://www.youtube.com/watch?v=CrXe6D8yMl0

Kittrie, N. N. (1971). *The right to be different: Deviance and enforced therapy.* Baltimore, MD: Penguin.

Kleiman, M. A. R. (2009). *When brute force fails: How to have less crime and less punishment.* Princeton, NJ: Princeton University Press.

Kleiman, M. A. R., Kilmer, B., & Fisher, D. T. (2014). Theory and evidence on the swift-certain-fair approach to enforcing conditions of community supervision: A response to Stephanie A. Duriez, Francis T. Cullen, and Sarah M. Manchak. *Federal Probation, 78*(2), 71–74

Kovandzic, T. V., & Vieraitis, L. M. (2006). The effect of county-level prison population growth on crime rates. *Criminology and Public Policy, 5,* 213–244.

Krikorian, G. (2001, August 21). 3 strikes targets less-violent, older offender, study finds. *Los Angeles Times.* Retrieved from http://articles.latimes.com/2001/aug/23/local/me-37482

Krisberg, B. (2006). *Focus: Attitudes of U.S. voters toward prisoner rehabilitation and reentry programs.* Oakland, CA: National Council on Crime and Delinquency.

Krohn, M. D., Lopes, G., & Ward, J. T. (2014). Effects of official intervention on later offending in the Rochester Youth Development Study. In D. P. Farrington & J. Murray (Eds.), *Labeling theory: Empirical tests* (Advances in Criminological Theory, Vol. 17, pp. 179–207). New Brunswick, NJ: Transaction.

Kruttschnitt, C., & Gartner, R. (2005). *Marking time in the Golden State: Women's imprisonment in California.* New York, NY: Cambridge University Press.

Kulig, T. C., Pratt, T. C., & Cullen, F. T. (2015). *Revisiting the Stanford Prison Experiment: A case study in organized skepticism.* Unpublished manuscript, University of Cincinnati.

Langan, P. A., & Levin, D. J. (2002). *Recidivism of prisoners released in 1994.* Washington, DC: Bureau of Justice Statistics, U.S. Department of Justice.

Lappi-Seppala, T. (2007). Penal policies in Scandinavia. In M. Tonry (Ed.), *Crime, punishment, and politics in comparative perspective* (Crime and Justice: A Review of Research, Vol. 36, pp. 217–296). Chicago, IL: University of Chicago Press.

Latessa, E. J., & Allen, H. E. (1982). Halfway houses and parole: A national assessment. *Journal of Criminal Justice, 10,* 153–163.

Latessa, E. J., Cullen, F. T., & Gendreau, P. (2002). Beyond correctional quackery: Professionalism and the possibility of effective treatment. *Federal Probation, 66*(2), 43–49.

Latessa, E. J., & Smith, P. (2011). *Corrections in the community* (5th ed.). Burlington, MA: Anderson.

Latimer, J., Dowden, C., & Muise, D. (2005). The effectiveness of restorative justice practices: A meta-analysis. *Prison Journal, 85,* 127–144.

Lattimore, P. K., Barrick, K., Cowell, A., Dawes, D., Steffey, D., Tueller, S., & Visher, C. A. (2012). *Prisoner reentry services: What worked for SVORI evaluation participants?* (Final Report). Washington, DC: National Institute of Justice.

Lattimore, P. K., Steffey, D. M., & Visher, C. A. (2009). *Prisoner reentry experiences of adult males: Characteristics, service receipts, and outcomes of participants in the SVORI multi-site evaluation.* Research Triangle Park, NC: RTI International.

Lattimore, P. K., & Visher, C. A. (2009). *The multi-site evaluation of SVORI: Summary and synthesis.* Research Triangle Park, NC: RTI International.

Laub, J. H., & Sampson, R. J. (2003). *Shared beginnings, divergent lives: Delinquent boys to age 70.* Cambridge, MA: Harvard University Press.

La Vigne, N. G., Visher, C., & Castro, J. L. (2004). *Chicago prisoners' experiences returning home.* Washington, DC: Urban Institute.

LeBel, T. P., Burnett, R., Maruna, S., & Bushway, S. (2008). The "chicken and the egg" of subjective and social factors in desistance from crime. *European Journal of Criminology, 5,* 131–159.

Lehrer, J. (2010, December 13). The truth wears off: Is there something wrong with the scientific method? *The New Yorker, 86,* 52–57.

LeMarquand, D., & Tremblay, R. E. (2001). Delinquency prevention in schools. In C. R. Hollin (Ed.), *Handbook of offender assessment and treatment* (pp. 237–258). Chichester, UK: Wiley.

Levitt, S. D. (2002). Deterrence. In J. Q. Wilson & J. Petersilia (Eds.), *Crime: Public policies for crime control* (2nd ed., pp. 425–450). Oakland, CA: ICS Press.

Levrant, S., Cullen, F. T., Fulton, B., & Wozniak, J. F. (1999). Reconsidering restorative justice: The corruption of benevolence revisited? *Crime and Delinquency, 45,* 3–27.

Lewis, M. (2003). *Moneyball: The art of winning an unfair game.* New York, NY: W. W. Norton.

Lewis, M. (2010). *The big short: Inside the doomsday machine.* New York, NY: W. W. Norton.

Lieberman, A. M., Kirk, D. S., & Kim, K. (2014). Labeling effects of first juvenile arrests: Secondary deviance and secondary sanctioning. *Criminology, 52,* 345–370.

Liedka, R. V., Piehl, A. M., & Useem, B. (2006). The crime-control effect of incarceration: Does scale matter? *Criminology and Public Policy, 5,* 245–276.

Lilly, J. R., Cullen, F. T., & Ball, R. A. (2015). *Criminological theory: Context and consequences* (6th ed.). Thousand Oaks, CA: Sage.

Lindquist, C. H., Lattimore, P. K., Barrick, K., & Visher, C. A. (2009). *Prisoner reentry experiences of adult females: Characteristics, service receipt, and outcomes of participants in the SVORI multi-site evaluation.* Research Triangle Park, NC: RTI International.

Link, B. G., Cullen, F. T., Struening, E., Shrout, P. E., & Dohrenwend, B. P. (1989). A modified labeling theory approach to mental disorders: An empirical assessment. *American Sociological Review, 54,* 400–423.

Link, B. G., & Phelan, J. C. (2001). Conceptualizing stigma. In K. S. Cook & J. Hagan (Eds.), *Annual review of sociology* (Vol. 27, pp. 363–385). Palo Alto, CA: Annual Reviews.

Lipsey, M. W. (1992). Juvenile delinquent treatment: A meta-analytic treatment inquiry into the variability of effects. In T. D. Cook, H. Cooper, D. S. Cordray, H. Hartmann, L. V. Hedges, R. J. Light, T. A. Lewis, & F. Mosteller (Eds.), *Meta-analysis for explanation: A casebook* (pp. 83–127). New York, NY: Russell Sage.

Lipsey, M. W. (1995). What do we learn from 400 research studies on the effectiveness of treatment with juvenile delinquency? In J. McGuire (Ed.), *What works: Reducing reoffending* (pp. 63–78). West Sussex, UK: Wiley.

Lipsey, M. W. (1999a). Can intervention rehabilitate serious delinquents? *Annals of the American Academy of Political and Social Science, 564,* 142–166.

Lipsey, M. W. (1999b). Can rehabilitative programs reduce the recidivism of juvenile offenders? An inquiry into the effectiveness of practical programs. *Virginia Journal of Social Policy and Law, 6,* 611–641.

Lipsey, M. W. (2009). The primary factors that characterize effective interventions with juvenile offenders: A meta-analytic overview. *Victims and Offenders, 4,* 124–147.

Lipsey, M. W., & Cullen, F. T. (2007). The effectiveness of correctional rehabilitation: A review of systematic reviews. *Annual Review of Law and Social Sciences, 3,* 297–320.

Lipsey, M. W., & Derzon, J. H. (1998). Predictors of violent or serious delinquency in adolescence and early adulthood: A synthesis of longitudinal research. In R. Loeber & D. P. Farrington (Eds.), *Serious and violent juvenile offenders: Risk factors and successful interventions* (pp. 86–105). Thousand Oaks, CA: Sage.

Lipsey, M. W., & Wilson, D. B. (1998). Effective intervention for serious juvenile offenders: A synthesis

of research. In R. Loeber & D. P. Farrington (Eds.), *Serious and violent juvenile offenders: Risk factors and successful interventions* (pp. 313–336). Thousand Oaks, CA: Sage.

Lipton, D., Martinson, R., & Wilks, J. (1975). *The effectiveness of correctional treatment: A survey of treatment evaluation studies.* New York, NY: Praeger.

Listwan, S. J., Cullen, F. T., & Latessa, E. J. (2006). How to prevent prisoner re-entry programs from failing: Insights from evidence-based corrections. *Federal Probation, 70*(3), 19–25.

Listwan, S. J., Jonson, C. L., Cullen, F. T., & Latessa, E. J. (2008). Cracks in the penal harm movement: Evidence from the field. *Criminology and Public Policy, 7,* 423–465.

Listwan, S. J., Sullivan, C. J., Agnew, R., Cullen, F. T., & Colvin, M. (2013). The pains of imprisonment revisited: The impact of strain on inmate recidivism. *Justice Quarterly, 30,* 144–168.

Littell, J. H. (2005). Lessons from a systematic review of effects of multisystemic therapy. *Children and Youth Services, 27,* 445–463.

Loeber, R., Farrington, D. P., Stouthamer-Loeber, M., Moffitt, T. E., Caspi, A., White, H. R., Wei, E. H., & Beyers, J. M. (2003). The development of male offending: Key findings from fourteen years of the Pittsburgh Youth Study. In T. P. Thornberry & M. D. Krohn (Eds.), *Taking stock of delinquency: An overview of findings from contemporary longitudinal studies* (pp. 93–136). New York, NY: Kluwer Academic/Plenum.

Lösel, F. (1995). The efficacy of correctional treatment: A review and synthesis of meta-evaluations. In J. McGuire (Ed.), *What works: Reducing reoffending* (pp. 79–111). West Sussex, UK: Wiley.

Lösel, F. (2007, September–October). It's never too early and never too late: Towards an integrated science of developmental intervention in criminology. *The Criminologist, 32*(5), 1, 3–9.

Loughran, T. A., Mulvey, E. P., Schubert, C. A., Fagan, J., Piquero, A. R., & Losoya, S. H. (2009). Estimating a dose-response relationship between length of stay and future recidivism in serious juvenile offenders. *Criminology, 47,* 699–740.

Lowenkamp, C. T., Flores, A. W., Holsinger, A. M., Makarios, M. D., & Latessa, E. J. (2010).

Intensive supervision probation? Does program philosophy and the principles of effective intervention matter? *Journal of Criminal Justice, 38,* 368–375.

Lowenkamp, C. T., & Latessa, E. J. (2002). *Evaluation of Ohio's community based correctional facilities and halfway house programs* (Technical Report). Cincinnati, OH: Center for Criminal Justice Research, University of Cincinnati.

Lowenkamp, C. T., Latessa, E. J., & Smith, P. (2006). Does correctional program quality really matter? The importance of adhering to the principles of effective intervention. *Criminology and Public Policy, 5,* 201–220.

Lux, J. L. (2010). *The effectiveness of multisystemic therapy: A review of the evidence.* Unpublished master's demonstration project, University of Cincinnati.

Lynch, J. P., & Sabol, W. J. (2000). Prison use and social control. In J. Horney (Ed.), *Criminal justice 2000: Vol. 3. Policies, processes, and decisions of the criminal justice system* (pp. 7–44). Washington, DC: National Institute of Justice, U.S. Department of Justice.

Lynch, M. J. (2007). *Big prisons, big dreams: Crime and the failure of America's penal system.* New Brunswick, NJ: Rutgers University Press.

MacKenzie, D. L. (2000). Evidence-based corrections: Identifying what works. *Crime and Delinquency, 46,* 457–471.

MacKenzie, D. L. (2006). *What works in corrections: Reducing the criminal activities of offenders and delinquents.* New York, NY: Cambridge University Press.

MacKenzie, D. L., Browning, K., Skroban, S. B., & Smith, D. A. (1999). The impact of probation on the criminal activities of offenders. *Journal of Research in Crime and Delinquency, 36,* 423–453.

Manchak, S. M., & Cullen, F. T. (2014). When troubled offenders come home: Removing barriers to reentry for offenders with mental illness. In M. S. Crow & J. O. Smykla (Eds.), *Offender reentry: Rethinking criminology and criminal justice* (pp. 251–269). Burlington, MA: Jones and Bartlett Learning.

Martin, S. S., Butzin, C. A., Saum, C. A., & Inciardi. J. A. (1999). Three-year outcomes of therapeutic community treatment for drug-involved offenders in

Delaware: From prison to work release to aftercare. *Prison Journal, 79,* 294–320.

Martinson, R. (1974). What works? Questions and answers about prison reform. *The Public Interest, 35*(Spring), 22–54.

Martinson, R. (1979). New findings, new views: A note of caution regarding sentencing reform. *Hofstra Law Review, 7*(2), 243–258.

Maruna, S. (2001). *Making good: How ex-convicts reform and rebuild their lives.* Washington, DC: American Psychological Association.

Matsueda, R. L., & Kreager, D. A. (2006). Deterring delinquents: A rational choice model of theft and violence. *American Sociological Review, 71,* 95–122.

Matthews, R. (2009, November). *The myth of punitiveness revisited.* Paper presented at the annual meeting of the American Society of Criminology, Philadelphia.

Matthews, R. (2014). *Realist criminology.* Houndmills, UK: Palgrave Macmillan.

Matthews, S. K., & Agnew, R. (2008). Extending deterrence theory: Do delinquent peers condition the relationship between perceptions of getting caught and offending? *Journal of Research in Crime and Delinquency, 45,* 91–118.

Matza, D. (1964). *Delinquency and drift.* New York, NY: John Wiley.

Mauer, M., & Ghandnoosh, N. (2013, December 20). Can we wait 88 years to end mass incarceration? *Huffington Post.* Retrieved from http://www .huffingtonpost.com/marc-mauer/88-years -mass-incarceration_b_4474132.html

McAlinden, A.-M. (2008). Are there no limits to restorative justice? The case of child sex abuse. In D. Sullivan & L. Tifft (Eds.), *Handbook of restorative justice: A global perspective* (pp. 299–310). New York, NY: Routledge.

McCold, P. (2008). The recent history of restorative justice: Mediation, circles, and conferencing. In D. Sullivan & L. Tifft (Eds.), *Handbook of restorative justice: A global perspective* (pp. 23–51). New York, NY: Routledge.

McCoy, C. (2011). Prosecution. In M. Tonry (Ed.), *The Oxford handbook of crime and criminal justice* (pp. 664–695). New York, NY: Oxford University Press.

McDonald, D., & Jonson, C. L. (2013). Easing the transition from prison to the community: An evaluation of a Second Chance Act Mentoring Grant Program. *Contemporary Journal of Anthropology and Sociology, 3,* 184–202.

McGarrell, E. F., & Hipple, N. K. (2007). Family group conferencing and re-offending among first-time juvenile offenders: The Indianapolis Experiment. *Justice Quarterly, 24,* 221–246.

McGuire, J. (2002). Criminal sanctions versus psychologically-based interventions with offenders: A comparative empirical analysis. *Psychology, Crime and Law, 8,* 183–208.

McGuire, J. (2013). "What works" to reduce re-offending: 18 years on. In L. A. Craig, L. Dixon, & T. A. Gannon (Eds.), *What works in offender rehabilitation: An evidence-based approach to assessment and treatment* (pp. 20–49). Chichester, UK: Wiley-Blackwell.

Meade, B., Steiner, B., Makarios, M., & Travis, L. (2013). Estimating a dose-response relationship between time served in prison and recidivism. *Journal of Research in Crime and Delinquency, 50,* 525–550.

Mears, D. P., & Cochran, J. C. (2015). *Prisoner reentry in the era of mass incarceration.* Thousand Oaks, CA: Sage.

Mears, D. P., Cochran, J. C., & Cullen, F. T. (2015). Incarceration heterogeneity and its implications for assessing the effectiveness of imprisonment on recidivism. *Criminal Justice Policy Review, 26,* 691–712.

Mears, D. P., Moore, G. E., Travis, J., & Winterfield, L. (2003). *Improving the link between research and drug treatment in correctional settings.* Washington, DC: The Urban Institute.

Menninger, K. (1968). *The crime of punishment.* New York, NY: Penguin.

Merton, R. K. (1972). Insiders and outsiders: A chapter in the sociology of knowledge. *American Journal of Sociology, 78,* 9–47.

Merton, R. K. (1973). *The sociology of science: Theoretical and empirical investigations* (N. K. Storer, Ed.). Chicago, IL: University of Chicago Press.

Metraux, S., & Culhane, D. P. (2004). Homeless shelter use and reincarceration following prison release: Assessing the risk. *Criminology and Public Policy, 3,* 201–222.

Miller, J. G. (1991). Last one over the wall: The Massachusetts experiment in closing reform schools. Columbus: Ohio State University Press.

Mills, L. G., Barocas, B., & Ariel, B. (2013). The next generation of court-mandated domestic violence treatment: A comparison study of batterer intervention and restorative justice programs. *Journal of Experimental Criminology, 9,* 65–90.

Mills, N. (1997). *The triumph of meanness: America's war against its better self.* Boston, MA: Houghton Mifflin.

Minton, T. D., & Golinelli, D. (2014). *Jail inmates at midyear 2013: Statistical tables.* Washington, DC: Bureau of Justice Statistics, U.S. Department of Justice.

Minton, T. D., & Zeng, Z. (2015). *Jail inmates at midyear 2014.* Washington, DC: Bureau of Justice Statistics, U.S. Department of Justice.

Mischel, W. (2014). *The marshmallow test: Mastering self-control.* Boston, MA: Little, Brown.

Moffitt, T. E. (1993). Adolescence-limited and life-course-persistent antisocial behavior: A developmental taxonomy. *Psychological Review, 100,* 674–701.

Moffitt, T. E. (2006). A review of research on the taxonomy of life-course persistent versus adolescence-limited antisocial behavior. In F. T. Cullen, J. P. Wright, & K. R. Blevins (Eds.), *Taking stock: The status of criminological theory* (Advances in Criminological Theory, Vol. 15, pp. 277–311). New Brunswick, NJ: Transaction.

Monachesi, E. (1972). Cesare Beccaria. In H. Mannheim (Ed.), *Pioneers in criminology* (2nd ed., pp. 36–50). Montclair, NJ: Patterson Smith.

Moon, M. M., Cullen, F. T., & Wright, J. P. (2003). It takes a village: Public willingness to help wayward youths. *Youth Violence and Juvenile Justice, 1,* 32–45.

Moon, M. M., Sundt, J. L., Cullen, F. T., & Wright, J. P. (2000). Is child saving dead? Public support for juvenile rehabilitation. *Crime and Delinquency, 46,* 38–60.

Morizot, J., & Kazemian, L. (Eds.). (2015). *The development of criminal and antisocial behavior: Theory, research and practical applications.* New York, NY: Springer.

Morris, B. (2014, July 24). Billion-dollar Billy Beane. *FiveThirtyEight.* Retrieved from http://fivethirty eight.com/features/billion-dollar-billy-beane/

Morris, N. (1974). *The future of imprisonment.* Chicago, IL: University of Chicago Press.

Morris, N., & Tonry, M. (1990). *Between prison and probation: Intermediate punishments in a rational sentencing system*. New York, NY: Oxford University Press.

Moskowitz, T. J., & Wertheim, L. J. (2011). *Scorecasting: The hidden influences behind how sports are played and games are won*. New York, NY: Crown Archetype.

Murray, C. (1984). *Losing ground: American social policy 1950–1980*. New York, NY: Basic Books.

Murray, J., & Farrington, D. P. (2010). Risk factors for conduct disorder and delinquency: Key findings from longitudinal studies. *Canadian Journal of Psychiatry, 55*, 633–642.

Mytton, J. A., DiGuiseppi, C., Gough, D. A., Taylor, R. S., & Logan, S. (2002). School-based violence prevention programs: Systematic review of secondary prevention tools. *Archives of Pediatric and Adolescent Medicine, 156*, 752–762.

Nagin, D. S. (1998). Criminal deterrence research at the outset of the twenty-first century. In M. Tonry (Ed.), *Crime and justice: A review of research* (Vol. 23, pp. 1–42). Chicago. IL: University of Chicago Press.

Nagin, D. S. (2013). Deterrence in the twenty-first century. In M. Tonry (Ed.), *Crime and justice in America, 1975–2025* (Crime and Justice: A Review of Research, Vol. 42, pp. 199–263). Chicago, IL: University of Chicago Press.

Nagin, D. S., Cullen, F. T., & Jonson, C. L. (2009). Imprisonment and reoffending. In M. Tonry (Ed.), *Crime and justice: A review of research* (Vol. 38, pp. 115–200). Chicago, IL: University of Chicago Press.

Nagin, D. S., Piquero, A. R., Scott, E. S., & Steinberg, L. (2006). Public preferences for rehabilitation versus incarceration for juvenile offenders: Evidence from a contingent valuation. *Criminology and Public Policy, 5*, 627–651.

Nagin, D. S., & Tremblay, R. E. (2005). What has been learned from group-based trajectory modeling? Examples from physical aggression and other problem behaviors. *Annals of the American Academy of Political and Social Science, 602*, 82–117.

Najaka, S. S., Gottfredson, D. C., & Wilson, D. B. (2001). A meta-analytic inquiry into the relationship between selected risk factors and problem behavior. *Prevention Science, 2*, 257–271.

National Conference of Commissioners on Uniform State Laws. (2010). *Uniform Collateral Consequences of Conviction Act*. Chicago, IL: Author.

National Institute of Justice. (2011). *About the serious and violent offender reentry initiative*. Washington DC: Author.

Ndrecka, M. (2014). *The impact of reentry programs on recidivism: A meta-analysis*. Unpublished doctoral dissertation, University of Cincinnati.

Newburn, T. (2007). "Tough on crime": Penal policy in England and Wales. In M. Tonry (Ed.), *Crime, punishment, and politics in comparative perspective* (Crime and Justice: A Review of Research, Vol. 36, pp. 425–470). Chicago, IL: University of Chicago Press.

Newman, G. (1983). *Just and painful: A case for corporal punishment of criminals*. New York, NY: Harrow and Heston/Macmillan.

Nieuwbeerta, P., Nagin, D. S., & Blokland, A. A. J. (2009). The relationship between first imprisonment and criminal career development: A matched samples comparison. *Journal of Quantitative Criminology, 25*, 227–257.

O'Connell, D., Visher, C. A., Brent, J., Bacon, G., & Hines K. (2013, November 21). *Utilizing swift and certain sanctions in probation: Final results from Delaware's Decide Your Time program*. Paper presented at the annual meeting of the American Society of Criminology, Atlanta, GA.

O'Connell, D., Visher, C. A., Martin, S., Parker, L., & Brent, J. (2011). Decide your time: Testing deterrence theory's certainty and celerity effect on substance-using probationers. *Journal of Criminal Justice, 39*, 261–267.

Ogloff, J. R. P., & Davis, M. R. (2004). Advances in offender assessment and rehabilitation: Contributions of the risk-needs-responsivity approach. *Psychology, Crime and Law, 10*, 229–242.

Olds, D. L. (with Hill, P. L., Mihalic, S. F., & O'Brien, R. A.). (1998). *Prenatal and infancy home visitation by nurses: Blueprints for violence prevention* (Book 7). Boulder: Institute of Behavioral Science, University of Colorado.

Olds, D. L. (2007). Preventing crime with prenatal and infancy support of parents: The nurse-family partnership. *Victims and Offenders, 2*, 205–225.

Olds, D. L., Hill, P., & Rumsey, E. (1998). *Prenatal and early childhood nurse home visitation.* Washington, DC: Office of Juvenile Justice and Delinquency Prevention, U.S. Department of Justice.

Olds, D. L., Kitzman, H., Knudtson, M. D., Anson, E., Smith, J. A., & Cole, R. (2014). Effect of home visiting by nurses on maternal and child mortality: Results of a 2-decade follow-up of a randomized clinical trial. *JAMA Pediatrics, 168,* 800–806.

Omori, M. K., & Turner, S. F. (2015). Assessing the cost of electronically monitoring high-risk sex offenders. *Crime and Delinquency, 61,* 873–894,

Onedera, J. D. (2006). Functional family therapy: An interview with Dr. James Alexander. *The Family Journal, 14,* 306–311.

Ouimet, M. (2002). Explaining the Canadian and American crime "drop" in the 1990s. *Canadian Journal of Criminology, 44,* 33–50.

Owens, M. (2009). More time, less crime? Estimating the incapacitative effects of sentence enhancements. *Journal of Law and Economics, 52,* 551–579.

Padgett, K. G., Bales, W. D., & Blomberg, T. G. (2006). Under surveillance: An empirical test of the effectiveness and consequences of electronic monitoring. *Criminology and Public Policy, 5,* 61–92.

Page, J. (2011). *The toughest beat: Politics, punishment, and the prison officers in California.* New York, NY: Oxford University Press.

Pager, D. (2007). *Marked: Race, crime, and finding work in an era of mass incarceration.* Chicago, IL: University of Chicago Press.

Pager, D., Western, B., & Bonikowski, B. (2009). Discrimination in a low-wage labor market: A field experiment. *American Sociological Review, 74,* 777–799.

Palmer, T. (1975). Martinson revisited. *Journal of Research in Crime and Delinquency, 12,* 133–152.

Palmer, T. (1978). *Correctional intervention and research.* Lexington, MA: Lexington Books.

Palmer, T. (1992). *The re-emergence of correctional intervention.* Newbury Park, CA: Sage.

Palmer, T. (1994). *A profile of correctional effectiveness and new directions for research.* Albany: State University of New York Press.

Palmer, T. (2002). *Individualized intervention with young multiple offenders.* New York, NY: Routledge.

Paparozzi, M. A., & Gendreau, P. (2005). An intensive supervision program that worked: Service delivery, professional orientation, and organizational supportiveness. *Prison Journal, 85,* 445–466.

Parks, G. (1998). *The High/Scope Perry Preschool Project.* Washington, DC: Office of Juvenile Justice and Delinquency Prevention, U.S. Department of Justice.

Paternoster, R. (1987). The deterrence effect of the perceived certainty and severity of punishment: A review of the evidence and issues. *Justice Quarterly, 4,* 173–217.

Paternoster, R. (2010). How much do we really know about criminal deterrence? *Journal of Criminal Law and Criminology, 100,* 763–823.

Paternoster, R., & Bachman, R. (2013). Perceptual deterrence theory. In F. T. Cullen & P. Wilcox (Eds.), *The Oxford handbook of criminological theory* (pp. 649–671). New York, NY: Oxford University Press.

Pearsall, B. (2014, March). Replicating HOPE: Can others do as well as Hawaii? *National Institute of Justice Journal, 273,* 1–5.

Petersilia, J. (1992). California's prison policy: Causes, costs, and consequences. *Prison Journal, 72,* 8–36.

Petersilia, J. (1999). Parole and prisoner reentry in the United States. In M. Tonry & J. Petersilia (Eds.), *Prisons* (Crime and Social Justice: A Review of Research, Vol. 26, pp. 479–529). Chicago, IL: University of Chicago Press.

Petersilia, J. (2003). *When prisoners come home: Parole and prisoner reentry.* New York, NY: Oxford University Press.

Petersilia, J. (2008). California's correctional paradox of excess and deprivation. In M. Tonry (Ed.), *Crime and justice: A review of research* (Vol. 37, pp. 207–278). Chicago, IL: University of Chicago Press.

Petersilia, J. (2009). Transformation in prisoner reentry: What a difference a decade makes. In *When prisoners come home: Parole and prisoner reentry* (pp. 249–264). New York, NY: Oxford University Press. ("New Afterword" added to the paperback edition issued in 2009)

Petersilia, J. (2011). Parole and prisoner re-entry. In M. Tonry (Ed.), *The Oxford handbook of crime and criminal justice* (pp. 925–952). New York, NY: Oxford University Press.

Petersilia, J., & Cullen, F. T. (2015). Liberal but not stupid: Meeting the promise of downsizing prisons. *Stanford Journal of Criminal Law and Policy, 2,* 1–43.

Petersilia, J., & Turner, S. (1993). Intensive probation and parole. In M. Tonry (Ed.), *Crime and justice: A review of research* (Vol. 17, pp. 281–335). Chicago, IL: University of Chicago Press.

Petrosino, A., Derzon, J., & Lavenberg, J. (2009). The role of the family in crime and delinquency: Evidence from prior quantitative reviews. *Southwestern Journal of Criminal Justice, 6,* 108–132.

Petrosino, A., Turpin-Petrosino, C., & Guckenburg, S. (2010). *Formal system processing of juveniles: Effects on delinquency.* Oslo, Norway: The Campbell Collaboration.

Pew Charitable Trusts. (2008). *One in 100: Behind bars in America 2008.* Washington, DC: Author.

Pew Charitable Trusts. (2009). *One in 31: The long reach of American corrections.* Washington, DC: Author.

Pew Charitable Trusts. (2014a). *Max out: The rise in prison inmates released without supervision.* Washington, DC: Author.

Pew Charitable Trusts. (2014b). *Mississippi's 2014 corrections and criminal justice reform.* Washington, DC: Author.

Piquero, A. R., Cullen, F. T., Unnever, J. D., Piquero, N. L., & Gordon, J. (2010). Never too late: Public opinion about juvenile rehabilitation. *Punishment and Society, 12,* 187–207.

Piquero, A. R., Farrington, D. P., & Blumstein, A. (2007). *Key issues in criminal career research: New analyses of the Cambridge Study in Delinquent Development.* New York, NY: Cambridge University Press.

Piquero, A. R., Farrington, D. P., Welsh, B. C., Tremblay, R., & Jennings, W. G. (2009). Effects of early family/parent training programs on antisocial behavior and delinquency. *Journal of Experimental Criminology, 5,* 83–120.

Piquero, A. R., Paternoster, R., Pogarsky, G., & Loughran, T. (2011). Elaborating the individual difference component in deterrence theory. *Annual Review of Law and Social Science, 7,* 335–360.

Piquero, A. R., & Steinberg, L. (2010). Public preferences for rehabilitation versus incarceration of juvenile offenders. *Journal of Criminal Justice, 38,* 1–6.

Platt, A. M. (1969). *The child savers: The invention of juvenile delinquency.* Chicago, IL: University of Chicago Press.

Pogarsky, G. (2009). Deterrence and decision-making: Research questions and theoretical refinements. In M. D. Krohn, A. J. Lizotte, & G. P. Hall (Eds.), *Handbook on crime and deviance* (pp. 241–258). New York, NY: Springer.

Pogarsky, G. (2010). Perceptual deterrence. In F. T. Cullen & P. Wilcox (Eds.), *Encyclopedia of criminological theory* (pp. 699–702). Thousand Oaks, CA: Sage.

Pogarsky, G., Kim, K., & Paternoster, R. (2005). Perceptual change in the National Youth Survey: Lessons for deterrence theory and offender decision-making. *Justice Quarterly, 22,* 1–29.

Pogarsky, G., & Piquero, A. R. (2003). Can punishment encourage offending? Investigating the "resetting" effect. *Journal of Research in Crime and Delinquency, 40,* 95–120.

Pope Francis. (2014, June 13). Letter of Pope Francis to participants in the 19th International Congress of the International Association of Penal Law and of the 3rd Congress of the Latin-American Association of Penal Law and Criminology. *L'Osservatore Romano, 24* (Weekly ed. in English). Retrieved from https://w2.vatican.va/content/francesco/en/letters/2014/documents/papa-francesco_20140530_lettera-diritto-penale-criminologia.html

Porporino, F. J. (2010). Bringing sense and sensitivity to corrections: From programs to "fix" offenders to services to support desistance. In J. Brayford, F. Cowe, & J. Deering (Eds.), *What else works? Creative work with offenders.* London, UK: Willan Publishing.

Pratt, J. (2007). *Penal populism.* London, UK: Routledge.

Pratt, T. C. (2009). *Addicted to incarceration: Corrections policy and the politics of misinformation in the United States.* Thousand Oaks, CA: Sage.

Pratt, T. C., & Cullen, F. T. (2005). Assessing macro-level predictors and theories of crime: A meta-analysis. In M. Tonry (Ed.), *Crime and justice: A review of research* (Vol. 32, pp. 373–450). Chicago, IL: University of Chicago Press.

Pratt, T. C., Cullen, F. T., Blevins, K. R., Daigle, L. E., & Madensen, T. D. (2006). The empirical status of deterrence theory: A meta-analysis. In F. T. Cullen, J. P. Wright, & K. R. Blevins (Eds.), *Taking stock: The status of criminological theory* (Advances in Criminological Theory, Vol. 15, pp. 367–395). New Brunswick, NJ: Transaction.

Presser, L. (2014). The restorative prison. In F. T. Cullen, C. L. Jonson, & M. K. Stohr (Eds.), *The American prison: Imagining a different future* (pp. 19–32). Thousand Oaks, CA: Sage.

Public Opinion Strategies and The Mellman Group. (2012). *Public opinion on sentencing and corrections policy in America*. Washington, DC: Pew Center on the States.

Raphael, S. (2014). The effects of conviction and incarceration on future employment outcomes. In D. P. Farrington & J. Murray (Eds.), *Labeling theory: Empirical tests* (Advances in Criminological Theory, Vol. 17, pp. 237–262). New Brunswick, NJ: Transaction.

Raynor, P., & Robinson, G. (2009). *Rehabilitation, crime and justice* (Rev. & updated ed.). Basingstoke, UK: Palgrave Macmillan.

Redcross, C., Millenky, M., Rudd, T., & Levshin, V. (2012). *More than a job: Final results from the evaluation of the Center for Employment Opportunities (CEO) Transitional Jobs.* Washington, DC: Office of Planning, Research and Evaluation, Administration for Children and Families, U.S. Department of Health and Human Services.

Reicher, S., & Haslam, S. A. (2006). Rethinking the psychology of tyranny: The BBC Prison Study. *British Journal of Social Psychology, 45,* 1–40.

Reiman, J. H. (1984). *The rich get richer and the poor get prison: Ideology, class, and criminal justice* (2nd ed.). New York, NY: John Wiley.

Reitz, K. R. (2011). Sentencing. In J. Q. Wilson & J. Petersilia (Eds.), *Crime and public policy* (pp. 467–498). New York, NY: Oxford University Press.

Renzema, M., & Mayo-Wilson, E. (2005). Can electronic monitoring reduce crime for moderate to high-risk offenders? *Journal of Experimental Criminology, 1,* 215–237.

Reynolds, A. J., Temple, J. A., Ou, S.-R., Arteaga, I. A., & White, B. A. B. (2011). School-based early childhood education and age-28 well-being: Effects by timing, dosage, and subgroups. *Science, 333*(July 15), 360–364.

Rhine, E. E. (Ed.). (1998). *Best practices: Excellence in corrections.* Lanham, MD: American Correctional Association.

Rhine, E E. (2011). The present status and future prospects of parole boards and parole supervision. In J. Petersilia and K. R. Reitz (Eds.), *The Oxford handbook of sentencing and corrections* (pp. 627–656). New York, NY: Oxford University Press.

Rhine, E. E., Mawhorr, T. L., & Parks, E. C. (2006). Implementation: The bane of effective correctional programs. *Criminology and Public Policy, 5,* 347–358.

Rhine, E. E., & Thompson, A. C. (2011). The reentry movement in corrections: Resiliency, fragility, and prospects. *Criminal Law Bulletin, 47,* 177–209.

Ritchie, D. (2011). *Does imprisonment deter? A review of the evidence.* Melbourne, Australia: Sentencing Advisory Council.

Robbins, C. A., Martin, S. S, & Surrat, H. L. (2009). Substance abuse treatment, anticipated maternal roles, and reentry success of drug-involved women prisoners. *Crime and Delinquency, 55,* 388–411.

Robins, L. N. (1966). *Deviant children grown up.* Baltimore, MD: Williams & Wilkins.

Robins, L. N. (1978). Sturdy childhood predictors of adult antisocial behaviour: Replications from longitudinal studies. *Psychological Medicine, 8,* 611–622.

Robinson, C., Lowenkamp, C. T., Holsinger, A. M., Benshoten, S., Alexander, M., & Oleson, J. C. (2012). A random study of Staff Training Aimed at Reducing Re-arrest (STARR): Using core correctional practices in probation interaction. *Journal of Crime and Justice, 35,* 167–188.

Rodriguez, N. (2005). Restorative justice, communities, and delinquency: Whom do we reintegrate? *Justice Quarterly, 4,* 103–130.

Rose, D. R., & Clear, T. R. (1998). Incarceration, social capital, and crime: Examining the unintended consequences of incarceration. *Criminology, 36,* 441–479.

Rosenfeld, R. (2009). Homicide and serious assaults. In M. Tonry (Ed.), *The Oxford handbook of crime and public policy* (pp. 25–50). New York, NY: Oxford University Press.

Rosenhan, D. L. (1973). Being sane in insane places. *Science, 179*(January 19), 250–258.

Ross, R. R. (1995). The reasoning and rehabilitation program for high-risk probationers and prisoners. In R. R. Ross, D. H. Antonowicz, & G. K. Dhaliwal (Eds.), *Going straight: Effective delinquency prevention and offender rehabilitation* (pp. 195–222). Ottawa, ON, Canada: Air Training and Publications.

Ross, R. R., & Fabiano, E. A. 1985. *Time to think: A cognitive model of delinquency prevention and offender rehabilitation.* Johnson City, TN: Institute of Social Sciences and Arts.

Rossi, P. H., Waite, E., Bose, C. E., & Berk, R. E. (1974). The seriousness of crimes: Normative structure and individual differences. *American Sociological Review, 39,* 224–237.

Rothman, D. J. (1971). *The discovery of the asylum: Social order and disorder in the new republic.* Boston, MA: Little, Brown.

Rothman, D. J. (1980). *Conscience and convenience: The asylum and its alternatives in Progressive America.* Boston, MA: Little, Brown.

Rothman, D. J. (2002). *Conscience and convenience: The asylum and its alternatives in Progressive America* (Rev. ed.). New York, NY: Aldine de Gruyter.

Rukus, J., & Lane, J. (2014). Unmet need: A survey of state resources at the moment of reentry. In M. S. Crow & J. O. Smykla (Eds.), *Offender reentry: Rethinking criminology and criminal justice* (pp. 155–180). Burlington, MA: Jones and Bartlett Learning.

Rydberg, J., & Clark, K. (2015). *Does the effect of incarceration length on parole failure vary across offense types? A dose-response analysis.* Unpublished manuscript, University of Massachusetts Lowell.

Sabol, W. J., & Lynch, J. P. (1997). *Crime policy report: Did getting tough on crime pay?* Washington, DC: Urban Institute.

Sabol, W. J., West, H. C., & Cooper, M. (2009). *Prisoners in 2008.* Washington, DC: Bureau of Justice Statistics, U.S. Department of Justice.

Sacks, S., Sacks, J. Y., & Stommel, J. (2003). Modified therapeutic communities for inmates with mental illness and chemical abuse disorders. *Corrections Today, 65*(6), 90–99.

Sampson, R. J. (2012). *Great American city: Chicago and the enduring neighborhood effect.* Chicago, IL: University of Chicago Press.

Sampson, R. J., & Laub, J. H. (1993). *Crime in the making: Pathways and turning points through life.* Cambridge, MA: Harvard University Press.

Sampson, R. J., & Laub, J. H. (2005). A life-course view of the development of crime. *Annals of the American Academy of Political and Social Science, 602,* 12–45.

Scally, C. P. (2005). Housing ex-offenders. *Shelterforce Online, 139.* Retrieved from http://www.nhi .org/online/issues/139/exoffenders.html

Schaefer, L., Cullen, F. T., & Eck, J. E. (2016). *Environmental corrections: A new paradigm for supervising offenders in the community.* Thousand Oaks, CA: Sage.

Schindler, H. S., & Yoshikawa, H. (2012). Preventing crime through intervention in the preschool years. In B. C. Welsh & D. P. Farrington (Eds.), *The Oxford handbook of crime prevention* (pp. 70–88). New York, NY: Oxford University Press.

Schriro, D. (2000). *Correcting corrections: Missouri's Parallel Universe* (Sentencing and Corrections: Issues for the 21st Century—Paper from the Executive Sessions on Sentencing and Corrections, No. 8). Washington, DC: Office of Justice Programs, U.S. Department of Justice.

Schriro, D. (2009). Getting ready: How Arizona has created a "Parallel Universe" for inmates. *NIJ Journal, 263,* 1–9.

Schriro, D., & Clements, T. (2001, April). Missouri's Parallel Universe: A blueprint for effective prison management. *Corrections Today,* pp. 140–143, 152.

Schwarz, A. (2004). *The numbers game: Baseball's lifelong fascination with statistics.* New York, NY: Thomas Dunne Books.

Schwarzenegger, A. (2010). Governor Schwarzenegger delivers 2010 State of the State Address. Sacramento, CA: Office of the Governor. Retrieved from http://gov.ca.gov/speech/14118/

Schweinhart, L. J. (2007). Crime prevention by the High/Scope Perry Preschool Program. *Victims and Offenders, 2,* 141–160.

Seiter, R. P., & Kadela, K. R. (2003). Prisoner reentry: What works, what does not, and what is promising. *Crime and Delinquency, 49,* 360–388.

Shapland, J., Atkinson, A., Atkinson, H., Dignan, J., Edwards, L., Hibbert, J., Howes, M., Johnston, J., Robinson, G., & Sorsby, A. (2008). *Does restorative justice affect reconviction? The fourth report from the evaluation of three schemes.* London, UK: Ministry of Justice.

Shaw, C. R. (1966). *The jack-roller: A delinquent boy's own story.* Chicago, IL: University of Chicago Press. (Original work published in 1930)

Shaw, C. R., & McKay, H. D. (1972). *Juvenile delinquency and urban areas* (Rev. ed.). Chicago, IL: University of Chicago Press.

Sherman, L. W. (1993). Defiance, deterrence, and irrelevance: A theory of the criminal sanction. *Journal of Research in Crime and Delinquency, 30,* 445–473.

Sherman, L. W. (1998). *Evidence-based policing.* Washington, DC: Police Foundation.

Sherman, L. W., & Strang, H. (2007). *Restorative justice: The evidence.* London, UK: Smith Institute.

Sherman, L. W., Strang, H., Mayo-Wilson, E., Woods, D. J., & Ariel, B. (2015). Are restorative justice conferences effective in reducing repeat offending? Findings from a Campbell Systematic Review. *Journal of Quantitative Criminology, 31,* 1–24.

Simon, J. (1993). *Poor discipline: Parole and the social control of the underclass, 1890–1990.* Chicago, IL: University of Chicago Press.

Simon, J. (2007). *Governing through crime: How the war on crime transformed American democracy and created a culture of fear.* New York, NY: Oxford University Press.

Simon, J. (2014). *Mass incarceration on trial: A remarkable court decision and the future of prisons in America.* New York, NY: The New Press.

Sinclair, U. (1960). *The jungle.* New York, NY: Signet. (Original work published in 1906)

Singer, R. B. (1979). *Just deserts: Sentencing based on equality and desert.* Cambridge, MA: Ballinger.

Skardhamar, T., & Savolainen, J. (2014). Changes in criminal offending around the time of job entry: A study of employment and desistance. *Criminology, 52,* 263–291.

Skardhamar, T., Savolainen, J., Aase, K. N., & Lyngstad, T. H. (2015). Does marriage reduce crime? In M. Tonry (Ed.), *Crime and justice: A review of research* (Vol. 44, pp. 385–446). Chicago, IL: University of Chicago Press.

Skelton, G. (2010). Arnold Schwarzenegger hits the right tone. *Los Angeles Times.* Retrieved from http://articles.latimes.com/2010/jan/07/local/la-me-cap7-2010jan07

Smith, P. (2006). *The effects of incarceration on recidivism: A longitudinal examination of program participation and institutional adjustment in federally sentenced adult male offenders.* Unpublished doctoral dissertation, University of New Brunswick, Canada.

Smith, P. (2013). The psychology of criminal conduct. In F. T. Cullen & P. Wilcox (Eds.), *The Oxford handbook of criminological theory* (pp. 69–88). New York, NY: Oxford University Press.

Smith, P., Cullen, F. T., & Latessa, E. J. (2009). Can 14,737 women be wrong? A meta-analysis of the LSI-R and recidivism for female offenders. *Criminology and Public Policy, 8,* 183–208.

Smith, P., Gendreau, P., & Swartz, K. (2009). Validating the principles of effective intervention: A systematic review of the contributions of meta-analysis in the field of corrections. *Victims and Offenders, 4,* 148–169.

Smith, P., Goggin, C., & Gendreau, P. (2002). *The effects of prison sentences and intermediate sanctions on recidivism: General effects and individual differences.* Ottawa, ON: Solicitor General of Canada.

Smith, P., Schweitzer, M., Labrecque, R. M., & Latessa, E. J. (2012). Improving probation officers' supervision skills: An evaluation of the EPICS model. *Journal of Crime and Justice, 35,* 189–199.

Snodgrass, G. M., Blokland, A. A. J., Haviland, A., Nieuwbeerta, P., & Nagin, D. S. (2011). Does the time cause the crime? An examination of the relationship between time served and reoffending in the Netherlands. *Criminology, 49,* 1149–1194.

Snodgrass, J. (1982). *The jack-roller at seventy.* Lexington, MA: Lexington Books.

Spector, M., & Kitsuse, J. I. (1977). *Constructing social problems.* Menlo Park, CA: Cummings Publishing Company.

Spelman, W. (2000a). The limited importance of prison expansion. In A. Blumstein & J. Wallman (Eds.), *The crime drop in America* (pp. 97–129). New York, NY: Cambridge University Press.

Spelman, W. (2000b). What recent studies do (and don't) tell us about imprisonment and crime. In M. Tonry (Ed.), *Crime and justice: A review of research* (Vol. 27, pp. 419–494). Chicago, IL: University of Chicago Press.

Spiegler, M. D., & Guevremont, D. C. (1998). *Contemporary behavior therapy* (3rd ed.). Pacific Grove, CA: Brooks/Cole.

Spohn, C., & Holleran, D. (2002). The effect of imprisonment on recidivism rates of felony offenders: A focus on drug offenders. *Criminology, 40,* 329–347.

Stemen, D., & Rengifo, A. F. (2011). Politics and imprisonment: The impact of structured sentencing and determinate sentencing on state incarceration rates, 1978–2004. *Justice Quarterly, 28,* 174–199.

Stouthamer-Loeber, M., Loeber, R., & Thomas, C. (1992). Caretakers seeking help for boys with disruptive and delinquent behavior. *Comprehensive Mental Health Care, 2,* 159–178.

Stouthamer-Loeber, M., Loeber, R., van Kammen, W., & Zhang, Q. (1995). Uninterrupted delinquent careers: The timing of parental help-seeking and juvenile court contact. *Studies on Crime and Crime Prevention, 4,* 236–251.

Strang, H., & Sherman, L. W. (2006). Restorative justice to reduce victimization. In B. C. Welsh & D. P. Farrington (Eds.), *Preventing crime: What works for children, offenders, victims, and places* (pp. 147–160). Dordrecht, The Netherlands: Springer.

Sullivan, C. J. (2013). Change in offending across the life course. In F. T. Cullen & P. Wilcox (Eds.), *The Oxford handbook of criminological theory* (pp. 205–225). New York, NY: Oxford University Press.

Sullivan, C. J., McKendrick, K., Sacks, S., & Banks, S. (2007). Modified therapeutic community treatment for offenders with MICA disorders: Substance use outcomes. *American Journal of Drug and Alcohol Abuse, 33,* 823–832.

Sullivan, D., & Tifft, L. (Eds.). (2008). *Handbook of restorative justice: A global perspective.* New York, NY: Routledge.

Sundt, J., Cullen, F. T., Thielo, A. J., & Jonson, C. L. (2015). Public willingness to downsize prisons: Implications from Oregon. *Victims and Offenders, 10,* 365–379.

Swanson, C. C., Schnippert, C. W., & Tryling. A. L. (2014). Reentry and employment: Employees' willingness to hire formerly convicted felons in Northwest Florida. In M. S. Crow & J. O. Smykla (Eds.), *Offender reentry: Rethinking criminology and criminal justice* (pp. 203–223). Burlington, MA: Jones and Bartlett Learning.

Sweeten, G., & Apel, R. (2007). Incapacitation: Revisiting an old question with a new method and new data. *Journal of Quantitative Criminology, 23,* 303–326.

Sykes, G. M. (1958). *The society of captives: A study of a maximum security prison.* Princeton, NJ: Princeton University Press.

Sykes, G. M. (1978). *Criminology.* New York, NY: Harcourt Brace Jovanovich.

Szasz, T. S. (1970). *The manufacture of madness.* New York, NY: Dell.

Tango, T. M., Lichtman, M. G., & Dolphin, A. E. (2007). *The book: Playing the percentages in baseball.* Washington, DC: Potomac Books.

Task Force on Corrections, President's Commission on Law Enforcement and Administration of Justice. (1967). *Task force report: Corrections.* Washington, DC: Government Printing Office.

Taxman, F. S., Pattavina, A., & Caudy, M. (2014). Justice reinvestment in the United States: An empirical assessment of the potential impact of increased correctional programming on recidivism. *Victims and Offenders, 9,* 50–75.

Taxman, F. S., Perdoni, M. L., & Caudy, M. (2013). The plight of providing appropriate substance abuse treatment services to offenders: Modeling the gaps in service delivery. *Victims and Offenders, 8,* 70–93.

Taxman, F. S., Perdoni, M. L., & Harrison, L. D. (2007). Drug treatment services for adult offenders: The state of the state. *Journal of Criminal Justice, 32,* 239–254.

Taxman, F. S., Young, D., & Byrne, J. M. (2004). With eyes wide open: Formalizing community and social control intervention in offender reintegration programmes. In S. Maruna & R. Immarigeon (Eds.), *After crime and punishment: Pathways to offender reintegration* (pp. 233–260). Cullompton, UK: Willan.

Terkel, A. (2014). Cory Booker and Rand Paul team up on criminal justice reform. *Huffington Post* (August 7). Retrieved from http://www.huffingtonpost.com/2014/07/08/cory-booker-rand-paul_n_5566800.html

Thaler, R. H., & Sunstein, C. R. (2008). *Nudge: Improving decisions about health, wealth, and happiness.* New Haven, CT: Yale University Press.

The Sentencing Project. (2014). *Fewer prisoners, less crime: A tale of three states.* Washington, DC: Author

Thielo, A. J., Cullen, F. T., Cohen, D. M., & Chouhy, C. (2016). Rehabilitation in a Red State: Public support for correctional reform in Texas. *Criminology and Public Policy, 14.*

Timmermans, S., & Berg, M. (2003). *The gold standard: The challenge of evidence-based medicine and standardization of health care.* Philadelphia, PA: Temple University Press.

Toby, J. (1964). Is punishment necessary? *Journal of Criminal Law, Criminology, and Police Science, 55,* 332–337.

Tocqueville, A. de. (1968). On prison reform. In S. Drescher (Ed. & Trans.), *Tocqueville and Beaumont on social reform* (pp. 70–97). New York, NY: Harper & Row. (Original work published 1844)

Tocqueville, A. de. (1969). *Democracy in America* (J. P. Mayer, Ed., & G. Lawrence, Trans.). New York, NY: Harper & Row. (Original work published 1835 and 1840)

Tonry, M. (1996). *Sentencing matters.* New York, NY: Oxford University Press.

Tonry, M. (1998). Intermediate sanctions. In M. Tonry (Ed.), *The handbook of crime and punishment* (pp. 683–711). New York, NY: Oxford University Press.

Tonry, M. (1999). *Reconsidering indeterminate and structured sentencing.* Washington, DC: National Institute of Justice, U.S. Department of Justice.

Tonry, M. (2004). *Thinking about crime: Sense and sensibility in American penal culture.* New York, NY: Oxford University Press.

Tonry, M. (2007). Determinants of penal policies. In M. Tonry (Ed.), *Crime, punishment, and politics in comparative perspective* (Crime and Justice: A Review of Research, Vol. 36, pp. 1–48). Chicago, IL: University of Chicago Press.

Tonry, M. (2008). Learning from the limitations of deterrence research. In M. Tonry (Ed.), *Crime and justice: A review of research* (Vol. 37, pp. 279–311). Chicago, IL: University of Chicago Press.

Tonry, M. (2009). The mostly unintended effect of mandatory penalties: Two centuries of consistent findings. In M. Tonry (Ed.), *Crime and justice: A review of research* (Vol. 38, pp. 65–114). Chicago, IL: University of Chicago Press.

Tonry, M. (2011a). *Punishing race: A continuing American dilemma.* New York, NY: Oxford University Press.

Tonry, M. (2011b). Punishment. In M. Tonry (Ed.), *The Oxford handbook of crime and criminal justice* (pp. 95–125). New York, NY: Oxford University Press.

Tonry, M. (2013). Sentencing in America, 1975–2025. In M. Tonry (Ed.), *Crime and justice in America, 1975–2025* (Crime and Justice: A Review of Research, Vol. 42, pp. 141–196). Chicago, IL: University of Chicago Press.

Tonry, M. (2014). Why crime rates are falling throughout the Western world. In M. Tonry (Ed.), *Why crime rates fall and why they don't* (Crime and Social Justice: A Review of Research, Vol., 43, pp. 1–63). Chicago, IL: University of Chicago Press.

Tonry, M., & Petersilia, J. (Eds.). (1999). *Prisons* (Crime and Social Justice: A Review of Research, Vol. 26, pp. 479–529). Chicago. IL: University of Chicago Press.

Travis, J. (2005). *But they all come back: Facing the challenges of prisoner reentry.* Washington, DC: Urban Institute.

Tremblay, R. E. (2006). Prevention of youth violence: Why not start at the beginning? *Journal of Abnormal Child Psychology, 34,* 481–487.

Tremblay, R. E., Japel, C., Perusse, D., McDuff, P., Boivin, M., Zoccolillo, M., & Montplaisir, J. (1999). The search for the age of "onset" of physical aggression: Rousseau and Bandura revisited. *Criminal Behaviour and Mental Health, 9,* 8–23.

Turner, M. G., Cullen, F. T., Sundt, J. L., & Applegate, B. K. (1997). Public tolerance for community-based sanctions. *Prison Journal, 77,* 6–26.

Turner, S., Chamberlain, A. W., Jannetta, J., & Hess, J. (2015). Does GPS improve recidivism among high risk sex offenders? Outcomes for California's GPS pilot for high risk sex offender parolees. *Victims and Offenders, 10,* 1–28.

Turner, S. F., David, L. M., Fain, T., Braithwaite, H., Lavery, T., Choinski, W., & Camp, G. (2015). A national picture of prison downsizing strategies. *Victims and Offenders, 10,* 402–421.

Turner, S., & Petersilia, J. (2012). Putting science to work: How the principles of risk, need, and responsivity apply to reentry. In J. A. Dvoskin, J. L. Skeem, R. W. Novaco, & K. S. Douglas (Eds.), *Using social science to reduce violent offending* (pp. 179–198). New York, NY: Oxford University Press.

Tyler, T. R. (2003). Procedural justice, legitimacy, and the effective rule of law. In M. Tonry (Ed.), *Crime, punishment, and politics in comparative perspective* (Crime and Justice: A Review of Research, Vol. 30, pp. 283–357). Chicago, IL: University of Chicago Press.

Tyler, T. R. (2009). Legitimacy and criminal justice: The benefits of self-regulation. *Ohio State Journal of Criminal Law, 7,* 307–359.

United States Census Bureau. (2014). *College enrollment declines for second year in a row, Census Bureau reports.* Washington, DC: United States Census Bureau.

Unnever, J. D., & Cullen, F. T. (2009). Empathetic identification and punitiveness: A middle-range theory of individual differences. *Theoretical Criminology, 13,* 283–312.

Unnever, J. D., & Cullen, F. T. (2010a). Racial-ethnic intolerance and support for capital punishment: A cross-national comparison. *Criminology, 48,* 831–862.

Unnever, J. D., & Cullen, F. T. (2010b). The social sources of Americans' punitiveness: A test of three competing models. *Criminology, 48,* 99–129.

Unnever, J. D., Cullen, F. T., & Jonson, C. L. (2008). Race, racism, and support for capital punishment. In M. Tonry (Ed.), *Crime and justice: A review of research* (Vol. 37, pp. 45–96). Chicago, IL: University of Chicago Press.

U.S. Department of Justice. (2014). *In a new step to fight recidivism, Attorney General Holder announces Justice Department to require federal halfway houses to boost treatment services for inmates prior to release.* Washington, DC: U.S. Department of Justice. Retrieved from http://www.justice.gov/opa/pr/new-step-fight-recidivism-attorney-general-holder-announces-justice-department-require

Useem, B., & Piehl, A. M. (2008). *Prison state: The challenge of mass incarceration.* New York, NY: Cambridge University Press.

van der Stouwe, T., Asscher, J. J., Stams, G. J. J. M., Deković, M., & van der Laan, P. H. (2014). The effectiveness of multisystemic therapy (MST): A meta-analysis. *Clinical Psychology Review, 34,* 468–481.

Van Ness, D. W., & Strong, K. H. (2010). *Restoring justice: An introduction to restorative justice* (4th ed.). New Providence, NJ: Anderson/LexisNexis.

Van Voorhis, P. (1987). Correctional effectiveness: The high cost of ignoring success. *Federal Probation, 51*(1), 59–62.

Van Voorhis, P., Braswell, M., & Lester, D. (Eds.). (2009). *Correctional counseling and rehabilitation* (7th ed.). New Providence, NJ: Anderson/LexisNexis.

Veysey, B. M., Christian, J., & Martinez, D. J. (Eds.). (2009). *How offenders transform their lives.* Cullompton, Devon, UK: Willan Publishing.

Villettaz, P., Gillieron, G., & Killias, M. (2015). The effects on re-offending of custodial vs. non-custodial sanctions: An updated systematic review of the state of the knowledge. *Campbell Systematic Reviews, 1,* 1–92.

Villettaz, P., Killias, M., & Zoder, I. (2006). *The effects of custodial vs. noncustodial sentences on re-offending: A systematic review of the state of knowledge.* Philadelphia, PA: Campbell Collaboration Crime and Justice Group.

Visher, C. A. (1987). Incapacitation and crime control: Does a "lock 'em up" strategy reduce crime. *Justice Quarterly, 4,* 513–543.

Visher, C., & Kachnowski, V. (2005). Finding work on the outside: Results from the "Returning Home" project in Chicago. In S. Bushway, M. A. Stoll, & D. F. Weiman (Eds.), *Barriers to reentry? The labor market for released prisoners in post-industrial America* (pp. 80–113). New York, NY: Russell Sage,

Visher, C., Kachnowski, V., La Vigne, N., & Travis, J. (2004). *Baltimore prisoners' experiences returning home.* Washington, DC: The Urban Institute.

Vito, A. G., & Vito, G. F. (2013). Lessons for policing from *Moneyball:* The views of police managers—A research note. *American Journal of Criminal Justice, 38,* 236–244.

von Hirsch, A. (1976). *Doing justice: The choice of punishments.* New York, NY: Hill and Wang.

von Hirsch, A., Ashworth, A., & Roberts, J. (Eds.). (2009). *Principled sentencing: Readings on theory and policy* (3rd ed.). Portland, OR: Hart.

Vose, B., Cullen, F. T., & Smith, P. (2008). The empirical status of the Level of Service Inventory. *Federal Probation, 72*(3), 22–29.

Wacquant, L. (2001). Deadly symbiosis: When ghetto and prison meet and mesh. *Punishment and Society, 3,* 95–134.

Wacquant, L. (2009). *Punishing the poor: The neoliberal government of social insecurity.* Durham, NC: Duke University Press.

Wakefield, S., & Uggen, C. (2010). Incarceration and stratification. *Annual Review of Sociology, 36,* 387–406.

Waller, I. (2006). *Less law, more order: The truth about reducing crime.* Westport, CT: Praeger.

Ward, T. (2002). Good lives and the rehabilitation of offenders: Promises and problems. *Aggression and Violent Behavior, 7,* 513–528.

Ward, T., Mann, R. E., & Gannon, T. A. (2007). The Good Lives Model of offender rehabilitation: Clinical implications. *Aggression and Violent Behavior, 12,* 87–107.

Ward, T., & Marshall, B. (2007). Narrative identity and offender rehabilitation. *International Journal of Offender Therapy and Comparative Criminology, 51,* 279–297.

Ward, T., & Maruna, S. (2007). *Rehabilitation: Beyond the risk paradigm.* London, UK: Routledge.

Ward, T., Yates, P. M., & Willis, G. M. (2012). The Good Lives Model and the risk need responsivity model: A critical response to Andrews, Bonta, and Wormith (2011). *Criminal Justice and Behavior, 39,* 94–110.

Weatherburn, D. (2013). A review of restorative justice responses to offending. *Evidence Base* (1), 1–20.

Webster, C. M., & Doob, A. N. (2007). Punitive trends and stable imprisonment rates in Canada. In M. Tonry (Ed.), *Crime, punishment, and politics in comparative perspective* (Crime and Justice:

A Review of Research, Vol. 36, pp. 297–370). Chicago, IL: University of Chicago Press.

Weigend, T. (2001). Sentencing and punishment in Germany. In M. Tonry & R. S. Frase (Eds.), *Sentencing and sanctions in Western countries* (pp. 188–221). New York, NY: Oxford University Press.

Welsh, B. C. (2003). Economic costs and benefits of primary prevention of delinquency and later offending: A review of the research. In D. P. Farrington & J. W. Coid (Eds.), *Early prevention of adult antisocial behaviour* (pp. 318–355). Cambridge, UK: Cambridge University Press.

Welsh, B. C., & Farrington, D. P. (2009). *Making public places safer: Surveillance and crime prevention.* New York, NY: Oxford University Press.

Welsh, B. C., & Farrington, D. P. (Eds.). (2012). *The Oxford handbook of crime prevention.* New York, NY: Oxford University Press.

Welsh, B. C., Farrington, D. P., & Gowar, B. R. (2015). Benefit-cost analysis of crime prevention programs. In M. Tonry (Ed.), *Crime and justice: A review of research* (Vol. 44, pp. 447–516). Chicago, IL: University of Chicago Press.

Welsh, B. C., Sullivan, C. J., & Olds, D. L. (2010). When early crime prevention goes to scale: A new look at the evidence. *Prevention Science, 11,* 115–125.

West, H. C., & Sabol, W. J. (2008). *Prisoners in 2007.* Washington, DC: Bureau of Justice Statistics, U.S. Department of Justice.

West, H. C., & Sabol, W. J. (2010). *Prisoners in 2009.* Washington, DC: Bureau of Justice Statistics, U.S. Department of Justice.

Western, B. (2006). *Punishment and inequality in America.* New York, NY: Russell Sage.

Western, B., & Pettit, B. (2010). Incarceration and social inequality. *Daedalus, 139*(3), 5–19.

Wexler, H. K., Lipton, D. S., & Johnson, B. D. (1988). *A criminal justice system strategy for treating cocaine-heroin abusing offenders in custody. Issues and practices.* Washington, DC: National Institute of Justice, U.S. Department of Justice.

White, P. (2014, February 11). Analytics filter down to field. *USA Today,* p. C9.

Whitehead, P. R., Ward, T., & Collie, R. M. (2007). Time for a change: Applying the Good Lives Model of rehabilitation to a high-risk offender. *International Journal of Offender Therapy and Comparative Criminology, 51,* 578–598.

Wicker, T. (1975). *A time to die*. New York, NY: Ballantine.

Wikström, P.-O. (2007). Deterrence and deterrence experiences: Preventing crime through the threat of punishment. In S. G. Shohan (Ed.), *The international handbook of penology and criminal justice* (pp. 345–378). Oxford, UK: Taylor & Francis.

Willis, G. M., & Ward, T. (2013). The Good Lives Model: Does it work? Preliminary evidence. In L. A. Craig, L. Dixon, & T. A. Gannon (Eds.), *What works in offender rehabilitation: An evidence-based approach to assessment and treatment* (pp. 305–317). Chichester, UK: Wiley-Blackwell.

Wilson, D. B., Bouffard, L. A., & MacKenzie, D. L. (2005). A quantitative review of structured, group-oriented, cognitive-behavioral programs for offenders. *Criminal Justice and Behavior, 32,* 172–204.

Wilson, D. B., Gottfredson, D. C., & Najaka, S. S. (2001). School-based prevention of problem behaviors: A meta-analysis. *Journal of Quantitative Criminology, 17,* 247–272.

Wilson, J. A. (2007). Habilitation or harm: Project Greenlight and the potential consequences for correctional programming. *National Institute of Justice Journal, 257,* 2–7.

Wilson, J. A., Cheryachukin, Y., Davis, R. C., Dauphinee, J., Hope, R., & Gehi. K. (2005). *Smoothing the path from prison to home: An evaluation of the Project Greenlight Transitional Service Demonstration Program.* New York, NY: The Vera Institute.

Wilson J. A., & Davis. R. C. (2006). Good intentions meet hard realities: An evaluation of the Project Greenlight Reentry Program. *Criminology and Public Policy, 5,* 303–338.

Wilson, J. Q. (1975). *Thinking about crime.* New York, NY: Vintage.

Wilson, J. Q. (2010). The future of blame. *National Affairs, 2*(Winter), 105–114.

Wilson, S. J., & Lipsey, M. W. (2007). School-based interventions for aggressive and disruptive behavior: Update of a meta-analysis. *American Journal of Preventative Medicine, 33,* S130–S143.

Wilson, S. J., Lipsey, M. W., & Derzon, J. H. (2003). The effects of school-based intervention programs on aggressive behavior: A meta-analysis. *Journal of Counseling and Clinical Psychology, 71,* 136–149.

Windzio, M. (2006). Is there a deterrent effect of pains of imprisonment? *Punishment and Society, 8,* 341–364.

Wines, E. C. (1910). Declaration of principles promulgated at Cincinnati, Ohio, 1870. In C. R. Henderson (Ed.), *Prison reform: Correction and prevention* (pp. 39–63). New York, NY: Russell Sage. (Original work published 1870)

Wolfers, J., Leonhardt, D., & Quealy, K. (2015). 1.5 million missing Black men. Retrieved from http://www.nytimes.com/interactive/2015/04/20/upshot/missing-black-men.html?abt=0002&abg=1

Wolfgang, M. E., Figlio, R. M., & Sellin, T. (1972). *Delinquency in a birth cohort.* Chicago, IL: University of Chicago Press.

World Prison Brief. (2013). King's College London, International Centre for Prison Studies website. Retrieved from http://www.kcl.ac.uk/depsta/law/research/icps/worldbrief

Wright, J. P., Tibbetts, S. G., & Daigle, L. E. (2008). *Criminals in the making: Criminality across the life course.* Thousand Oaks, CA: Sage.

Wright, K. A., & Cesar, G. T. (2013). Toward a more complete model of offender reintegration: Linking the individual-, community-, and system-level components of recidivism. *Victims and Offenders, 8,* 373–398.

Zimbardo, P. G. (2006). On rethinking the psychology of tyranny: The BBC Prison Study. *British Journal of Social Psychology, 45,* 47–53.

Zimbardo, P. G. (2007). *The Lucifer effect: Understanding how good people turn evil.* New York, NY: Random House.

Zimbardo, P. G., Banks, W. C., Haney, C., & Jaffe, D. (1973, April 8). A Pirandellian prison: The mind is a formidable jailer. *New York Times Magazine,* pp. 38–60.

Zimring, F. E. (2007). *The great American crime decline.* New York, NY: Oxford University Press.

Zimring, F. E., Hawkins, G., & Kamin, S. (2001). *Punishment and democracy: Three strikes and you're out in California.* New York, NY: Oxford University Press.

Index

Aase, K. N., 198

Abramsky, S., 114

Abuse of discretion, 175

Accountability/social exchange model, 153

Addicted to Incarceration: Corrections Policy and Politics of Misinformation in the United States (Pratt), 114

ADHD. *See* Attention deficit hyperactivity disorder (ADHD)

Adolescence, 243

Adolescence-limited offenders (ALs), 243–246

African Americans
  get tough laws and, 72–73
  incapacitation effect on, 137–138
  incarceration of, 2
  in Perry Preschool Program, 254, 256

Age-crime curve, 136, 243–244

Aggregation bias, 141

Aging effect, 136–137

Agnew, R., 95

Akers, R., 264

Alarid, L. F., 237

Alexander, J., 261–262, 268

Alexander, M., 15, 196, 216, 236

Allen, F. A., *x*, 151, 173–174, 179, 241, 285

Allen, H. E., 226

Allen, R., 117

Alm, S. S., 100–102

Alper, J. S., 245

ALs. *See* Adolescence-limited offenders (ALs)

American exceptionalism, 123–124

American Friend Service Committee Working Party, 67

American Furies: Crime, Punishment, and Vengeance in the Age of Mass Imprisonment (Abramsky), 114

America's Toughest Sheriff (Arpaio), 110

Andrews, D. A., 13, 63, 100, 130, 161–162, 165, 167–169, 171–172, 181–182, 184, 188, 190–196, 199, 201, 230–233, 254, 284–285

Anson, E., 254

Antisocial behavior
  genetic factors in, 245
  history of, 194
  MST effect on, 268–269
  onset of, 246
  theory of, 243

Antisocial development
  model for, 263
  pathway for, 269
  risk factors for, 252

Aos, S., 268, 271–274, 272 *(table)*

Apel, R., 79, 87, 135–137

Applegate, B. K., 46, 75, 99–100, 221

Ariel, B., 160–162, 166

Arpaio, J., 110–111

Arthur, M. W., 263

Ashworth, A., 51

Asscher, J. J., 269

Assessment stage, 261

At-risk families, 259–260

At-risk mothers, 251–254

At-risk youths
  antisocial development in, 252
  developmental tracks of, 264
  educational failure of, 254, 263
  generality of deviance in, 256
  intellectual development of, 255
  intervention system for, 287
  interventions for, 242–244
  juvenile court system and, 70, 242, 260
  nurse home visitation programs for, 251–254
  parental management of, 258–259
  preschool programs for, 254–258
  studies on, 242–244

Attention deficit hyperactivity disorder
    (ADHD), 245, 257, 258, 259
Attica Prison riot, 65–66
Austin, J., 124
Aviram, H., 114
Ayres, I., 19, 195, 280

Bachman, R., 98
Bacon, G., 103
Baldry, A. C., 263
Bales, W. D., 100–101
Ball, R. A., 13, 264
Ballot-box approach, 177–178
Banks, S., 225
Banks, W. C., 60
Barnes, G. C., 105, 260
Barnoski, R., 271, 272 (table)
Barocas, B., 161
Barrick, K., 100, 233–234
Bartlett effect, 184
Baseball theory, 21–25
Bateman, R. W., 228
Bazemore, G., 168
Beane, B., 23–25
Beaumont, G. de, 241
Beccaria, C., 83
Beck, A. J., 137
Becker, T. E., 249
Beckett, K., 73
Beckman, M., 41
Beckwith, J., 245
Behavior
    antisocial, 268–269
    change in, 262
    determination of, 52–54
Behrman, R. E., 253
"Being Sane in Insane Places"
    (Rosenhan), 64–65
Bellah, R. N., 275
Bennett, W. J., 125
Benshoten, S., 196
Benson, M. L., 53, 56, 197, 237
Berg, M., 19
Berger, P. L., 212, 280
Berglund, L., 263
Berk, R. E., 48
Bernburg, J. G., 100
Bewley-Taylor, D., 117
Bhati, A. S., 135
Bias, 141
Big Four criminogenic
    needs, 193–194, 200

Big Prisons, Big Dreams: Crime and the
    Failure of America's Penal System
    (Lynch), 114
Bivariate studies, 89–90
Blevins, K. R., 96, 97 (table), 100
Blokland, A. A. J., 108–109, 135
Blomberg, T. G., 101
Blueprints, 3
Blumstein, A., 117, 121, 140, 244
Bonczar, T. P., 2, 125, 196, 215–216
Bonikowski, B., 217
Bonta, J., 13, 63, 105, 130, 156, 161–162,
    165, 167–169, 171–172, 181–182,
    188, 190–191, 193, 195–196, 199,
    201, 230–233, 254, 284–285
Bontrager, S., 100
Borduin, C. M., 268
Bose, C. E., 48
Bottom-up approach, 132, 139–141
Bouffard, L. A., 188, 223
Bourgon, G., 196
Bradshaw, W., 161
Braithwaite, J., 12, 51, 146–147, 150–151,
    155, 157–161, 169
Braswell, M., 188
Brayford, J., 161, 197
Brent, J., 103
Brodeur, J.-P., 119–120
Brodeur, P., x
Bronfenbrenner, U., 251
Brown v. Plata, 72, 115
Browning, K., 142
Brutalization effect, 87
Bulmer, M., 207
Burke, C., 227–228
Burnett, R., 237
Burton, V. S., Jr., 237
Bush, George, 220
Bushway, S. D., 135, 216, 237
But They All Come Back: Facing the
    Challenges of Prisoner Reentry
    (Travis), 218
Butzin, C. A., 224
Byrne, J. M., 100, 238

Calder, M. C., 157
California, 71–72, 214
Cambridge Study in Delinquent
    Development, 259–260
Caplan, J. M., 210
Caputo, G. A., 100
Carich, M. S., 157

Carich, P. A., 157

Carson, E. A., 2, 11, 14–15, 121, 213

Castro, J. L., 225

Catalano, R. F., 263–265

Caudy, M., 215

Causes of Delinquency (Hirschi), 243

Cavender, G., 56

CEO program. *See* Center for Employment Opportunities (CEO) program

Center for Employment Opportunities (CEO) program, 227

Cernkovich, S. A., 231

Cesar, G. T., 236, 238

Chamberlain, A. W., 101

Chen, M. K., 110

Cheryachukin, Y., 233

Child development, 245

Children. *See* At-risk youths

Chin, G. J., 236

Chiricos, T., 100

Chouhy, C., 42, 96

Christian, J., 161

Christianity, 33–34

Chronic offenders
    crimes committed by, 127
    defined, 127
    selective imprisonment of, 127–131

Cid, J., 108

Cincinnati Congress of 1870, 33–34, 290

Clark, K., 109

Class X felonies, 71

Classical School of criminology, 83

Clear, T. R., 15, 72, 77, 114, 137–138

Clements, T., 223, 231

Client-centered counseling, 190

Cloward, R. A., 199, 243

Cochran, J. C., 15, 109, 212, 221, 230, 232, 238, 286

Cognitive-behavioral programs
    emphasis of, 169
    reliability of, 188
    responsivity principle and, 194

Cohen, A. K., 243

Cohen, D. M., 42

Cohen, J., 121

Cohen, M. A., 271, 273

Coid, J. W., 249

Cole, R., 254

Collateral consequences, 236–237

Collective incapacitation
    concept of, 126–127
    defined, 10
    selective incapacitation vs., 129

Collie, R. M., 199

Community control (deterrence) programs
    description of, 98
    HOPE example, 100–103
    overview of, 98
    Rand ISP study of, 103–105
    review of, 100–101
    support for, 99

Community corrections
    defined, 37
    get tough policies and, 120
    movement for, 98

Community-based reentry programs, 226–229

Co-morbidity of problems, 256

Concentrated incarceration, 137–138

Conflicting-personal-experience problem, 21

Conrad, J., 67

Consequences, 77–78, 80

Conservatives
    abuse of discretion view of, 175
    data selectivity by, 90
    deterrence support from, 82
    intermediate punishment views of, 99
    just deserts opposition by, 46
    justice model and, 74
    rehabilitation opposed by, 38–39
    restorative justice view of, 152–153
    retribution view of, 7

Context, influence of, 4

Context-theory-policy linkage, 27–28

Coolidge, S., 105

Cooper, A. D., 214, 235

Cooper, M., 38

Cormier, R., 161

Correctional institutions. *See* Prisons

Correctional quackery, 5
    defined, 19
    effects of, 173
    insider knowledge and, 20
    therapeutic integrity vs., 183

Correctional system
    future of, 289–290
    just deserts in, 45
    organization of, 278
    population increases in, 2–3
    size of, x
    statistics regarding, 2

Correctional treatments
    bases of, 191
    individualized, 35–36, 174

paradigm for, 172
recidivism model, 74
Costs
  early intervention programs, 270–274
  intangible, 272–273
  mass incarceration, 113, 121–123
  opportunity, 11
  prisons, 11
  punishment, 10
  tangible, 272
Cowe, F., 161, 197
Cowell, A., 233–234
Crime
  data collection, 85
  expected utility of, 81
  longitudinal studies of, 94
  politicization of, 72
  predictors for, 94–95
Crime, Shame and Reintegration (Braithwaite),
  146, 158
Crime control
  decay in effects, 87
  harsh punishment and, 13
  public mandate for, 75–76
  rehabilitation and, 28–29
  RJ effects on, 158–161
  situational, 88
  utilitarian goal of, 10, 46
Crime in America: Uniform Crime Reports, 88–89
Crime in the Making (Sampson, Laub), 107
Crime rates
  cross-national, 3
  incarceration and, 132, 139–141
  macro-level study of, 88–92
  publishing of, 88
  use of, 87
Criminals. *See* Offenders
Criminogenic needs, 199
Criminogenic risk factors, 13–14, 191, 241
Criminology
  environmental, 87
  history of, 36–37
  just deserts and, 52–54
  life-course, 246
  Positivist School of, 84
Cross-sectional study, 247
Crow, M. S., 221
Culhane, D. P., 229
Cullen, F. T., 4–5, 9, 11–13, 19–22, 24, 26,
  28, 31, 38–39, 41–42, 44–49, 52–61,
  66, 68–71, 73–76, 78–79, 87, 90, 91 *(table),*
  94–96, 97 *(table),* 99–103, 105–109, 111,
  114–119, 124, 128, 130–131, 134, 138,

  141–143, 146–148, 151–156, 158–162, 165,
  167–169, 171–173, 175–176, 179, 181–182,
  184, 188, 191–192, 195–201, 203, 209–210,
  213–215, 218, 221–223, 230, 232, 237–238,
  242, 244, 247, 249–250, 253, 255–256,
  259–261, 264, 266–271, 274–290
Culross, P. L., 253
Cumulative continuity, 245
Cumulative risk, 258
Currie, E., 77, 142
Curtis, N. M., 268
Cwick, J. M., 100

Daigle, L. E., 96, 97 *(table),* 160
Daly, K., 154–156, 160
Data. *See also* Crime rates
  collection of, 85
  importance of, 3
  macro-level, 92
  perceptual deterrence studies, 86 *(table)*
  selectivity of, 90
  statistical, 23–24
Dauphinee, J., 233
David, S. L., 249
Davies, P., 19
Davis, M. R., 191
Davis, R. C., 223, 233
Davis, S., 288
Decker, S. H., 217
"Declaration of Principles," 34
Deering, J., 161, 197
Dehumanization, 61
Deindividuation, 61
Deinstitutionalization, 70
Dekovic, M., 269
Delinquency in a Birth Cohort
  (Wolfgang et al.), 127
Democracy in America (de Tocqueville), 32
Denver Youth Survey (DYS), 248
Dependent variables, 88
DePodesta, P., 24
Derkzen, D., 225
Derzon, J. H., 246, 258, 263
Desistance-based rehabilitation, 196–198
Determinate sentencing
  crime rates and, 73
  criminal code for, 48
  justice model support for, 67
  legislative process and, 72
  state passage of, 210
Deterrence
  bases of, 77, 83
  community control programs for, 98–103

effectiveness of, 79
imprisonment's effects on, 105–112
individual differences and, 78–79
National Youth Survey, 95–96
punishment and, 81, 85, 87–88
specific. *See* Specific deterrence
studies of, 84–85, 86 *(table)*
types of, 80–81
Deterrence effect
defined, 80
evidence of, 111–112
studies of, 139
Deterrence theory, 278
appeal of, 78
assumptions of, 82–84
ideology of, 81–82
limits of, 111–112
policies favored by, 9
predictions by, 80
principles of, 8–10
rational choice in, 107
recidivism rates and, 106
Developmental criminology.
See Life-course criminology
Dhami, M. K., 156
Di Tella, R., 101
DiGuiseppi, C., 263
DiIulio, J. J., Jr., 51, 125, 134, 136, 138, 287
Discovery of the Asylum (Rothman), 32
Discretion, 47, 55
diZerega, M., 225
Do no harm theory, 59, 281
Dog Day Afternoon, 65
Doherty, E. E., 100
Dohrenwend, B. P., 237
Doob, A. N., 87, 120
Dowden, C., 161
Drago, E., 110
Drake, E. K., 268, 271–272, 274
Due process rights movement, 67
Duncan, G. J., 258
Duriez, S. A., 101
Durlauf, S. N., 102, 284
Durose, M. R., 214, 235
Dynamic predictors, 192
DYS. *See* Denver Youth Survey (DYS)

Early interventions
appeal of, 16, 256–257
childhood studies and, 242–246
cost effectiveness of, 270–274
description of, 16
DYS, 248

functional family therapy for, 258–263
goals of, 31
multisystemic therapy for, 266–269
need for, 246–249
nurse home visitations for, 251–254
overview of, 240–242
policy implications of, 269–270
preschool programs for, 254–258
public support for, 274–275
PYS, 247–249
researcher effect and, 250
RNR paradigm in, 250–251
school-based, 263–266
technology transfer in, 249
wisdom of, 276
Eck, J. E., 196
Ecological fallacy, 92–93
Ecological-level study. *See* Macro-level study
Effect size
defined, 90, 185
estimates, 91 *(table)*
heterogeneity of, 187–189
homogeneity of, 186
overall, impact of, 186–187
positive, impact of, 186
"Effective Correctional Treatment: Bibliotherapy
for Cynics" (Gendreau, Ross), 182
Effective interventions, 13–14
characteristics of, 168
preschool, 257–258
RJ programs for, 168
scientific criminology and, 162
Electronic monitoring, 101
Empathy, 289
Empirical issues
defined, 8
MST, 267–269
theories and, 18
Employment
after reentry, 227, 230
recidivism affected by, 230–231
Engagement stage, 261
Enlightenment Era, 83
Ensminger, M. E., 100
Environmental criminology, 87
Eraser justice, 72
Esbensen, F., 248
Espiritu, R., 248–249
Evidence-based corrections, 5
baseball analogy for, 21–25
consequences of, 280–281
crime theories and, 76
knowledge factors in, 20–21, 173

overview of, 19
professional responsibilities in, 20
purpose of, 3
Experience
  personal, 20, 22
  personal, conflicts in, 21
  social, 107
Experiential effect, 94
External constraints, 265

Fabiano, E. A., 233
Fagan, J., 108
False positives, 130–131
Farrington, D. P., 16, 53, 88, 96, 125, 158, 226, 242,
    244, 246, 249, 253, 257–260, 263, 268, 271,
    274, 287
FBI (Federal Bureau of Investigation), 88, 92
Feld, B., 38
Felson, M., 88
FFT. See Functional family therapy (FFT)
Figlio, R. M., 127
Fisher, B. S., 46, 221
Fisher, C., 237
Fisher, D. T., 103
Flores, A. W., 105
FOCUS: Offender Re-entry Mentoring Project,
    226–227
Fogel, D., 67, 71
Fox, D., 156
France, A., 56
Francis, Pope, 288–289
Frazier, B. D., 223
Free will. See Human agency
French, S. A., 191
Fulton, B., 154
Functional family therapy (FFT)
  cost effectiveness of, 272 (table)
  defined, 261
  effective change from, 262
  orientation of, 261–262
  overview of, 258–259
  stages of, 261–262
Future consequences, 78

Gaes, G., 231
Galbiati, R., 110
Gannon, T. A., 199–200
Garland, B., 211, 222, 230, 238
Garland, D., 4, 69–70, 153, 288
Gartner, R., 72, 114, 214
Gatti, U., 100
Gawande, A., 116
Gaylin, W., 59

Gehi, K., 233
Geis, G., 83
Gendreau, P., 5, 19, 41, 59, 100, 105, 108,
    171–172, 181–184, 188, 190–192, 195,
    232, 236, 238, 279–280
General deterrence, 80–81
General deterrent effect, 111
Generality of deviance, 256
Generalizability, 20
Generalization stage, 262
Genetic fatalism, 245, 259
Ghandnoosh, N., 115
Gideon, L., 221–222, 286
Gilbert, K. E., 4, 26, 31, 38–39, 41,
    66, 69–71, 114, 153–154, 171,
    209–210, 214
Gileno, J., 225
Gill, C. E., 105
Gillieron, G., 108
Giordano, P. C., 231
Giving Kids a Fair Chance (Heckman), 257
Gladwell, M., 287
Glasser, I., 59
Glaze, L. E., 2, 121, 212
GLM. See Good Lives Model (GLM)
Glueck, E., 107
Glueck, S., 107
Gobeil, R., 225
Goggin, C., 100, 108, 191, 236
Golden Rule, 56
Golinelli, D., 14, 213
Gomby, D. S., 253
Good Lives Model (GLM), 198–201
Goodman, A., 251, 253
Gordon, D. R., 73
Gordon, J., 275
Gottfredson, D. C., 197, 263
Gottfredson, M. R., 9, 40, 179, 257
Gottschalk, M., 42, 58
Gough, D. A., 263
Gouldner, A. W., 28, 279
Gowar, B. R., 271, 274
Grattet, R., 41
Gray, S., 22, 24
Great American City (Sampson), 206
Great Society, 70
Green, K. M., 100
Greenwood, P. W., 249, 253, 257, 259,
    271, 273–274
Griffin, M. L., 110–111
Griggs, R. A., 60, 62
Griset, P. L., 69–70
Guckenburg, S., 100

Guerra, N. G., 249
Guevremont, D. C., 188
Gunnison, E., 15, 212, 221, 230, 238

Hagan, J., 56, 220
Hairston, C. F., 225
Hakes, J. K., 25
Half-empty reviews, 178
Half-full reviews, 178–181
Halfway houses, 226, 232
Hallam, C., 117
Handwerk, A. M., 226
Haney, W. C., 60
Hanlon, T. E., 228
Harland, A. T., 100
Harris, J. R., 258
Harrison, L. D., 41, 215, 224
Harrison, P. M., 137
Haslam, S. A., 62
Haviland, A., 109
Hawaii's Opportunity Probation with Enforcement
    (HOPE) program, 100–103
Hawken, A., 101–102
Hawkins, G., 71, 107, 114
Hawkins, J. D., 263–266
Heckman, J., 257
Hedberg, E., 217
Helfgott, J. B., 15, 212, 221, 230, 238
Henggeler, S. W., 266–268, 271
Hepburn, J. R., 110–111
Herberman, E. J., 2, 125, 196, 212
Hess, J., 101
Hickey, J. E., 67
High/Scope Educational Research
    Foundation, 254
High/Scope Perry Preschool
    Program, 254–258, 272 (table)
Hill, K. G., 264
Hill, P. L., 252
Hines, K., 103
Hipple, N. K., 161–162, 164, 167
Hippocratic Oath, 280–281
Hirschi, T., 9, 197, 257, 264
Hoge, R. D., 194, 232
Holleran, D., 108
Holsinger, A. M., 105, 196
Holzer, H. J., 216
Homelessness, 216, 229
Homish, D. I., 125
Hooper, R. M., 224
HOPE. See Hawaii's Opportunity
    Probation with Enforcement
    (HOPE) program

Hope R., 233
Hot-stove phenomenon, 78
Housing, after reentry, 228–229
Howell, J. C., 276
Hudson, J., 67, 71
Huizinga, D., 248–249
Human agency, 52
Hunt, K. S., 109
Hyatt, J. M., 105

Imprisoning Communities: How Mass Incarceration
    Makes Disadvantaged Neighborhoods Worse
    (Clear), 114
Imprisonment. See also Mass incarceration
    concentrated, 137–138
    deterrence and, 107–111
    effects of, 105–111
    incapacitation effect of, 116
    international rates of, 119 (table)
    judicious use of, 120–121
    rates from 1925–1970, 122 (figure)
    rates from 1970–2013, 122 (figure)
    studies of, 85, 86 (table)
    youths at risk for, 261
Impulsivity, 257
Incapacitation
    collective, 126–127
    concept of, 126–131
    logic of, 123
    policy conundrum in, 123–125
    power of, 124
    problems with, 283
    rehabilitation vs., 123
    selective, 127–131
Incapacitation effect
    aging effect on, 136–137
    benefits of, 124
    bottom-up studies of, 132, 139–141
    complexity of, 141–143
    defined, 10
    estimation of, 131–141
    inmate self-report studies on, 132–134
    labeling effect on, 137
    longitudinal studies on, 134–136
    macro-level studies of, 139–141
    on African Americans, 137–138
    replacement effect on, 137
    small unit study of, 141
    top-down studies of, 132, 139–141
Incapacitation theory
    core principles of, 10–11
    goals of, 10
    limitations of, 10–11

measurement of, 89
overview of, 113–117
Inciardi, J. A., 224
Indeterminate sentencing
  criminal code for, 47
  decline of, 38
  discretionary power in, 72
  goals of, 34
  purpose of, 34–35
  replacement of, 67
  therapeutic system and, 63–64
Individual differences, 160
Individual psychotherapeutic model, 267
Individual traits
  deterrence and, 78–79
  free will vs., 53
  macro-level data on, 92
  un-chosen, 53, 245
Individualized treatment
  paradigm of, 36
  rehabilitation, 174
  rise of, 35
Inequality, 54–57
Inference, 92
Inmate self-report studies, 132–134
Insider knowledge
  baseball analogy for, 22–23
  defined, 20
  over-reliance on, 279
  problems associated with, 20–21
  risk of, 25
Intangible costs, 272–273
Intelligence enrichment programs, 257–258
Intensive supervision programs, 103
Intermediate punishment movement
  emergence of, 98–99
  HOPE program, 100–103
  ideological perspectives on, 99
Interrupted time-series studies, 85
Interventions. *See also* Early interventions;
    Effective interventions
  boosting self-esteem in, 190
  character-building programs for, 190
  client-centered, non-directive, 190
  cognitive-behavioral programs, 188–189
  defined, 85
  effect size in, 185–189
  failed, 280–281
  hubris in, 18
  medical, 30
  meta-analysis reviews of, 184–189
  principles of, 172

punishment-oriented programs for, 190
studies, 86 *(table)*
success predictors for, 192–195
treatment paradigm for, 172
Irwin, J., 31, 124

*The Jack-Roller: A Delinquent Boy's
    Own Story* (Shaw), 206–208, 215
Jackson, D., 288
Jacobs, J. B., 15, 237
Jacobson, M., 284
Jacoby, J. E., 48
Jaffe, D., 60
James, B., 23–24
Jannetta, J., 101
Jennings, W. G., 253, 271
Jeong, S., 161–162, 164, 167
Jesseman, R., 161
Jo, H.-j., 225
Johnson, B. D., 210, 228
Johnson, D. T., 118
Johnson, R., 51
Johnstone, J. G., 156
Jolliffe, D., 125, 226, 260
Jonson, C. L., 4, 9, 11–13, 21, 24, 28, 31,
    41–42, 44–45, 47–49, 52–58, 60–61,
    68–70, 73–76, 78–79, 87, 94–96,
    100–103, 105–106, 108, 111, 116–117,
    119, 124, 128, 130–131, 134, 138, 141–142,
    146–148, 151–152, 154–156, 158–162, 165,
    167–169, 172–173, 175, 179, 181–182, 188,
    191–192, 196, 199–201, 203, 213, 221–223,
    226, 237, 242, 244, 247, 249–250, 253,
    255–256, 259–261, 264, 266–271, 275,
    276–279, 281–288, 290
Judicial discretion, 35–36
Just and Painful (Newman), 52
Just deserts theory
  challenges for, 46
  concept of, 7
  crime control and, 74–76
  criminology problem for, 52–54
  expectations of, 17–18
  ideological split on, 46
  inequality problem for, 54–57
  liberal support for, 58–66, 175
  major principles of, 50
  measure of, 17–18
  overview of, 44–46
  prison problem for, 51–52
  punishment concept in, 47
  utility problem for, 57–58

Justice model
  acceptance of, 68–70
  crime control and, 74–76
  development of, 58–66
  failure of, 70–75
  history leading to, 65–66
  limits of, 76
  main components of, 67–68
  predictions about, 171
  purpose of, 146
  rehabilitation failure and, 58–66
  rights to, 281
Juvenile courts
  creation of, 36
  harsher approach by, 38
  initiation of, 37
Juvenile delinquency, 242, 259–260
Juvenile Delinquency and Urban Areas
    (Shaw and McKay), 206
Juvenile reformatories, 70

Kachnowski, V., 224
Kadela, K. R., 229, 234
Kaeble, D., 2, 121
Kahnenman, D., 20, 97
Kalb, L. M., 260
Kamin, S., 71, 114
Kant, I., 50–51
Kasich, J., 289
Kazemian, L., 249
Keaton, S., 227–228
Kennedy, J. F., 4, 279
Kennedy, R. F., 279
KEY/Crest Substance Abuse
    Program, 224–225
Killias, M., 108
Kilmer, B., 103
Kim, K., 95, 100
King, M. L., Jr., 279
Kinnevy, S. C., 210
Kirk, D. S., 100
Kitsuse, J. I., 212, 217
Kittrie, N. N., 38, 63, 67
Kitzman, H., 254
Kleiman, M. A. R., 101–103, 284
Knowledge. *See* Insider knowledge;
    Outsider knowledge
Knudtson, M. D., 254
Koegl, C. J., 271
Kosterman, R., 264
Kovandzic, T. V., 141
Kreager, D. A., 95

Krikorian, G., 128
Krisberg, B., 221
Krohn, M. D., 100, 237
Kruttschnitt, C., 72, 114, 214
Kulig, T. C., 60

La Vigne, N. G., 224–225
Labeling effect, 137
Labeling theory, 96, 107
Labrecque, R. M., 196
Lambert, S., 260
Lane, J., 216
Langan, P. A., 213–214, 235
Lappi-Seppala, T., 118
Late onset offenders, 241
Latessa, E. J., 5, 19, 22, 24, 41, 105, 130,
    172, 183, 196, 209, 226, 230, 232,
    238, 280–281
Latimer, J., 161
Lattimore, P. K., 220, 233–234
Laub, J. H., 107–108, 161, 197, 231, 244, 246
Lavenberg, J., 258
LCPs. *See* Life-course-persistent
    offenders (LCPs)
LeBel, T. P., 237
Legal sanctions, 97
Legislation, 72
Lehrer, J., 60
LeMarquand, D., 263
Leonhardt, D., 2
Lester, D., 188
Level of Service Inventory (LSI), 195, 228
Levin, D. J., 214, 235
Levitt, S. D., 87, 109
Levrant, S., 154
Levshin, V., 227
Lewis, M., 22, 24, 56
Liberals
  abuse of discretion view of, 175
  data selectivity by, 90
  deterrence support from, 82
  intermediate punishment views of, 99
  just deserts support by, 46
  justice model advocacy by, 68–70
  parole boards and, 209
  rehabilitation opposed by, 38–39,
      58–59, 63–64
  restorative justice view of, 152–153
  retribution view of, 7
Lieb, R., 271, 272 *(table)*
Lieberman, A. M., 100
Liedka, R. V., 141

Life-course criminology
  defined, 244
  lessons from, 241
  school interventions and, 264
Life-course-persistent offenders (LCPs)
  defined, 244
  early interventions for, 246, 269
  identification of, 245–246
  stability of, 246
Lilly, J. R., 13, 264–265
Lin, J., 41
Lindquist, C. H., 233
Link, B. G., 48, 237
Lipsey, M. W., 167, 184, 189, 191,
    194, 246, 258, 263
Lipton, D. S., 184, 228
Listwan, S. J., 41, 230, 232
Littell, J. H., 268–269
Little, T., 191
Loeber, R., 125, 247–249, 260, 263
Logan, S., 263
Lombroso, C., 84, 245
Longitudinal studies
  cost effectiveness of, 247
  defined, 94
  example of, 134–136
  follow-ups in, 256
  omission of, 247
Lopes, G., 237
Los Angeles Times, 113, 128
Lösel, F., 184, 242, 276
Losoya, S. H., 108
Loughran, T. A., 98, 109
Loveland, N., 222
Lowenkamp, C. T., 105, 172, 196, 232
LSI. See Level of Service Inventory (LSI)
Luckmann, T., 212, 280
Lux, J. L., 221, 269
Lynch, J. P., 124, 138, 215
Lynch, M. J., 114
Lyngstad, T. H., 198

Maakestad, W. J., 56
MacKenzie, D. L., 19, 100–101, 142, 169,
    176, 188, 191, 223, 231, 280
Macro-level study
  conducting, 88–90
  data from, 86 (table)
  defined, 85
  inference of, 92
Madensen, T. D., 96, 97 (table)
Madsen, R., 275

Magnuson, K., 258
Makarios, M. D., 105, 109
Managerial parole, 210
Manchak, S. M., 101, 215
Mann, R. E., 199–200
Mantle, G., 156
Marcus, S., 59
Marshall, B., 199
Martin, S. S., 224
Martinez, D. J., 161
Martinson, R., 28, 39–40, 172, 175–182, 184–185,
    187, 189, 266, 279
Maruna, S., 197, 199–200, 231, 237
Maslach, C., 62
Mass incarceration
  costs of, 113, 121–123
  crime rates and, 138
  cross-cultural comparisons of, 117–120
  debate over, 114–117
  diminishing returns of, 141
  factors causing, 120–121
  folly of, 113
  policy factors in, 122–123
  problems with, 283–284
  statistics of, 212–213
  theoretical perspective of, 120–123
Matsueda, R. L., 95
Matthews, R., 114, 124–125
Matthews, S. K., 95
Maturational reform, 243
Matza, D., 243
Mauer, M., 115
Mawhorr, T. L., 232
Mayo-Wilson, E., 101, 160–162, 166
McAlinden, A.-M., 157
McAnoy, K., 156
McCold, T., 149
McCoy, C., 56
McDonald, D., 226
McGarrell, E. F., 161–162, 164, 167
McGuire, J., 100, 187, 191, 194
McKay, H. D., 206
McKendrick, K., 225
McKinney, K. C., 263
Meade, B., 109
Meanness, theory of, 288
Mears, D. P., 15, 109, 212, 221, 224,
    230, 232, 238, 286
Medical model, 30, 174
Menninger, K., 31, 59
Mental health, 227–228
Mental illness, 64–65

Mentoring, 226–227
Merton, R. K., 20, 28, 192
Meta-analysis
    advantages of, 173
    defined, 90
    effect size in, 185–189
    interventions, 184–189
    perceptual deterrence studies, 95–96
    quantitative synthesis of, 185
    questions answered by, 90–91
    restorative justice, 167–169
Methodological issues, 89
Metraux, S., 229
Micelli, S. L., 100
Millenky, M., 227
Miller, J. G., 70
Miller, M. G., 268
Mills, L. G., 161
Mills, N., 153
Minton, T. D., 213
Miranda decision, 67
Mischel, W., 97
Misspecified model, 89
Modified Therapeutic Community for Offenders
    with Mental Illness and Chemical
    Abuse (MICA)
    Disorders, 223
Moffitt, T. E., 53, 243–246
Moirizot, J., 249
Monachesi, E., 83
*Moneyball: The Art of Winning an
    Unfair Game* (Lewis), 22–25
Moon, M. M., 100, 275
Moon, S. H., 257
Moore, G. E., 224
Morris, B., 25
Morris, N., 63, 67, 99
Motivation stage, 261
MST. *See* Multisystemic therapy (MST)
Muise, D., 161
Multisystemic therapy (MST)
    case load limits of, 267
    cost effectiveness of, 272 *(table)*, 273
    defined, 266–267
    empirical research on, 267–269
    invention of, 266–267
Multivariate studies
    controls for, 93
    defined, 88
    findings from, 90–92
    methodological issues with, 89
    on punishment effects, 96

Mulvey, E. P., 108
Murray, C., 153
Murray, J., 96, 158, 246
Myer, A. J., 22, 24
Mytton, J. A., 263

Nagin, D. S., 11, 77, 79, 85, 87, 95–96, 102,
    108–109, 137, 213, 243–244, 275, 282, 284
Najaka, S. S., 263
Narrative reviews
    ballot-box approach to, 178–181
    defined, 177
    description of, 177–178
    meta-analysis vs., 189
    rebuttal of, 178–181
National Longitudinal Study of Youth (NLSY),
    135–136
National Youth Survey, 95–96
Natural experiment, 109
Naturalistic desistance, 197
Ndrecka, M., 227, 229, 234
Need principle, 250
Neuropsychological deficits, 245
Newburn, T., 118
Newman, G., 52
NFP. *See* Nurse-Family Partnership (NFP)
Nieuwbeerta, P., 108–109, 135
Nirvana story, 155–156
NLSY. *See* National Longitudinal Study of
    Youth (NLSY)
Noble lie, 63
N-of-1 problem, 20
Non-directive counseling, 190
Non-utilitarian theories
    defined, 8
    just deserts as, 45
    restorative justice as, 12
Nothing works doctrine
    debate over, 172
    meta-analysis and, 189–191
    origins of, 39–40
    responses to, 178–189
Nurco, D. N., 228
Nurse home visitation program,
    251–254, 272 *(table)*
Nurse-Family Partnership (NFP), 253

Obama, Barack, 288
O'Connell, D., 103
Offenders
    categories of, 126
    children as, 242–246

chronic, 127–131
coddling of, 31
false positives, 130–131
high-risk, 194
historical views of, 83
late onset, 241
reforming of, 33–34
self-reporting survey of, 132–134
social psychology of, 192
social stigma associated with, 237
Ogloff, J. R. P., 191
O'Grady, K. E., 228
Ohlin, L. E., 243
Olds, D. L., 16, 249–254, 271
Oleson, J. C., 196
Olson, J. J., 263
Omori, M. K., 101
Onedera, J. D., 261–262
Opportunity cost, 11
Ortiz, N. R., 217
Ouimet, M., 120
Outsider knowledge, 20
Owens, M., 135

Pacino, A., 65
Padgett, K. G., 101
Page, J., 72, 114, 214
Pager, D., 216–217
Palmer, T., 40, 178–181, 189
Paparozzi, M. A., 105
Parallel Universe program, 223, 231
Parental management, 258–259
Parenting style, 258
Parks, E. C., 232
Parks, G., 254–256
Parole
    crimes ineligible for, 210
    determinate sentencing versus, 210
    disciplinary, 209
    historical description of, 209–210
    managerial, 210
    reentry versus, 209–211, 218
Parole boards, 210–211
Parole officers, 35
Parsons, B., 261
Paternoster, R., 79, 94–95, 98, 135
Pattavina, A., 100, 215
Pealer, J. A., 221, 275, 285
Pearsall, B., 102
Penitentiary
    invention of, 32
    rationality of, 32–33
    religious nature of, 33–34

Perception, 23, 96
Perceptual deterrence studies
    data from, 86 (table)
    defined, 85
    ecological fallacy of, 92–93
    individuals and, 93–95
    meta-analysis, 95–96
    National Youth Survey, 95–96
Perdoni, M. L., 41, 215
Personal decisions, 24
Personal experience
    conflict of interest in, 21
    effective intervention and, 191
    empirical data vs., 279–280
    insider knowledge and, 20–21, 25
    recidivism predications based on, 130
    selective perceptions in, 21
    value of, 20
Personalities, criminal, 78–79
Personality-situation debate, 60–61
Petersilia, J., 11, 14–15, 41–42, 71, 103–104,
        114–115, 125, 143, 210–211, 214,
        216, 218–221, 223–225, 227, 232,
        235, 238, 286, 288
Peterson, A., 109
Peterson, K., 226
Petrosino, A., 100, 258–259
Pettit, B., 54
Pettit, P., 51
Pew Charitable Trusts, 2, 121
PFV. See Private Family Visiting (PFV) program
Phelan, J. C., 237
Philosophies of punishment. See Theories of
        corrections
Phipps, P., 271, 272 (table)
Piehl, A. M., 114, 134, 136, 141
Pinto, R., 257
Piquero, A. R., 95, 98, 108, 244, 253,
        259–260, 271, 273, 275
Piquero, N. L., 275
Pittsburgh Youth Study (PYS), 247–249,
        259–260
Platt, A. M., 37
Plea bargaining, 55
Pogarsky, G., 87, 95, 98
Polanzi, C. W., 48
Policies
    changes in, 85, 86 (table), 87–88
    critical issue of, 92
    deterrence favored, 9
    early interventions and, 269–270
Poor Discipline: Parole and the Social Control of the
        Underclass, 1890–1990 (Simon), 209

Porporino, F. J., 191
Positivist School, 84
Poverty, cycle of, 254
Pratt, T. C., 2, 41, 60, 90, 91 *(table)*, 94–96, 97 *(table)*, 100, 114, 118, 284
Predistribution, 257
Pregnancy, 251–254
Presser, L., 156
The Prison (Hawkins), 107
Prison State: The Challenge of Mass Incarceration (Useem, Piehl), 114
Prisons. *See also* Imprisonment
    brutal environment in, 59–61
    costs of, 11
    inequality in, 54–57
    as just communities, 68
    just deserts and, 51–52
    mentally ill in, 64–65
    rise of, 37
    RJ effects on, 156–157
    Stanford experiment, 60–64
    therapeutic system in, 63–64
    warehouse, 124
Private Family Visiting (PFV) program, 225
Probation officers, 35
Procedural justice, 159
Progressive era, 36–37
Proietti-Scifoni, G., 160
Project Greenlight, 223, 232
Propensity-score matching, 135
Prosecutorial discretion, 55
Prosocial attitudes
    community involvement and, 262, 265–266
    development of, 257, 265, 285
    mate selection and, 260
    pursuit of, 188–189
    relationships and, 158
    values and, 194
The Psychology of Criminal Conduct (Andrews, Bonta), 195
Public Safety Realignment Act, 115
Pugh, C., 261
Punishment. *See also* Imprisonment; Just deserts
    certainty and severity of, 81–82, 85, 93
    costs of, 10
    increasing, policy change-induced, 85, 87–88
    individual's perception of, 93–95
    intermediate, 98–100
    just deserts view of, 47–49
    justice model approach to, 67–68
    limits of, 281–282
    macro-level study of, 88–92
    perceptual studies of, 92–98
    philosophy of, 6–8, 39
    rewards vs., 34
    white-collar criminals, 56–57
Punishment-oriented programs, 190
Punitive-oriented correctional sanctions, 112
PYS. *See* Pittsburgh Youth Study (PYS)

Quealy, K., 2

Racism-punitiveness connection, 73
Rand ISP study, 103–105
Raphael, S., 216, 237
Rational choice theory
    deterrence theory and, 107
    implications of, 83
Rationality, 24
Raynor, P., 161, 168, 197
Reaffirming Rehabilitation (Cullen, Gilbert), 4, 69, 171
Reagan, R., 4
Recidivism
    Big Four criminogenic needs and, 193–194, 200
    collateral consequences and, 237
    community supervision effects on, 196
    correctional theories and, 6
    effect size in, 185–187
    employment effects on, 230–231
    halfway houses' effect on, 232
    imprisonment effects on, 213
    prevention of, 211
    reentry programs effect on, 234
    risk factors for, 192–193
    RJ's effects on, 163–165
    statistics regarding, 213–214
    studies of, 163–164
    treatment model and, 75
    variation in, 106
Redcross, C., 227
"Redeem Act," 237
Reentry
    barriers faced by prisoners after, 215–216
    barriers to effectiveness of, 229–235
    books about, 221
    collateral consequences, 236–237
    "coming home" after, 235
    components of, 15
    correctional component of, 15
    criminology of, 239
    definition of, 15
    description of, 14–15
    drug treatment before, 214–215

effectiveness of, 229–235
employment barriers after, 216
failure of, 235–236
good will and, 238
history of term, 211, 217–219
homelessness after, 216, 229
importance of, 286
institutionalization of, 221
lack of treatment services' effect
    on, 214–215
lack of vocational services' effect on, 216
normative side of, 211
parole and, 209–211, 218
prescriptive side of, 211
present-day interest in, 219–222
problem of, 212–222
reintegration component of, 15
Serious and Violent Offender Reentry Initiative
    (SVORI), 220, 233–234
statistics regarding, 14, 286
stigma after, 237
Reentry programs
case studies of, 223–225
community-based, 226–229
conclusions regarding, 235
description of, 211
development of, 234–235
diversity of, 229–230
employment, 227, 230
familial bonds as focus of, 225
halfway houses, 226, 232
housing, 228–229
implementation issues for, 232–233
increases in, 221
institutional, 223–225
lack of credible theory in, 230–232
mental health treatment as
    part of, 227–228
mentoring as part of, 226–227
public support for, 221–222
recidivism affected by, 234
RNR model as basis for, 232
setting of, 222
state spending on, 221
substance abuse treatment
    in, 224–225, 228
Reflexive sense, 279
Reformatory. See Juvenile reformatories
Reformatory discipline, 34
Reformers
history of, 32–33
motives of, 33
religious nature of, 33–34

Rehabilitation
advantages of, 284–286
concept of, 29, 173–176
correctional institutions and, 37
defined, 173
desistance-based, 196–198
distinctiveness of, 30
end of, 41–42
fundamental components of, 35–36
goals of, 13
Good Lives Model (GLM), 198–201
half-empty reviews of, 178
half-full reviews of, 178
hegemony of, 174
implications of, 13
incapacitation vs., 123
individualized treatment in, 33–34
liberal abandonment of, 58–66
meta-analysis of, 184–189
narrative reviews of, 176–183
new penology and, 33–34
nothing works doctrine
    and, 39–40, 189
opposition to, 38–40
overview of, 31, 171–173
predictions by, 13–14
Progressive era and, 36–37
relational, 168–169
rise of, 28
RJ and, 162–163
societal benefits from, 74
studies, conclusions of, 201–203
voluntary, 67–68
Reicher, S., 62
Reiman, J. H., 56, 114, 203
Reitz, K. R., 210
Relational rehabilitation, 168–169
Rengifo, A. F., 73
Renzema, M., 101
Replacement effect, 137
Researcher effect, 250
Responsivity principle, 194, 250
Restorative justice (RJ)
advocates of, 146–147
appeal of, 151–154
approach to, 149
core principles of, 149
corruption of, 154
criminological problem in, 158–161
defined, 11, 148
focus of, 159
goals of, 31
implementation of, 11–12

justice problem in, 154–156
limitations of, 162–163, 169–170
meta-analysis of, 167–169
prison problem in, 156–157
procedural justice versus, 159
recidivism and, 163–164
recidivism study of, 164–165
scenario for, 150–151
studies of, 161–169
Restoring harm, 150, 152
Retribution. *See also* Just deserts theory
core principles of, 7–8
demands of, 46
expectations of, 17–18
utility linked to, 7–8, 74
Rhine, E. E., 210–211, 220–221, 232, 281
The Rich Get Richer and the Poor Get Prison
(Reiman), 56
Risk principle, 165, 194, 250
Risk-need-responsivity (RNR) model
community supervision applications of, 196
core principles of, 195
description of, 192
for early interventions, 250
as evidence based, 202
FFT and, 262
MST and, 268
for Perry Preschool Program, 254
reasons for developing, 196
reentry programs based on, 232
studies of, 232
Risks
criminogenic, 13–14
cumulative, 258
insider knowledge, 25
Ritchie, D., 108
Rivera, C. J., 100
RJ. *See* Restorative justice (RJ)
RNR. *See* Risk-need-responsivity
(RNR) model
Robbins, C. A., 224
Roberts, J., 51
Robins, L. N., 246
Robinson, G., 161, 168, 196–197
Rodriquez, N., 161
Rollin, J., 225
Ronan, K. R., 268
Rooney, J., 105, 156
Rose, D. R., 138
Roseborough, D., 161
Rosenfeld, R., 140
Rosenhan, D. L., 64–65
Ross, R. R., 182–184, 190–191, 233

Rossi, P. H., 48
Rothman, D. J., 32, 35, 37, 64, 69–70,
72–73, 154, 174, 209
Rudd, T., 227
Rudolph, J. L., 231
Rugge, T., 161, 196
Rukus, J., 216
Rumsey, E., 252
Rydberg, J., 109

Sabermetrcians, 25
Sabol, W. J., 38, 114, 121, 124, 138, 215
Sacks, J. Y., 225
Sacks, S., 225
Sampson, R. J., 107–108, 161, 197, 206, 231,
244, 246
Sanctions. *See also* Imprisonment; Mass
incarceration; Punishment
certainty of, 284
community, 3, 48
intermediate, 101
longitudinal studies of, 134–136
noncustodial, 98, 106, 108
process prior to, 155
punitive-oriented, 112
punitive-oriented correctional, 112
RJ v., 167–168
simple justice and, 44
state, 8, 67
utilitarian goals for, 8, 174
Santana, S. A., 221
Sauer, R. D., 25
Saum, C. A., 224
Savelyev, P. A., 257
Savolainen, J., 198, 231
Scally, C. P., 228–229
Schaefer, L., 196
Scharf, P. L., 67
Schargrodsky, E., 101
Schnippert, C. W., 216
School-based interventions
effectiveness of, 263
example of, 264–266
preschool programs, 254–258
Schriro, D., 223, 231
Schubert, C. A., 108
Schuhmann, R., 222
Schwarz, A., 22–23
Schwarzenegger, A., 113–114
Schweinhart, L. J., 254–257, 271
Schweitzer, M., 196
Science of sophomores.
See Stanford prison experiment

Scientific evidence, 24
Scientific method, 20–21
Scott, E. S., 275
Scott, T.-L., 196
Seattle Social Development Project (SSDP), 264–266, 272 *(table)*
Second Chance Act, 220, 226
Secondary goods, 199
Seiter, R. P., 229, 234
Selective incapacitation, 10, 127–131
Selective perception, 23
Selectivity-of-perceptions problem, 21
Self-esteem, 190, 193
Self-report survey, 93, 132
Self-selection, 280
Sellin, T., 127
Sentencing. *See also* Determinate sentencing; Indeterminate sentencing
    guidelines for, 48
    justice model approach to, 67
    proportionality in, 49
    reforms, 69–70
Serious and Violent Offender Reentry Initiative (SVORI), 220, 233–234
Shaming, 158–159
Shapiro, J. M., 110
Shapland, J., 161
Shaw, C. R., 206–208, 215
Sherman, L., 110–111
Sherman, L. W., 19, 79, 111, 159–162, 164–167
Shriver, M., 113
Shrout, P. E., 237
Simon, J., 4, 41, 72, 114–115, 209–210, 220, 288
Simple justice, 48
Simpson, O. J., 148
Sinclair, U., 207
Singer, R. B., 67
Situational crime prevention, 87–88
Skardhamar, T., 198, 231
Skelton, G., 113
Skroban, S. B., 142
Smith, B. H., 264
Smith, D. A., 142
Smith, J. A., 254
Smith, P., 105, 108, 130, 172, 191–192, 195–196, 209, 226, 232
SMSA. *See* Standard Metropolitan Statistical Area (SMSA)
Smykla, J. O., 221
Snodgrass, G. M., 109
Snodgrass, J., 207

Snyder, H. N., 214, 235
Social construction of reality, 212
Social context
    broader, 28
    consequences of, 279–280
    influence of, 27
    prevailing, 4–5, 27
    prevalence of, 279
    punishment, 57
    rehabilitation demise and, 36–39
    relevance of, 4
    state power, 63
Social development model, 264–265
Social experience, 107
Social problems, 212, 217
Social psychologists, 60
Social welfare, theory of, 288
Social welfare model, 153, 174
Social-ecological model, 267
The Society of Captives (Sykes), 59, 66
Solitary system, 33
Soucy, G., 249
Specific deterrence, 9
    defined, 81
    effectiveness of, 81, 285
    punishment levels and, 282
Specific deterrent effect, 112
Spector, M., 212, 217
Spelman, W., 139–140, 142
Spiegler, M. D., 188
Spohn, C., 108, 217
SSDP. *See* Seattle Social Development Project (SSDP)
Stams, G. J. J. M., 269
Standard Metropolitan Statistical Area (SMSA), 88
Stanford County Prison, 61
Stanford prison experiment
    academic view of, 63
    description of, 60–62
State enforced therapy, 38
State power, 66–68
Static predictors, 192
Statistics, 23–25
Steffey, D. M., 233
Steinberg, L., 275
Steiner, B., 109
Stemen, D., 73
STICS. *See* "Strategic Training Initiative in Community Supervision" (STICS)
Stohr, M. K., 41, 287
Stoll, M. A., 216
Stommel, J., 225

Stouthamer-Loeber, M., 247–248, 260
Strang, H., 160–162, 164–167
"Strategic Training Initiative in Community Supervision" (STICS), 196
Strong, K. H., 148
Struening, E., 237
Substance abuse treatment, in reentry programs, 224–225, 228
Sullivan, C. J., 198, 225, 249–250
Sullivan, D., 148
Sullivan, W. M., 275
Sundt, J. L., 75, 152, 222, 275
Sung, H.-E., 221
"Sunset laws," 237
Super-predators, 241, 249
Surrat, H. L., 224
Sutherland, E., 264
SVORI. See Serious and Violent Offender Reentry Initiative (SVORI)
Swanson, C. C., 216
Swartz, K., 191, 195
Sweeten, G., 135–137
Swidler, A., 275
Sykes, G., 59, 66, 68
Szasz, T. C., 217

Tangible costs, 272
Task Force on Corrections, 37
Tastes, concept of, 78
Taxman, F. S., 41, 215, 238
Taylor, R. S., 263
Technology transfer, 249–250
Terkel, A., 237
Theories of corrections
    basic assumption of, 91
    components of, 3
    consequences of, 278
    context definitions in, 4
    core themes of, 5
    deterrence, 8–10
    early intervention, 16
    empirical issue of, 18
    evidence for, 76
    expectations and, 17–18
    incapacitation, 10–11
    overview of, 6–7
    reentry. See Reentry
    rehabilitation, 12–14
    restorative justice, 11–12
    retribution, 7–8
    social context in, 27–29, 36–39, 279–280
    summary of, 17 (table)
Theory of outs, 23

Therapeutic system, 63–64
Thielo, A. J., 42, 222
Thinking About Crime (Wilson), 114, 128
Thomas, C., 247
Thompson, A. C., 211, 220–221
Tibbetts, S. G., 160
Tifft, L., 148
Timmermans, S., 19
Tipping point, 287
Tipton, S. M., 275
Toby, J., 31, 59
Tocqueville, A., de, 32, 241
Tonry, M., 2–3, 38, 41, 70, 72–73, 87, 99–100, 114, 117–118, 120, 210, 218
Top-down approach, 132, 139–141
Trager, J. S., 100
Travis, J., 14–15, 211–212, 216, 218–219, 221, 224–225, 227–228, 286
Travis, L., 109, 147, 171
Treatments. See Correctional treatments
Tremblay, R. E., 53, 100, 243–244, 253, 263
Trinity of components, 278
Tryling, A. L., 216
Tueller, S., 233–234
Turner, M. G., 75
Turner, S., 101, 103–104, 232, 235, 238, 253, 257, 259
Turpin-Petrosino, C., 100
Tyler, T., 159

Uggen, C., 54
Un-chosen individual traits, 53
Unfettered discretion, 36
Uniform Collateral Consequences of Convictions Act, 237
Uniform Determinate Sentencing Act, 71
Unnever, J. D., 73, 275, 288
Useem, B., 114, 141
Utilitarian theory
    deterrence, 10
    empirical issues in, 18, 76
    goals of, 10, 17–19, 30
    public support for, 57–58
    restorative justice, 12
    retribution, 7–8, 74
Utility
    bases, of, 76
    expected, of, 81
    intended, 18
    just deserts, 57–58
    retribution linked to, 7–8, 74
    risk to, 18
    value of, 5, 18

van der Laan, P. H., 269
van der Stouwe, T., 269
van Kammen, W., 248
Van Ness, A., 117
Van Ness, D. W., 148
Van Voorhis, P., 188, 202, 280
Vertova, P., 110
Veysey, B. M., 161
Victimization, 38–39
Victim-offender conference, 149–151
Vieraitis, L. M., 141
Villabos Agudelo, S., 225
Villetez, P., 108
Visher, C. A., 103, 126, 129, 134, 220,
   224–225, 233–234
Vitaro, E., 100
Vito, A. G., 22
Vito, G. F., 22
von Hirsch, A., 44, 51, 67
Vose, B. A., 195, 275

Wacquant, L., 31, 54, 72, 137
Waite, E., 48
Wallace-Capretta, S., 105, 156
Waller, I., 284
Wallman, J., 140
Walters, J. P., 125
Ward, J. T., 237
Ward, T., 199–201
Warehouse prisons, 124
Washington State Institute
   for Public Policy, 271
Weatherburn, D., 161–162, 168
Webster, C. M., 87, 120
Weigend, T., 118
Weiher, A. W., 248
Weikart, D., 254–255
Weiman, D. F., 216
Welsh, B. C., 16, 53, 88, 201, 242, 246,
   249–250, 253, 257–259, 263, 268,
   270–271, 274, 287
West, D., 260
West, H. C., 38, 114
Western, B., 54, 137, 217
Wexler, H. K., 228
What Works in Corrections (MacKenzie), 169

"What Works? Questions and Answers About
   Prison Reform" (Martinson), 175
When Brute Force Fails: How to Have Less Crime
   and Less Punishment
   (Kleiman), 284
When Prisoners Come Home: Parole and
   Prisoner Reentry (Petersilia), 218–219
White, P., 25
White-collar criminals, 56–57
Whitehead, P. R., 199
Wicker, T., 65
Wikström, P.-O, 87
Wilks, J., 184
Willis, G. M., 199–201
Wilson, D. B., 184, 188, 223, 263
Wilson, J. A., 223–224, 233
Wilson, J. Q., 53, 113–114, 128–129
Wilson, S. J., 263
Wines, E. C., 34, 290
Winterfield, L., 224
Within-group variation argument, 54
Wodahl, E., 211, 222, 230, 238
Wolfers, J., 2
Wolfgang, M. E., 127–128
Woods, D. J., 160–162, 166
World Prison Brief, 117–118,
   119 (table), 120, 124
Wormith, J. S., 199
Wortzik, S., 65
Wozniak, J. F., 152, 154
Wright, J. P., 99–100, 160, 245–246,
   258, 275, 289
Wright, K. A., 236, 238

Yates, P. M., 199
Yavitz, A., 257
Yessine, A. K., 196
Young, D., 238

Zeng, Z., 213
Zhang, Q., 248
Zimbardo, P. G., 60–64
Zimring, F. E., 71, 114
Zinger, I., 232
Zito, B., 24
Zoder, I., 108

About the Authors

Francis T. Cullen is Distinguished Research Professor Emeritus in the School of Criminal Justice at the University of Cincinnati, where he also holds an appointment as Senior Research Associate. He received a Ph.D. (1979) in sociology and education from Columbia University. Professor Cullen has published more than 300 works in the areas of criminological theory, corrections, white-collar crime, public opinion, and the measurement of sexual victimization. He is author of *Rethinking Crime and Deviance Theory: The Emergence of a Structuring Tradition* and is coauthor of *Reaffirming Rehabilitation, Corporate Crime Under Attack: The Ford Pinto Case and Beyond, Criminology, Combating Corporate Crime: Local Prosecutors at Work, Unsafe in the Ivory Tower: The Sexual Victimization of College Women, Criminological Theory: Context and Consequences*, and *Environmental Corrections: A New Paradigm for Supervising Offenders in the Community*. He also is coeditor of *Criminological Theory: Past to Present—Essential Readings, Taking Stock: The Status of Criminological Theory, The Origins of American Criminology*, the *Encyclopedia of Criminological Theory, The Oxford Handbook of Criminological Theory, The American Prison: Imagining a Different Future, Challenging Criminological Theory: The Legacy of Ruth Rosner Kornhauser*, and *Sisters in Crime Revisited: Bringing Gender into Criminology*. Professor Cullen is a Past President of the American Society of Criminology and of the Academy of Criminal Justice Sciences. In 2010, he received the ASC Edwin H. Sutherland Award.

Cheryl Lero Jonson is Assistant Professor in the Department of Criminal Justice at Xavier University. She received a Ph.D. (2010) in criminal justice from the University of Cincinnati. She is coeditor of *The Origins of American Criminology, Sisters in Crime Revisited: Bringing Gender into Criminology, The American Prison: Imagining a Different Future*, and *Deterrence, Choice, and Crime: Contemporary Perspectives*. Her published work has appeared in *Criminology and Public Policy, Crime and Justice: A Review of Research*, and *Victims and Offenders*. Her current research interests include correctional policy, the impact of incarceration on recidivism, the use of incentives to downsize American prisons, inmate adjustment to conditions of confinement, strategies to prevent school shootings, and work reactions among criminal justice employees. From 2012 to 2015, she served as an Executive Counselor of the Corrections Section of the Academy of Criminal Justice Sciences.